THE CHALLENGE
OF THE CONCORDANCE

Some New Testament words studied in depth

HAROLD K. MOULTON

Deputy Translations Secretary, Bible House, London
Formerly New Testament Professor,
United Theological College, Bangalore

SAMUEL BAGSTER & SONS LTD · LONDON

SAMUEL BAGSTER & SONS LTD
A member of the Pentos group
1 Bath Street
London EC1V 9QA

© The Senate of Serampore College

First British edition 1977
Reprinted October 1977

ISBN 0 85150 124 9

Printed in Great Britain by
Hollen Street Press Ltd, Slough
771089L510

THE CHALLENGE OF THE CONCORDANCE

To

THE UNITED THEOLOGICAL COLLEGE,
BANGALORE

Where I was a student for twenty-five years
and where many taught me much

ABOUT THE AUTHOR

Dr. Harold K. Moulton, a noted New Testament scholar, belongs to a family highly distinguished in the field of New Testament studies. His grandfather, W. F. Moulton, was one of the outstanding New Testament scholars of his day, and a member of the English Revised Version Committee of 1881. His father, James Hope Moulton, was a pioneer in the linguistic studies of Egyptian papyri which have deepened our understanding of the New Testament. His books still remain standard works. Harold Moulton himself, a Methodist minister, who read classics and theology at Cambridge, worked as a missionary in South India from 1927-1957. During most of that period he was New Testament professor at the United Theological College, Bangalore. He was a member of the Tamil Bible Revision Committee from 1939-1950. From 1957-1971 he served in the Translations Department of the British and Foreign Bible Society, before returning to Bangalore for a further two years. He is now lecturing in New Testament Studies at New College, University of London. He is the author of a number of books on New Testament subjects, and he edited the fourth edition of Moulton and Geden's *Concordance to the Greek Testament*.

FOREWORD

As stated in the Introduction, this volume began with articles published in the *South India Churchman*. These were then collected and published in book form in the Christian Students' Library Series. I happened to show the book to Principal C. S. Duthie of New College, London, who suggested that an edition published in England might find readers. The Co-ordinating Committee of the Indian Theological Library (as the Christian Students' Library is now called) has graciously given permission on the sole condition that this edition is not distributed in Asia. The copyright remains with the Senate of Serampore College.

The book was written primarily for readers in India and rightly contains references with Indian settings. These will, however, rarely be obscure to readers in another country. They remain in gratitude to the land where I have lived so long and which I love so much—and the Word of God is valid for every land.

HAROLD K. MOULTON

New College
University of London

NOTE ON THE BRITISH EDITION

THE CHALLENGE OF THE CONCORDANCE has developed from articles originally written for the *South India Churchman* and published in book form for the Christian Students' Library. By their kind permission the British edition is now published.

CONTENTS

IV. THE CHRISTIAN YEAR

V. WORSHIP

VI. THE CHRISTIAN LIFE

VII. CHRISTIAN CHARACTER

VIII. THE SCRIPTURES

INTRODUCTION

Most people find a Concordance useful for looking up a text —and allow its usefulness to end there. They fail to see the other gifts that it can bring: its collection of *all* the instances of a word, spreading them before our eyes so that we may take them in as a whole; its indication of the preferences of the various writers for different words and the ideas that go with them; its underlining of the great New Testament themes by the sheer quantity of the references; and, above all, its stimulation of our imagination and its challenge to our way of living by the varied repetition of a Christian word. I was once taken to task for suggesting that a Concordance could be 'challenging'. I remain quite impenitent. I have found no book more so: to the intellect, to right living, and to the knowledge of God.

My own first deep appreciation of the Concordance began when I was a member of the Tamil New Testament Revision Committee which worked during the Second World War and included such fine men as the Reverend C. H. Monahan (the chairman), Bishops V. S. Azariah and Stephen Neill, and the Danish Lutheran, Hans Bjerrum. It was my task to keep an eye on variant translations of the same Greek word to see if they were justified or merely accidental.

Some years later I experimented with a brief devotional Concordance study when taking prayers in the chapel of the United Theological College, Bangalore. I was then asked to adapt this study for an article in the *South India Churchman*. In the end I wrote exactly one hundred articles, of which eighty-six are reproduced in this book.

What was borne in upon me increasingly was that it was not my business just to use the Concordance as a tool for my own purposes but to *let it teach me*. I tried to come to a word with as open a mind as possible and sort out all its instances into groups.

I could then arrange these groups in some kind of logical order, hoping that in the end I would see what this complete survey of a New Testament word had to show me.

To give one straightforward illustration: in preparing the article on Wisdom (Number 9), I found that the first two references were to wisdom in the Old Testament, the next four referred to the wisdom of Jesus, then came some more under the Old Testament category, then several which spoke of the wisdom of God. The next new types were human wisdom, approved or neutral, and human wisdom condemned. A considerable number then fitted into one or other of these categories, and the only further new category required—though it proved to be a large one—was that of wisdom as a gift from God or Christ or the Spirit.

The logical order, beginning with the lowest, then appeared to be: 1. Human wisdom condemned. 2. Human wisdom approved or neutral. 3. The wisdom of the Old Testament. 4. The wisdom of the incarnate Jesus. 5. The wisdom of God or Christ. 6. Wisdom as the gift of God to men. (Actually that seemed to be the pattern of so many New Testament words: first human failure, then God's perfection, and then the gift from God to men of what they cannot acquire by themselves.)

After this preparation I was ready to begin writing the article. Before taking up the different headings, I nearly always gave the figures of the occurrences of the word, or words—because many articles include two or three similar words. Figures are never really dull, and usually they are very revealing. The total figure indicates how large or small a part a word plays in the New Testament. The figures for the different books (a detail which I came to give increasingly as I went along) show if a word is evenly distributed, or if it is a special favourite of Luke, or John, or Revelation. The figures, by the way, are obtained by the simple process of counting the references, and rechecking one's first count, not forgetting that a word may occur twice or three times in one verse.

The article then writes itself. Put together all the instances in each group, and it is easy to see their message as a whole, with its emphasis on some aspect of man's weakness, of God's greatness, and of his gracious goodness to us, his children. No article left itself up in the air. It always came down in the end to practical realities of Christian life and character.

I used the *Concordance to the Greek Testament*, of which the first edition was prepared by my grandfather, Dr. W. F. Moulton, and Dr. A. S. Geden, but Young's *Analytical Concordance* in English is a fine piece of scholarship and gives the Greek underlying the English of the Authorised Version.

The selection of words is not systematic. Indeed I deliberately avoided such great Christian words as sin, salvation, and love. These are fully treated in so many places. I wanted to call attention to others which have received less notice. For the book I classified the articles and was not a little surprised to find that the section on The Christian Life turned out to be far the longest. Yet surely that is right. The New Testament is not content even with proclaiming the greatness of God and the saving act of Christ. It goes on to emphasise that unless we 'live up to our calling' (see Eph. 4:1, N.E.B.) all God's love and all his grace offered through the Spirit are, so far as we are concerned, useless. This book has been written in the hope that the New Testament may challenge and guide us to the life to which it calls us.

I. JESUS

1. 'HE WHO WAS SENT'

In Hebrews 3:1 there is a familiar New Testament word which is applied in that place alone to Jesus. The writer says: 'Consider the *Apostle* ... of our confession, even Jesus'. We begin this book by studying our Lord as *the* missionary to this world, the pattern of all subsequent Christian mission.

Though the noun Apostle, or missionary, is nowhere else used of Him, the verb frequently describes God's sending of His Son. Actually there are two verbs in the Greek: *apostellō*, which occurs in this sense 30 times, and *pempō*, which is identical in meaning and occurs 27 times in the same sense. Of these 57 uses of the word to describe God's sending of Jesus, no fewer than 46 are found in St. John's Gospel and First Epistle. The whole series gives a full picture of the meaning and purpose of the Incarnation.

We shall consider first the relation of the 'Apostle' to His Father and the commission with which He was sent; then the response which He expected from men; and finally the link between Himself as the first Apostle and those whom He Himself sent out as apostles.

1. He stresses first of all that He really is an Apostle. He did not come of Himself but God sent Him, and the God who sent Him is true (Jn. 8:42, 7:28). The Father had 'sanctified' Him, that is, He had set Him apart for this purpose, and sent Him into the world (Jn. 10:36). Jesus 'knew' His Father who sent Him; He was in intimate personal touch with Him (Jn. 7:29). In the same way, the Father who sent Him was with Him (Jn. 8:29). The Father witnessed to Him (Jn. 5:37, 8:18), particularly perhaps at His Baptism and Transfiguration, but also at every moment of His apostolic task. The very works that He did bore continual witness to the fact that the Father had sent Him (Jn. 5:36).

And what were those works? Not simply what we usually call His miracles, but the whole of His miraculous life. The Father sent the Son to be the Saviour of the world (1 Jn. 4:14). He sent Him not primarily to judge but to save (Jn. 3:17). He sent Him both to the lost sheep of the house of Israel (Mt. 15:24), and also to the nations all over the world (Acts 28:28).

He was sent 'for sin' (Rom. 8: 3, RSV), that is, to deal with sin as a whole.   He was sent to bless men in turning them away from their iniquities (Acts 3: 26).   He was sent to be the 'propitiation' for their sins (1 Jn. 4: 10)—not, that is, to propitiate the Father who sent Him, but to disinfect men from their sins so that they could be fit to come into the presence of God's purity. He was sent to do all God's will (Jn. 5: 30, 6:38, 6: 39). That meant doing the work of Him who sent Him (Jn. 4: 34, 9: 4). It meant seeking God's glory throughout (Jn. 7: 18). It meant sharing with the Father the task of judgment, even though that was not His primary task (Jn. 8: 16). It meant speaking what God had sent Him to say: 'He whom God has sent speaks the words of God' (Jn. 3: 34); 'My teaching is not mine but His who sent me' (7:16); 'He that sent me is true, and the things which I heard from Him, these speak I unto the world' (8:26); 'The Father who sent me has given me a commandment what I should say' (12:49); 'The word which you hear is not mine but the Father's who sent me' (14: 24). The Father who sent Him would draw men to Him, and so His work would be accomplished (6: 44). Then He would return to Him who sent Him (7:33, 16: 5) and, to complete all, the Lord would send Him again (Acts 3:20).

2.   And what was the response that He expected from men? First of all, that He should be received, because those who received Him received the God who sent Him. All four gospels contain this sentence (Mt. 10:40; Mk. 9:37; Lk. 9:48; Jn. 13:20). Unless men are willing to receive Christ, He cannot make the first beginning with them.

Then He is sent in order that men may know Him and the God who sent Him. This is especially emphasised in the High Priestly prayer of John 17 (vv. 3, 23, 25). If men do not know the God who sent Jesus, all manner of evil and oppression will take place (Jn. 15:21). He was sent also that men should behold in His person the God who sent Him (Jn. 12:45).

He was sent further that men should believe and have faith. Six times over this is emphasised. Receiving, knowing and beholding are not enough if they do not issue in a new relationship of faith.   To the Jews, characteristically asking what works they must do, He replies, 'This is the work of God, that you have faith in Him whom He has sent' (Jn. 6:29).   The resurrection of Lazarus was done so that the people might believe that God had sent Him (Jn. 11:42).   His chosen Twelve believed that God had sent Him, and the result of their unity with one another and with Christ, and the unity of all subsequent believers, is to be that the world will really believe that God did send His Son (Jn. 17:21). Those who do not believe the One whom God sent are completely out of touch with Him (Jn. 5:38), but those who have faith in Christ are carried on to faith in God who sent Him (Jn. 12:44). This faith in Christ and in the God who sent Him gives the believer that life which has the quality of eternity (Jn. 5: 24), and he who assimilates Christ has life, because Christ Himself has been sent by the living Father (Jn. 6:57). God sent His Son that we might live through Him (1 Jn. 4: 9). No wonder that the Son is to be honoured, because dishonouring Him implies dishonouring the Father who sent Him (Jn. 5: 23). Yet of course honouring must not be taken as mere lip service. In perhaps the most searching of all the parables, one repeated in all three Synoptic gospels, the Owner of the vineyard sends His Son that He may receive the fruits that are His due (Mt. 21: 37; Mk. 12:6; Lk. 20:13). He says 'Surely they will reverence my Son', but they do not. They are set only on keeping the fruits for themselves. These words are a parable for more than the Jews to whom they were first addressed.

3. The link between Jesus as the first Apostle and those whom He sent out as apostles is, if taken seriously, both astounding and almost unbearable. It is contained in two further verses in St. John's gospel: '*As* Thou didst send me into the world, *so* I have sent them' (17:18), and '*As* the Father has sent me, *even so* send I you' (20:21). Consider what this means. *In the same way* that God has sent His Son—to do His works, to bring His salvation, to deal with sin, to do His will, to seek His glory, to speak His words; that men may receive Christ, know God, believe in Him, behold Him, find life in Him, render fruit to Him—*in that same way*, and for that same purpose, He sends His followers, first the original twelve, and then all who are His apostles, that is, all His church, for all in their different vocations are called to apostleship and mission. There is no evading the implications of the study of this word 'send'. What God sent Jesus to do, He sends us to do also, not usurping the place of Jesus, but being as deeply committed as He was. I said above that this link, this implication, was almost unbearable. So it is, but not quite, because to the apostles whom He still sends He gives His Holy Spirit, as He gave Him on the Day of Pentecost. That, and that alone, is enough for every apostle commissioned to do His service.

2. THE MANNER OF HIS SPEAKING

When we consider the words of Jesus, we are chiefly concerned—and rightly so—with their revealing, challenging, loving content. So much so that we seldom pause to consider the verbs with which the evangelists introduce them. In fact, when we quote the words, we usually omit the introduction as mere framework, forgetting that a good frame is important for a good picture. Its purpose is to show it up to perfection. At its best it becomes all of a piece with the picture itself, blending with it into one.

Three in particular of the 'introductory' words which the gospels use throw a fuller light on the character and actions of our Lord.

1. The first is *proskaloumai*, normally used in the phrase 'He called unto Him'. It is found in the Synoptic gospels only, where it occurs 19 times. Ten times Jesus calls His disciples to Him, three times the crowd, once or twice the children or His enemies. Twice He Himself uses the word in a parable. It is never used to describe the first call of a disciple. The word for that is different. It is not 'as of old St. Andrew heard it', but '*day by day* His sweet voice soundeth'—though the voice is often stern as well as sweet. It is the calling of committed persons, and of others, who need bringing close to Him for definite instruction or warning.

'He called unto Him His twelve disciples and gave them authority . . . saying, Go to the lost sheep . . . and as ye go, preach' (Mt. 10:1 ff.). Here is the personal instruction, personally given, not formally communicated. Here is the hand that beckons towards before it points outward, so that along with instruction it may give effectiveness.

'He called unto Him His disciples and said, I have compassion on the multitude . . . and He took the loaves . . . and gave . . . and they did all eat and were filled' (Mt. 15:32). The disciples needed bringing to His side to join in His compassion. Until they were there, they felt only the bother and nuisance of the emergency. When they were by Him, they could see the crowd with His eyes and share in His work of love.

'He called them to Him and saith unto them, They which are accounted to rule over the Gentiles lord it over them . . . but it is not so among you . . . whosoever would become great among

you shall be your minister ... for verily the Son of Man ...'
(Mk. 10:42). How ashamed ever after Peter must have been
to remember that day and that call, and the disgraceful situation
that lay behind it. Jesus quietly says, 'Come here, all of you.
I want you'. It is the way a good parent speaks to a naughty
child. And how reluctantly the child sometimes comes. But
the disciples never forgot what Jesus said when they came close.
It was no lecture from a distance that He gave them; it was the
quiet searching presence of God Himself. And it worked.

'He called to Him the multitude and said unto them, Hear
me, all of you and understand' (Mk. 7:14). These were no casual
words to passers-by, but a winning of their attention before
speaking, so that the message would be sure to go home.

'Jesus called them unto Him, saying, Suffer the little children
to come unto me' (Lk. 18:16). The parents and children were
going away, their spirits dashed by the harsh words of the
disciples. And then they hear the voice: 'Come back here a
minute. I want you'. And they come—and are given the
true and tender humanity of the love of God.

Why do men call each other? (a) Because they are *superior*.
The master does not go to the servant; he summons him for
orders. 'He called them ... and said, *Go*' (Mt. 10:1, 5). We
would most of us be the better for the spirit of obedience. We
are far too ready to pick and choose, even with the commands of
the Master. (b) Because they have something to *say*. It is a
psychological fact that you pay more attention when you are
called than when someone comes to you. 'He called them and
said, *Hear*' (Mk. 7:14). (c) Because they have something to *give*.
A parent calls his child to give him something. If he comes, he
gets it. If he doesn't, he has to wait. 'He called the children
to Him and blessed them, saying, For of such (Does that
mean those who *came*?) is the Kingdom of God' (Lk. 18:16;
Mk. 10:16).

2. Our second word is *epitimaō*, translated either '*charge*'
or '*rebuke*'. The word was first used of the judge assessing the
deserved penalty and delivering the sentence with authority.
It comes 28 times in the Synoptic gospels and twice in the epistles,
being used 17 times of Jesus. We are never to forget that He is
the Commander, and that He always speaks with authority.

So the evangelists use it of the Lord's authority over devils:
'Jesus rebuked him, saying, Hold thy peace and come out of

him' (Mk. 1:25); over disease: 'He stood over her and rebuked the fever and it left her' (Lk. 4:39); over nature: 'He awoke and rebuked the wind, and said unto the sea, Peace, be still' (Mk. 4:39).

But they use it more often of His words of authority to men: 'He charged them much that they should not make Him known' (Mk. 3:12). His message must remain at first in His own hands, lest it be misused, and His word of authority here is absolute. 'Then He charged the disciples that they should tell no man that He was the Christ' (Mt. 16:20) — again the word of authority to quench misguided enthusiasm. And as the climax of this series: 'He charged them that they should tell no man ... save when the Son of Man should have risen again from the dead' (Mk. 9:9). They could not understand Jesus till after the resurrection, because the whole story was not there. The whole story never is there without the Resurrection. That is both our justification for preaching now, and Christ's warning as to how we must preach. The incarnation, the teaching, even the cross itself, are not enough unless in some way every time we proclaim the triumphant power of God.

But there were occasions when other people tried to deliver sentence without the charity and understanding that were the Lord's. The gospels leave us in no doubt about His reaction to them: 'They brought unto Him little children ... and the disciples rebuked them' (Mk. 10:13). We know the Lord's strong indignation then. 'Many rebuked him that he should hold his peace' (Mk. 10:48)—but the Lord will not let Bartimaeus be held back. 'Lord, do you want us to bid fire come down from heaven and consume them? But He turned and rebuked them' (Lk. 9:54, 55). No man is to rebuke His way of love, whether it be for the children, or for the blind, or for the hated Samaritans.

The hardest word is for poor Peter! He has ventured to rebuke the Lord for linking up the cross with His Messiahship. Instead of dealing with him privately, Jesus makes a public example of him: '*Seeing His disciples*, He rebuked Peter and saith, Get thee behind me, Satan' (Mk. 8:32, 33). These were the same words that He had used at His first temptation, when He was facing the whole problem of gaining His purpose in the world. They were very hard on Peter, but Peter knew that they were right, or He would not have told Mark. Unless a man accepts the cross, for Jesus first and for himself afterwards, he has hardly a clue as to why Christ came.

Yet let not that be the final example.   Let us look at Lk. 19:39:
'Master, rebuke Thy disciples . . . If these shall hold their peace,
the stones will cry out'.   For those who will proclaim Him with
joy and assurance, acknowledging Him as their King and the
King of all the world, there is no rebuke.   There is always His
approval and support.   In that confidence we too must cry out,
'Blessed is the King who comes in the name of the Lord'.

3.   Our third word is one of the most frequent in the gospels:
Apekrithē, 'He answered'.   We give no figures here; the uses
in the gospels and the Acts cover two full pages in the Concordance.   But as we glance down them, it is remarkable how many
times comes the phrase 'Jesus answered'.   Some are the ordinary
answerings of conversation: the to-and-fro with Nathanael,
Nicodemus, the woman of Samaria, for example.   For all that
Jesus had such truth to utter, He did not monopolize conversa-
tions like many people we know—ourselves excepted, of course!
He was always ready to listen, to take His turn.   He did not
offend people by not letting them get a word in.   There is no
record of His prosing along, or being guilty of rude interruption.
He must have been a most stimulating, because a most courteous,
conversationalist.

Others of His answers deal with the great problems of the day:
'What commandment is first of all? Jesus *answered* . . . ' (Mk.
12:28, 29); 'Who did sin, this man or his parents. . . . ? Jesus
answered. . . .' (Jn. 9:2, 3).   He does not fight shy of the big
problems of the mind, nor retreat into narrow devotionalism.

Others deal with dire need.   Look at Mt. 15:22-28 with its
four answers to the Syrophoenician woman, testing her step by
step till at last she is ready for the answer, 'O woman, great is
thy faith'.   Or see Jn. 11:9: 'Jesus answered, Are there not
twelve hours in the day?', and He resists the well-meant efforts
of His disciples to keep Him in safety, and goes to meet the need
of the stricken family in Bethany, and the need of the world on
the Cross.

Others answer no questions, but sensitively sum up a situation
without needing to have it explained to Him—seeing and dealing
with a person's need before it is put into words: 'And he, casting
away his garment, sprang up and came to Jesus.   And Jesus
answered him . . .' (Mk. 10:51).   Bartimaeus had said nothing,
but Jesus needed no words from him.   'At that season Jesus
answered and said . . . Come unto Me' (Mt. 11:25).   There

had been no question—but Jesus saw the need of the world and answered it before men fully saw it themselves. Some translations do not use the word 'answered', just because there is no direct question to answer. That betrays a lack of spiritual insight. Jesus has always answered need rather than words.

But sometimes there is no answer: 'Master, this woman . . . What then sayest thou of her? But Jesus stooped down and with His finger wrote on the ground' (Jn. 8:4-6). 'Answerest thou nothing? Behold, how many things they accuse thee of. But Jesus no more answered anything, insomuch that Pilate marvelled' (Mk. 15:4, 5). Silence itself was the perfect answer in both cases, commanding a response from guilty consciences that might have faced up to argument, but not to the empty echo of their own voices.

Paul uses the word once only, in Col. 4:6: 'Let your speech be always with grace . . . that you may know how you ought to answer each one'. Jesus alone knew that perfectly, because He alone is *the* answer. But the grace of God can make it possible for even us to answer as we ought. Two last answers from the gospels show us how that grace is made available: 'The tempter came and said unto Him . . . and He answered . . .' (Mt. 4:4). All Christ's answers to the tempter came from God's Word. That is where, rightly interpreted, the answers are always to be found. And then Mt. 28:5: 'The angel answered and said unto the women, Fear not . . . He is risen'. Humbly confident in that answer to our hearts also, we can give an answer by word and deed for the faith that is in us.

3. THE SEEING OF JESUS

In the previous chapter we looked at some of the words with which the evangelists introduce the *sayings* of Jesus. In this chapter we shall consider another series of introductory words connected with *seeing*. Two of them are characteristic of Jesus, the third of His followers. All of them are striking because they demonstrate the speaker brought into personal contact with the object of his vision before ever he opens his mouth.

The first word is *periblepomai*, 'look round about on'. It comes only seven times in the gospels, six of them in Mark, and every time but once it is used of Jesus. I am sure that it goes back to the personal memory of Peter. He could not forget the well-beloved ways of the Lord, the sweeping look by which He included all His audience in what He was going to say, not letting anyone feel that He was not speaking personally to him or to her. He might be including them all in His anger, as when He was about to defy them by healing the man with the withered hand (Mk. 3:5; Lk. 6:10). He might be including them all in the great Christian family (Mk. 3:34). He might be looking round at all so as to select one, as when He looked round after He was touched by the woman with the issue of blood (Mk. 5:32). He might be looking round in order to gain attention for a devastating word such as His saying about riches in Mk. 10:23, or to sum up a situation for action, as He did when He looked round the temple in Mk. 11:11.

But whatever the circumstances in which that look was used, it took in everything. Most of us live in blinkers, with a minimum field of vision. I have known two men, one old, one young, who preach with their eyes literally shut, making no attempt to gather their congregations to them. Whether we follow that actual practice or not, we rarely look around as we should, either in the pulpit or outside it. We are too unloving, too self-centred, too burdened ourselves, to take in comprehensively the needs of others as we look at the world. We need to pray for a look like our Lord's which can take in both the needs of men and the glory of God.

Our second word, *emblepō,* is rather different. It means literally 'look *into.*' It is used sometimes of plain physical sight, for example the blind man's restored sight in Mk. 8:25, or Paul's description of his inability to see after his vision in Acts 22:11. It is also used metaphorically, as when Jesus in Mt. 6:26 asks us to *behold* the birds. (Luke 12:24 uses a different word, *consider*).

But its outstanding use in the N.T. is of the penetrating gaze of Jesus. Our first word saw Him looking *extensively.* Here we have Him looking *intensively.* He not only includes everyone in His look; He looks right into their hearts. He looks searchingly at Peter, and sees the character of the man and what he will become (Jn. 1:42). He looks into the rich young ruler and sees the unsurrendered part of his heart, and challenges him with it because He loves him (Mk. 10:21). And immediately afterwards (Mk. 10:27; cp. Mt. 19:26) He looks into the minds of His disciples and sees their puzzlement and their self-satisfaction with their poverty—and He puts to them too the challenge that they need.

He goes on to look with the same penetrating gaze into the hearts of His enemies (Lk. 20:17) and to say, 'The stone which the builders rejected, the same was made the head of the corner'. And finally there was the most heartbreaking look of all. Silly Peter had been first rash, and then scared—and the result was the denial of all that the greatest period of his life had meant to him. 'And the Lord turned and looked into Peter. And Peter remembered ...' (Lk. 22:61). He never forgot again, because that look brought him back to where Jesus wanted him to be, and his tears were the tears of true repentance.

Our third word, *atenizo*, is a word that is not used of Jesus. Ten of its fourteen occurrences in the N.T. come in the book of Acts. But it is a word worth examining because it describes one of the ways of looking which the Christian has learnt through his Master. It is the fixed gaze of concentration, of single purpose, sometimes in giving, sometimes for receiving. It is the gaze of Stephen (Acts 7:55) looking into heaven with eyes for nothing but his Lord as he passes from death into life. It is the gaze of Cornelius (Acts 10:4), as he looks in astonishment, and yet surely with some premonition of what is to come, at the angel visitor appearing to put him in touch with the realities after which he has been groping. It is the gaze of Peter (Acts 3:4) and of Paul (14:9) on those whom they were about to heal, concentrating the whole power of the gospel on them, mediated through their attentive love. It is the gaze of Paul on the Sanhedrin (23:1), as he bends his whole mind to set forth the essentials of the gospel to those hardened religionists.

But it began with the concentrated attention which Jesus Himself always called forth from those who listened to Him or watched Him. The word is used only twice to describe the way in which people looked at Him, but it is significant that the first occasion is at the beginning of His ministry, and the second describes the last physical sight of Him that men have ever had. Within these two the whole story is comprehended.

The first is in the synagogue at Nazareth (Lk. 4:20): the eyes of all are *fastened* on Him, determined to let nothing distract them from missing a word, even though so far He has done nothing but read the lesson. Rarely, as readers or speakers, do we compel such attention or, as hearers, give it. The second is at the Ascension (Acts 1:10), when the disciples are looking *intently* (NEB) into heaven as He is going, determined to keep Him in sight till the last, as we look after a train bearing away a loved one until long after the handkerchief waving from the window has become indistinguishable. The two men in white tell them that they need not concentrate so much upon the physical; this, after all, is not a last look. But there can be nothing but praise for the intenseness of their purpose.

There is another word for looking at Jesus, which is used only in Heb. 12:2. It is a beautiful and striking word, because it really means 'looking away'—looking away from everything else as secondary, and fixing the eyes upon Him who alone is worth looking at. That was what men found themselves compelled to do when He was here on earth. That is the direction in which our looking must continue to be towards Him who alone is the 'author and perfecter of faith'.

4. THE CONTACTS OF JESUS

After looking at the links of Jesus with men through speech and through sight, we turn to the link of actual physical touch. The gospels use three words in particular to describe this.

The first is *haptomai*, which sometimes means to touch and sometimes to take hold of. Nearly always it is used in connection with healing—of Jesus touching or taking hold of others, or of their doing the same with Him. The leper in Mk. 1:41 is, of course, the most striking example: that Jesus should actually touch a man with that dreadful contagious disease, whom everyone else wanted to keep at a distance! But there is a beautiful significance in His touching the tongue of the deaf and dumb man in Mk. 7:33. Here is a person deprived of the normal means of communication, and therefore very probably retarded in mental development. Jesus meets him in the only way, perhaps, that he can understand. It is no good trying to talk to him, but the touch will make His intention clear to the simplest mind.

Then, on the other hand, there are those who wanted physical contact with Him: the woman with the issue of blood in Mk. 5:27 who believed that that simple contact would cure her. So she comes behind Him in the crowd and gently takes hold of that most sacred part of a Jew's garment, the fringe thrown back over the shoulder which reminds him of the observance of the Law. But the pull, though gentle, is purposeful amid all the other accidental jostling. Jesus at once senses it—and the cure is effected, with that touch as the means of grace.

The people in Mk. 10:13 who brought their children to Jesus that He should touch them (the gospels do not actually use the word 'mothers') had probably something of the same thought in their minds. Here is someone kind and loving, and they believe that somehow His touch will do the children good. And who is to say that they were wrong? Anyhow Jesus, in the face of His disciples, puts His arms round them and blesses them, laying His hands on them. He loved to symbolise by a physical act His communication of *Himself*.

Contrast St. Paul who uses the word only three times (1 Cor. 7:1; 2 Cor. 6:17; Col. 2:21) and always in the form 'Don't touch', though once he is quoting his opponents. Paul is like the anxious parent with the fiddling child who might break something! John's only use too is negative: 'The evil one touches him not' (1 Jn. 5:18). But Jesus is always positive. The one exception might seem to be Jn. 20:17, when He says to Mary: 'Touch me not', though the more accurate translation is 'Do not cling to me' (NEB). But that too is really positive. He wants to assure her that He is not disappearing yet. He will be staying with her and the others, and there is no need to try to hold Him back.

By a beautiful Greek idiom, the same word 'touch' is used for kindling a light: bringing it into flame by touching it with your own. That was what Jesus always did with men and women: He set them alight by touching them with Himself.

Our second word is actually a phrase: 'He laid His hand(s) upon'. It comes eleven times in the gospels, nearly always in connection with the healing ministry of Jesus (Mt. 9:18, 19:13, 15; Mk. 5:23, 6:5, 7:32, 8:23, 25; Lk. 4:40, 13:13; the exception is Mk. 16:18). As with the previous word, there was a power in Him which could somehow be communicated by a physical touch, not in any superstitious sense, though some of those He helped may have thought of it that way, but because it was the personal touch of One who cared. We know how a hand on someone's shoulder, or a firm hand-shake, convinces far more than almost any number of words. In that way the hand of Jesus had the capacity to convince men of His caring, and so to heal.

When we come to Acts, we find the Apostles laying their hands on men for the same healing purpose, and for other purposes as well. In 8:17 and 19:6 it is the act connected with the receiving of the Holy Ghost. In 13:3 it is the commissioning for a missionary journey. We may be sure that the apostles copied not only their Master's action but also His spirit of caring love. In the later Church the laying on of hands has been connected with confirmation and ordination, and often there has been a danger of the act being mechanically given and superstitiously received. Surely again its value depends on its being a sign of the caring love of him who gives it and of the Church behind him. Without that love it sinks into a formality. Simon Magus (Acts 8:19) thought that this value could be bought, and we have coined the word 'simony' for that type of ecclesiastical mentality. But its efficacy depends neither on cash nor on ceremony. It depends on the inheritance of the caring love of Christ when He laid His hands upon men.

The third word which the gospels use of Jesus's physical contact with people is *paralambanō*, I take on one side. It is used several times when He wishes to say something special to His disciples or do something special with them. He takes them by the arm and says, 'I want you on your own with me for a bit'. He does that with Peter and James and John before the Transfiguration (Mk. 9:2), giving a personal invitation to that sublime revelation. He does it with all the Twelve in Mk. 10:32, when He wants His chosen band in particular to learn something of the way of the Cross that lies ahead of Him. He does it with the inner three again in Gethsemane (Mk. 14:33), that He may have their support in this last crisis that He can share with them. And when in Jn. 14:3 He says, 'I come again and will take you unto myself', it is only an extension and completion of the same thing that He has been doing with them all through His time on earth. Here it had been intermittent and occasional. In heaven it is to be permanent. But wherever it is, we have the personal touch: no command, no coercion, only the gentle leading of the individual to where He can open his eyes and use him and give to him.

That is how He calls us too to act with other people. There are several easy, natural, 'small' uses of this word in Acts. The Philippian jailor (16:33) takes Paul and Silas on one side for special treatment apart from the rest of the prisoners and washes their stripes. Paul takes along those four poor men who cannot afford the money for the sacrifices, and helps them to fulfil their vows in the temple (21:26). The centurion in 23:18 puts a kindly hand on the arm of the rather nervous young nephew of Paul and leads him reassuringly along to the chief captain. Barnabas takes Mark along with him in 15:39 after the quarrel with Paul. Rightly or wrongly he feels that Paul has been too hard on him. He wants to restore his confidence by this personal contact.

But whether it is the little things, or the glory of Mount Hermon, or the agony of Gethsemane, it is this personal contact which counts. We can be ready for all things if Christ has hold of us. And He can use us in His service with our fellow men only if we are ready to take hold of them with the love with which we ourselves have been grasped and held.

5. THE JOURNEYING OF JESUS

Jesus was always on the move, and the Gospels use several words to describe His journeyings. The one which we shall mainly, though not exclusively, examine now is the verb *poreuomai* ('journey', 'go') which, in its simple form or compounded with some preposition that further defines it, occurs in all the Gospels, but most frequently in Luke—so much so that Luke has been called 'The Gospel of the Road'.

The English dictionary says that 'travel' and 'travail' are etymologically the same. Travelling can be very hard work, and few people manage to make the best of it. It is easier to be selfish while travelling than almost anywhere else. Rarely do we manage to be 'travelling givers'. Normally we endure travel only as an interlude between periods of comfort.

No doubt Jesus would have liked a job like mine was for many years, with but two minutes walk from my house to my classroom, leaving all His physical energies conserved for teaching and service. Yet He never let physical difficulties detract from His mission, never failed to make His travelling sacramental. Look at Him in Mk. 2:23 as He journeys through the cornfields. His disciples are hungry. He probably is too. Yet He has the spiritual energy left to give His critics some of His most penetrating teaching: 'The Sabbath was made for man, and not man for the Sabbath'. Look at Him again in Jn. 4:6 sitting 'wearied with His journey' by the well. Yet He can turn that very weariness into the means of saving a soul and ultimately a city (vv. 39-42). What a lesson for us!

We are not told the purpose of those two journeys, but much of His travelling is *strategic*. Sometimes it involves evasive action, escape: 'But He, passing through the midst of them, went His way' (Lk. 4:30). Note in particular that astonishing circuitous route in Mk. 7:31, which, as the map shows, trebles the length of His journey. It is like travelling from Bangalore to Vellore via Guntakal, Bezwada and Madras! Professor F. C. Burkitt suggested that He did it in order to avoid trouble from Herod. Jesus was not afraid to run away. He would have been wrong to blunder into danger at some futile moment, wasting His mission by meeting His death up some side-track. But when the strategic moment does come, He goes forward gladly without hesitation, knowing that the end will be the Cross.

The key verse is Lk. 9:51: 'When the days were fulfilled that He should be taken up, He set His face like a flint to journey to Jerusalem'. That is the irrevocable stroke, perfectly timed, at God's hour. His first action (9:52) was to journey through that Samaritan village where He was so discourteously received. Jn. 4:4, describing another journey in that area, says 'He *must needs* pass through Samaria'. There was no necessity so far as geography was concerned. Most Jewish pilgrims from Galilee to Jerusalem went down the Jordan valley expressly to avoid Samaria; but the necessities of Jesus are the necessities of God's planning.

There was also the time when He journeyed into Judaea to awake Lazarus out of sleep (Jn. 11:11). A crazy journey the disciples thought it, though Thomas was ready to journey with Him whatever the consequences (v. 16). But He who had seen that it was right to avoid the Nazareth mob and Herod had no hesitation here. During the war, when travel was discouraged in England, there were notices at railway booking offices saying, 'Is your journey really necessary?' That depends on a person's standards and his objectives. Jesus states His own dominant objective in one of His parables: 'Does he not leave the ninety and nine . . . and journey after that which is lost until he find it?' That is really the sole test of necessity, both for His journeying and for ours.

How was the journey begun in Lk. 9:51 completed? Its next stage was when He journeyed into Jerusalem on Palm Sunday

(Lk. 19:36) to conquer the city in meekness.   It continued as the disciples in Acts 1:10 gazed steadfastly into heaven watching Him still journeying, as the Forerunner entering in beyond the veil.   And He Himself stated its ultimate intention in Jn. 14:2: 'I journey on to prepare a place for *you*'.

But the Lord's journeying is not something that He does alone, leaving His disciples to stay behind, sitting still.   Look at the number of times that He commands other people to *go*, times when the gospel makes it clear that the effectiveness of Jesus' word or action depends upon the obedience of those whom He commands.   He says to the nobleman in Jn. 4:50: '*Go your way;* your son lives'—and as the man believes and obeys, his servants meet him with the glad news.   He says to the ten lepers in Lk. 17:14: '*Go* and show yourselves to the priests'. 'And . . . *as they went*, they were cleansed'.   His last word to the lawyer to whom He has told the parable of the Good Samaritan is '*Go*, and do thou likewise' (Lk. 10:37).   Look too at His admiration of the centurion's directness in Lk. 7:8: 'I say to this one, *Go*, and he goes'.   Things happen when people obey and go. When they don't, nothing gets done.   That explains quite a bit of our ineffectiveness.

Then there are His commands to go and *continue His work*: '*Go* . . . to the lost sheep of the house of Israel' (Mt. 10:6); '*Go* to the partings of the highways, and as many as ye shall find, bid to the marriage feast' (Mt. 22:9); '*Go* unto my brethren, and say to them, I ascend unto my Father and your Father' (Jn. 20:17); '*Go* . . . and make disciples of all the nations' (Mt. 28:19). We too are to be a journeying community—in body, in mind, in love—if we are to carry on the Master's work.

Lastly, 'Go' is not only a command; it is a gift.   'Thy faith hath saved thee; *journey out* into peace' (Lk. 7:50).   The blessing and the command are given together.   As the disciples were journeying to Emmaus, 'Jesus Himself drew near and journeyed with them' (Lk. 24:15).   He still does.   And He always will.

II. SOME CHRISTIAN BELIEFS

6. THE ONLY ONE

Christianity has always claimed to be unique. 'Although there may be so-called gods in heaven or on earth ... yet for us there is one God, the Father ... and one Lord, Jesus Christ', says St. Paul in 1 Cor. 8:5, 6 (R.S.V.), and every true Christian has always made the same confession. We should therefore expect to find this truth strongly entrenched in the N.T., and so it is—in many ways. We shall look at just one of them now: the N.T. use of the Greek adjective *monos*, usually translated either 'only' or 'alone'. The corresponding adverb is normally translated in the same way, and it may seem strange that some uses of the English words have been included and some omitted. The reason is simply that we are restricting ourselves to the Greek adjective, which has more striking uses than the adverb.

The adjective occurs in all 47 times—7 in Matthew, 4 in Mark, 8 in Luke, 10 in John, 9 in Paul, 4 in the Pastoral Epistles, and 5 in the remaining books.

Some of its uses merely illustrate the normal sense of the word. A man against whom a fellow-Christian has sinned must first of all speak to him alone with no one else present (Mt. 18:15). In Mk. 4:10 Jesus is alone with His disciples away from the crowd. In Jn. 6:22 the disciples sail away alone without Jesus. These are simple statements without ethical judgment or theological significance.

A larger number of cases, however, though not concerned with the uniqueness of the Christian faith, are important because of the ethical judgments of approval or fault-finding attached to them. There are 11 of the former and 10 of the latter.

Approval. In Mt. 12:4 and Lk. 6:4 the priests are noted as special people who alone were allowed to eat the shewbread. In Mk. 9:2 three disciples are given the privilege of being taken by Jesus to the Mount of Transfiguration by themselves alone. In Rom. 16:4 Prisca and Aquila receive the gratitude not of Paul alone but of all the Gentile churches. In Gal. 6:4 a man's worth is to be judged on his own merits alone and not by comparison with his neighbour. In Phil. 4:15 the Philippians are commended because they alone stood by Paul in his need.   So too in Col. 4:11 there is a small group whom alone Paul singles out as his fellow-workers and his strength.   In 1 Thess. 3:1 he speaks of himself as having remained alone in Athens in order that his companion Timothy might go back to Thessalonica. 2 Tim. 4:11 singles out another individual for praise: 'Luke alone is with me'.   2 Jn. 1 parallels Rom. 16:4: the church to which John is writing is loved not by John alone but by all who know the truth.   And finally Heb. 9:7 carries Mt. 12:4 a big stage further.   One refers to the ordinary priests who alone have the privilege of eating the shewbread; the other speaks of the single man who alone has the dread responsibility of entering the Holy of Holies.

Fault-finding.   In 10 places 'only' and 'alone' are used to note some fault or defect or indicate some criticism.   'Man shall not live by bread alone' (Mt. 4:4; Lk. 4:4).   'My sister left me to serve alone' (Lk. 10:40).   'Do you alone sojourn in Jerusalem and not know what has happened?' (Lk. 24:18).   'Jesus was left alone, and the woman', by those who could not stand up to His searching question (Jn. 8:9).   'Except a grain of wheat fall into the earth and die, it abides by itself alone' and useless (Jn. 12:24). 'You shall be scattered, every man to his own, and shall leave me alone' (Jn. 16:32).   Similarly Paul quotes Elijah: 'I am left alone, and they seek my life' (Rom. 11:3).   Two verses in 1 Corinthians complete this section: Paul first complains that he and Barnabas are singled out as alone having no right to forbear working (9:6), and he finishes by criticising the Corinthians' individualistic attitude: 'Did the word of God come to you alone?' (14:36).

All the above instances, however, are of far less significance than the remaining ones which stress the uniqueness of God and of Christ.

There are four places in the Gospels where Jesus is spoken of as being physically alone, but where much more than His physical aloneness is implied.   After the feeding of the five thousand, Matthew, Mark and John all in different ways refer to this aloneness. Matthew tells how He compelled the disciples to go away, and goes on to say that when evening came He was alone in the mountain praying (14:23).   Mk. 6:47 says essentially the same.   Jn. 6:15 does not mention the prayer, but stresses that He withdrew alone so that He should not be made into an earthly king. In each case there is a distinction between Him and the multitude, between Him and His disciples. He is not on an equal footing with them; He is apart and unique. Luke also has an 'alone' after the feeding of the multitude, but in a different connection: 'As He was praying alone' (9:18). Christ's prayer life, like so much else, is distinct from ours.

The heart of the N.T. message, however, comes with that repeated phrase, 'The Only God'. Jn. 5:44 speaks of 'the glory that comes from the only God'. He is 'the only true God' (Jn. 17:3), 'the only wise God' (Rom. 16:27), 'the only God' again in 1 Tim. 1:17, 'the blessed and only Potentate' (1 Tim. 6:15), the One 'who only hath immortality' (1 Tim. 6:16), 'the only God our Saviour' (Jude 25), the One to whom it must be said, 'Thou only art holy' (Rev. 15:4).

Because He is the only God, there are things that He alone can do. 'Who can forgive sins but God alone?' (Lk. 5:21). No one knows what the future will be, 'but the Father only' (Mt. 24:36). And the command which rebukes Satan, and which is passed on to us through Christ, is 'Him only shalt thou serve' (Mt. 4:10; Lk. 4:8).

What is true of the Father is true also of the Son. Jude 4 speaks of Him as 'our only Master and Lord'. The R.V. margin points out that it is possible to translate this 'the only Master (i.e. God), and our Lord Jesus Christ', and some commentators agree with this. Either translation is equally good Christian truth. The disciples from the earliest times had regarded Jesus as their only Master: 'To whom else shall we go?' (Jn. 6:68), and the chosen three at the Transfiguration, after they had looked at the great lawgiver, Moses, and the representative of the prophets, Elijah, finally 'saw no one, save Jesus only' (Mt. 17:8; Mk. 9:8). Lk. 9:36 adds something more: 'When the voice came, Jesus was found alone'. God's word 'This is my Son' was meant only for Him, and for no one else, however great.

There is a final word which unites the Two who are alone: 'I am not alone, but I and the Father that sent me' (Jn. 8:16). 'He that sent me is with me; he has not left me alone' (Jn. 8:29). 'Yet I am not alone, because the Father is with me' (Jn. 16:32). All this is part of the paradox of the Trinity, but it is Christian truth. The Father is unique, and so is the Son. Each can be spoken of as 'alone' and yet, because they are one, they are together.

Courteously, yet firmly, the Christian must always proclaim this truth.   There is much good elsewhere, and we are wrong if we deny or condemn it.   God has not left Himself without witness in many ways.   Yet He stands alone as the Bible declares Him, and His unique revelation, far beyond any other way in which even He has revealed Himself, is in His Son, Jesus Christ. We need not simply to declare that with our lips, but to be sure of it in all our thinking, and to act upon it in all our living.

7. THE TRANSCENDENCE OF GOD

The classic reply of the Hindu monist when anyone seeks to define God is to say *Neti, Neti*.   He is not like that, He cannot be defined.   The Christian faith is not content with such a merely negative answer.   God *has* been defined.   Jesus, in His word and even more in His life, has defined Him.   And yet *defined* is not an adequate word.   Strictly speaking, it means *limited*, and there are no limits to God.

The N.T. is very clearly aware of this and so, in addition to the abundant revelation of God that is given us there, it keeps on reminding us of what still lies beyond what we know now. This it does in many ways.   One way is to use the negative method that the ancient Hindus used, though with a fundamental difference.   Greek, like Sanskrit, puts the letter *a*- before many of its words to negative their meaning, as English puts *un*- or *in*-.   (*Suttham, a-suttham* give the pattern in Indian languages). And so the N.T. uses word after word beginning with *a*- to emphasise the transcendence of God in what He is and what He does.   He is wonderfully revealed to us in Jesus, and yet all the time we are to remember how much there is beyond our knowledge.   Seventeen of these 'negative' words will be briefly examined in this chapter, though the picture with which they will leave us will not be negative, but very positive.

1.   God is *invisible, unseen* (Rom. 1:20; 1 Tim. 1:17).   He is not to be thought of as material, however much we may be tempted to put Him in the categories that we understand.   He is visible only to the spiritual eye of faith (Heb. 11:27), and pre-eminently in Jesus.

2.   He is also *incorruptible*, not liable to the corruption of this earth, undying, eternal (Rom. 1:23; 1 Tim. 1:17), and He bestows

something of His nature upon us. He raises the dead incorruptible (1 Cor. 15:52). He gives us the incorruptible crown of life (1 Cor. 9:25). He has begotten us out of His own incorruptible nature (1 Pet. 1:23) for an incorruptible inheritance (1 Pet. 1:4).

3. This life of His he has shared especially with Jesus, our great High Priest, appointing Him 'according to the power of an *indissoluble* life' (Heb. 7:16); that is to say, a life that cannot be broken up and destroyed but remains one and whole for ever.

4. The same emphasis on God's undying eternity is further made in another metaphor, this time from the realm of botany. The inheritance that He will give us is *unfading* (1 Pet. 1:4); we shall have an *unfading* wreath of glory from Him (1 Pet. 5:4). The coveted garland which was the prize for the victor in Greek races soon faded, however valued it was. What God has to give us is something that will not fade throughout eternity. It will always be fresh and living.

5. God is also *immutable*, unchanging in His purposes and decisions (Heb. 6:17, 18). He is not like what we so often are: thinking one thing one day and another the next, altering our plans so that no one can depend on us. Hebrews uses the metaphor of a solemn oath, such as men intend to be final, to show that when God once makes a promise we can count on Him. He will never break it.

6. This thought is also expressed by another word in Rom. 11:29: 'The gifts and the calling of God are *unrepented of*'. Sometimes we give away something and then later on we wish that we had not done so. God is not like that. He does not make mistakes in what He gives, and so He has no need to wish to change His mind after the gift has been made.

7. Another way in which His constancy is expressed is by the word in Heb. 12:28: *unshakable*. All earthly power is so easily shaken. The whole of history is the story of empires that last for a while and then topple over. But the kingdom that God gives to those who obey Him and are ready to serve Him is the unshakable kingdom of His own power.

8. This power is never power on the material level. The Jews relied too much on the material. Their temple, and the rite of circumcision, both central to their religion, were things made or done with hands. Jesus emphasises that God's future temple will be *un-hand-made* (to give the Greek literally), not made with hands out of earthly material (Mk. 14:58). So also the heavenly body which will finally be ours will be 'not made

with hands' (2 Cor. 5:1); and the 'circumcision of Christ', the putting off of our earthly nature by a spiritual action not done with hands, supersedes the external Jewish act of circumcision (Col. 2:11).

What is true of God's transcendence over us on the metaphysical level is equally true on the moral.

9.   James 1:13 uses a remarkable word about Him, saying that He is *'untempted* by evil', or perhaps *'inexperienced* in evil'. We are far too experienced in it. Here is possibly the only sphere in which God is less experienced than we are.

10.   The divine moral transcendence is carried yet further by the word *undefiled*, used of Jesus in Heb. 7:26, and of our prospective inheritance in 1 Pet. 1:4. Things and people on this earth are so easily polluted by the smuts of ubiquitous dirt or the stain of filthy sin. In Him there is no defilement. Everything is spotless and pure.

11.   In the same verse in Hebrews (7:26) our great High Priest is also spoken of as *guileless*, the actual word being simply the negative of the word *bad*. The phrase 'not bad' has unfortunately somewhat changed its meaning these days, but if we give it its full literal sense, it means that Jesus and His Father with Him are the very opposite of all that is evil, the very perfection of goodness, utterly beyond the goodness of mortal men in themselves, apart from the grace that comes from God alone.

12.   From every angle we apply to God that common adjective *true*, and it is included in this list because by derivation the Greek word is a negative: *a-lēthēs, unconcealing*, that which does not hide reality, or deceive as men do. It is an adjective that is rarely applied to men in the N.T. It is rightly reserved almost exclusively for God and for His Son—for examples see Jn. 3:33 and Mk. 12:14.

Finally we come to four words by which St. Paul and St. Peter, with their sense of the greatness and majesty of God, attempt to say what they know cannot really be said.

13.   There is the word translated *unsearchable* in Eph. 3:8 and 'past tracing out' in Rom. 11:33. It is a metaphor from hunting. The trained shikari does not find it hard to track down an animal. Foot-marks, broken twigs, remains of the animal's prey, are all clear guides. God's ways, and His riches in Christ, are not so simply explored. They go too deep.

14. God's judgments too are *unsearchable* (Rom. 11:33). The English translation is the same, but the metaphor is different. They cannot be fathomed by investigation such as a clever lawyer might undertake successfully. They are beyond our efforts to comprehend fully.

15. Even the gift of God's grace which He Himself puts within us is ultimately *indescribable* (2 Cor. 9:15). It goes beyond all our powers of speech.

16. And yet, despite this, we can rejoice with joy *unspeakable* (1 Pet. 1:8), with emotions that we cannot put into words.

The grammatical form of all these words may be negative. There is nothing negative about what they give us. Here is a God far above our comprehension, far purer than our imperfection and sin, but not cut off from us. All the while He is ready to share with us as much as our poor capacity can receive. We have (17) an *unfailing* treasure laid up for us in the heavens (Lk. 12:33), and the unchanging, undefiled, unfailing God has us in His care and love.

8. THE REVELATION OF GOD

Christianity is not essentially a philosophy or a code of morals, though it includes both. It is essentially a revelation, given to us from above. We therefore expect to find the word *Revelation* frequently in the New Testament.

The Greek noun is *apokalupsis*, which occurs 18 times, and the verb *apokalupto*, 'I reveal', comes 26 times, making a total of 44 uses which we may treat together. The words are not specially frequent in the Gospels. Matthew has the verb four times, Luke has it five times and the noun once, John has the verb once. Their great user is Paul, who has the two words 26 times in all, though 1 Peter with its six occurrences has a greater proportion compared with its length. The Book of Revelation has the noun as its first word, but that is all.

Revelation has three aspects: the one who reveals, the content of the revelation, and the person or persons to whom the revelation is made. We shall be dividing the N.T. references under these three heads.

1. *The Revealer.* The person of the revealer is not always explicitly stated, but where no name is mentioned it may usually be taken to be God Himself. Assuming this, He is the Revealer in three-quarters of our instances. Outstanding examples are

Christ's word to Peter: 'Flesh and blood hath not revealed it unto thee, but my Father who is in heaven' (Mt. 16:17), and Paul's description of his conversion: 'It pleased God to reveal His Son in me' (Gal. 1:16). In cases such as Eph. 3:3, when Paul speaks of the mystery that was made known to him 'by revelation', it is clear that he is thinking of God as the Revealer. A few instances present difficulty. Who is Jesus thinking of when in Mt. 10:26 He says, 'There is nothing hidden that shall not be revealed'? T. W. Manson is probably right when he suggests that Jesus is addressing His opponents and referring to their evil thoughts that God will reveal at the Judgment Day. And who reveals the Man of Sin in 2 Thess. 2:3, 6, 8? Probably again it is God, according to Paul's belief. Even the movements of the Evil One are controlled by Him. God will not allow him to get out of hand.

But Christ is also the Revealer. He reveals the Father to men (Mt. 11:27; Lk. 10:22). His incarnation reveals the thoughts out of many hearts (Lk. 2:35). Paul knows Him by special revelations (2 Cor. 12:1, 7; Gal. 1:12). The whole of the last book of the N.T. is a revelation from Jesus, given to Him by God to reveal (Rev. 1:1).

Paul speaks of the Gospel also as a revealer: 'I am not ashamed of the gospel ... In it is revealed a righteousness of God' (Rom. 1:17). And even men can be revealers, when God gives them a revelation to pass on (1 Cor. 14:6, 26).

2. *The Content of the Revelation.* This is astonishingly full and varied. It may be a revelation of some special aspect of the nature or power of God: John 12:38 quotes Isaiah's words about the revelation of 'the arm of the Lord', His strength. Paul speaks in one verse of the revelation of His righteousness, and in the next of the revelation of His wrath (Rom. 1:17, 18). He goes on to speak of the revelation of His glory (Rom. 8:18), and of the depths in Him that are revealed by the Spirit (1 Cor. 2:10). There is also knowledge of Himself that God reveals (Eph. 1:17). But greatest of all is His Son's revelation of Him as Father (Mt. 11:27; Lk. 10:22).

Next we see how Christ Himself is revealed. That took place first at the Incarnation, when He was a light that would be a revelation to the Gentiles (Lk. 2:32). It continues when every Christian has Christ revealed in his heart, as Paul had on the Damascus road (Gal. 1:16). The complete revelation will be

at the End, when the Son of Man will be revealed (Lk. 17:30).
We do not know when or in what form that revelation will be,
but three times over the New Testament speaks of its coming:
we are to wait for it (1 Cor. 1:7); it will bring rest (2 Thess. 1:7),
and at it our stedfast faith will receive recognition from God
(1 Pet. 1:7). That will be a faith in Jesus as Messiah, as it was
revealed to Peter (Mt. 16:17), with all that that faith implies.
And the revelation will come by God's grace at the end (1 Pet.
1:13), as it will have been by His grace throughout. The Day
will be associated with the fire of testing (1 Cor. 3:13), but it
will be a day of salvation (1 Pet. 1:5). The whole creation eagerly
looks for that time of glory, when the sons of God will be revealed
(Rom. 8:18; cp. 1 Pet. 4:13, 5:1), and the time will certainly
come because, as the first verse of the book of Revelation indicates,
the whole of the future is in God's hands.

The first generation of Christians may have expected that
revelation very soon. It has not yet come as they expected it.
Yet they received revelation not only for the future but for the
present. Paul declares that he received the whole gospel message
through revelation (Gal. 1:12). Revelations of any kind could
come to Christians as they worshipped (1 Cor. 14:6, 26, 30).
Jesus Himself had declared that God reveals His truth to babes
(Mt. 11:25; Lk. 10:21). He still continues to do so. The
revelation may be simple guidance for a new step to be taken
(Gal. 2:2) or the gift of clear Christian thinking (Phil. 3:15).
It may be the ineffable revelation that came to Paul in rapturous
ecstasy (2 Cor. 12:1, 7), or it may be the revelation of the secret
that was so hard for the Jew to accept: that the Gentiles have
an equal share with the Jews in the heritage of the Gospel
(Rom. 16:25; Eph. 3:3, 5). It is a revelation of the centrality
of faith (Gal. 3:23), and a revelation not meant for ourselves alone
but, as the prophets of old were made to see, a revelation meant
to be passed on to others (1 Pet. 1:12).

But the revelation is not only of what God has to give. It is
also a revelation of what we are. Christ's coming meant that
the thoughts of many hearts were revealed (Lk. 2:35), and even
the coming of the Man of Sin is spoken of as a revelation (2 Thess.
2:3, 6, 8). He will himself be exposed, and his coming will
show men in their true nature.

3. *The Receivers of the Revelation.* These too are many and
varied. There were the prophets of old (1 Pet. 1:12). There

are Christians in general, as in Rom. 8:18; 1 Cor. 2:10; Eph.1:17; Phil. 3:15; Rev. 1:1.   In a number of cases the recipients are not mentioned, e.g. Rom. 8:19.   In two cases they are mentioned individually: Peter in Mt. 16:17, and Paul many times (2 Cor. 12:1, 7; Gal. 1:12, 16, 2:2; Eph. 3:3).   Revelation is also made to those who are men of faith (Rom. 1:17; Gal. 3:23), whoever they are.   Simeon at the beginning saw that the revelation included the Gentiles (Lk. 2:32).   Jesus is really saying the same thing when He says that revelation is given to babes (Mt. 11:25; Lk. 10:21), those who do not trust in their own efforts but know that they must rely entirely upon God.   And He makes it clear that revelation is not something that we deserve, but is entirely in His hands, when He says that it is made to whomsoever the Son wills (Mt. 11:27; Lk. 10:22).

But the revelation may not always be to people eager to receive it.   There is the wrath of God revealed to the ungodly in Rom. 1:18, and the judgment of God revealed to the impenitent in Rom. 2:5.   And sometimes there may be no one who will receive the revelation: 'To whom has the arm of the Lord been revealed ?' cries John (12:38), in grief that those to whom Jesus came would not listen to His revelation.   Revelation is always a two way affair: what He gives evokes a response, and His revelation itself reveals the thoughts of men's hearts to Him, so that He knows what they are (Lk. 2:35).   How do *we* stand in the light of His very varied revelation to us ?

9. WISDOM

We should expect to find Wisdom as one of the important words of the New Testament—and indeed it is.   The noun comes 51 times; the adjective 'wise' 20 times, and the verb 'to make wise' twice.   Their combined distribution is interesting. Matthew has them five times, Mark only once, Luke and Acts eleven, John never, Paul 44 times (including 26 in 1 Corinthians 1-3), James five times and the other books seven.

The surprising thing about Wisdom in the New Testament is that it is very far from being generally praised.   In nearly one third of its mentions it is quite clearly condemned.   It meets with approval under only certain very definite conditions. There is no *gnāna mārga*, as generally understood, in the New Testament.   Human wisdom, as Paul argues especially in the opening chapters of 1 Corinthians, confers no benefit on man. It is only the wisdom that is God's gift which is worth possessing.

We may therefore divide the uses of the words into six sections: 1. Mere human wisdom, usually condemned; 2. Human wisdom spoken of in a neutral sense or with a measure of approval; 3. The Wisdom of God in the sense in which the Old Testament uses the word; 4. The wisdom of Jesus in His incarnate life; 5. The wisdom of God in heaven or of the Exalted Christ; 6. The gift of wisdom to men from Father, Son or Spirit.

1. The condemnation of human wisdom is found especially when Paul is writing to a Greek church at Corinth because Greeks sought wisdom (1 Cor. 1:22) and thought that they could be saved by it. Normally, however, it led men astray; 'the world by its wisdom knew not God' (1:21), its wisdom was foolishness in His sight (3:19). 'The wisdom of this age' (2:6) is not God's wisdom at all; He has made it foolish (1:20), and has chosen the things that in the world's sight are foolish to put to shame those who think themselves to be wise (1:27). So Paul speaks of God's destroying the wisdom of the wise (1:19), of His taking the wise in their craftiness (3:19), of His knowing the reasonings of the wise, that they are vain (3:20). And he learns from God to say 'Where is the wise man?' (1:20), and to come to Corinth 'not in wisdom of speech' (1:17), 'not with excellency of speech or wisdom' (2:1), 'not in persuasive words of wisdom' (2:4), 'not in words which man's wisdom teaches' (2:13), so that his hearers' faith may stand 'not in the wisdom of men but in the power of God' (2:5). If anyone thinks that he is wise, it is better for him to become a fool in the world's eyes (3:18), and Paul can thank God that 'not many wise after the flesh' had been called (1:26).

This teaching, so strongly emphasised in 1 Corinthians, is echoed elsewhere. Rom. 1:22 speaks of those who professed to be wise and become fools, 2 Cor. 1:12 contrasts fleshly wisdom with the grace of God. Col. 2:23 talks of the human things that have a mere show of wisdom. Jas. 3:15 describes the wisdom that does not come from above as 'earthly, sensual, devilish'. 2 Pet. 1:16 has the phrase 'cunningly devised fables', which is literally 'fables that have been made wise', too wise, too clever in fact. All this condemnation of the wrong kind of wisdom is very strong but very necessary.

2. There is a human wisdom, however, that does not need to be condemned. Jesus in Mt. 11:25 and Lk. 10:21, speaks of things that are hidden from the wise and understanding, but

He does not specially condemn them for their wisdom.   Moses was 'instructed in all the wisdom of the Egyptians (Acts 7:22), and very noble wisdom it was.   Paul speaks of himself as a debtor both to wise and to foolish (Rom. 1:14).   He urges the Romans to be wise as regards that which is good (16:19), and asks the Corinthians 'Is there not one wise man among you ?' (1 Cor. 6:5). The Ephesians are bidden to 'walk, not as unwise but as wise' (5:15), and the Colossians to 'walk in wisdom towards them that are without' (4:5).   Paul is the last person to rant indiscriminately against wisdom as a whole.

3.   Even if he had wanted to, the Old Testament would not have allowed him.   Jesus Himself speaks of the wisdom of Solomon (Mt. 12:42; Lk. 11:31).   He also lets the Wisdom of God speak, as it were, as a separate person (Lk. 11:49), as she does, for example, in the eighth chapter of Proverbs.   And when, in Mt. 11:19 and Lk. 7:35, He describes Wisdom as being proved right by her works (or her children), He is thinking in Old Testament terms of God's Wisdom, which has sent both the Baptist and Himself into the world.

4.   The New Testament also emphasises Jesus' own wisdom when He was here on earth.   He grew up, filled with wisdom (Lk. 2:40), and advanced in wisdom as He advanced in age (2:52). There was a wisdom about Him that astonished men (Mt. 13:54; Mk. 6:2).

5.   But this is transcended by the New Testament description of the wisdom of God in heaven and the wisdom of the Exalted Christ.   'Oh the depth of the riches of the wisdom of God', sings Paul (Rom. 11:33), such wisdom that even His foolishness is wiser than men   (1 Cor. 1:25), and by His wisdom men are kept from knowing Him by their own wisdom (1:21).   For He is 'the only wise God' (Rom. 16:27), to whom alone can be ascribed 'blessing and glory and wisdom' (Rev. 7:12), and by whose 'manifold wisdom' (Eph. 3:10) His purposes were revealed in Jesus Christ.   That means that Christ alone is 'the wisdom of God' (1 Cor. 1:24) and has become to us 'wisdom from God' (1:30).   He is the One 'in whom all the treasures of wisdom are hidden' (Col. 2:3).   And so of Him also it can be sung that He is 'worthy . . . to receive the power, and riches, and wisdom' (Rev. 5:12).

6.   This means that in nearly every case in the New Testament where men possess wisdom it has come to them as a gift from God —the Father, the Son, or the Spirit.   There are 23 such instances

(strangely enough the same number as the instances of human wisdom condemned in our first section). It is Christ who sends wise men into the world (Mt. 23:34). When the disciples are being persecuted, it is Christ who will give them 'a mouth and wisdom' (Lk. 21:15). It was because Stephen and the other deacons were filled with the Spirit that they were filled with wisdom (Acts 6:3, 10). Stephen himself emphasises that it was God who gave Joseph his wisdom (7:10). If Paul can speak wisdom to the Corinthians, it is because it is the wisdom of God (1 Cor. 2:6, 7). If he is a 'wise master-builder' (3:10), it is only according to the grace of God given to him. If anyone wants to become wise, he must become a fool or he will not be receptive to God (3:18), and it is only through the Spirit that men are given a word of wisdom (12:8). Any wisdom that we have is what God made to abound to us (Eph. 1:8). It is He who gives us a spirit of wisdom (1:17), and who fills us 'with the knowledge of His will in all spiritual wisdom' (Col. 1:9). If Paul can 'teach every man in all wisdom', it is only because Christ works in Him mightily (1:28, 29). If the Colossians are to possess wisdom, it is only when the word of Christ dwells in them richly (3:16). The Scriptures are written according to the wisdom given by God to their writers (2 Pet. 3:15), and therefore they are able to make their readers 'wise unto salvation' (2 Tim. 3:15). Where there are difficult passages, as in Revelation, the writer can exclaim: 'Here is need of wisdom' (Rev. 13:18, 17:9—Kingsley Williams), and the need is supplied only by God.

And so St. James has the final word: 'If any of you lacks wisdom, let him ask God, who gives to all liberally' (Jas. 1:5). Then he will be able to show that he is wise, by a life lived 'in meekness of wisdom' (3:13), for the truly wise man is never conceited. He knows that all that he has is God's gift. 'And the wisdom that comes from above is first pure, then peaceable, gentle, open to reason, full of mercy and good fruits, without uncertainty or insincerity' (3:17, R.S.V.). I like to remember that those words, in the original Greek, stand on my father's memorial tablet in the chapel of the college where he taught them to his students in the class-room and by his example. They were true of him, and they are the true *gnāna mārga*, not a way *to* God, but a way of living given *by* Him.

10. AUTHORITY

Authority plays an essential part in everyone's life. The dictionary defines it firstly as 'the right to command, or give an ultimate decision', and secondly as 'derived or delegated power'. All of us, to a greater or lesser degree, have certain rights and powers of our own; all of us also have other rights and powers which we owe to the authority given to us by someone above us. A dictator has absolute authority. Democratic 'authorities' have only the power delegated to them by the nation as a whole. At the other end of the scale, a small child has no authority over others except the rights and claims upon them that he possesses as a human being.

In the light of all this, what has the New Testament to say ? The word for us to study is *Exousia*, which is variously translated 'authority', 'right', and 'power', though when the latter word is used, we must be careful to understand it not as mere strength but as the power associated with authority.

The word comes 102 times in the New Testament. It is divided up as follows: Matthew 10, Mark 10, Luke 16, John 8, Acts 7, Paul 26, other epistles 4, Revelation 21—a fairly even distribution, though the occurrences in Revelation are somewhat outstanding.

1. It is used in the sense of *personal human rights* eleven times, nine of them by St. Paul. In 1 Cor. 9 he speaks six times of his 'right' to be supported by the church to which he ministers (verses 4, 5, 6, 12 (twice), 18), and he makes the same point in 2 Thess. 3:9. In 1 Cor. 8:9 he speaks of the right, or liberty, of men to eat what they choose, to be vegetarians or not. No one has ever been sure what he means in 1 Cor. 11:10 when he says that in church a woman ought 'to have a sign of authority on her head' (R.V.). Some take it as meaning a sign of man's authority over her. Others would put it in this class of human rights: the wearing of the veil or sari or hat is a sign of her dignity, her right to respect in God's presence. The other two uses in this sense of 'right' are in Heb. 13:10, where it is stated that the Jewish priests have no right to share in the Christian sacrifice on Calvary, and in Rev. 22:14, where those who have cleansed themselves have the right to share in the life of the heavenly city.

Yet a Christian always hesitates to talk about his rights, even when he is disclaiming them. He knows that they are not absolutely his. They come from God. If Paul has rights, they are only rights in the gospel (1 Cor. 9:18), and in Revelation, as we shall see, no one has rights or authority of his own, but only what he is *given*.

2. From personal human rights we pass on to *human authority*. About many of the seventeen uses of the word in this sense there is little to be said. When Jesus, in Lk. 12:11, speaks of 'the authorities', He uses the word just as we should, to refer to those in charge of administering justice. The same is true when Luke himself (20:20) speaks of 'the authority of the governor', and of the 'authority (or jurisdiction) of Herod' (23:7). The same is true of the 'authority' from the chief priests with which Paul went to Damascus (Acts 9:14, 26:10, 12). In a somewhat more individual sense it is true of a person's possessions being within his own power or authority (Acts 5:4; Rom. 9:21), and of a man's will being within his own authority (1 Cor. 7:37). But both Jesus and Paul make it very clear that such human authority is not absolute; it is only delegated. Pilate says to Jesus, 'Do you not know that I have authority to release you and authority to crucify you'? and Jesus's reply is, 'You would have no authority except it were given you from above' (Jn. 19:10, 11). And when in Rom. 13:1-3 Paul speaks of the authorities, or the powers that be (compare also Tit. 3:1), he says most emphatically, 'There is no authority but of God'. Even that unpleasant person, Simon Magus, when he asks for power and authority to confer the Holy Spirit on men, realises that the power must be *given* him; it is not his own (Acts 8:19).

3. The same double aspect of authority can be seen *in Jesus Himself*. Twenty-seven times His authority is mentioned in the gospels. Sometimes that authority is spoken of as His own, or its source is not mentioned. People saw Him 'as having authority' when He taught (Mt. 7:29; Mk. 1:22). He spoke of Himself as having authority to forgive sins (Mt. 9:6; Mk. 2:10; Lk. 5:24). He commanded 'with authority' (Mk. 1:27; Lk. 4:36). His word was 'with authority' (Lk. 4:32).

But more often the emphasis is on the God-given nature of His authority. The centurion sees Him as one under authority, like himself (Mt. 8:9; Lk. 7:8). The crowds glorify God, who has given Him the power and authority to forgive sins and work miracles (Mt. 9:8). The argument with the chief priests and

others about His authority (the word is used eleven times in the
three accounts in Mt. 21:23-27; Mk. 11:28-33; Lk. 20:2-8)
turns on its origin, and though Jesus refuses to tell His opponents
where it comes from, lest they misuse His words, He makes it
perfectly clear what is in His mind. His final words in Matthew's
gospel (28:18) begin with 'All authority has been *given* to me'.
The same truth is underlined in St. John. The Father *gives*
the Son authority to execute judgment (5:27). If He has
authority to lay down His life and authority to take it again, it is
because of the commandment that He has received from
His Father (10:18). And in His final prayer He prays to
the Father who has given Him authority over all flesh
(17:2). Even He, God's Son, looks up to the One Absolute
Authority.

4. If this is true of Him, it must be even more *true of His
disciples and of any of God's agents.* Their authority is not their
own; it is always *given.* He gave them authority over unclean
spirits (Mt. 10:1; Mk. 3:15, 6:7; Lk. 9:1), and over other forces
of evil (Lk. 10:19). In His parables people have their authority
given to them (Mk. 13:34; Lk. 19:17). Supremely He *gives*
men their right to become children of God; they do not have it of
themselves (Jn. 1:12).

Paul too speaks of his authority in the same terms. It is
something that the Lord has *given* him (2 Cor. 10:8, 13:10).
And the agents in the Book of Revelation—some obviously,
some more mysteriously, agents to God's will—are all *given*
their authority: the victor in trial is given authority over the nations
(2:26); Death and Hades are given authority over a quarter of
the earth (6:8); the monstrous locusts (9:3) and the fierce horses
(9:19) are given their power; so are the two witnesses (cp. 11:6
with 11:3); so even is the Beast, permitted by God to exercise his
authority for a time (13:5, 7); the eagle in 14:18 comes from God's
altar and so has His authority; and the kings of Rome, with all
their authority, have it only as 'received' (17:12). Whatever the
interpretation of all these passages, the note of God as the source
of all authority runs throughout.

The other heavenly authorities also—those strange powers of
which the first century thought so much and we think so little—
are creations of God through Christ (Col. 1:16), under Christ's
headship (2:10), subject to Him (1 Pet. 3:22), and in need of
learning the manifold wisdom of God (Eph. 3:10). They have
no authority of their own.

5. Yet *the powers of evil* try to set up their own authority in opposition to God. Satan claims to possess it (Lk. 4:6). Even Jesus admits their power (Lk. 22:53; Acts 26:18). Paul too knows the authority of evil (Eph. 2:2; Col. 1:13), and Revelation speaks of the powers of evil delegating their authority even as God does (13:2, 4, 12). Most astonishing of all, the kings who have been given God's authority delegate that authority to the Beast (17:12, 13). How true that has often been! This opposition to God's authority is so determined that one of the New Testament names for the powers of evil is 'the authorities' (1 Cor. 15:24; Eph. 6:12; Col. 2:15).

6. None of their efforts, however, have final power. Over those whom God has raised, death has no authority (Rev. 20:6). For *the only ultimate authority is God* Himself. It is He alone who has power to cast into hell (Lk. 12:5). It is He who sets times and seasons within His own authority (Acts 1:7). It is He who has the power over the terrors in Revelation (16:9). It is from Him alone that the angel can come 'with great authority' (18:1). It is His Christ whose authority is shown in the destruction of Satan (12:10). And so Jude concludes his letter with the tremendous words: 'To the only God our Saviour, be glory, majesty, dominion and *authority* . . . now and for evermore'.

Thus the New Testament knows only one real Authority. We had better not claim personal authority, but if we may, it is only as given by God. The State has no authority except what God gives it. Even the Church dare claim no authority except under God. Evil may have temporary authority, but God's alone is final. Wherefore let all men be subject to Him, that He may be all in all.

11. FAITH, AS SHOWN IN THE LETTER TO THE HEBREWS

Faith is fundamentally the same throughout the New Testament, but different writers show us different aspects of it. For its basic definition we should rightly turn to Paul's letter to the Romans, but we should be very much the poorer if we lacked the special emphasis laid on it by the unknown author of Hebrews. He uses the word thirty-two times, in comparison with the thirty-eight or thirty-nine times in Romans, and Hebrews is only three-quarters the length of Romans.

Hebrews makes Paul's contrast between faith and works (6:1), but it chiefly attempts to bring its message home by personal illustration. Personal examples nearly always make a meaning clearer than abstract argument. Whereas Paul brings in only Abraham and Sarah, and even in their case does not attempt to give us a personal picture, Hebrews, in the great eleventh chapter in which the word *faith* occurs twenty-four times, refers to no fewer than fifteen Old Testament characters by name, and to a host of others anonymously. It is the living historical method. The other eight uses of the word in the epistle are the application of what is so vividly portrayed in chapter eleven by historical example.

The list in this chapter is most carefully, as well as vividly, compiled. It begins in verse one with a definition of what faith is, defining it by two words not found elsewhere in the New Testament. The first is translated *assurance* in the Revised Version. *Confidence* and *certainty* are words used in other translations. The Authorised Version and the Revised Version margin use the word *substance*, because that is the meaning of the Greek word elsewhere. All these translations help to give us the sense of what was in the writer's mind. It has been noticed that in the legal documents of the period, dug up in modern times from the sands of Egypt, the word is used for the title-deeds of a piece of property, the papers which give a man the assurance that the property belongs to him, even though he may never have seen it. The second word, *proving* or *proof*, has the same implication of certainty about something on which a man has not actually set eyes. If faith is essentially trust in God, in this letter it is, as Alexander Nairne says in his beautiful commentary, 'trust intensified by hope and love'.

After the definition, we have in verse two a summary of all that is about to be emphasised in the list which follows, and in verse thirty-nine there is the same phrase, summarising all that has been said. All the people given as examples 'had witness borne to them' by their faith. The phrase is old-fashioned. We may say 'won their reputation', as in the Bible Society translation, or 'stand on record,' or 'are commemorated' (N.E.B.) because of their faith. It is this faith which has caused them to be remembered to this day.

But before we come to the names we do have a theological assertion: it is by a sheer act of trust that we believe that God created the world out of nothing (v. 3), and if He can do that, there is nothing that He cannot do. And there is a further linking of faith with theological assertion in v. 6: He who comes to God must perform the great act of faith in His existence and in His meeting with men. It is no use talking about men of faith until these articles of the Creed are established. Then the writer can go ahead on the personal level.

He begins with two rather difficult examples: Abel and Enoch. The Old Testament nowhere says that Abel's sacrifice was offered 'by faith' (v. 4). It says only that God accepted it. Nor does the O.T. say that Enoch had faith (v. 5), or even that he was 'well-pleasing to God'. That is the phrase that the Greek translation of the O.T. substitutes for the Hebrew 'walked with God'. But the writer of Hebrews wants to include everyone possible in this category of faith, and so he assumes that both these men must have been acceptable to God on this ground. In this universal category he later includes others: the parents of Moses (v. 23) —'two commonplace people', as Chrysostom says—, the reluctant Israelites who crossed the Red Sea inspired only by the faith of Moses (v. 29), Rahab, the Jericho prostitute, who accepted the spies as God's messengers (v. 31), and the long list, named and unnamed, in vv. 32-38. Half way through he has paused to say 'These all died according to faith' (v. 13), 'on the journey of faith', as Nairne puts it, with faith as their sphere and standard, to use Moffatt's words in the International Critical Commentary. Men of faith are not merely those with the great names; they are many, and in all walks of life.

And how is faith shown? 1. It is shown by *obedience*. Noah built the ark by faith, obeying God's command, and so saved both the animal and the human race (v. 7). By faith Abraham obeyed God's command, left his secure life, and went out to found the people of God (v. 8). Through Israel's act of obedience to God in faith, the walls of Jericho fell down, and the way into the promised land was opened (v. 30).

2. Faith is shown in absolute *trust*. To paraphrase the latter part of v. 7, Noah became the possessor of the right relationship with God which comes only to those who put their trust in Him. Sarah received power beyond the course of physical nature because she trusted God's promise (v. 11). Abraham put absolute trust in God when he offered up Isaac, even though it seemed to involve throwing away all that God had originally promised (v. 17).

3. Faith always *looks forward in hope*, however unfavourable the present circumstances may be. Abraham, though only a

temporary sojourner, looked forward by faith to his permanent home (vv. 9, 10). Isaac blessed his sons 'concerning things to come' (v. 20). By faith Jacob blessed Joseph's sons, even though he was far away from the promised land (v. 21). By faith Joseph looked forward to the Exodus (v. 22). By faith Moses refused present privilege, looking forward to God's ultimate reward of His people (vv. 23-26). After killing the Egyptian, he left Egypt 'not because he feared the king's anger' (v. 27, N.E.B.), but by faith. His motive was not escape, but the future deliverance of Israel. His celebration of the Passover and smearing of the blood to save the firstborn were also 'by faith'. They looked forward to the protection and the future of God's people (v. 28).

In the references to faith outside chapter eleven, the message is applied both to the first readers of the letter, and to us. Faith is that which unites the community of those who obey God (4:2). Imitation of those whose faith and endurance has brought them fulfilment enables us too to receive God's promises (6:12). We need the full assurance that comes through faith, in order that we may be able to draw near to God (10:22). It is through faith that we find life and salvation (10:38, 39). And all this comes not only by imitating the men of the distant past, but by imitating those whom we know and remember (13:7). Too often we idealise those who lived long ago, and do not value sufficiently the faith of men of today.

But the supreme source of our faith is not the imitation of human heroes. The greatest word on faith is 'Look unto Jesus, the author and perfector of faith' (12:2). He begins it in us, because it is God's gift, as Paul tells us in Eph. 2:8. He alone can complete it, and He alone is its perfect example. The true Christian takes Him as his pattern and his power.

12. EACH ONE

Both Church and Society today lay great emphasis upon the corporate. And rightly so. Selfish individualism is fatal. We are members of one Body, and we ignore that fact at our peril. Yet the New Testament never lets us forget the other side of the picture. The Body is composed of individual members, and but for the individual parts there could be no Body. Each member has its value, and its particular duty.

The Greek adjective *hekastos*, therefore, has its important place in the theology of the New Testament. Its primary translation is 'each'. Occasionally, for the sake of idiom, it must be translated 'every', but in most instances that is unnecessary. In this chapter it will be translated 'each' whenever possible, in order to indicate its fundamental significance.

It occurs eighty-two times in the New Testament: Matthew 4; Mark 1; Luke 5; John 4; Acts 11; Paul 42 (22 of them in 1 Corinthians); Hebrews 5; James 1; 1 Peter 2, and Revelation 7.

1. Sometimes it simply denotes the individual, without any further special significance. At the enrolment in Lk. 2:3 they went 'each one to his own city'. 'Does not each one of you on the Sabbath loose his ox ?' (Lk. 13:15). 'He called to him each one of his lord's debtors' (16:5). 'They went each man to his own house' (Jn. 7:53). 'You shall be scattered each man to his own' (16:32). 'They made four parts, to each soldier a part' (19:23). 'Let each man have his own wife, and each woman her own husband' (1 Cor. 7:2). 'Each in his own order: Christ, then they that are Christ's' (15:23). 'Twenty-four elders, having each one a harp' (Rev. 5:8). 'Each of the gates was of one pearl' (21:21). None of these uses needs any comment, except perhaps to call attention to the loneliness of grief and defeat in Jn. 16:32.

2. Sometimes the emphasis is on the collection of the units into a single whole, so that none are left out: 'that each may take a little' (Jn. 6:7); 'he rehearsed each one of the things that God had done' (Acts 21:19); 'exhort one another each day' (Heb. 3:13); 'the tree yielding its fruit each month' (Rev. 22:2). The whole is always the sum of its parts, though it is more as well.

3. Before we go further we must note that the N.T. does not forget that there is such a thing as selfish individualism, but the word occurs only four times in this sense: 'Each one of you says, I am of Paul, I of Apollos . . .' (1 Cor. 1:12); 'each takes his supper before the other person' (11:21); 'each one has a psalm, a teaching' etc. which he is tempted to utter selfishly (14:26); 'not looking each of you to his own things' (Phil. 2:4).

4. The characteristic N.T. emphasis begins from this point. In the first place, each individual is bidden to care for others. The danger is always to leave caring to other people, and fail to take it as our own personal task. *Each one* must forgive his brother (Mt. 18:35). *Each one* must please his neighbour for

his neighbour's good (Rom. 15:2). In the matter of financial giving, *each one* must set aside his contribution (1 Cor. 16:2), *each one* must keep to his intentions and do so cheerfully (2 Cor. 9:7). *Each one* must speak truth with his neighbour (Eph. 4:25), and love his own wife (5:33). *Each one* must look at the needs of others (Phil. 2:4). The love of *each one* towards all in the Church must abound (2 Thess. 1:3). Until God's day of perfect fulfilment comes, *each one* must teach his fellow-citizen, and *each man* his brother, to know the Lord (Heb. 8:11).

5. Similarly the Christian message is meant for each individual. It is not just a general thing. When numbers of sick people were brought to Jesus, He laid His hands on *each one* of them (Lk. 4:40). At Pentecost, *each man* heard the message that he could understand (Acts 2:6, 8), and Peter's speech was an appeal to *each one* to repent and be baptized (2:38). Peter takes up the same theme in 3:26, when he tells his audience how God in Christ has blessed them in turning *each one* away from his sins. Paul too calls to mind how he had admonished *each one* of the elders at Ephesus (20:31). Nor was this individual application simply verbal. It was worked out practically as well. In the early Jerusalem church, 'distribution was made unto *each*, according as anyone had need' (Acts 4:35). Paul went through the ceremonies for the four Jewish Christians, 'until the offering was offered for *each one* of them' (21:26). That action was in accord with the individual attention that he always gave: 'we dealt with *each one* of you, as a father with his children' (1 Thess. 2:11). Jacob had dealt in that way with his own grandchildren, blessing *each* of the sons of Joseph (Heb. 11:21). And the Christian's task is to pass on that message individually; he must have enough grace and wisdom to know how to answer *each one* (Col. 4:6).

6. Christian responsibility is also an individual matter. It must, of course, be collective to be fully effective, but it cannot begin to be effective unless it is accepted by each individual. The Lord gives responsibilities 'to *each* according to his ability' (Mt. 25:15); *each one* is given his work (Mk. 13:34), and then *each* separate part of the whole must work in its proper measure (Eph. 4:16). *Each* tree will be known by its own fruit (Lk. 6:44).

That fruit of individual responsibility is very various. It involves *each man* making material contributions to the needy according to his ability (Acts 11:29). It involves *each man* having clear convictions in his own mind (Rom. 14:5). *Each man* also must 'take heed how he builds' (1 Cor. 3:10), be free from restlessness about his condition in life (7:20, 24), test the quality of his own work (Gal. 6:4), bear his own load (6:5), be responsible for his own sexual purity (1 Thess. 4:4; Jas. 1:14), and show the same diligence that others before him have shown (Heb. 6:11). *Each one* must be deeply sensitive lest in any way he may be betraying his Lord (Mt. 26:22).

7. In order that the Christian may meet his responsibilities, God for His part gives His gifts to each individually. At Pentecost the fire sat upon *each* of the apostles (Acts 2:3). Nor is it limited to the apostles: 'to each of us is given the manifestation of the Spirit' (1 Cor. 12:7), which God distributes 'separately to each individual' (12:11, N.E.B.). God gives 'to *each man* a measure of faith' (Rom. 12:3), to *each* of His servants the power for his work (1 Cor. 3:5), to *each man* his own different gift (7:7, 17; 1 Peter 4:10), to *each* his own calling (1 Cor. 7:17). *Each* of us receives grace (Eph. 4:7). God gives *each* part of His creation its own body (1 Cor. 15:38), and sets *each* member in its own place in the Body (12:18). Nor is a single one of those who have died for their faith forgotten; *each* is given his white robe (Rev. 6:11). Paul sums it all up when he says to the Athenians that God 'is not far from *each one* of us' (Acts 17:27).

8. Yet God who gives to each man judges each man. He will render to *each man* according to his works (Mt. 16:27; Rom. 2:6; Rev. 2:23, 20:13, 22:12—the wording varies only very slightly in all these five verses). At the end, the quality of *each man's* work will be made manifest, and proved by fire (1 Cor. 3:13). Some will have commendation and reward for the good that they have done, and *each* will receive it if he deserves it (1 Cor. 4:5; Eph. 6:8), just as *each* worker on earth receives the reward of his labour (1 Cor. 3:8). But whether what we receive is commendation or punishment (2 Cor. 5:10), *each of us* will have to 'give account of himself to God' (Rom. 14:12), and God judges 'without respect of persons according to *each man's* work' (1 Pet. 1:17).

How awe-inspiring—and how strengthening—to know that we are, *each one of us*, eternally in God's hands!

13. DEATH

Few of our word-studies reveal a greater difference between ordinary thinking and New Testament thinking than a study of the word *Thanatos*, Death. It occurs frequently, as we should expect, coming no less than a hundred and twenty times in all. Twenty-eight of these occurrences are in the Gospels, eight in Acts, twenty-two in Romans, seventeen in 1 and 2 Corinthians, six in Philippians, ten in Hebrews, six in 1 John, four in the remaining epistles, and nineteen in Revelation. The verb *die* (*apothnēskō* or *thnēskō*) occurs exactly the same number of times, with roughly the same distribution, though it is found much more frequently in John's gospel and less often in Revelation. It covers the same ground, however, as the noun, to which we will now limit our attention. It will tell us most of what the New Testament has to say.

We do, of course, find in the New Testament a number of instances of the ordinary uses of the word. There are fifteen references to natural death: in the promise to Simeon (Lk. 2:26), in the promise to some of the disciples (Mk. 9:1; Mt. 16:28; Lk. 9:27), two uses of the word in the account of the raising of Lazarus (Jn. 11:4, 13), Jesus' word in Gethsemane: 'My soul is almost dead with sorrow' (Mk. 14:34; Mt. 26:38 — C.K. Williams), 'neither death nor anything else can separate us from God's love' (Rom. 8:38, 39), the references in Hebrews to natural death: of priests (7:23), of a man whose will and testament thereby becomes effective (9:16)—and to the death which Enoch did not see (11:5); and finally the references to the death of the Beast (the Roman emperor Nero, who was expected to be revived and return again) in Rev. 13:3, 12.

There are also fifteen references to the death penalty in a court of law: general legal condemnation (Mk. 7:10; Mt. 15:4), the condemnation of Jesus (Mk. 10:33, 14:64; Mt. 20:18, 26:66; Lk. 23:15, 24:20; Acts 13:28), the charge from which Paul was exonerated (Acts 23:29; 25:11, 25; 26:31; 28:18), and Paul's own condemnation of evil-doers in Rom. 1:32.

The New Testament further recognizes the very natural and general fear of death. When Jesus came, it was to those who sat in the shadow of death (Mt. 4:16; Lk. 1:79). Hebrews 2:15 speaks of those who throughout their life are enslaved by this fear. Even Jesus Himself in Gethsemane had to fight against this temptation. It is part of the humanity that He shared with us.

But these are not the distinctive attitudes of the New Testament towards death. Death is one of the possible consequences of persecution, and persecution is a consequence of the acceptance of Christ. Death in persecution may therefore be something to be accepted without fuss (Mk. 13:12; Mt. 10:21; Lk. 22:33; Acts 22:4; 2 Cor. 11:23), or it may be something whereby we can glorify God (Jn. 21:19), something which demands the ultimate faithfulness towards Him (Rev. 2:10, 12:11). This is a very different thing from the death which comes into the world as part of the punishment of God (Rev. 6:8, 18:8).

The kind of death which troubles New Testament writers far more than physical death is what they call 'the death of sin', that state of opposition to God which cuts us off from Him who is the only source of true life. Thirty-five uses of the word 'death' are in this sense, fifteen of them in Romans 5 to 8. The argument of Romans 5 (verses 12, 14, 17, 21) is that Adam's sin started off a chain of consequences whereby his descendants were caught up in his disobedience and this state of being cut off from God was firmly established. The next chapters describe some of the things that follow from this: we become slaves of sin so that we are cut off (6:16), the end of it all is inevitably separation (6:21), we get our wages for our action and those wages are in the form of separation from God (6:23). Our sinful passions have this death as their fruit (7:5). Even God's law, because men cannot obey it, brings death (7:10); it shows men how terrible sin is, but it cannot provide the remedy (7:13); it is in fact a law of sin and death (8:2), as is the whole mind of the flesh (8:6)—and all that Paul can do is to cry out to be delivered from it (7:24). The reference to Adam occurs again in 1 Cor. 15:21, where Paul is discussing physical death, but he does not let it remain merely physical; the real sting of death is not in mere dying, it is in sin (15:56). And the same link between sin, death and law continues in 2 Cor.: Christian preaching has the threat of death in it for sinful men (2:16), the law of Moses may well be described as 'the ministration of death' (3:7), and the remorse of sinners does not bring them any nearer to the life of God (7:10).

James, so different from Paul in many ways, still links sin and death: when sin reaches maturity, its child is death (1:15), and he who converts a sinner saves him from death (5:20). Yet another character continues the same link: John says characteristically that a man who does not know how to love is living in death (1 Jn. 3:14), and at the end of his letter (5:16, 17) he distinguishes between those whose sins land them in this state and those whose sins do not. The writer of Revelation four times refers to 'the second death' (2:11; 20:6, 14; 21:8): he is thinking of physical death as the first and less important, and of the second as ultimate separation from God.

To this terrible picture of the death of sin the New Testament provides the answer: Jesus Christ. He is the answer, both as Redeemer from death and as Victor over death; and we share both in the redemption and in the victory.

He Himself spoke of drawing all men to Him by His death (Jn. 12:32, 33), and John saw the working out of that in the crucifixion (18:32). Paul goes on to speak of our being reconciled to God through the death of His Son (Rom. 5:10; Col. 1:22), and of our baptism being like His death, an act of release from all that holds us away from God; our old self is drowned and we can begin a new life, united with Him (Rom. 6:3-5). Paul also links the other great sacrament with Christ's death: 'As often as ye eat this bread and drink the cup, ye proclaim the Lord's death' (1 Cor. 11:26). His death took place to deliver us from our transgressions (Heb. 9:15). It was for this purpose that He was honoured by God, so that He tasted death for us all (Heb. 2:9) when He became obedient unto death, the death of the cross (Phil. 2:8). In this death we share (Phil. 3:10), not only benefiting from it ourselves but joining in His redeeming work. Whatever the issue of Paul's trial, whether life or death, Christ is to be magnified by it (Phil. 1:20). However near to death Epaphroditus was, it was working for Christ on behalf of the Philippians that brought him there (Phil. 2:27, 30). Christ's followers must always be at death's door for His sake, so that they may bring life to those whom they serve (2 Cor. 4:11, 12).

But even above redemption from death comes victory over death—Christ's victory, and ours in Him. This is the theme of twenty references. At the resurrection God loosed the pangs of death for His Son (Acts 2:24). Christ abolished death and brought life and immortality to light (2 Tim. 1:10). Through His death He destroyed the effectiveness of the devil with his power of death (Heb. 2:14). Death no more has any dominion over Him (Rom. 6:9). He has the keys of death and of Hades (Rev. 1:18), and though death is the last enemy to be completely destroyed (1 Cor. 15:26), yet the time will come when death and

Hades will give up the dead that are in them (Rev. 20:13), and be cast into the lake of fire (20:14), and be no more (21:4).

Christ's victory, past and future, is ours too. If we keep His word, we shall never see death in the deepest sense (Jn. 8:51). If we believe God (Jn. 5:24), and if we love as He commanded us, we have already passed out of death into life (1 Jn. 3:14). When Paul was under actual sentence of death, God delivered him, and he can trust Him for all future deliverance (2 Cor. 1:9, 10). Under all circumstances, physical and spiritual, we too can say, because of Christ, 'Death is swallowed up in victory— O death, where is thy victory? O death, where is thy sting?' (1 Cor. 15:54, 55). All things, including death itself, are ours, because we belong to Christ, and He belongs to God (1 Cor. 3:22, 23).

This is our message, not only for Good Friday and Easter, but for the whole year round: redemption through Christ's death, victory with Him over death. May we know the message to be true for ourselves, so that we may proclaim it to others with assurance!

14. LIFE

When the apostles in Jerusalem were released from their imprisonment, they were bidden by the angel to go and speak 'all the words of *this life*' (Acts 5:20). We could find no better description of what Jesus and His resurrection gave to His first disciples, and what they have gone on giving ever since.

This chapter will therefore take the noun 'Life' (*Zōē*), and try to see something of what the New Testament says about it. We shall not attempt the verb. The noun itself occurs 135 times, and that will be more than enough.

The word is, of course, used in the sense of ordinary physical life; e.g. in Paul's speech at Athens, when he speaks of God's gift of 'life and breath and all things' (Acts 17:25), or in his word to the Philippians that Christ will be magnified in his body 'whether by life or by death' (Phil. 1:20). But at the most this sense comes only thirteen times, and several of the occurrences bear an additional deeper meaning.

It is remarkable how the vast majority of instances of the word are essentially connected with Christ, with who He is and what He does. 'In Him was life' (Jn. 1:4), so that Paul can speak about 'the life of Jesus' (2 Cor. 4:10-11), as he speaks in Eph. 4:18 about 'the life of God'. That means that we have life in Him (2 Tim. 1:1; 1 Jn. 5:11). He is 'the Prince of Life' (Acts 3:15). He is 'the Bread of Life' (Jn. 6:35, 48), the bread that gives life to the world (6:33), the bread which is His flesh, given 'for the life of the world' (6:51). His words are life (6:63, 68). In fact He is 'the Word of life' (1 Jn. 1:1). As the Revised Version margin shows, it is open to us to use a capital letter here or not. John may be thinking of the word or message of life, as Paul is when he is writing to the Philippians (2:16), or he may be thinking of Christ as the incarnate Word. Ultimately those two are the same. Christ *is* His message.

Through Him life is manifested (1 Jn. 1:2), or brought to light (2 Tim. 1:10). In fact John identifies life and light (Jn. 1:4), and later records Jesus' saying that He is the Light of the world (8:12). It is not that light and life are one and the same thing, but that both physically and spiritually they go closely together. You rarely find physical life which is not dependent on light; and when a man is spiritually illuminated, he normally has a great access of vitality.

This Christ-given life links us with God. In fact the true Christian's life is one that is 'hid with Christ in God' (Col. 3:3). We are 'saved by His life' (Rom. 5:10). Indeed Christ *is* our life (Col. 3:4); because He is 'the Resurrection and the Life' (Jn. 11:25), our reception into fellowship with Him is 'life from the dead' (Rom. 11:15). That means that in Him we 'walk in newness of life' (Rom. 6:4), and through Him we 'reign in life' (5:17). In fact our whole life has been 'justified' (5:18); that is to say, it has been set right in God's sight so that we can live as He means us to live. We are able to obey His 'commandment for life' (7:10 — note the great use that Paul makes of this word in Romans), and in the end we can confidently believe that 'what is mortal' in us will be fully 'swallowed up by life' (2 Cor. 5:4), and we shall experience that 'power of an endless life' which Hebrews attributes to our great High Priest (7:16).

So far we have not looked at the outstanding New Testament phrase 'Eternal life'. Paul uses it only five times. For him the simple word 'life' conveys the same idea, but the phrase comes altogether forty-three times in the N.T., and of these twenty-three are in St. John's gospel or his first epistle. Six of the remaining uses are in the three accounts of the rich young ruler's visit to Jesus, so that the balance is scattered rather thinly.

The phrase is pre-eminently John's. What exactly does he mean by it?

Its literal translation is 'the life of the age', that is, of the age to come. Jews thought not so much in terms of two worlds, the earthly and the heavenly, as in terms of two ages: the present, imperfect one, and the future one, here or elsewhere, in which all would be according to God's will. Jesus taught that the *quality* of life expected in that future age could be realised through Him here and now. That is why the translation 'eternal life' is better than 'everlasting life'. It is, of course, everlasting, but it is its nature, rather than its duration, that Jesus emphasises.

It is not the same as mere immortality. People have believed in immortality without even a belief in God. This is life that is not automatically ours; it is the gift of Christ (Jn. 17:2), and it becomes the possession only of those who believe on Him (3:15, 16, 36).

But we do not have to wait for it till we have left this world. It can be our possession here and now. 'He that believeth on the Son *has* (not *shall have*) eternal life' (Jn. 3:36). 'He that eats my flesh and drinks my blood *has* eternal life' (6:54). In gospel and epistle John uses the verb 'to have' with 'eternal life' or with the simple word 'life' seventeen times, and in every single case it is used in the present tense. Present possession is the essential significance of the phrase, so that the full translation, of, e.g., Jn. 6:47 would be 'He that believes actually possesses eternal life here and now'. In two cases John goes even further and uses the perfect tense: 'He that believeth ... *has passed* out of death into life' (5:24); 'We *have passed* out of death into life because we love the brethren' (1 Jn. 3:14).

Other books of the New Testament express this same idea of a present fact in different terms. The Jerusalem church glorifies God because He has granted the Gentiles 'repentance unto life' (Acts 11:18). They are not thinking of future life; they have just heard the account of the gift of the Spirit. In fact, three times over in Romans 8 Paul connects the Spirit with life: 'the Spirit of life' (v. 2), 'the mind of the Spirit is life' (v. 6), 'the Spirit is life' (v. 10). Paul had experienced the revitalizing power of the Holy Spirit both in himself and in thousands of others. In 2 Cor. 4:12 he says, 'Life *works* in you', using a verb which means the working of supernaturally-given energy. In 2 Cor. 2:16 he describes the apostolic ministry as a sweet savour of

Christ 'from life to life', that is, a scent of the life of God which, as it comes to men's nostrils, puts new life into them.

The book of Revelation, with its love of concrete imagery, speaks in terms of the Book of Life (3:5; 13:8; 17:8; 20:12, 15; 21:27), a phrase which Paul also uses in Phil. 4:3.   There is, as it were, a register of the names of the citizens of heaven; but the important thing is not just the fact that our names are there, but that Christ has given us the life of which this book is the record.   Revelation also writes of the Tree of Life (2:7; 22:2,14) and of the Waters of Life (7:17; 21:6; 22:1, 17, 19)—again true and beautiful symbols, especially that of water.   Jews knew the pains of thirst and consequent loss of vitality in a hot country where water was scarce.   Under God's perfect rule this faintness would disappear.   Revelation chiefly emphasises the future, but not entirely.   All the references to the Book of Life state that men's names are already written there, or that their exclusion is already decided.   We must be careful, however, to treat its symbolism as symbolism and not take it too materialistically.   John is not really talking about books and trees and water.   He is seeing beyond them to the life-giving power of God, and trying (as we all have to try) to express what he sees with his heart in imperfect material terms.   Let us never fail to look behind his language to what it symbolises.

In Christ God has given us 'the grace of life' (1 Pet. 3:7), 'has granted us all things that pertain unto life ... through the knowledge of Him' (2 Pet. 1:3).   And His word to us still stands: 'Lay hold on the life that is really life' (1 Tim. 6:19).

15. AMEN

'Amen' is such a well-known New Testament word that it is often ignored or misunderstood.   It really means 'truth' or 'certainty', and when we say it at the end of a creed or prayer, we ought to mean 'I affirm that this is true', or 'I would have this become true'.   In some ways it is the most important word of all, though we often mumble it without much thought.

It is used in this sense often in the epistles, perhaps about thirty times in all, though it is not easy to be exact, as in many places some manuscripts include and some omit it.   Phil. 4:20 is a typical example: 'Now unto our God and Father be the glory for ever and ever. Amen'. (Note in passing how many benedictions there are in the epistles that we never use in public worship).

This chapter, however, will be dealing with another use of the word, a use which in the New Testament is found in the words of Jesus alone. He had a characteristic way of opening a sentence with the phrase 'Verily, I say unto you (or thee)', meaning, 'In solemn truth I tell you'. This phrase comes forty-nine times in the Synoptic gospels (thirty in Matthew, thirteen in Mark, six in Luke), and twenty-five times in John, where it is always doubled: 'Verily, verily'. This makes a total of seventy-four occurrences, sixty-five of them addressed to a group ('you'), and nine to individuals ('thee').

This is not Jesus' only method of emphasis, and indeed there are none of His words that do not need attention. But it does seem that often when He wanted particular attention He prefaced His remark with this phrase. It is therefore worth while to collect these specially emphasised sayings, and to try to see what He wanted His hearers on no account to miss. The sayings may be divided into six groups.

1. First of all there are sayings about His own Person and Work, all of them in St. John's Gospel. '*Verily, verily, I say unto you*, The Son can do nothing of Himself, but what He sees the Father doing (Jn. 5:19)'; 'before Abraham was, I am' (8:58); 'I am the door of the sheep' (10:7); 'except a grain of wheat fall into the ground and die . . . (12:24); he who receives him whom I send receives Me, and he who receives Me receives Him who sent Me (13:20); if you ask anything of the Father, He will give it you in My name (16:23)'. In other words, Jesus is saying: 'I lay particular stress on My dependence on God, Myself as the entrance into the security and the life of the Christian fellowship, My fruitful death, My disciples' close link with Myself and with God, and on prayer in My name'. It would be a searching enough test for us to ask ourselves if these are the stresses that we lay when we think of Him.

Along with this emphasis on Himself comes an emphasis on His message: '*Verily I say unto you*, many . . . desired to see the things which you see . . . and to hear the things which you hear' (Mt. 13:17); he rejoices over the lost sheep 'more than over the ninety and nine' (18:13); 'whatever you bind on earth shall be bound in heaven' (18:18). Again to paraphrase, Jesus is saying: 'I lay especial stress on the surpassing greatness of what I have brought, on God's love and longing for every individual, on the terrible responsibility of declaring in this world God's standards and judgments'.

2.   There are two sayings about Faith which are introduced by this phrase. '*Verily I say unto you*, I have not found so much faith with anyone in Israel (Mt. 8:10); if you have faith like a grain of mustard seed, you will say to this mountain . . .' (Mt. 17:20; cp. 21:21 and Mk. 11:23). Faith is another of the qualities that Jesus could not leave unemphasised.

3.   John's gospel brings us a group of five emphatic sayings on Life: '*Verily, verily I say unto you:* he who hears My word and believes Him who sent Me has Eternal Life (Jn. 5:24); not Moses . . . but My Father gives you the true bread out of heaven . . . which gives life unto the world (6:32, 33); he who believes has eternal life (6:47); unless you eat the flesh of the Son of man and drink His blood, you have not life (6:53); if a man keep My word, he will never see death (8:51)'. Spiritual life is one of the 'verily' essentials.

4.   There is also a large group of some nineteen sayings, dealing with men's character and conduct, and sometimes with their reward. On character we have: '*Verily I say unto you*: there has not arisen a greater than John the Baptist (Mt. 11:11); unless you turn and become as little children, you shall never enter the kingdom of heaven (18:3); it is hard for a rich man to enter into the kingdom of heaven (19:23); a servant is not greater than his master (Jn. 13:16); except a man be born again of water and spirit . . . (3:5). These sayings are a very adequate summary of what Christian character should be: straightforward, childlike, unmaterialistic, a servant of others, a new creature in Christ.

On conduct we have: '*Verily I say unto you:* thou shalt by no means come out (from the prison where failure to agree has led a man) until thou hast paid the last farthing (Mt. 5:26); inasmuch as ye did it to one of these My brethren, ye did it unto Me (25:40); this poor widow has cast in more than they all (Mk. 12:43); he who believes on Me, greater works than these shall he do (Jn. 14:12)'. Agreement with adversaries, caring love, costly sacrifice, effective belief—this list covers a very large part of the sphere of Christian conduct.

On reward we have: '*Verily I say unto you:* whoever gives a cup of cold water, he shall not lose his reward (Mt. 10:42); he will set the faithful servant over all that he has (24:47); wherever this gospel is preached, this woman's act shall be spoken of (26:13; Mk. 14:9); there is no man who has left ... but he shall receive a hundredfold (Mk. 10:29; Lk. 18:29); he will gird himself and come and serve those whom he finds watching (Lk. 12:37)'. We are often exhorted to labour and to *seek for no reward*; yet the gospel has a great deal to say about reward. But the word to be noted is *seek*. None of these people were seeking reward. It came because they were simply doing God's will.

5. Yet Jesus prefaces not only promises but also rebukes in this solemn way, and His first two rebukes are concerned with people who are seeking reward: '*Verily I say unto you*, They have received their reward' (Mt. 6:2, 16). They will get nothing more from God—only the praise from men that they have been looking for. The other rebukes are: '*Verily I say unto you:* it shall be more tolerable for the land of Sodom than for that city (Mt. 10:15); the publicans and harlots go into the kingdom of God before you (21:31); all these things shall come upon this generation (23:36); one stone shall not be left upon another (24:2); I know you not (25:12;) inasmuch as ye did it not unto one of these least, ye did it not unto Me (25:45); one of you will betray Me (26:21; Mk. 14:18; Jn. 13:21); before the cock crow, you will deny Me thrice (Mt. 26:34; Mk. 14:30; Jn. 13:38); whoever blasphemes against the Holy Spirit is guilty of eternal sin (Mk. 3:28, 29); no sign shall be given to this generation (8:12); whoever does not receive the kingdom of God as a little child shall never enter in (Mk. 10:15; Lk. 18:17); no prophet is acceptable in his own country (Lk. 4:24); you seek me not because you saw signs but because you ate of the loaves (Jn. 6:26); everyone who commits sin is the slave of sin (8:34); he who enters not through the door is a thief and a robber (10:1); we speak what we know, and you do not receive our witness (3:11)'. Nearly all this long list of rebukes is addressed to people who refused to accept Jesus and His message. He cannot regard that refusal lightly.

6. Finally, many of these emphasised sayings are connected with 'the last things'. We can never rule eschatology out of the mind of Jesus, whatever variation of interpretation is possible. Some of the rebukes in the previous section had eschatology in them, but in addition there are: '*Verily I say unto you:* till heaven and earth pass away, one jot or one tittle shall not pass away from the Law (Mt. 5:18); you will not have completed the cities of Israel till the Son of man be come (10:23); some of those standing

C

here shall not taste of death till they see the Son of man already come in His kingdom (Mk. 9:1; cp. Mt. 16:28); in the regeneration you shall sit on twelve thrones judging (Mt. 19:28); this generation shall not pass away till all these things are accomplished (Mt. 24:34; Mk. 13:30; Lk. 21:32); I will no more drink of the fruit of the vine till I drink it new in the kingdom of God (Mk. 14:25); today you will be with me in Paradise (Lk. 23:43); you shall see the heaven opened and the angels ascending and descending upon the Son of man (Jn. 1:51); the hour comes and now is when the dead shall hear the voice of the Son of God (Jn. 5:25)'. The emphasis is abundantly clear that, whatever men may do with space and with history, Christ is the ultimate Lord.

The book of Revelation sums all this up by calling Him 'the Amen' (Rev. 3:14), the One who not only emphasises truth, but Who is Himself all truth. 'To Him be the glory . . . unto all generations for ever and ever. *Amen*'. (Eph. 3:21).

III. THE CHURCH

16. THE PEOPLE OF GOD

One of the fundamental ideas of the Old Testament is that the Israelites are the People of God. The New Testament takes over this idea and carries it on with the declaration that the true People of God are not simply those who are Jews racially, but those of every race who have accepted God in Christ.

The New Testament therefore very frequently uses both these words—People and Israel—in this sense, as well as in a variety of others. The figures are as follows:

People (Greek, *Laos*): Matthew fourteen times, Mark two, Luke thirty-six, John three, Acts forty-eight, Paul eleven (all in quotations from the Old Testament), Pastoral Epistles one, Hebrews thirteen, other epistles five, Revelation nine, making a total of 142. One striking point about these figures is that the Gentile Christian, Luke, makes such full use of this especially Jewish word; he provides nearly sixty per cent of the instances.

Israel: Matthew twelve times, Mark two, Luke twelve, John four, Acts fifteen, Paul seventeen, Hebrews three, Revelation three, making a total of sixty-eight. Again Luke provides a large proportion, nearly forty per cent.

We may treat the two words together. Many of their occurrences have no special spiritual significance. About a third of them simply describe the people of Palestine without any particular emphasis on their relationship with God. When Mt. 4:23, for example, speaks of Jesus healing all manner of disease among the people, this probably means no more than the people in general. In fact the words *people* and *multitude* are sometimes used interchangeably.

The word *people* is also used some ten times to refer to the peoples of the outside world; e.g. 'Why did the Gentiles rage, and the *peoples* imagine vain things?' (Acts 4:25). The book of Revelation uses it seven times (5:9; 7:9; 10:11; 11:9; 13:7; 14:6; 17:15) in its lists of synonyms for the nations of the earth.

But the most frequent use in the New Testament is for the Jews as the People of God. The word *People* comes in this sense some sixty-five times, though there are places where it is difficult to decide whether the word has a special significance or not.

The word *Israel* for the Jews as God's People comes about another forty times. Together the two words have half their instances
in this sense.   The coming of Jesus, and the Baptist's preparation
for it, are to be for the benefit of God's People, Israel: 'Thou
shalt call His name Jesus, for it is He that shall save His People
from their sins' (Mt. 1:21); 'Blessed be the Lord, the God of
Israel, for He hath visited and wrought redemption for His
People' (Lk. 1:68); 'Behold, I bring you good tidings of great
joy, which shall be to all the People' (Lk. 2:10); 'God has visited
His People' (7:16).   And because of the coming of Christ,
Paul can quote Deut. 32:43 with a new application and say,
'Rejoice, ye Gentiles, with His People' (Rom. 15:10).

On many occasions the two words are used together: 'Out
of thee shall come forth a governor, who shall be shepherd of
My People Israel' (Mt. 2:6).   Simeon in the Temple speaks of
Jesus as 'a light for revelation to the Gentiles, and the glory
of Thy People Israel' (Lk. 2:32).   Peter in Acts proclaims
Jesus 'to all the People of Israel' (4:10), and the early church
takes note before God of the resistance of the Peoples of Israel
to His holy Servant (4:27).   Paul carries on the use of the double
phrase in his speech at Antioch.   His opening sentence speaks
of 'the God of this People Israel' (Acts 13:17), and he goes on to
mention the Baptist's preaching 'to all the People of Israel'
(13:24).

Yet the tragedy is that God's People turned away from Him,
both in the days before the coming of Christ, and especially when
He came in order to make them more truly God's People than
before.   The New Testament often lays sad emphasis on this
apostasy: 'This People's heart is waxed gross' (Mt. 13:15;
Acts 28:27); 'This People honours me with their lips, but their
heart is far from me' (Mk. 7:6; Mt. 15:8); 'All the day long did
I spread out my hands to a disobedient and gainsaying People'
(Rom. 10:21); 'Israel, following a law of righteousness, did not
arrive at that law' (9:31); 'That which Israel seeketh for, that he
attained not' (11:7).   In fact, all through Romans 9-11 Paul
is grappling with this problem of Israel's perversity.   He knows
her failure, but he still believes in her ultimate salvation along
with the Gentiles: 'A hardening in part has befallen Israel, until
the fulness of the Gentiles come in; and so all Israel shall be
saved' (Rom. 11:25, 26).   On the day of the Crucifixion, 'All
the People answered and said, His blood be on us, and on our
children' (Mt. 27:25), but that word uttered in anger is not the

final word. 'Did God reject His People ?' asks Paul in Rom. 11:1, and his instantaneous reply, which he develops all through that chapter, is 'Never!'

The old Israel will be saved, but she will be saved in the context of God's new Israel, His new People, the Church of Christ. It is the establishment of this new People to which the whole of the Bible story leads up. John the Baptist is sent 'to make ready for the Lord a People prepared for Him' (Lk. 1:17). He declares in Jn. 1:31 that he has come baptizing 'that He should be made manifest to Israel', and Nathanael recognizes Him as the 'king of Israel' (1:49). But the gospel writers knew well enough that it was only the Israel after the Spirit which truly accepted Him as King. The crowd in Jn. 12:13 could shout at the Triumphal Entry: 'Blessed . . . is the King of Israel', but they did not as yet (not even the disciples—Jn. 12:16) realize the meaning of what they were shouting. Even the disciples on the road to Emmaus had not seen it when they said: 'We hoped that it was He who should redeem Israel' (Lk. 24:21).

But the apostles later see clearly the implications of this long process of the bringing into being of God's true People. James, at the Council of Jerusalem, realizes that the significance of what happened in the house of Cornelius was that God had visited the Gentiles, 'to take out of them a People for His Name' (Acts 15:14). The Lord's words to Paul in the vision at Corinth: 'I have much people in this city' (18:10), are applied by Paul in the letter he writes later to that very city: 'I will be their God, and they shall be My People' (2 Cor. 6:16). Hebrews five times speaks of Christians as the People of God: Jesus, our High Priest, makes propitiation and offerings for the sins of the People (2:17; 5:3); the Sabbath rest remains for God's new People (4:9); the old Covenant will vanish, and in the new one 'they shall be to me a People' says the Lord (8:10); and, finally, Jesus sanctifies the People through His own blood (13:12).

Probably 1 Pet. 2:9 puts the whole thing most clearly when it says: 'You are a People for God's own possession', i.e. 'You Christians now hold the special title of God's Chosen People, which first belonged to the Jews'. Paul, speaking to Gentile Christians, reminds them how previously they were 'alienated from the commonwealth of Israel' (Eph. 2:12), but now in Christ they are united in one body with all who accept Him. Thus he can conclude his letter to the Galatians (6:16) by describing this new unity with the beautiful phrase 'the Israel of God'.   Jesus speaks of the apostles as finally sitting on thrones 'judging the twelve tribes of Israel' (Mt. 19:28; Lk. 22:30)—not an easy saying, but we may link it up with the picture in Revelation (7:4; 21:12) of the Israel of God finally redeemed in heaven, and so bring the biblical evidence to its conclusion.

We today are the heirs of that evidence, the People of God—provided that we do not turn away as the old Israel did, but accept God's promises.   He has said that in time past we were no People, but now are the People of God (1 Pet. 2:10).   And the essential reason for our possessing that privilege is that we may show forth the excellencies of Him who called us out of darkness into His marvellous light (2:9).

17. 'GOD'S PEOPLE'

The previous chapter dealt with two of the regular New Testament words which describe God's chosen People.   This chapter will look at another, which describes them from a slightly different angle.   It is the word *Hagios*, one of the most important words in the Book, and one of the most difficult to translate adequately.   It is often translated 'holy', and in the plural the traditional translation is 'saints'.   These renderings, however, can be misleading, as can Indian translations such as *parisutthar*, 'very clean or pure people'.

The primary meaning of the word *Hagios* is 'set apart for God'. It can be used of a place, such as Jerusalem, which was not holy in a moral sense, but which was regarded as particularly belonging to God (Mt. 4:5).   It can be used of a baby, dedicated to God before his moral character has been formed (Lk. 2:23).   Moral goodness should, of course, be expected of people dedicated to God, but it comes as the consequence of their dedication; it is not a separate quality in itself.   We lose a great deal in our understanding of the New Testament by equating 'holy' with 'very good', and a 'saint' with a person of outstanding moral character.

The New English Bible helps us here, as it does in so many other places.   It frequently and rightly translates *Hagios* in many places by 'holy'.   It always does, for instance, in the case of the Holy Spirit.   In many places, however, it deliberately avoids both 'holy' and 'saint'.   The purpose of this chapter will be to look at those places and see what light they have to show on the real meaning of the word.

There are ninety of them in all: three in the Gospels, four in Acts, fifty-four in Paul, fourteen in the other epistles, and fifteen in Revelation. The simple sense of an object being 'consecrated' to God is found in Rom. 11:16, where a lump of dough and a root are spoken of in this way. The word 'sacred' is used in the same sense in 2 Pet. 1:18, where the Mount of Transfiguration is spoken of as 'the sacred mountain'. The 'sacred scriptures' (Rom. 1:2) and 'the sacred commandments' (2 Pet. 2:21) mean those which belong to God, and the phrase 'your most sacred faith' (Jude 20) may also mean 'that faith which sets you apart for God'. Twice the word 'belong' is used: the first-born male is 'deemed to belong to the Lord' (Lk. 2:23), and the children of a mixed marriage do (belong to the Lord) if one parent is Christian (1 Cor. 7:14). The traditional translation of 'do (belong to the Lord)' is simply 'holy', which is not nearly so clear or accurate.

This leads us to the standard New English translation of *Hagioi*, which is not 'saints' but 'God's people' (or 'his people', 'thy people', 'the people of God'). This describes much more satisfactorily such folk as the Corinthians, who were far from being saints in the usual sense, but who certainly belonged to God and were set apart for Him from the rest of the world, however often they failed Him. The phrase, in its slightly varying forms, comes no fewer than fifty-four times. It is a regular description of a church in a particular place: 'God's people in Lydda' Acts 9:32), 'God's people at Corinth' (2 Cor. 1:1) God's people at Ephesus' (Eph. 1:1), 'God's people who live at Philippi' (Phil. 1:1), 'God's people at Colossae' (Col. 1:2). Sometimes there are references to the persecution of 'God's people' (Acts 9:13; 26:10; Rev. 13:7; 16:6; 17:6; 18:24; 20:9). Sometimes the emphasis is on the satisfaction of the needs of the poor among God's people by others who are able to help them (Rom. 12:13; 15:25, 26, 31; 1 Cor. 16:1,15; 2 Cor. 9:1, 12; 1 Tim. 5:10; Philemon 5, 7; Heb. 6:10). Sometimes God's people are spoken of as a group acting together in welcome and greeting (Rom. 16:2; 2 Cor. 13:13; Phil. 4:22). Sometimes God's people are a group who are greeted (Rom. 16:15; Phil. 4:21—where the greeting is to each individual member of the group—Heb. 13:24). Sometimes God's people are praying, or being prayed for (Eph. 1:18; 3:18; 6:18; Rev. 5:8; 8:3, 4). Sometimes there is an underlining of their unity: they are 'the community of God's people' (1 Cor. 6:1), 'all the congregations of God's people (14:33), 'all God's people' (Eph. 1:15). The Gentiles are 'fellow-citizens with God's people' (2:19). The Colossians 'bear love towards all God's people' (Col. 1:4), and 'share the heritage of God's people' (1:12). Sometimes the emphasis is on God's action towards His people: He has chosen them (Col. 3:12), He has disclosed His secrets to them (1:26), He has entrusted the Faith to them (Jude 3). Sometimes the emphasis is on the qualities and duties of God's people themselves: humility (Eph. 3:8), purity of speech (5:3), faithfulness (Rev. 13:10), fortitude (13:10; 14:12), joy because of God's activity (18:20), righteous deeds (19:8), work in God's service (Eph. 4:12), judgment of the world by their new manner of life (1 Cor. 6:2).

Our response to God's choice of us must be dedication, and that word is used eleven times as a translation of *Hagios*. Rom. 1:7 links together God's choice and man's dedication: 'whom God has called to be His dedicated people'. Our commitment is stressed also in Rom. 12:1 ('dedicated and fit for his acceptance'), 1 Cor. 7:34 ('dedicated in body as in spirit'), Eph. 1:4 ('He chose us . . . to be dedicated'), 3:5 ('his dedicated apostles and prophets'), Col. 1:22 ('dedicated men without blemish'), 2 Tim. 1:9 ('He . . . called us to a dedicated life'), 1 Pet. 2:9 ('you are . . . a dedicated nation'), 2 Pet. 3:11 ('what devout and dedicated lives you should live!'). We are God's 'dedicated people' (Rev. 11:18), and the last page of the New Testament says, 'Let the dedicated man be true to his dedication' (Rev. 22:11).

We may omit three or four usages that are not especially significant, but we should certainly note some that underline what has already been said. In six places the word 'own' is added to the word 'people', to give it additional force. The Spirit 'pleads for God's own people in God's own way' (Rom. 8:27). We are claimed by God as 'his own' (1 Cor. 1:2). Our Lord Jesus will come 'with all those who are His own' (1 Thess. 3:13), and will 'be glorified among His own' (2 Thess. 1:10). The prophets are 'God's own' (2 Pet. 3:2), and so, says John, are those who share in the first resurrection (Rev. 20:6).

Two other phrases in the New English Bible are striking. Instead of 'ministering to the saints' we have 'service to their fellow-Christians' (2 Cor. 8:4); and instead of 'holy brethren' we have 'brothers in the family of God' (Heb. 3:1).

What a wealth of privilege and of responsibility all this is!

We are no 'saints' in the usual sense, but we *are* God's people, His own, chosen by Him, and in return He demands from us entire dedication. Those are the two sides of Holiness. One beautiful practice of the Syrian Church, gratefully adopted by the Church of South India, could regularly remind us of both sides. Four times in his letters St. Paul bids his readers salute one another 'with a holy kiss' (Rom. 16:16; 1 Cor. 16:20; 2 Cor. 13:12; 1 Thess. 5:26). The New English New Testament translates it 'with the kiss of peace', using the definite article because Paul is reminding his readers of a custom they know well. We know it too, and observe it in our Communion Service with a touch of the hands going from end to end of the congregation. That touch is 'holy', because it reminds us that we too are God's people, chosen by Him, united in Him, called by Him for His service in full dedication. 'Greet one another with the kiss of peace'—every time we obey this command, may we be given grace to accept all that it means.

18. BROTHERHOOD IN THE NEW TESTAMENT (i)

Brotherhood is one of the great Christian words. As we shall see, it is not restricted to Christians, even in the New Testament, and it was used to denote members of the same religious community in several places in Egypt more than a century before Christ. But it is the New Testament that has given the word its extensive usage, and a Concordance study is very rewarding, though the different uses of the word are so numerous that this study will be spread over two chapters.

The word *brother* (*adelphos*) occurs 341 times, but 79 of these describe an ordinary blood relationship and we shall not be concerned with them. The word *sister* (*adelphē*) occurs 26 times, of which 19 are in a metaphorical sense. *Brotherhood* (*adelphotēs*) comes twice, both metaphorical. *Love of the brethren* (*philadelphia*) is found six times, and the adjective formed from it, *loving as brethren* (*philadelphos*), occurs once.

The distribution of these words, which will be considered together, is interesting. They are not very common in the Gospels, only 29 times in all. In Acts, when the Church begins to grow, they occur 54 times, though nineteen of the instances are used by, or with reference to Jews. Paul develops the use of the words extensively. He has them no less than 132 times, most frequently in Romans and Corinthians, though it is remarkable to find them twenty times in a short letter such as 1 Thessalonians. They are not common in the Pastoral Epistles —only five times in all—one of the many instances of the differences in vocabulary between these letters and Paul's. Hebrews has eleven examples, James has no fewer than twenty. 1 Peter has only five, but uses all the different words, except *sister*. 2 Peter has four, the Johannine letters seventeen (contrast the Gospel with only two), and Revelation has five.

Jewish Brethren

As indicated above, the words *brother* or *brethren* are used not infrequently in connection with Jews. In addition to the nineteen references in Acts there are two in Hebrews (7:5; 8:11) and one in Romans (9:3). A few examples only need be given. At Pentecost, Peter addresses the crowd of Jews as 'Brethren' (Acts 2:29). Moses several times speaks of the Hebrews as a group of brethren; see Acts 3:22 (repeated in 7:37), and 7:26 when the two men quarrelling are reminded of their spiritual kinship. In fact, the Jews speak of themselves occasionally as a community of brothers, just as the Christians do to a much greater extent. Saul of Tarsus went with letters to 'the brethren' in Damascus, his fellow-Jews (Acts 22:5), and the Jews in Rome use the same word in telling Paul of their fellow-Jews from Jerusalem (28:21). Jews even use the word to address Christians, not only at the beginning (2:37), but even at Pisidian Antioch much later on, when the division between Jew and Christian was more definite (13:15).

But this maximum of twenty-one uses is in strong contrast to the use of the word within the Christian fellowship. It represents less than seven per cent of the whole.

The Natural Form of Christian Address

No fewer than ninety-nine times is the word 'Brother' used in addressing a single Christian, or 'Brethren' in addressing a group. Paul says it seventy-one times, and in nearly all his letters. He does not use it in Ephesians or Colossians, perhaps because he had not personally visited the churches to which he writes these letters, though he uses it ten times in his letter to Rome, another church unvisited at the time of writing. He uses it twenty-one times in addressing the Thessalonians, and six times to the Philippians, two churches with which he had the happiest relations. He also uses it twice in addressing his dear friend Philemon (verses 7 and 20). But he does not refrain from using it when writing more difficult letters. He had many stern things to say to the Galatians, yet he calls them 'Brethren' nine times. The Corinthian church had given him endless trouble, but in his first letter, which deals fully and faithfully with the various aspects of the trouble, he calls them 'Brethren' twenty times, and in the second letter he uses the word thrice. The Church is a family, and even if it needs rebuke, that rebuke is made within the family. The word 'brother' applies, whether it is uttered in praise or in blame.

James uses this form of address fifteen times, an even higher proportion than Paul, considering that Paul's words occupy sixteen times as many pages of the New Testament as James's. The theology of Paul and James has often, though unjustifiably, been contrasted. No contrast can be made between their attitudes towards the Christian family. The word that comes readily to the pens of both is the word 'Brother'.

Acts has the form of address seven times. 1:16 and 6:3 are what we should expect: the natural way of Christian speaking to Christian. All the remaining uses are striking. Ananias, whom Saul came to Damascus to imprison, obeys the command of his Lord to visit his would-be persecutor, and his first words to him are 'Brother Saul' (9:17; 22:13). Paul gives the second of these two accounts himself, and he does not forget the first Christian word ever spoken to him after the shattering experience of his conversion. The other three instances in Acts are in the context of the delicate question of relationships between Jewish and Gentile Christians. This question might easily have split the Church, but at the Council of Jerusalem Peter on the one hand and James on the other are determined that it should not. Each in turn addresses the gathering as 'Brethren' (15:7, 13). And later, when the Jerusalem church wants Paul to do something that he perhaps does not consider necessary but that would help to unite the two parts of the Church, they address him as 'Brother' (21:20), using the same word on this final occasion of his freedom as Ananias had used the first time that Paul ever heard a Christian greeting.

Hebrews, a letter written to a Christian congregation in danger of reverting to Judaism, uses the word 'Brethren' when reminding its readers of their heavenly vocation (3:1), when warning them against falling away (3:12), when urging them to enter into the fulness of their faith (10:19), and when exhorting them to accept the message that they are reading (13:22). Throughout, the letter is written to members of the family, however great the danger of their leaving it.

The remaining two of these ninety-nine vocatives are in 2 Pet. 1:10 and 1 Jn. 3:13.

The Brother by Name

The New Testament, however, is not content to deal with brothers anonymously and leave it at that. The word is seventeen times linked with a personal name: Phoebe our sister (Rom. 16:1), Quartus the brother (16:23), Sosthenes our brother (1 Cor. 1:1), Apollos the brother (16:12), Timothy our brother (2 Cor. 1:1; Col. 1:1; 1 Thess. 3:2; Phm. 1; Heb. 13:23), Titus my brother (2 Cor. 2:13), Tychicus the beloved brother (Eph. 6:21; Col. 4:7), Epaphroditus my brother (Phil. 2:25), Onesimus the faithful and beloved brother (Col. 4:9), Apphia our sister (Phm. 2), Silvanus our faithful brother (1 Pet. 5:12), our beloved brother Paul (2 Pet. 3:15). Brothers and sisters in Christ are not left vague and general. They are made definite and personal.

19. BROTHERHOOD IN THE NEW TESTAMENT (ii)

The Christian Brotherhood

It naturally follows that a word used to address and describe individual Christians will also be used to describe them in larger groups or as a whole. Jesus sometimes uses the word in this way: the man who leaves blood-relations for the sake of the Gospel will receive a hundredfold by way of brothers and sisters in the new fellowship (Mk. 10:29, 30), though a Christian's personal relationships are not to be restricted to his spiritual brethren alone (Mt. 5:47). But the term comes into fuller use with the early Church. John has it at the end of his gospel (21:23). Acts uses it to describe many varieties of Christian groups: the first disciples (1:15), Christians in Jerusalem and Judaea (9:30; 11:1, 29; 12:17; 15:22; 21:17), in Joppa (10:23; 11:12), in Iconium (14:2; 16:2), in Antioch (15:1, 23, 32, 33, 40), in Phoenicia and Samaria (16:3), in the cities of the first missionary journey (15:36), in Lystra (16:2), in Philippi (16:40), in Thessalonica (17:10), in Beroea (17:14), in Corinth (18:18), in Ephesus (18:27), in Ptolemais (21:7), and in Rome (28:15). An ecumenical list indeed!

To it may be added references in the epistles at 1 Cor. 15:6; Eph. 6:23; Col. 1:2; 4:15, and also the word *brotherhood* in 1 Pet. 2:17; 5:9. But the most notable word in the epistles is a word which was coined by Christians, the word *brotherly-love*. It is found very occasionally in non-Christian writers to describe love between two blood brothers, but never in the sense of a relationship between members of a spiritual family. The New Testament has it six times (Rom. 12:10; 1 Thess. 4:9; Heb. 13:1; 1 Pet. 1:22; 2 Pet. 1:7 [twice]). Perhaps they may all be summed up in the verse from Hebrews: 'Let love of the brethren continue'.

Brother=Christian

There are many places where this equation is very clear, so much so that the New English Bible does not hesitate to translate the word *brother* by *Christian* in suitable contexts. This is most noticeable in 1 Corinthians, e.g. 'If *a Christian* has a heathen wife', instead of 'If *any brother* has an unbelieving wife' (7:12). See also 5:11; 6:5; 7:14, 15; 9:5. It is used too in Phil. 1:14: 'fellow-Christians' (brethren in the Lord), 1 Thess. 4:10 and 3 Jn. 5. It could have been used in Acts 17:6, where 'certain brethren' means 'certain Christians'. It *is* used in 28:14: 'There we found fellow-Christians'.

The New English Bible sometimes uses the happy translation, 'friends': 'our friend Apollos' (1 Cor. 16:12), 'these friends' (2 Cor. 9:3, 5), 'our friends' (11:9), 'our friend' (12:18). See also 1 Cor. 16:11; Gal. 1:2; 3 Jn. 3.

Other passages where the translation 'brother' in the usual versions means simply 'brother-Christian' are 2 Cor. 8:18, 22, 23; Phil. 4:21; Rev. 1:9; 6:11; 19:10; 22:9.

The Local Church a Brotherhood

This fact is stated explicitly in 2 Jn. 13, where the local church in a particular place is spoken of in the singular as the 'sister' of a church elsewhere. Each church is a united family, closely related to the other small families in the Great Family of God.

The implication is equally clear in Rom. 16:14, where certain

Christians are greeted by name, along with 'the brethren that are with them', that is, the rest of the local brotherhood.   The same is true in 1 Cor. 16:20, where 'all the brethren', the whole local church, send greetings.   Compare also 1 Thess. 5:26, 27; 1 Tim. 4:6 and 2 Tim. 4:21.

How not to act to the Brethren

To call fellow-Christians our brothers is not, however, enough. The New Testament has much to say about how we should not, and how we should, treat them.   We are not to be angry with them (Mt. 5:22), not to see their small faults and miss our own big ones (Mt. 7:3-5; Lk. 6:41, 42), not to fail in forgiveness (Mt. 18:35).   We are not to judge, despise, grieve or trip up our brother (Rom. 14:10-21), not defraud him (1 Cor. 6:5), nor wound his conscience, seeing that he is 'the brother for whose sake Christ died' (8:11, 12).   We are not to overreach him to gratify our sexual passions (1 Thess. 4:6), nor to take advantage of the fact that he is a Christian (1 Tim. 6:2).   We are not to fail him if he lacks food or clothing, or to disparage him in any way (Jas. 2:15; 4:11).   We are not to hate him or fail to love him (1 Jn. 2:9, 11; 3:10, 15; 4:20), or shut our hearts against him when we have this world's goods (3:17).   We are not to reject him so that we may be the more prominent (3 Jn. 10).   All this is the way of the Devil, whom Revelation describes as 'the accuser of the brethren' (12:10).

How to act to the Brethren

Instead of all this, we are to follow the positive way of reconciliation with our brother (Mt. 5:23, 24), helping him quietly to see where he has gone wrong (18:15), avoiding practices that will make him stumble (1 Cor. 8:13), admonishing him 'as one of the family' (2 Thess. 3:15, New English).   We are to treat all as brothers and sisters (1 Tim. 5:1, 2).   The master is to treat his servant as 'a brother beloved' (Phm. 16).   The Christian in a humble position is not to grumble but to rejoice (Jas. 1:9). Above all things, we are to love our brothers (1 Jn. 2:10; 3:14, 16); that is the way of light and life and sacrifice.   We are to 'lend strength' (Lk. 22:32, New English) to the brethren who need it; and by our prayers we are to do our utmost to save our brother from sin (1 Jn. 5:16).   1 Pet. 3:8 sums it all up with the compound adjective: Be ye all 'loving-as-brethren'.

Christ our Brother

Yet the New Testament does not simply urge us to live as brothers in a family, separate from Christ. It makes it clear that He too is in the family, Himself our Brother: 'Behold, my brethren! Whosoever shall do the will of my Father, he is my brother and sister' (Mt. 12:49, 50; Mk. 3:34,35; Lk. 8:21). He is indeed our superior, our teacher where we are all brethren (Mt. 23:8), but at the same time even the least of us are His brethren (25:40). Nor is this true only during His incarnate life. Among His first words after His resurrection is the command, 'Go tell my brethren' (Mt. 28:10; Jn. 20:17). Incarnate or glorified, He is not ashamed to call us brethren (Heb. 2:11,12), because He was made in all things like unto us, His brethren (2:17). This is why He can set before us the ideal and the precept of being a Family. He Himself is in all respects our Brother.

This has been a somewhat intricate study of a common and apparently simple word. It will have served its purpose if it has reminded us of what brotherhood in Christ means. It means that we cannot evade responsibility for our fellow-Christians. If we disclaim our family relationship, we are acting like Cain towards Abel, or the older brother towards the prodigal. It means that brotherhood must be personal and individual, that it must embrace the whole Church, and that it must be world-wide. It means that it must be not just a name, but a life of forbearance from evil, and of action for good. And because we can do so little of this in our own strength, Christ Himself delights to become our Brother and guide us in the way that He wants us to go.

IV. THE CHRISTIAN YEAR

20. THE 'COMING' OF JESUS

The Coming of Jesus is the centre of our thoughts at Christmas. Yet how much we miss if we limit our thought of His coming to the time of His birth. Every moment of His time on earth was 'Coming'. It was the whole purpose of the Incarnation.

The study of a very simply New Testament word lights up that truth. The ordinary verb *erchomai*, I come, occurs a large number of times in many connections. It is, however, used some seventy-six times in connection with the coming of Jesus to this world and with His 'comings' when He was in it. We shall not now consider His ordinary geographical comings and goings, though they might well be included, nor shall we take up what He says about His coming again. We shall find enough to satisfy us in what relates directly to Christmas and springs out of it.

We shall look first at the purpose of His coming. The New Testament shows it as five-fold.

1. He came simply to live with men at their own level. 'He came and dwelt in Capernaum' (Mt. 4:13, cp. 9:1) is more than a geographical statement. It is part of the meaning of the Incarnation. 'The Son of man came eating and drinking' (Mt. 11:19; Lk. 7:34), and He continued to join in ordinary human activity even in His resurrection body: 'He came and took the bread' (Jn. 21:13). From the beginning of His ministry He had come right down to men's level, to the Baptist's utter astonishment: 'Do you come to me?' (Mt. 3:14), and this humility continued throughout, up to the Last Supper itself: 'He took a towel . . . so He comes to Simon Peter' (Jn. 13:6).

2. He came to fulfil all that His people had long been hoping for. He came to fulfil the Law and give it new meaning (Mt. 5:17). He came as their long-expected prophet (Jn. 6:14), as the Messiah (Jn. 4:25-26; 11:27), as the King hoped for by Zechariah (Mt. 21:5; Jn. 12:15), and as the One who received the pilgrim welcome to Jerusalem: 'Blessed is he who comes in the name of the Lord' (Mt. 21:9; Mk. 11:9; Lk. 19:38; Jn. 12:13), the words of the Psalmist in Ps. 118:26, but with the word 'King' added in Luke and John. The crowds knew that He was more than a pilgrim. He was One who was stronger and better not only than the Baptist (Mt. 3:11; Mk. 1:7; Lk. 3:16; Jn. 1:15,

27, 30), but than all whom He 'came after'. That 'coming after' was in time only, not in degree.

3. He came for healing and helping and serving and teaching. He said to the centurion, 'I will come and heal' your son (Mt. 8:7). Immediately after, He came to Peter's house and healed his wife's mother (8:14). Jairus besought Him, saying 'Come and lay thy hands on my daughter' (Mk. 5:23; Mt. 9:18). 'In the fourth watch of the night He came' to his disciples in trouble on the sea, and the wind ceased (Mt. 14:25; Mk. 6:48). They had been in sore need when 'Jesus had not yet come to them' (Jn. 6:17). He longed that all men, especially wayward Jerusalem, should call on His help and be ready to say, 'Blessed is he that cometh in the name of the Lord' (Mt. 23:39; Lk. 13:35). He 'came not to be ministered unto but to minister' (Mt. 20:28; Mk. 10:45), and even a half-blind man like Nicodemus could acknowledge Him as 'a teacher come from God' (Jn. 3:2).

4. But He came for more than service. He came to save, and to give light and life. He 'came . . . to call sinners' (Mt. 9:13; Mk. 2:17; Lk. 5:32). He 'came not to judge the world but to save the world' (Jn. 12:47). 1 Tim. 1:15 carried on the Gospel message: 'Christ Jesus came into the world to save sinners'. John loves to speak of Him as the light that has come into the world (1:9; 3:19; 12:46), and as the One who has come that men may have life (10:10). He brings this life physically to Lazarus, coming to the tomb where he lay (11:17, 38), and in His own resurrection life He comes back to His disciples and stands in their midst (20:19), comes even though the doors are shut (20:26), and revives their drooping spirits.

5. Yet this 'Coming' is for Him no easy matter. It means coming to a place named Gethsemane (Mt. 26:36; Mk. 14:32). It means that He has to answer His own prayer for physical safety with the words 'But for this cause *came* I unto this hour' (Jn. 12:27). He is ready to let His 'coming' continue to the ultimate sacrifice.

Despite His purpose of love and service, however, His coming was so often regarded with suspicion and hostility. 'He came unto His own, and they that were His own received Him not' (Jn. 1:11). One can understand this suspicion on the part of the demoniacs: 'Art thou come hither to torment us ?' (Mt. 8:29), but when He came into His own place, Nazareth, what evil power prevented them from welcoming Him ? (Mt. 13:54; Mk. 6:1). Jesus has to meet this suspicion and lack of response to His coming with stern and challenging statements of its purpose: 'For judgment came I into this world' (Jn. 9:39).   (In 12:47 He says that He came not to judge but to save, but it makes all the difference whether He is speaking to the rebellious or to the obedient.)   He came seeking fruit from men (Lk. 13:6; Mt. 21:19; Mk. 11:13), and would not accept excuse for its absence.   He came to show men their sin (Jn. 15:22).   He came to bear witness to the truth, and to speak of it fearlessly to the highest authority (Jn. 18:37).   He came with a stern challenge that would not be peace but a sword (Mt. 10:34), that would divide families (10:35), that would scorch like fire (Lk. 12:49).   And His words in Gethsemane to His disciples are all the more stern for their tender restraint.   He who had come there to make the uttermost sacrifice (Jn. 12:27) comes to His disciples and finds them sleeping (Mt. 26:40; Mk. 14:37)—'Could you not watch with me one hour?'

He had the right to speak like this, because He is not a mere human leader, seeking obedience from His followers.   He has not come of His own accord; it is God who has sent Him (Jn. 7:28; 8:42).   He has come in His Father's name (5:43).   He has come from above, from heaven (3:31), and that gives Him supreme rights.   Nor is He a self-deluded boaster; He knows for certain whence He has come (8:14).

From all this it is clear why St. John in his letters emphasises the fundamental importance of belief in the Incarnation.   Those who will 'not acknowledge Jesus Christ as coming in the flesh' (2 Jn. 7, N.E.B.) are deceivers, they are antichrist himself. They are attacking the very basis of the Faith.   But 'every spirit which acknowledges that Jesus Christ has come in the flesh is from God' (1 John 4:2); he has the root of the matter in him. He can overcome all the attacks of the evil world because He believes in Jesus, 'He who came with water and blood' (1 John 5:6), that is, He who came to be baptized with us and to die for us.   If all that the New Testament says about His 'coming' is untrue, there is very little substance left in Christianity.

In John 16:28 Jesus says, 'I *came* from the Father and *have come* into the world' (N.E.B.).   In Greek there is a significant difference between the two tenses of the verb.   The first refers to the single moment of His coming into the world, His actual birth; the second denotes a permanent, lasting effect.   It is true that, as He immediately says, He has physically left the world and gone back to the Father.   But the permanent, lasting effect of the Incarnation remains. He is still here in His Word, in His Church, in His Spirit, in His personal communication with His disciples. He *has come*, and has not gone away. That—not the Birth alone—is the complete Christmas message.

21. PEACE

Christmas is the traditional season of peace, celebrated in a world which is far from knowing the secret of peace. What has the New Testament to say about peace?

The word (Greek, *eirēnē*) occurs no fewer than ninety-two times, twenty-five of the uses being in the Gospels and forty-three in the Pauline letters. Derivations from it occur another eight times, bringing the total to just over a hundred. It is obviously a word to which the New Testament pays great attention.

From this extensive use we shall take only samples, but six distinct senses of the word can be found:

1. There is the ordinary secular sense — absence of armed fighting. Jesus uses that sense in Lk. 14:32. It comes twice in Acts (12:20 and 24:2), and once in Revelation 6:4. That, I think, is all. The New Testament is not unaware of the secular sense, but it makes little use of it.

2. More frequently we find, especially in the Gospels, the ordinary Jewish use of the word as a salutation, corresponding to the Muslim 'Salaam': 'Whatever house you enter, first say, Peace be to this house' (Lk. 10:5; cp. Mt. 10:13). And this is the primary meaning of the only use of the word in Mark, when Jesus says to the woman whom He has healed: 'Go in peace' (5:34). His words there are more than a merely conventional Good-bye. He bids the woman enter into a new state of peace, arising out of her contact with Him.

3. In fact there is a special peace which the New Testament describes as 'the peace of Christ'. Jesus Himself speaks of '*my* peace' in Jn. 14:27, and in 16:33 He says that He has spoken 'that *in me* you may have peace'. Paul picks up the thought in Col. 3:15, and elaborates it in Eph. 2:14-17: He *is* our peace, making Jew and Gentile into one new humanity, so making peace; and He comes and preaches peace to them that are afar off and them that are nigh.

4. Yet in the New Testament peace goes back fundamentally behind even Christ Himself to God the Father. It is essentially His gift to men. It is a remarkable fact that every Pauline epistle begins with the salutation, very slightly varied: 'Grace to you and peace from God our Father and the Lord Jesus Christ'. In the body of the epistles a still deeper phrase is used, when God is spoken of as 'the God of peace': 'The God of peace be with you all' (Rom. 15:33); 'The God of peace shall bruise Satan under your feet shortly' (Rom. 16:20); 'God is not a God of confusion but of peace' (1 Cor. 14:33); 'The God of peace and love shall be with you' (2 Cor. 13:11); 'The God of peace shall be with you' (Phil. 4:9); 'The God of peace Himself sanctify you wholly' (1 Thess. 5:23); 'The Lord of peace Himself give you peace at all times in all ways' (2 Thess. 3:16); 'The God of peace make you perfect in every good thing' (Heb. 13:20, 21). If we are to have that 'peace on earth' of which the angels sang in Lk. 2:14, it comes as His gift, because it is part of His nature.

The gift of God's peace comes to men in two ways:

5. Firstly, in the personal reconciliation through Christ between us and God that Peter preached in Acts 10:36, the peace that is the result of forgiveness (10:43). Paul in Rom. 5:1 spoke of this peace as the consequence of the new faith-relationship with God in Christ, and in Col. 1:20 went on to describe it as intended to include all creation. It is no use our trying to set the world right until we ourselves have been set right with Him through the One whom He sent to bring about this 'reconciliation'. That is why human efforts at peace-making never succeed for very long, and why even Christian peace-making fails when it is mere patching up on the human level. It is only the peace of God, which passes all merely human understanding, that can really guard our hearts and thoughts and make true peace possible (Phil. 4:7). We often talk about 'arbitration' in industrial and international disputes, meaning an attempt to reach a compromise with which both sides will be reluctantly satisfied. The New Testament also uses the word, in Col. 3:15: 'Let the peace of Christ arbitrate (R.V. margin) in your hearts'. The word was used by the Greeks of the judges in athletic contests. Paul is saying that no other referee than Christ's peace can really keep the struggle of life under control.

6. Secondly, when Christians have learnt what peace with God and the peace of God really mean, then they are given a task to perform in the world, the task of following up the work

that Christ began. We are to 'give diligence to keep the unity of the Spirit in the bond of peace' (Eph. 4:3). 'Diligence' is not a very good translation here; it suggests something rather pedestrian. 'Eagerness' would be better. We are to be as eager for unity and peace as some people are for war, or for the advancement of their own selfish interests. And peace is something that essentially *binds* us together, that makes us one outwardly because we have become one at heart. As Paul says in the previous verse, that takes a great deal of mutual forbearance and love, but it is the calling wherewith we were called, and we are to walk worthily of it. This teaching is applied to a specific instance in 1 Cor. 7:15: 'God has called us in peace', says Paul, and he is referring to a husband and wife with very different outlooks on life. One has become a Christian, with all that that implies of change of thought and life. The other has not. Are these differences to separate them? Paul will not compel them to remain together; they are not under bondage. But how much better if they can stay together in peace. Who knows what consequences for good it may not have, if the believing partner really holds on to what the peace of God means?

The Christian life is to be a life of peace, of the peace of God. And that means that the abstract noun, however rich its content, is not enough. Four times over, the New Testament has a verb which has been formed from the noun — action, not merely abstraction, 'peacing' rather than just peace. 'Live-at-peace with one another', says Jesus in Mk. 9:50. 'If it be possible, as much as in you lieth, be-at-peace with all men', says Paul in Rom. 12:18, with apparent caution. Is he thinking of the frailty of human nature, even in Christians? I doubt if he would have let his readers down so lightly. It is rather that peace in this world does not depend entirely on ourselves; there is the other party too. But our task is clear: 'So far as it depends on *you*, be-at-peace with all men'. And unless we are ready to live-in-peace, we cannot expect the God of peace to be with us; 2 Cor. 13:11 links the two very closely together. Whether it is the difficult Corinthians or the simple-hearted Thessalonians (1 Thess. 5:13), 'be-at-peace among yourselves' is Paul's word for them.

Yet even that is not the last word. We are not only to live quietly, causing no trouble. We are to engage in the much harder task of *creating* peace. 'Blessed are the peace-*makers*, for they shall be called the sons of God' (Mt. 5:9). They will follow in the footsteps of what their Father has done in Christ, who came 'that He might create in Himself of the two one new man, so *making* peace' (Eph. 2:15). That is always the Christian's God-given task: to make two people or parties into one, by the peace of Christ who died that all might be one. Only so can the world become what it was intended to be: 'the harvest of right-eousness is sown in peace by those who *make* peace' (James 3:18; R.S.V.).

The Christmas message of peace to those in whom God can take pleasure because they accept His peace is therefore threefold: (1) that we should be utterly willing to be at peace with Him, with no rebellion against Him left in our hearts; (2) that with His peace in our hearts we should be eager to go out far beyond our own mere rights to be at peace with one another for Christ's sake; and (3) that we should never stop short of being peace-*makers*, sharing the creative activity of God, in our home, our church, our country, and the world.

22. HE MUST REIGN

We often use the word King when we speak of God and of Christ. We do not so often stop to think of what the use of that word really implies. This chapter will therefore examine two words in the New Testament vocabulary and see what they have to say to us, particularly in relation to Christmas and Epiphany.

The two words are the noun *Basileus*, a king, and the verb *Basileuō*, I reign as a king, rule. (This chapter will not deal with the equally frequent and important word *Basileia*, kingship, kingdom). *Basileus* occurs one hundred and fifteen times in all (twenty-two in Matthew, twelve in Mark, eleven in Luke, sixteen in John, twenty in Acts, thirteen in the epistles and twenty-one in Revelation). *Basileuō* occurs twenty-one times (four in the Gospels, ten in the epistles and seven in Revelation). A form of the verb meaning 'I reign with' occurs twice, so that our total for examination now is one hundred and thirty-eight.

Thirty-three of these instances refer to an unnamed earthly king, or kings: 'You shall be brought before governors and kings for my sake' (Mt. 10:18; Mk. 13:9; Lk. 21:12); 'Honour the king' (1 Pet. 2:17); 'The ruler of the kings of the earth' (Rev. 1:5). Another thirty-two refer to earthly kings by name: one or other of the Herod family (Mt. 2:1; Mk. 6:14; Acts 25:13 etc.), Pharaoh (Acts 7:10 etc.), David (Mt. 1:6; Acts 13:22), and others. There is no need to look at the full list. All we need to do is to remember the absolute power of a king in those days, power that was often used cruelly and selfishly but that was none the less absolute. A king might consult advisers or might rule alone, he might be hated or loved, but in every case he had the last word. It was the subject's business to obey without question. It is this note of authority that we bring into our understanding of the kingship of God and of Christ. The baser characteristics of earthly kings have no place in the divine kingship, but the authority is absolute there, to a degree that it can never be with an earthly king.

At His trial and crucifixion Jesus was often called king. The word is used twenty-six times in the gospel stories by the Jews and Pilate. Yet it is used only on the political level, with no realisation of what His spiritual kingship means. Pilate cries out, 'Behold your king!', and the answer comes, 'We have no king but Caesar' (Jn. 19:14,15). This is mere underlining of the Jews' tragic misunderstanding of the true nature of Messiahship. Even the title above the Cross, in slightly differing forms in the four Gospels (Mt. 27:37; Mk. 15:26; Lk. 23:38; Jn. 19:19) but all containing the phrase 'King of the Jews', has no hint of what the word King has come to mean for all who, through that Cross, have sworn loyalty to the Bearer of the name.

The list of the loyal ones does, however, begin the New Testament itself. Dimly or clearly, partially or fully, there are those who understand that word King, and who use it as it ought to be used of Jesus. The Wise Men, earnestly seeking, come with the words 'Where is He that is born King of the Jews?' (Mt. 2:2). Gabriel says to Mary, 'He shall reign over the house of Jacob for ever' (Lk. 1:33). Nathanael at his first meeting with Jesus says, 'Rabbi, thou art King of Israel' (Jn. 1:49). The crowd in Jn. 6:15 wanted to make Him king and, though their understanding and their motive were wrong, their desire arose out of admiration and respect. Three of the four evangelists speak of the Triumphal Entry as the coming of a king (Mt. 21:5; Lk. 19:38; Jn. 12:13, 15). Mark 11:10 has the word Kingdom in the popular patriotic sense. He portrays the crowd as even more blind, but still he makes their enthusiasm plain.

Jesus Himself, in two of His parables, spoke of His own kingship. In the parables of the Pounds the verb 'reign' comes twice (Lk. 19:14,27). This is not an easy parable to understand, but the nobleman is clearly Jesus. He demands that His followers be usefully employed between His Ascension and His Return, but there are those who do not want Him to reign over them. Their punishment is not arbitrary or vindictive; it is the parabolic way of expressing the doom of those who will not accept Christ's kingship. The other parable is easier. In Mt. 25:34,40 the King who sits as judge is Jesus Himself. We often think of the judge here as God, and it makes no serious difference; but a careful reading of Mt. 25:31,34 makes it clear at once. This declaration of the kingship of Jesus is continued after His earthly life is ended. Paul and Silas proclaim in Thessalonica that there is 'another king, one Jesus' (Acts 17:7). The author of the epistle to the Hebrews takes Melchizedek as a prototype of Jesus, and introduces him as 'King of Salem, King of Peace' (Heb. 7:1, 2). Paul speaks of Christ reigning till He has put all His enemies under His feet (1 Cor. 15:25), and then handing over the kingdom to God, though there is no ultimate distinction here between the Father and the Son. We may compare Rev. 11:15, where the angel says, 'The kingdom of the world is become the kingdom of our Lord (i.e. God) and of His Christ; and *He* shall reign for ever and ever'. Who is this 'He'? 'There is no indication as to who is meant', says Professor Anderson Scott; 'it is sufficient to observe that the Apostle draws no distinction'.

Yet of course the New Testament also speaks of God as King, both directly and indirectly. The parable of the Unforgiving Servant begins with the king who wanted to make a reckoning with his servants (Mt. 18:23), and the king is clearly God. So is the king who made a marriage feast for his son (Mt. 22:2,7, 11,13). When Jesus refers to Jerusalem as the 'city of the great King' (Mt. 5:35), He means God. So does the first epistle to Timothy with those two glorious ascriptions to 'the King eternal . . . the only God' (1:17) and to 'the blessed and only Potentate, the King of kings and Lord of lords' (6:15). Shall we include here that phrase of Paul's in Rom. 5:21 about grace reigning? We might well, because after all grace is the grace of *God*. But it is, of course, the book of Revelation that especially emphasises the kingship of God. He is 'King of the ages' (15:3). The four and twenty elders worship Him, saying 'Thou hast taken Thy great power and begun to reign' (11:17, R.S.V.), and the voice as of a great multitude, as of many waters, and as of mighty thunders, says 'Hallelujah! for the Lord our God, the Almighty, reigneth' (19:6).

But the New Testament also warns us that evil can and does reign. Death reigns through man's sin (Rom. 5:14, 17, 21). The story of the Fall is the story of man's sin, and of all the deathly consequences, physical and moral, that are due to sin. 'Let not sin therefore reign in your mortal body' (Rom. 6:12). When Paul says to the Corinthians, 'Already ye have reigned without us' (1 Cor. 4:8), is he thinking of the sin of self-will that had led them to separate themselves from their teacher and from God? Rev. 9:11 speaks of the creatures who 'have over them as king the angel of the abyss'. There is indeed another king whom man can choose instead of God — call him sin, death or Satan, as you will.

But the alternative of the right choice is always there also. If the Corinthians really reigned in God's kingdom, Paul could reign with them (1 Cor. 4:8). If death has power to reign, much more have we the power to reign in life through grace (Rom. 5:17). If we endure with Christ, we shall also reign with Him (2 Tim. 2:12). The final picture in Revelation is of men who reign: those who have been purchased by Christ's blood (5:9, 10), those who have been martyred (20:4, 6), those who do God service in heaven (22:3, 5). But all of them have first learnt to acknowledge Him and Him alone as King.

Here then is the message for Christmas: 'Where is He that is born King?' (Mt. 2:2). If we look for Him, we must look for Him as King of our lives. And here is the message for Epiphany: 'The kings of the earth do bring their glory into it', that is, into the New Jerusalem (Rev. 21:24). This was what the Three Kings did, laying their kingship at the feet of Jesus. This is what all must do, whether their authority is great or small, since only when that authority is completely submitted to Him can they reign for the good of His world.

23. NEWNESS

The beginning of the new calendar year comes not long after the beginning of the new Christian year, and both put thoughts of newness into our minds. It is therefore suitable to see what the New Testament has to say about this theme.

It uses two words. The first, *Neos*, comes in varying forms twenty-four times; the second, *Kainos*, forty-five times, also in varying forms. There is an essential difference of emphasis in the two, though (as we shall see) it is not invariably observed.

Neos means primarily new in time, recent, young. *Kainos* means new in quality, different from what has gone before.

Neos is therefore the word for the new wine of which Jesus speaks in Mk. 2:22 and parallels. It is not specially new in quality, different from any other wine previously made. It has simply been recently produced, freshly made. *Neos* is also the regular word for a young person; e.g. the younger son in Lk. 15:12, the young men in Acts 5:6, the young men and women who are advised in 1 Tim. 5:1 ff. It is found in Neapolis (Acts 16:11), the 'new city' founded long ago and named without thought that it would soon grow old. (We do the same with our Puthur, our Hospet, our Newcastle.) There was no suggestion that Neapolis differed in quality from earlier cities; it was only that it was newly built. *Neos* is the world's idea of newness —something that is fresh at the moment compared with things that have gone before it, but that will itself inevitably grow old before long.

Kainos, on the other hand, is the Christian word. Here is a newness, not merely of time but of quality, a newness that will not grow old as the years go by. The word is not, of course, confined to religion. After Jesus has spoken of the freshly-made wine in Mk. 2:22, He goes on to speak of wine-skins that must be not merely freshly made but different in quality from old ones, supple and elastic instead of hard and brittle, able to fulfil a new purpose. The same is true of the new patch on the old garment in Mk. 2:21. It is different in quality from the old— unshrunk, reacting very differently to the attentions of the dhobi! We find the same distinction with regard to the 'new tomb' in which Jesus was laid (Mt. 27:60; Jn. 19:41). The evangelists are not simply stating that it was newly constructed. They are emphasising that it was unused, different from other tombs, fit for the Lord of newness who was laid in it.

This brings us over into the spiritual sphere. We find the scribes in Mt. 13:52 who have become disciples, bringing out of their treasures things of a new quality, as well as the old, well-loved ones in which Matthew himself delights. We find the people in Mk. 1:27 astonished at the new quality of Jesus' teaching, different from anything that they have heard before. We find even the dilettante Athenians in Acts 17:19 recognising the new quality of what Paul had to say. They spent their time (v. 21) looking for this kind of thing, but they rarely found it. The commandments that Jesus gave to men were not just to be numbered serially after the original Ten. They were of a new quality (Jn. 13:34). John himself later on (1 Jn. 2:7, 8; 2 Jn. 5) describes them as both new and not new. In the sense that the Lord had told him them many years before, they were not new, and yet they had never lost their newness of quality. In Horatius Bonar's words, they were 'eternal and yet ever new'.

The word *kainos* is the obviously right word for the essential Christian book: The *New* Testament, The *New* Covenant. Though there is a sense in which the New Testament continues from the Old, it is not simply Volume Two, the second part of a long book divided into two manageable halves, with the second merely the continuation of the first. Jesus lifts the divine revelation on to a new level, and the covenant relationship with God henceforth has a quality about it different from anything that has gone before. That is what He means when He speaks of the New Covenant in His blood (Lk. 22:20), the phrase that Paul repeats in 1 Cor. 11:25 and that he extends from the Sacrament to the whole of the Christian message in 2 Cor. 3:6. Hebrews three times over (8:8,13; 9:15) applies the same words to the priestly work of Christ. The New Testament is so called because it speaks of One who was Himself different from all who had gone before, and whose work differed essentially in quality from theirs. It was effective where the work of others had never been.

This means that if any man is in Christ, he is a new kind of creature (2 Cor. 5:17; see also Gal. 6:15), or perhaps we should translate it 'there is a new act of creation', different in quality from what God did when He made Adam. Humanity can be made new and different (Eph. 2:15; 4:24). Newness of life (Rom. 6:4) and newness of spirit (7:6) can be truly ours. We can be transformed by the renewing of our mind (12:2). The renewing power of the Holy Spirit is something that God has sent down upon us plentifully through Jesus Christ our Saviour (Tit. 3:5, 6, N.E.B.). Nor does this depend upon congenial outward circumstances. In 2 Cor. 4:7-16 Paul speaks of all his physical troubles—his treasure is indeed in an earthen vessel—but though his outward man is decaying, yet his inward man is being renewed day by day (v. 16). The quality of the new life never decays.

And so he urges the Colossians to live as those who 'have put on the new man, which is being renewed unto knowledge after the image of Him that created him' (Col. 3:10). This is one of the places where the two words for newness are not distinguished: *new* here is *neos,* whereas *renewed* is a form of *kainos.* So also Hebrews (12:24) once uses *neos* for the New Covenant; and in 1 Cor. 5:7 we might have expected *kainos* rather than *neos* for the 'new lump' of the purified Christian community.

But these are the only exceptions in the New Testament. We return to the distinction when we look at what it has to say about the future. When Jesus spoke in Mk. 14:25 about drinking of the fruit of the vine *new* in the kingdom of God, it was of a new quality of feasting that He was thinking. This will be when new heavens and a new earth will come (2 Pet. 3:13; Rev. 21:1), when there will be a new kind of Jerusalem (Rev. 3:12; 21:2), not just fresh bricks and mortar to replace the rubble of the old, and when men will have new names (Rev. 2:17; 3:12) that will not be merely aliases of what they have been called before but will be a gift from Christ Himself of a new quality of nature. Under these new conditions we shall sing 'a new song' (Rev. 5:9; 14:3)—not just a supplement to Hymns Ancient and Modern ('modern' is *neos,* not *kainos*), but a song as different in quality as is the singing of Caruso from the croaking of a frog. And if any details have been omitted from this catalogue, they are covered in the final New Testament use of the word in Rev. 21:5: 'He who sits on the throne said, Behold, I make all things new'.

In the New Year, therefore, we must not be satisfied with simply having turned over another page, not essentially different from the one we were on last year. This is not the newness to which Christ has called us. The newness that He offers, and that He demands, is on a new level of existence. We cannot climb to it ourselves, but He can lift us there. That is why He came.

> 'Darkness and dread we leave behind;
> New light, new glory still we find,
>   New realms divine possess;
> New births of grace, new raptures bring;
> Triumphant, the new song we sing,
>   The great Renewer bless.'

24. SELF-DENIAL AND SUFFERING

Self-denial is one of the most misused of all Lenten words. It is so often prostituted to the level of appeals to give up smoking for a few weeks, or meat on Fridays—or to contribute a few annas more to charity.

The best corrective to this is to study the use of the word *deny* as we find it in the New Testament. In two slightly different forms: *arneomai* and *aparneomai*, it occurs forty-three times—twenty-five in the Gospels, four in Acts, twelve in the epistles, and two in Revelation. Sometimes it is an ordinary denial of fact, e.g. Lk. 8:45: 'When all denied' that they had touched Jesus in the crowd. But far more often the word has a religious, particularly personal sense, which is peculiar to the New Testament and to Christianity. This is one of the many words that our faith uses distinctively. The New Testament uses it in three special ways:

1. With regard to the denial of Christ. Here 'disown' or 'say No to' would bring out the meaning more fully. 'Whoever disowns me before men, I will disown him before my Father in heaven' (Mt. 10:33, N.E.B.). This is what Peter's 'denial' involved. When he said, 'I know not this man' (Mk. 14:71), he was fulfilling the Lord's warning 'You will disown me thrice' (Mk. 14:30). He himself later used the same word about the Jews: 'Ye disowned the Holy One' (Acts 3:14). They had done so when they said, 'His blood be on us and on our children'. Nor was it the first time that they had disowned a God-sent leader. They had disowned Moses in the same way (Acts 7:35).

The word is not a Pauline word, but we find it in the Pastoral Letters, where 2 Tim. 2:12 repeats the Lord's warning of Mt. 10:33. 'If we disown Him, He also will disown us'. And the New Testament closes with 2 Pet. 2:1 speaking of those who disown the Master who bought them, and 1 Jn. 2:22 labelling the antichrist as the one who disowns the Father and the Son.

2. The expression is also used to indicate denial of the Faith which Christ brought. 1 Tim. 5:8 speaks of the nominal believer who does nothing for his own family as one who has in fact disowned his Faith. 1 Jn. 2:22 declares that the man who 'says No' to the statement that Jesus is the Messiah is a liar. Rev. 2:13 and 3:8 speak of those who have not disowned their faith, nor disclaimed the name of Christian.

3.   It is with this background that we must look at the command 'Let him deny himself' (Mk. 8:34; Mt. 16:24; Lk. 9:23).
We are not concerned with trifles here.   The most central of sins
is to disown Christ and our Faith.   We are rejecting our Lord
and the truth of God which He has given us.   But just because
we are not to disown His lordship, we must always say 'No' to our
own.   Not merely on the circumference but at the centre we
must say to our self: 'You are not the master; Christ is'.   That
is the only real self-denial.   Of Christ alone does the New
Testament say, 'He cannot disown Himself' (2 Tim. 2:13).
For us His command is to ignore, to refuse to recognize, ourselves
and to recognize only Him.

A second word that is often on our lips during Lent, and that
again we fail to understand in full, is the word *Suffering*.

The Greek verb *paschō*, I suffer, occurs forty-two times;
the noun *pathēma*, suffering, sixteen times, and other forms make
up our total to sixty-two.

The word is used for physical human suffering, e.g. in Mt.
17:15 and Mk. 5:26.   But of course its primary use in the New
Testament is in connection with the sufferings of Christ (twenty-
eight times).   We know how hard it was to make a Jew believe
that the Messiah must, or even could, suffer.   He was to be a
glorious deliverer, above anything degrading of that sort.   Hence
Jesus's strong emphasis (Mk. 8:31; Mt. 16:21; Lk. 9:22) on the
necessity for His suffering: 'The Son of man *must* suffer'.   Paul
describes this to Agrippa in Acts 26:23 as one of the main themes
of his preaching.   It had been hard even for a close disciple
like Peter to accept the idea at first (see Mk. 8:32), but it was not
very long before he himself was speaking of Christ's suffering
as the way by which He brought men to God (1 Pet. 3:18).

How this works has never been fully explained, but the fact
is that it does.   Peter himself hints that simply looking at Christ's
sufferings has something to do with it (1 Pet. 5:1).   Hebrews
(5:8, 9) connects obedience with suffering.   Christ Himself
learnt obedience through suffering, and so He could offer salvation
to all who obey Him.   1 Pet. 2:21 goes on to speak of Christ's
suffering as an example for us to copy in dying to self.   The New
Testament does not go further than this with the word 'suffering'.
It is in connection with Christ's *death*, not simply with His
suffering, that Paul, for example, has his deepest things to say.
He uses the noun only twice, and the verb never, in speaking
of Christ.

But in speaking of suffering the New Testament does not limit itself to the sufferings of Christ. It lays equally upon Christians the necessity of suffering for their faith. In this connection the two words come twenty-two times. There is no virtue in suffering for its own sake; that is mere asceticism. But if we are wholly committed to the truth as Christ has shown it to us, that means holding on to it whatever the cost. It may be the cost of ridicule and persecution (Heb. 10:32-33), or of death itself (Rev. 2:10), or of the minor troubles and inconveniences that we find harder to meet than perhaps something bigger and more challenging would be. The New Testament makes it very clear that we are not to expect the Christian life to go smoothly and easily. The very name of Christian itself may be enough to make things difficult (1 Pet. 4:16). Sometimes parents avoid giving their children specifically Christian names for this very reason. The word of the Gospel is that we are to *accept* suffering as an essential part of the Christian life under the circumstances of this world —not to take every possible step to avoid it, as we often do. Col. 1:24 goes even further. Paul says: 'I *rejoice* in my sufferings', in being imprisoned and faced with death. He sees that they are part and parcel of Christ's way, and that by them the Church is not damaged or destroyed, but actually built up.

How can we have the will and power to accept and rejoice in suffering? It may be theoretically fine, but practically it can be very depressing. The New Testament says two things to encourage us:

1. Christ knows all about suffering, and shares it with us. 'In that He Himself has suffered being tested, He is able to succour them that are tested' (Heb. 2:18). We are 'partakers of *His* sufferings' (1 Pet. 4:13). 'As ye are partakers of the sufferings, so also are ye of the comfort' (2 Cor. 1:7). And Heb. 2:9-11 speaks of His oneness with us, a oneness that links up our salvation with His suffering, and His perfect power with the way in which He became one with suffering men.

2. The second thing that the New Testament says about suffering is that it is inextricably linked with Glory. That is seen most clearly in 1 Peter, and when the Quaker saint, Rendel Harris, wrote on that epistle, he rightly called his book 'The Sufferings and the Glory'. Peter puts the two words together four times: 'the sufferings of Christ and the glories that should follow them' (1:11); 'as ye are partakers of Christ's sufferings, rejoice; that at the revelation of His glory also ye may rejoice'

(4:13); 'a witness of the sufferings of Christ, who am also a partaker of the glory ' (5:1); 'God . . . who called you to His eternal glory in Christ, after you have suffered' (5:10). But the combination is not only in 1 Peter. It comes twice over in Heb. 2:9, 10; and its foundation is in the heavenly places: 'Worthy is the Lamb who has been slain, to receive . . . glory' (Rev. 5:12).

And let us not forget that in the New Testament glory is not just later grandeur, given to compensate for present misery. It is the manifested perfection of God, hereafter *and* here. That perfection is not revealed by the absence of suffering, but by suffering itself. Refusal to suffer means refusal to exhibit God's glory. But unreserved willingness to suffer shows that God's glory and God's Spirit rest upon us (1 Pet. 4:14), and go out from us.

25. THE CROSS

In Lent it is our business to think and speak increasingly about the Cross, and always we are in danger of being both conventional and sentimental. It is hard for us to have any new realization of its meaning, and much of our thought is far away from the plain reality of the New Testament. This chapter will therefore try to go back to the pages of Scripture, so that all our thinking and praying may be firmly based upon what it has to say to us, and not be so vague and general that it is not truly Christian.

The noun *stauros*, cross, occurs only twenty-seven times in all. The verb *stauroō*, crucify, is found forty-six times, and there are two compound verbs, *anastauroō*, crucify again (once), and *sunstauroō*, crucify with (five times), making a total in all of seventy-nine. The figures for the different writers are: Matthew sixteen, Mark thirteen, Luke nine, John sixteen, Acts two, Paul twenty, Hebrews two and Revelation one.

Much the largest number of references (fifty-six) are simply to the *physical* cross by means of which Jesus was put to death, or to the physical crucifixion of others. (In perhaps six of these instances the writer has also the spiritual message of the cross in mind, but his primary intention is to state a plain stark physical fact). Five uses are in the words of Jesus to His disciples *before* His own death, and need special attention. Thirteen, all in St. Paul, deal with the Christian *message of the cross* in its grace

and power.   One (Heb. 6:6) is the only New Testament instance
of the emphasis that we often lay today on men's *continuing to
crucify Christ* by their sin.   And finally four, again all in St. Paul,
speak of our being *crucified with Christ*.   The proportions are
significant, and we will examine the various divisions in the order
in which they are here listed.

The Physical Cross

It is striking to find that nearly three-quarters of the New
Testament uses of the words refer only to this.   To Pilate, to
the Jews, even to the disciples on Good Friday, crucifixion was
simply the normal means of Roman execution, with no more
spiritual significance attached to it then than the gallows or the
guillotine have today.   We must do our best to put into the word at
this stage no more meaning than it always had before the death
of Jesus transformed its meaning for ever.   We shall try to look
at it here in as matter-of-fact way as possible.

When Jesus predicted His own death, He mentioned quite
simply the way in which it would be carried out (Mt. 20:19;
26:2; Lk. 24:7), just as He mentioned the way in which other
servants of God would be killed (Mt. 23:34).   When the crowd
and the chief priests called out for His execution (Mt. 27:22, 23;
Mk. 15:13, 14; Lk. 23:21, 23; Jn. 19:6, 15), they were thinking
of getting rid of Him in the usual way, and of nothing more.
The same was true of Pilate's words as he discussed the matter
with the Jews and with Jesus (Jn. 19:6, 10, 15), and when he
finally handed Him over (Mt. 27:26; Mk. 15:15; Jn. 19:16).
The soldiers had nothing more in mind when they led Him away
to crucify Him (Mt. 27:31; Mk. 15:20), bearing the cross-bar of
the cross (Jn. 19:17—the whole cross was too heavy for any
criminal to carry), and when they compelled Simon of Cyrene to
carry it for Him after it proved too much for Him (Mt. 27:32;
Mk. 15:21; Lk. 23:26).   It is the physical action also of which
the evangelists spoke when they said 'They crucified Him'
(Mk. 15:25; Lk. 23:33; Jn. 19:18), and with Him the two robbers
(Mt. 27:38, 44;   Mk. 15:27, 32), and when the soldiers after
crucifying Him divided His garments between them (Mt. 27:35;
Mk. 15:24; Jn. 19:23).   When Pilate had the title put on the
cross (Jn. 19:19), when the mockers called on Him to come
down from the cross (Mt. 27:40, 42; Mk. 15:30, 32), when the
women stood by the cross (Jn. 19:25), when in order that the
bodies should not remain on the cross over the Sabbath the legs

D

of the crucified robbers were broken (Jn. 19:31, 32), when the place of crucifixion is described as being near the city and with a garden near it (Jn. 19:20, 41), still the reference is always physical. Even afterwards, when the Church looked back, it was often to the sheer physical event—to the action of the authorities of this world (Lk. 24:20; Acts 2:36; 4:10; 1 Cor. 2:8), to the weakness and torment of His end (2 Cor. 13:4; Phil. 2:8), to the endurance with which He faced that physical end (Heb. 12:2).

Now and then the physical thought is carried a little further. When the angel in Mt. 28:5 (the young man in Mk. 16:6) speaks of Him as 'the crucified', he means it literally, but he is beginning to suggest more than that, because the form of the verb in Greek indicates one who has been permanently crucified, not one for whom it was only a temporary experience.   And when Rev. 11:8 interjects that stark clause 'where also their Lord was crucified', the historical event is recalled, but its spiritual significance is also in the writer's mind.

Jesus' Words to His Disciples

One reason why it is necessary to stress that the cross, until it was linked with the death of Jesus, was nothing more than the physical means of legal execution, is that only so can we understand the words of Jesus to His disciples when He talked to them about taking (Mt. 10:38), taking up (Mt. 16:24; Mk. 8:34; Lk. 9:23) or bearing (Lk. 14:27) their cross.   It is so easy to read these words in the light of what we know of Christ's cross, but what would they mean to the disciples when they first heard them ? They did not know the future meaning of the cross.   All they knew was that they had often seen condemned criminals carrying the bar of their cross on their shoulders and walking to their place of execution.   The disciples would not think of that as in any way a redemptive action, nor primarily as an illustration of bearing suffering, great or small.   Their first thought as they looked at such men would be that they had finished with this world. Henceforward its concerns were no concerns of theirs. And that was what Jesus meant His disciples to think about their own lives.   They were not to lose sympathy for this world, but they were to give up being attached to it and to its advantages; they were to be ready to lose themselves as completely as those condemned criminals were going to lose their physical lives on those crosses that they carried.   And when Jesus said, 'Let him deny himself', that also was what He meant—not a small act of so-called self-denial, but a denial of one's own rights to life as complete as that which the condemned criminal had to make as he went to his execution.

The Message of Christ's Cross

It is St. Paul in particular who finds in this means of Christ's physical death a central part of the Christian faith. To us 'the word (or message) of the cross' (1 Cor. 1:18) is a well-known phrase. To its first hearers it must have sounded as strange as 'the message of the gallows' would sound to us. Paul himself described it as 'foolishness'. It was just a stumbling-block to many (Gal. 5:11); it stirred up nothing but hostility in them (Phil. 3:18). Yet Paul's experience was that this dying of Christ on the cross was what reconciled men to one another and to God (Eph. 2:16; Col. 1:20). Somehow when men looked at that dying and realized the love behind it, they could no longer remain at enmity with each other and with their Father. They saw that He had forgiven them, wiping out the evidence against them and nailing the document on which it had been written to that very cross which showed that it had disappeared (Col. 2:14). So, whatever others preached, Paul preached 'Christ crucified' (1 Cor. 1:23). With glorious overemphasis he refused to acknowledge anything but 'Christ and Him crucified' (1 Cor. 2:2). He placards 'Christ crucified' before men's eyes like a bold advertisement in a prominent place (Gal. 3:1); and in each of these three passages he uses that tense which means 'permanently crucified'. The influence of the cross would never pass away, nor be forgotten like a bad dream. The cross is therefore the only thing in which Paul can boast (Gal. 6:14). He had nothing to boast of in himself; he had not been crucified for anybody (1 Cor. 1:13), and his only ambition was that Christ's cross should not fail to have its effect on anyone who heard the good news that it brought (1 Cor. 1:17).

Crucifying Christ, and Being Crucified with Him

Even in New Testament times there were those who went through the sin of Good Friday again, crucifying the Son of God afresh by their own sin (Heb. 6:6). But the New Testament prefers to emphasise the positive aspect of the cross. When a man is willing to be crucified with Christ, then the cross is truly effective. Paul, because he had seen what the cross meant, had through it been crucified to the world and the world to him (Gal. 6:14). He knew even better than the first disciples what it meant to take up his cross and be finished with the selfish attractions of the world. 'I have been crucified with Christ' was his description of his new life (Gal. 2:20), and in both these verses he uses that tense which we have already examined, the tense which implies permanent crucifixion. As with his Lord, so for Paul there was nothing fleeting and temporary about this experience. Thus he can go on to write to all his readers: 'They that are of Christ Jesus have crucified the flesh' (Gal. 5:24). Our old nature was 'crucified with Him' (Rom. 6:6), put to death for ever.

That was what Good Friday was meant to do, and what it can do for everyone who accepts the message of Christ's cross and lets himself be crucified with Him.

26. THE HEIGHTS OF GOD

Height is a word that is used metaphorically in most forms of literature, and the New Testament is no exception. The ordinary Greek noun *hupsos* occurs six times, another form *hupsōma* twice. The adjective *hupsēlos*, high, is found twelve times, and the superlative *hupsistos*, highest, thirteen. The verb *hupsoo*, lift on high, exalt, occurs twenty times, and the strengthened form *huperhupsoō*, exalt highly, once. Thus in one form or another the word is found fifty-four times.

Very rarely is the word used in the ordinary physical sense. When Jesus takes His disciples to a high mountain to witness the Transfiguration (Mt. 17:1; Mk. 9:2), the mountain may indeed be physically high, but the gospel writers are thinking also of its remoteness from the ordinary world. When Paul in Eph. 4:8 quotes from Ps. 68:18, he may have in mind the original picture of the king ascending Mount Zion, but in saying 'When he ascended *on high*', he has primarily in his thoughts the Ascension of Christ. Similarly the 'mountain great and high' to which the angel carried St. John the Divine (Rev. 21:10) is introduced as a spiritual vantage point rather than a literal Himalayan peak, and the city which John saw with its high wall (21:12) and its height equal to its length and breadth (21:16) is not measured for the sake of its material dimensions but to show the security which it gives and its all-inclusive capacity. Paul is thinking on the same lines when he writes of the all-inclusive love of Christ with its breadth and length and height and depth (Eph. 3:18).

Yet the New Testament tells also of heights of evil as well as of heights of good. Jesus took his disciples to a high mountain to show them God's glory. The devil had already taken Him to a high mountain to tempt Him with earthly glory (Mt. 4:8). The powers of evil can spread almost as widely as the love of Christ, and it is to these powers of evil that Paul refers in Rom. 8:39, when he says that 'neither height nor depth' can separate us from Christ. In 2 Cor. 10:5 he may also be referring to the powers of evil who are lifting themselves on high against God. It is with this opposition between the heights of God and the heights of evil that the New Testament is largely concerned.

But before we come to this opposition and contrast let us continue to look at the record of the heights of God. Our words in one form or another are often used as synonyms for heaven. This heavenly reference occurs many times during the incarnate life of Jesus. Zacharias rejoices that in Christ 'the dayspring from on high hath visited us' (Lk. 1:78). At His birth the angels sing 'Glory to God in the highest' (2:14). At His last entry into Jerusalem the crowds sing 'Hosanna in the highest' (Mt. 21:9; Mk. 11:10), or 'Glory in the highest' (Lk. 19:38). The New English Bible translates these phrases: 'Hosanna in the heavens', 'Glory in highest heaven'. Among the last words of Jesus to His disciples is the command to wait until they are 'clothed with power from on high' (Lk. 24:49), and Heb. 1:3 writes of Him as having 'sat down at the right hand of the Majesty on high'.

But the word is used not only of heaven. It is used to describe the greatness of God. Eight times, by a wide range of persons, He is spoken of as 'the Most High': by the angel Gabriel at the Annunciation (Lk. 1:32, 35), by Zacharias (1:76), by Jesus Himself (6:35), by Stephen (Acts 7:48), by the writer to the Hebrews (7:1), and even by mentally deranged people such as Legion (Mk. 5:7; Lk. 8:28) and the girl at Philippi (Acts 16:17). All alike acknowledge His supremacy. Nor is He is supreme only in rank. He is supreme also in what He does: He exalts on high the slave nation of Israel and brings them out of Egypt 'with a high arm', lifted up against all possible opposition (Acts 13:17).

This pre-eminent power of His He used to exalt His Son. Peter emphasises this twice in his preaching. It is part of his message at Pentecost that Jesus was exalted, lifted on high, by

God's right hand (Acts 2:33), and Peter repeats the message before the Council in Acts 5:31. Heb. 7:26 takes up the same theme when it speaks of Jesus as 'made higher than the heavens'. This exaltation is not for His own glorification. In each passage the thought goes on: He is exalted so that He may pour forth the Holy Spirit (Acts 2:33), become a Prince and a Saviour (5:31), and offer Himself for mankind (Heb. 7:27).

This brings us to the essential New Testament reversal of human values. The unregenerate man seeks high position in order to increase his own importance in the eyes of the world. The teaching of Jesus is that 'whosoever shall exalt himself shall be humbled; and whosoever shall humble himself shall be exalted' (Mt. 23:12; Lk. 14:11; 18:14). A place such as Capernaum, which hoped to 'be exalted unto heaven', would find itself going down to Hades (Mt. 11:23; Lk. 10:15), 'for that which is exalted among men is an abomination in the sight of God' (Lk. 16:15). Before the Lord's birth, His mother had sung, 'He has put down princes from their thrones, and has exalted them of low degree' (Lk. 1:52), and this was the effect of His ministry—not through the processes of bloody revolution, but by the demonstration in word and action of the true values of God.

The apostles continued that demonstration. Paul humbles himself that the Corinthians may be exalted (2 Cor. 11:7), and begs the Romans not to be highminded or to set their mind on high things (Rom. 11:20; 12:16). James bids the lowly brother glory in his high estate (1:9), and urges all his readers to humble themselves in the sight of the Lord; only then will He exalt them (4:10). 1 Peter 5:6 uses almost the same words, and 1 Tim. 6:17 makes its appeal to the rich 'that they be not highminded'.

But this paradox was not limited to mere words. It was worked out and driven home on the Cross. The Fourth Gospel uses the verb *hupsoō* (exalt, lift on high, lift up) five times, and each time it is in connection with the lifting up of Jesus on the Cross: 'As Moses *lifted up* the serpent in the wilderness, even so must the Son of man be lifted up' (3:14); 'When you have *lifted up* the Son of man, then you shall know that I am he' (8:28); 'I, if I be *lifted up* from the earth, will draw all men unto myself' (12:32, see also 12:34). Lifting a person up on a cross was the ultimate humiliation for him. In the case of Jesus it was the effective symbol of God's standard of values, His ultimate way of bringing them into the world. It is only *after* and *because*

Christ has been lifted up on the Cross that God can exalt Him over and above everything else in heaven and earth (Phil. 2:9).

'Set not your mind on high things, but condescend to things that are lowly' (Rom. 12:16).　That word is at the heart of the Gospel, and no one has truly accepted the Gospel until he has become willing to obey it.

27.　THE　RESURRECTION

The Resurrection is the most joyous of all Christian events. Any word-study of it ought to do all it can to make it as fresh and living for us as it was for the New Testament Church, which had not had time to become over-familiar with it as we tend to be.

To take all the New Testament references to it would be too big a task for one chapter.　We will therefore leave on one side the two verbs that are used for our Lord's rising or being raised, and concentrate on the single noun *Anastasis*, Resurrection.

This occurs forty-two times in all, in connection either with the resurrection of Christ or with human resurrection. (The one exception is Lk. 2:34, where it simply means rising as opposed to falling.)　The other uses are well distributed: four in Matthew, two in Mark, five in Luke, four in John, eleven in Acts, seven in Paul, one in Second Timothy, three in Hebrews, two in First Peter and two in Revelation.

When today we speak of 'the resurrection', we mean first and foremost the resurrection of Jesus.　His resurrection has the centre of our thought and belief, and any other thought comes only as a consequence of His rising.　He Himself, however, found the word in common use among His own people.　It was one of the main words of current controversy.　The Sadducees, whose beliefs were very conservative, argued that there was no reference to resurrection in the books of the Law, and that therefore it could not be accepted as an established fact.　The Pharisees more liberal in their thinking, included it as part of their belief. Hence the heated argument that we find in several places in the New Testament.　The Sadducees, 'who say that there is no resurrection' (Mt. 22:23; Mk. 12:18; Lk. 20:27), come to Jesus with one of those questions that appear perfectly logical, but which are intended as a trap.　Jesus exposes their question as being merely silly because it is based on false premises.　A woman has seven husbands, one after the other. If there is a resurrection, what will be the position when they all meet in heaven (Mt. 22:28; Mk. 12:23; Lk. 20:33)? Very clever! But Jesus shows what nonsense it really is. The conditions of the resurrection life will not be physical; they will be spiritual. There will be no need then for marriage in the human sense (Mt. 22:30; Lk. 20:35). If we are accounted worthy to attain to the resurrection, we shall be 'sons of the resurrection', which means being 'sons of God', no longer living under the conditions of this earth (Lk. 20:36). And even in the books of the Law, Jesus goes on to say, resurrection is taken for granted. God, who spoke to Moses *after* the deaths of Abraham, Isaac and Jacob, still said 'I *am* their God', not 'I *was*'. They still live (Mt. 22:32).

But the Sadducees learn nothing. The apostles in Acts are still engaged in the same battle. In 4:2 the Sadducees arrest Peter and John because they proclaim in Jesus the resurrection from the dead. Later on Paul shows up the depth of the division between Pharisee and Sadducee by declaring himself on the side of the Pharisee over this matter of resurrection (23:6-8). The whole issue of the controversy between Jew and Christian really hung on this one point of the resurrection of Jesus (23:6; 24:21). Paul had a right to expect the Pharisees to support him there.

In fact quite a number of places in the New Testament assume this Jewish belief in the resurrection of the dead. Jesus, in Lk. 14:14, speaks of the resurrection of the just, and in Jn. 5:29 of the resurrection to life or to judgment. Martha says that she knows that her brother Lazarus will rise 'in the resurrection at the last day' (Jn. 11:24). Paul, in Acts 24:15, speaks of his common ground with his opponents in believing that there will be a resurrection of just and unjust. Heb. 11:35 writes of people before Christ who, like the widow of Zarephath, had their dead restored to them, and of others who were martyred, hoping for 'a better resurrection'. Rev. 20:5, 6 speaks of a coming resurrection which the writer does not link directly with the resurrection of Christ.

But so far, perhaps, this chapter has not been as 'fresh and living' as was promised in its first paragraph! The reason, of course, is not far to seek. All the quotations up till this p oint have come from periods before the resurrection of Christ, or from verses not closely connected with it—and it is the resurrection of Christ that makes all the difference, lifting the word out of controversy into living experience. Our actual

word comes only once in this sense in the Gospels, but it is a
thrilling, central word when it does come. To a grief-stricken·
woman Jesus says 'I am the Resurrection and the Life' (Jn. 11:25).
He demonstrated that on the first Easter Day, and it has been
the proclamation and experience of His followers ever since.
The apostles in Acts are full of that message. Judas' successor
must above all things be a witness of Christ's resurrection (1:22).
Peter's first Christian sermon declared that the revered Psalmist-
King had foreseen that resurrection (2:31). The first assault of
persecution did not stop the apostles giving their witness to the
resurrection of the Lord Jesus 'with great power' (4:33). When
Paul preached in Athens, he made so much of the resurrection
that the puzzled Greeks seem to have thought that *Anastasis*
was a goddess! (17:18). They mocked him later (17:32),
but their attitude did not detract from the effectiveness of Paul's
preaching. Later on he did not hesitate to tell Festus and Agrippa
how Christ's resurrection was a message of light to Jew and Gentile
alike (26:23). Nor does the witness end with Athens and Caesarea.
It goes on to Rome itself in the opening words of Paul's letter to
the Christians there: 'Declared to be the Son of God with power
. . . by his resurrection from the dead' (Rom. 1:4).

That is the Good News of the Resurrection which the apostles
proclaimed, and which we proclaim again every Easter Day. Yet
Christ's resurrection by itself is not the whole of the message.
By Him comes also *our* resurrection from the dead (1 Cor. 15:21).
This verse comes from the Epistle for Easter Sunday, part of
that great combination of argument and triumph song by which
Paul links Christ's resurrection with ours: 'If Christ is preached
as raised from the dead, how say some that there is no resurrection?
If there is no resurrection, neither has Christ been raised' (15:12,
13). And from those verses we go on to drink in verse forty-
two and all that follows it: *we* are raised in incorruption, glory,
power, because Christ Himself became a life-giving spirit.

Our baptism itself was like the resurrection (Rom. 6:5). Our
old nature was then drowned. We rose from the water with
new life, as Christ rose from the tomb. Peter makes the same
connection in a rather difficult verse, which J. B. Phillips translates simply and effectively: 'There is in every true baptism the
virtue of Christ's resurrection from the dead' (1 Pet. 3:21). The
Christian life is the life that knows 'the power of His resurrection'
(Phil. 3:10).

There were those in the early Church who had wrong or

imperfect ideas about the resurrection. Some said that our resurrection was past already (2 Tim. 2:18). Some needed reminding that resurrection from the dead was one of the elements of the faith, an element that could not just be repeated as an article of the Creed, but that needed building on like a foundation (Heb. 6:2). But Peter had the final word that has given Christians certainty and joy ever since the day he wrote it. It was Peter who, hearing that the Lord's body had disappeared, ran with John that first Easter morning to the tomb. It was he who entered in with John and, with him, saw and believed. And, remembering that unforgettable moment, he writes, 'Blessed be the God and Father of our Lord Jesus Christ, who according to His great mercy begat us again unto a living hope by the resurrection of Jesus Christ from the dead' (1 Pet. 1:3). It was by that hope that Peter lived. It is by that hope that Easter Day bids us live also.

28. REJOICE

'The disciples rejoiced when they saw the Lord' (Jn. 20:20). That is the record of the first Easter Day, and it has been the true message of Easter ever since. Nor is it limited to one period of the year, because we are commanded to 'rejoice always' (1 Thess. 5:16). What should make a Christian rejoice? The New Testament answers that question, and in this chapter we look at just one of its words for rejoicing—the verb *chairō*, 'I rejoice', 'I am glad', and its compound form *sunchairō*, 'I rejoice together with'.

Chairō in the sense of 'rejoice' occurs sixty times in the New Testament. (It is also used twelve times as a form of greeting, but we are not now concerned with that.) Of the sixty times, three are in Matthew, one in Mark, eleven in Luke, eight in John, five in Acts, twenty-seven in Paul, one in 1 Peter, two in John's letters and two in Revelation. *Sunchairō* comes three times in Luke and four in Paul. The alternative translation 'be glad' is sometimes found in the English Bible, but the Greek word behind the two translations is the same.

The central, fundamental reason for Christian rejoicing is simply the fact of Christ Himself. At the very beginning of His time on earth, the wise men saw His star and 'rejoiced with great joy' (Mt. 2:10). John the Baptist, at whose own birth many were to rejoice (Lk. 1:14), rejoiced in His coming with as deep a satisfaction as a man has when his friend is getting married, even though it meant that John's followers would turn away from him to Jesus (Jn. 3:29). Jesus Himself looks right back into history, and pictures Abraham rejoicing at the prospect of the day of Christ (8:56). He bids His followers rejoice even when He is about to leave them, because He will be able to do more for them when He is with the Father (14:28). But He promises to return, so that they may have a joy based on more familiar foundations (16:22).

This joy in Christ is taken up by Paul in the letter to the Philippians, the great epistle of joy. He rejoices, and will continue to rejoice, that Christ is proclaimed (1:18). He urges the Philippians to 'rejoice in the Lord' (3:1), 'rejoice in the Lord always' (4:4) and again to rejoice (4:4). Finally, he himself returns to rejoicing in the Lord, because of the way in which the Philippians took thought for him (4:10).

And the closing scene of the New Testament, like the opening one, is a scene of joy in Christ. St. John the Divine hears the voice of a great multitude in heaven, saying 'Let us rejoice and be exceeding glad . . . for the marriage of the Lamb is come' (Rev. 19:7).

This rejoicing is to be not only for what Christ is in Himself but also for the things that He does. In Lk. 13:17 'the multitude rejoiced for all the glorious things that were done by Him', and again at the Triumphal Entry they did the same (19:37). Jesus Himself rejoiced that the disciples were going to see the raising of Lazarus, because it would give them a deeper faith (Jn. 11:15).

Yet He deliberately turns His disciples' interest from the physical to the spiritual: 'Rejoice not that the spirits are subject to you, but rejoice that your names are written in heaven' (Lk. 10:20). Salvation is the act of Christ over which there is to be the deepest rejoicing. There is His own rejoicing when He puts the lost lamb on His shoulders (Lk. 15:5) and 'rejoices over it more than over the ninety and nine which have not gone astray' (Mt. 18:13). There is the rejoicing of the Father when the prodigal returns (Lk. 15:32). There is the rejoicing of Zacchaeus (19:6) when Jesus goes to stay with him and says 'Today is salvation come to this house'. There is Jesus' comment on the quick response of the Samaritans to His message, so quick that the sower and the reaper can rejoice together (Jn. 4:36).

Acts continues the theme when the Ethiopian eunuch goes on his way rejoicing at his having been brought to Christ (8:39), and the book especially underlines the joy at the salvation of the Gentiles: Barnabas rejoices at what the grace of God has done in Antioch (11:23); the Gentiles in the other Antioch, in Pisidia, rejoice when they hear Paul's message of universal salvation (13:48); and the Christians in Syrian Antioch rejoice when they hear that the Jerusalem church is going to put no serious restrictions on the free acceptance of that salvation (15:31).

Paul, as we should expect, rejoices over every aspect of salvation, whether he looks at its theology or at its practical effects. He bids the Romans rejoice in the hope that lies before them (12:12), and he himself rejoices in their obedience (16:19). He rejoices in the way that the Corinthians have responded to the appeal of Titus (2 Cor. 7:7, 9), and rejoices also because he himself has had his confidence in them restored (7:16). He can even rejoice when he is weak in contrast with their strength, provided only that they are being perfected (13:9). He rejoices —perhaps even more—when he sees the 'solid steadfastness' (J. B. Phillips) of the Colossians' faith in Christ (2:5).

John shares that spirit of rejoicing. He is delighted that he has found some who walk in the truth (2 Jn. 4), and some who could come and bear witness to their fellow-Christians' truth of life (3 Jn. 3). The Church is built on people like that.

Yet throughout the New Testament there is another, and most unexpected, cause for rejoicing. It comes first in the words of Jesus: 'Blessed are ye when men shall persecute you for my sake. Rejoice and be exceeding glad' (Mt. 5:11, 12; Lk. 6:23). Suffering, if it is for Christ, is a thing to rejoice in. The apostles did not forget that lesson. We find them in Acts (5:41) 'rejoicing that they were counted worthy to suffer dishonour for the Name'. We find Paul 'sorrowful yet always rejoicing' (2 Cor. 6:10), rejoicing in his sufferings for the sake of the Colossians (1:24), rejoicing even if his service to the Philippians is going to result in his death (2:17), and calling on the Philippians also to rejoice with him (2:18). Lastly we find Peter addressing a persecuted church and bidding them rejoice because they are partakers in Christ's sufferings (1 Pet. 4:13).

On the other hand, like all good things, rejoicing can be perverted, done for a bad reason. The chief priests rejoiced when Judas came to betray Jesus (Mk. 14:11; Lk. 22:5). Herod rejoiced when Pilate sent Jesus to him (Lk. 23:8), but only because he wanted to see Him do a miracle. Jesus Himself warned His disciples that the world would rejoice when He died (Jn. 16:20). Paul spoke of that attitude which rejoices in unrighteousness (1 Cor. 13:6); and one of the mysterious passages of the Book of Revelation is that where God's two witnesses are killed by the Beast, and the peoples of the earth rejoice over their death (Rev. 11:10). God keep us from rejoicing in evil!

The final New Testament teaching about rejoicing is that it is not a solitary thing. In Lk. 1:58 the neighbours rejoice with Elisabeth at the birth of John. In the parables, the friends and neighbours rejoice with the shepherd and the woman when they find what they have lost (Lk. 15:6, 9). Paul bids the Romans 'rejoice with them that rejoice' (12:15), and himself rejoices at the coming of his friends from Corinth (1 Cor. 16:17), at the joy of Titus over the success of his mission there (2 Cor. 7:13), and at the steadfastness of the Thessalonians (1 Thess. 3:9). He even shares his joy with the Philippians at the prospect of his death and bids them share with him in return (2:17, 18). He hates to have sorrow from those with whom he ought to be able to rejoice (2 Cor. 2:3), because in the unity of a true body all the members rejoice together (1 Cor. 12:26). In fact, wherever there is truth, real love always rejoices with it (1 Cor. 13:6).

So, although there is a sense in which we must sit loose to this world and, even if we rejoice, be as if we rejoiced not (1 Cor. 7:30), there is so much ground for a Christian to rejoice that he would fail to be a true Christian if he did not. If *we* do not rejoice, have we failed to understand our faith?

29. POWER

The key-note of Easter is Power: the Power of God that raised Christ from the dead, and the Power that is available for us as a result. Paul prays that he may know Christ and the power of His resurrection (Phil. 3:10), and that prayer was certainly fulfilled. Jesus, after His resurrection, promises His disciples that they shall receive power when the Holy Spirit is come upon them (Acts 1:8), and Acts is the account of how that promise was fulfilled.

The New Testament therefore has inevitably a great deal to say about Power, and its vocabulary for this word is very rich. In Eph. 1:19 Paul collects four words which he piles one on top of the other to show what God has done for us in Christ: 'the exceeding greatness of His *power* to us-ward who believe, according to that *working* of the *strength* of His *might* which He wrought in Christ when He raised Him from the dead. . . .' It is these four words which we shall look at in this chapter.

1.   The Greek for the first word is *dunamis*. This word and its associated verb and adjective are the most frequent of all. They occupy over four pages in the Concordance.   They are the words from which we derive 'dynamic' and 'dynamite'. Their root idea is the ability to get things done, effectiveness. In themselves they have no special supernatural connotation, but in the New Testament their central emphasis is that God and His Son and His Spirit are effective, that man by himself is not, but that man with God's aid is effective as God is.   Let us look at some examples of this.

(*a*) The effectiveness of God: 'The word of the cross is . . . unto us who are being saved *the power of God* (1 Cor. 1:18); 'Christ *the power of God*' (1:24); 'that your faith should . . . stand . . . in *the power of God*' (2:5); 'the gospel . . . is *the power of God* unto salvation' (Rom. 1:16).   And the verb ('can', 'be able') is used in the same sense: 'Unto *Him that is able* to do exceeding abundantly above all that we ask or think' (Eph. 3:20); 'unto *Him that is able* to guard you from stumbling' (Jude 24).   In fact Jesus Himself speaks of God as 'the Power' in Mk. 14:62, where the true translation should be 'sitting at the right hand of the Power'.

(*b*) The effectiveness of Christ: His miracles are more often described as 'powers' (mighty acts) than in any other way; but it is in Hebrews that his effective power is most beautifully proclaimed —He *is able* to succour them that are tempted (2:18), He *is able* to bear gently with the ignorant and erring (5:2), He *is able* to save to the uttermost them that draw near to God through Him (7:25).   His enemies said that there was one thing He could not do: He could not save Himself (Mk. 15:31)—but that was the most effective thing about Him.

(*c*) The effectiveness of the Spirit: Jesus Himself returns in *the power of the Spirit* from His temptation in the wilderness (Lk. 4:14).   Paul speaks of his ministry to win the obedience of the Gentiles as having been 'energised' (our second word) by Christ through him in *the power of the Spirit* (Rom. 15:18-19).

The 'cannots' of the New Testament are to be found when God, Christ and the Spirit are not in a man's life: 'Whosoever does not

bear his own cross and come after me, *cannot* be my disciple'
(Lk. 14:27); the disciples, when Jesus was away from them,
could not cast out the demon (Mk. 9:28). In John the Jews
cannot come where Jesus goes (7:34,36; 8:21,22), they *cannot*
hear His word (8:43), they *cannot* believe (12:39)—all because
they will not fundamentally accept Him; the natural man *cannot*
know the things of the Spirit of God (1 Cor. 2:14) because they
are spiritually judged, and he will not come under the judgment
of Christ.

But when we are willing to be strong in the Lord and receive
His armour, we *are able* to stand against the wiles of the devil
(Eph. 6:10, 11). When the power of Christ rests upon us, then
that power is made perfect in our dependence on Him (2 Cor.
12:9). John even dares to say that the man who is begotten of
God *cannot sin*. He is set free from the habit of sinning, because
he has become truly God's child (1 Jn. 3:9).

2. Paul's second word in Eph. 1:19, translated 'working'
in the English Bible, is the word from which our word *energy*
is derived. In its various forms—noun, verb and adjective—
it comes thirty-one times in the New Testament, and is always
used of *supernatural* activity working in a man. Five times,
three of them in 2 Thessalonians, that activity is of the forces
of evil: sinful passions working in our members to bring forth
fruit unto death (Rom. 7:5), the spirit now working in the sons of
disobedience (Eph. 2:2), the working of lawlessness and Satan
and error (2 Thess. 2:7,9,11).

All the other instances are of divine activity: God working
all things in all (1 Cor. 12:6), God's action making Peter an
apostle to the Jews and Paul an apostle to the Gentiles (Gal. 2:8),
God working in us, inspiring both the will and the deed (Phil. 2:13,
N.E.B.), God's word living and *working* (Heb. 4:12). In two
places the word is translated 'effectual': in 1 Cor. 16:9 Paul
speaks of the 'great door and effectual' that is opened for him in
Ephesus. When Paul uses a passive like 'is opened', he usually
means that it is God's action—and so he is here saying that God
has made a great opening for His own activity. In Philemon 6
Paul prays that the fellowship of faith in Philemon's household
'may become effectual', that is, that God may use their faith
effectively so that they may find Christ.

The realisation that the root meaning of this word is of divine
activity throws light on one more instance: Jas. 5:16 is translated
in the Revised Standard Version 'The prayer of a righteous man

has great power *in its effects*'. The Authorised Version has 'The *effectual* fervent prayer of a righteous man availeth much'. But if the word connotes divine activity, then a closer translation would be 'the *inspired* prayer'. It is prayer that is effective because God is working in the man who prays.

3. Paul's third word, translated 'strength' in the Revised Version and 'mighty' in the Authorised, denotes supreme power. The Greek word is *kratos*, the word found in the English auto-*crat* and demo*crat*, the individual or the people with supreme power. As a noun it comes twelve times in the New Testament, and in every case but one it refers to the supreme power of God. It comes six times in doxologies ascribing power to God or Christ (1 Tim. 6:16; 1 Pet. 4:11; 5:11; Jude 25; Rev. 1:6; 5:13). It is Mary's description of the meaning of the Annunciation (Lk. 1:51), and Luke's description of the power of the Christian message in Acts 19:20. Its benefits are available for us: 'Be strong in the Lord, and in the *strength* of His might' (Eph. 6:10); 'Be ... strengthened with all power, according to the *might* of His glory' (Col. 1:11). The only reference to any other strength but God's is in Heb. 2:14, where the devil has the *power of death*—but that power is mentioned only in order to show that Christ is bringing it to nought. Neither we, nor even the devil, have any ruling power of our own. 'All power is to our Jesus given.'

4. The last word for power in Eph. 1:19, *ischus*, translated 'might' at this point in the Revised Version, is a more general word for strength, human or divine. The noun comes ten times in the New Testament, and its corresponding verb twenty-eight times. In many cases it is used without particular religious reference, for example in Mt. 5:13, where tasteless salt is described as 'able for nothing'. But it is remarkable how often the same contrast between human weakness and divine strength occurs with this word also. The father of the epileptic boy in Mk. 9:18 complains to Jesus that he had asked the disciples to cast out the demon 'and they had no strength'. The disciples in Gethsemane 'had no strength to watch one hour' (Mk. 14:37). Acts 19:20 does not give Paul any credit for what has happened. He would not have wanted it. It is the word of the *Lord* that has grown mightily and has *had strength* (prevailed). In Phil. 4:13 Paul says 'I *have strength* for all things', but that is only in Him who 'empowers' him (our first word). And, going back to Jas. 5:16 it is this same word which is translated 'avails', but James makes clear that prayer only avails because it is itself inspired by God.

Our utter weakness by ourselves, God's fulness of power, that power at our disposal — that is the message of these four New Testament words, the message that Easter always offers us for our acceptance.

30. ASCENSION

To describe our Lord's Ascension the New Testament often uses the very common verb *anabainō*, I go up, come up, arise, ascend. The word occurs eighty-two times: nine times in each of the Synoptic Gospels, sixteen times in John, nineteen in Acts, seven in Paul, and thirteen in Revelation.

It is not the only word used for the Ascension. In Acts 1:9 Jesus 'was taken up'; in 1:11 He 'was received up'. But He uses the word in Jn. 6:62, where He speaks of Himself 'ascending where He was before'. In 3:13 He says 'No man hath ascended into heaven, but He that descended out of heaven', and in 20:17 He says to Mary, 'I am not yet ascended unto the Father .... I ascend unto my Father'. At Pentecost Peter does not use the actual word with regard to Jesus, but he implies it by contrast when he says, 'David ascended not into the heavens' (Acts 2:34); and Paul in Eph. 4:8-10 makes an interesting use of the sixty-eighth Psalm in connection with the Ascension. The Psalm really refers to the Hebrew king ascending Mount Zion, but Paul transfers the meaning to cover the Ascension of Christ, whereby He included the whole universe in His sphere.

The physical meaning of ascending cannot be pressed. We know that heaven is not physically above us; it is a spiritual state. But somehow it is natural to think of good things as being on high and bad things as being below, and many uses of the verb *anabainō*, though their first meaning is quite literal, carry with them a secondary meaning of ascending to something better.

There are plenty of instances where this secondary meaning must not be forced. 'The fish that first comes up' (Mt. 17:27) means no more than rising to the surface. So with the crowd that 'went up' to Pilate (Mk. 15:8), or with Zacchaeus going up into the sycomore tree (Lk. 19:4), though Zacchaeus certainly found something good through that action. Similarly, when 'it came up into' the heart of Moses to visit his brethren (Acts 7:23), or when Paul speaks of things which have not come up into the heart of man (1 Cor. 2:9), the phrase means no more than the occurrence of a thought, just as the eunuch's invitation to Philip 'to come up and sit with him' (Acts 8:31) had only a physical implication. Nor does the phrase 'tidings came up to the chief captain' (Acts 21:31) mean more than it says.

The word is used four times for 'going up' into a ship or boat (Mt. 14:32; Mk. 6:51; Jn. 21:11; Acts 21:6). Here again it is a natural term, but there is a slight undertone of reaching safety, though in the two instances of Jesus going up into the boat it was safety for the disciples, not for Himself.

A very frequent use of the word is in connection with 'going up' to Jerusalem, for a feast or for some other reason. Jesus goes up at the time of Passover, when He was crucified (Mt. 20:17, 18; Mk. 10:32, 33; Lk. 18:31). The other twenty-one references need only be listed, as they are all of the same nature (Lk. 2:4, 42; 19:28; Jn. 2:13; 5:1; 7:8 [twice], 10 [twice]; 11:55; 12:20; Acts 11:2; 15:2; 18:22; 21:12, 15; 24:11; 25:1, 9; Gal. 2:1, 2). Of these instances Lk. 2:4 refers to Bethlehem. The others all refer to Jerusalem, including most probably Acts 18:22, though Luke does not actually mention the place. Jerusalem is high up in the hills, but we always speak of 'going up' to any capital city because of its importance, even though it may be at sea level. 'Going up' in this instance means doing an important act.

There is a similar, though shorter, series when the 'going up' is to an upper room or roof-top. The men go up to the house top to let the paralytic down (Lk. 5:19). The disciples go to the upper room after the Lord has ascended (Acts 1:13). Peter goes to the house top to pray (10:9), and Paul goes up again to the upper room to continue the worship after the raising of Eutychus (20:11). In each case the physical act has an additional spiritual purpose. This is also true, of course, when there is a going up to the temple to pray (Lk. 18:10), or to teach (Jn. 7:14), or to worship (Acts 3:1). It was particularly true of Jesus when he went up into the mountain to teach, or to pray, or to heal, or for His Transfiguration (Mt. 5:1; 14:23; 15:29; Mk. 3: 13; Lk. 9:28). The physical act was subordinate to the spiritual intention. And when the New Testament speaks of prayer 'going up', the physical term is used only as a metaphor (Acts 10:4; Rev. 8:4).

But the New Testament does not forget that evil also tries to ascend, to put itself into a more powerful position. The thorns 'come up' and choke the growing seed (Mt. 13:7; Mk. 4:7). Doubts and hesitations 'arise' in men's hearts (Lk. 24:38). The thief 'goes up' to try and rob the fold (Jn. 10:1). In

Revelation the smoke of evil and torment goes up (9:2; 14:11; 19:3); the beast comes up out of various deep places (11:7; 13:1, 11; 17:8); the nations go up to attack the saints (20:9). Evil does not take things lying down.

Against this, however, good is also striving always to rise. Two of Jesus' parables about the Kingdom speak of the seed coming up and increasing (Mk. 4:8) and of the mustard seed coming up and becoming greater than all the herbs (4:32). Moreover, the act of baptism, the beginning of the new life in Christ, is completed by the coming up out of the water in order to start life anew (Acts 8:39). Even Jesus, in a sense, shared in that experience (Mt. 3:16; Mk. 1:10).

All this fits in with the references to heaven as the place to which we *ascend*. John hears a voice saying, 'Come *up* hither' (Rev. 4:1). The two slain prophetic witnesses were finally bidden, 'Come up hither', and they went up into heaven (11:12). The angel in 7:2 is naturally spoken of as ascending, though Rom. 10:6 warns us not to think of heaven as too literally above us. Yet Jesus Himself uses the metaphor in Jn. 1:51, when He says that He is the communicating ladder between heaven and earth, upon whom angelic messengers can go up to heaven with men's needs and return with God's answers. That is the simplest understanding of His words here.

The message of Ascensiontide is underlined in the Collect for the Day: 'like as we believe . . . our Lord Jesus Christ to have *ascended* into the heavens, so we may also in heart and mind thither *ascend*'. The analysis of this common New Testament word shows how God is always bidding us to come up to Him —realising His importance, turning to Him in quiet and prayer, leaving behind the things that drag us down, being ready to accept a new, upward-turned life, living in touch with heaven. Let Ascensiontide make us obey God's Word, and truly ascend!

31. THE SPIRIT

Pentecost brings us back each year to the Spirit, and to what the New Testament has to say about Him. The Concordance has four and a half pages of references to the word 'spirit'. Many of them are to the spirit of man, or to evil spirits. We are not now concerned with those. Many which refer to the Holy Spirit speak of Him as the gift of God or of Christ (e.g. Jn. 20:22), or in some way as the object or instrument of God's action.

We are not now concerned with those either. We are concerned only with the places where the Spirit is spoken of as acting personally, where He is actually or in effect the subject of a verb. One of our great difficulties is to realise that the Spirit is personal, and it may help us to do so now if we collect and examine a number of the instances where the New Testament speaks of Him as engaged in personal action. I find no fewer than seventeen different activities of the Spirit in the New Testament, but perhaps they may be classified under five heads.

1. First of all, there are His activities that are most closely linked with the heavenly world. He comes upon Mary (Lk. 1:35, cp. Mt. 1:18), so that Jesus is born of her. He comes upon men too (Acts 10:44; 19:6), so that they are born of the Spirit (Jn. 3:5, 6, 8). He descends upon Jesus at His baptism (Mk. 1:10 and all the gospels). In all these cases He is spoken of as bringing this world into direct contact with the heavenly world. This is of course true in every other instance, but in these places it is especially emphasised.

He also links men with God through His Word. Men may be the mouthpieces that He uses, but they are moved by the Holy Spirit (2 Pet. 1:21; Acts 1:16; 28:25;1 Pet. 1:11). Hebrews does not even mention the human author; the Spirit Himself is the giver of the Word (3:7; 9:8; 10:15).

Nor is the link only a descending one from God. It is an ascending one to Him also, making intercession for us to help our feeble prayers (Rom. 8:26).

2. Secondly, the Spirit is closely concerned with the inward nature of man, speaking to him, transforming him. He reveals to us the deep things of God (1 Cor. 2:10; cp. Lk. 2:26; Eph. 3:5). He quickens us (Jn. 6:63). He dwells in us (Jn. 14:17; Rom. 8:9, 11; 1 Cor. 3:16; 1 Pet. 4:14). He teaches us (Jn. 14:26) He bears witness in our hearts and in the world (Jn. 15:26; Acts 5:32, 20:23; Rom. 8:16; 1 Jn. 5:7).

3. Thirdly, He takes control of our actions. He led Jesus into the wilderness (Mk. 1:10; Mt. 4:1), and He led Him *in* the wilderness (Lk. 4:1). He will guide us into all the truth (Jn. 16:13). It was He who caught Philip away after the baptism of the Ethiopian eunuch (Acts 8:39). It was He who bound Paul to go to Jerusalem (20:22), and warned him of what was coming (21:11). It is He who leads God's sons (Rom. 8:14). Not only does He lead; He also commands. 'The Spirit said to Philip, Go near, and join thyself to this chariot' (Acts 8:29).

'The Spirit said to Peter, Arise and go' (10: 19, 20). 'The Holy Spirit said, Separate me Barnabas and Saul' (13:2). And the command is sometimes one which forbids: 'They were forbidden by the Holy Spirit to speak the word in Asia' (16:6), and when they tried to go into Bithynia, 'the Spirit of Jesus suffered them not' (16:7). Yet, whether He is commanding or forbidding, the Spirit is always there to help us. 'He helps our infirmity' (Rom. 8:26), and the Church can walk in His 'comfort' (Acts 9:31). In fact, in John's Gospel (14:16, 26; 15:26; 16:7) He is described as the Comforter, the same Greek root being used. It is an impossible word to translate fully. It means much more than mere consolation, though in Rev. 14:13 the Spirit does promise us final rest from our labours. It includes the work of strengthening, of encouraging, and of speaking on behalf of a person who is too weak or too confused to present his case for himself. Not that He needs to plead with a loving Father who has Himself sent Him to help us, and who knows us through and through. But we do need one who can make us see our sins, encourage us in our despair, and bring us where God can pardon and restore us.

The Spirit, however, does not control the actions of individuals alone. He controls the actions of the Church. Baptism is not a human action; it is the Holy Spirit sealing us. This is the force of Paul's allusion in Eph. 1:13. Nor is ordination a human appointing. When Paul is speaking to the Ephesian elders in Acts 20:28, he says, 'The Holy Spirit has made you bishops (overseers)'. The whole relationship of the Spirit to the Church is summed up in 1 Cor. 12:11. After describing the various types of ministry and relating each one to the Spirit, Paul finally says, 'All these are inspired by one and the same Spirit, who apportions to each one individually as He wills' (R.S.V.).

4. But Christians are not simply to *receive* from the Spirit. They are to *give* by His help. Especially are they to speak in the power that He gives them. Jesus tells His disciples that they are not to be anxious what to say before a hostile audience. They will be told what to say: 'for it is not ye that speak, but the Holy Spirit (Mk. 13:11; cp. Mt. 10:20). And on the day of Pentecost, when the witness of the Church began, the disciples spoke 'as the Spirit gave them utterance' (Acts 2:4). Again, when 1 Tim. 4:1 begins a prophecy with the words 'The Spirit says expressly', the reference is not to any Scripture of the past, but to the word of the Spirit uttered in the present, either through the writer

himself or through some other Christian of the time. So, when St. John the Divine writes to the seven churches of Asia, he does not claim that his words are his own. Each letter closes with the same refrain: 'He who has an ear, let him hear what *the Spirit* says to the churches' (Rev. 2:7 etc.).

5. This belief in the personal activity of the Spirit, not argued but assumed, continues up to the closing words of the New Testament, the great invitation (Rev. 22:17) where 'the Spirit and the bride say, Come'.

The New Testament is not a theological text-book on the Trinity. That work was left for later generations, the best of which have confessed that they have done it inadequately. What the New Testament does is to give us the words of the early disciples and of Jesus Himself about the Father, the Son and the Spirit—words that we believe were given to them by God. And one of the most striking things about these words is that they normally refer to the Spirit as personal. In Eph. 4:30 Paul says, 'Grieve not the Holy Spirit of God'. You cannot grieve an influence; you can only grieve a person. It is this person, one with the Father and the Son but a person Himself, whose activity we call to mind at Pentecost, and we pray that, as He acted in the first days of the Church, so He will continue to act today.

32. CHRISTIAN CONDUCT

The main events of the Christian Year are crowded into its first six months. We celebrate in succession Christ's birth, death, resurrection, ascension and the coming of the Spirit, all of which stimulate our thoughts and wills as they were intended to do. Then we settle down to a more humdrum period. It is impossible to get wildly enthusiastic about, say, the twenty-second Sunday after Trinity.

But this is the period in which our reaction to the great Christian events is put to the test. Believing in the work of Christ, are we going to live according to what He has given us? The Church of South India has wisely emphasised this by speaking not of Sundays after Trinity, but as Sundays after Pentecost, the time when we prove the gift of the Holy Spirit. It might have been even better if we had decided to call them Sundays *in* Pentecost.

The New Testament has a great deal to say about the stupend-ous act of God in sending Christ. It also has much to say about the life expected from Christians in the light of that act. We should therefore be quite wrong if we left our studies on the Christian Year without an examination of some of the New Testament words for *Conduct*. Conduct is no substitute for Faith. It is a feeble thing without God's power. But the New Testament makes clear that it is an essential consequence of what God has done for us in Christ. We are not saved by our good works, but God has 'created us in Christ Jesus *for* good works . . . that we should walk in them' (Eph. 2:10).

So we look first of all at the word *peripateō*, 'walk', which is used no less than forty-six times in the New Testament in this metaphorical sense of Conduct. Jesus Himself uses it twice (Jn. 8:12; 12:35), but thirty-one of its uses are by St. Paul. The man who was sure that he was saved by grace was equally sure that his own conduct and that of all Christians must be according to the salvation that he had experienced.

Probably the best picture of the use of the word can be given by making two divisions, negative and positive. We are NOT to walk in darkness (Jn. 8:12; 1 Jn. 1:6; 2:11), nor according to the flesh (Rom. 8:4; 2 Cor. 10:2) though we have to walk *in* the flesh (2 Cor. 10:3). Nor are we to walk 'after the manner of men' (1 Cor. 3:3). In this verse the reference is to jealousy and strife, but the phrase sums up many other instances: we are not to walk in craftiness (2 Cor. 4:2), in sins (Eph. 2:2; Col. 3:7), in 'vanity', that is, emptiness (Eph. 4:17), in a disorderly way (2 Thess. 3:6, 11), by meats, that is, by merely human scruples (Heb. 13:9). Phil. 3:18 speaks of those who walk 'as enemies of the Cross of Christ'. That describes the essential nature of the anti-Christian world of New Testament times and of today.

On the other hand we ARE to walk in an entirely different atmosphere: in the light, not in the darkness (Jn. 12:35; Eph. 5:8; 1 Jn. 1:7; Rev. 21:24), in newness of life (Rom. 6:4), 'honestly' (Rom. 13:13; 1 Thess. 4:12), that is, in a manner becoming to the Christian faith. We are to walk according to love (Rom. 14:15; Eph. 5:2), as God has called (1 Cor. 7:17), worthily of our calling (Eph. 4:1), worthily of the Lord (Col. 1:10), worthily even of God (1 Thess. 2:12). We are to walk by faith (2 Cor. 5:7), in the Spirit (Rom. 8:4; 2 Cor. 12:18; Gal. 5:16), in good works (Eph. 2:10), 'not as unwise but as wise' (Eph. 5:15), and 'as you have us for an example' (Phil. 3:17). Paul is several times very bold in asking people to imitate him, but it is only because he believes that he is walking in Christ, a phrase which he uses in Col. 2:6. We are also to walk in wisdom (Col. 4:5), in truth (2 Jn. 4; 3 Jn. 3:4), according to the commandments (2 Jn. 6) and as we have 'received' (1 Thess. 4:1). John sums it up by saying that we are to walk 'as Christ' (1 Jn. 2:6).

What a magnificent standard for Christian conduct all this is! How far short we always fall! And yet we dare not adopt any lower standard, because the power for this is what God offers us in Christ.

We turn now to a second word, *anastrephō*, which, in its noun and verb forms, is used metaphorically nineteen times. It literally means 'turning to and fro', and in the older English versions was translated 'conversation', a literal rendering into a Latin form which will not do now because we have limited it to the to and fro of speech alone. Hence we now have words for it such as 'life', 'manner of life' or 'behaviour'.

Again the same negative and positive divisions will bring out the picture. We are NOT to go to and fro among the sons of disobedience (Eph. 2:3). We are to escape from those who go to and fro in a state of wandering from God (2 Pet. 2:18). We are not to imitate Paul's former manner of life in persecuting the Church of God (Gal. 1:13), nor to cling on to the 'old man' of our former life (Eph. 4:22), that life which 1 Pet. 1:18 speaks of as vain and empty, and which Lot in Sodom found to be un-ashamedly indecent (2 Pet. 2:7). The list is very similar to the previous one, though not so full.

On the other hand, we ARE to live in the grace of God (2 Cor. 1:12), in the house (or the church) of God (1 Tim. 3:15). We are to be prepared to join those who move to and fro in persecution (Heb. 10:33). We are to live 'honestly', as Heb. 13:18, says. The Greek word simply means 'well', that is, as a Christian ought to live. That will include living in the fear of God (1 Pet. 1:17). Just previously Peter has also written of living in holiness (1:15), and James as usual brings out the practical implications: 'Let him show his works by his good manner of life' (Jas. 3:13).

This good life is not to be for ourselves alone. It is also to be an example to others (1 Tim. 4:12), so that the Gentiles may see it and glorify God (1 Pet. 2:12), so that Christian wives may win over their non-Christian husbands (1 Pet. 3:1, 2), and so that people who revile may be put to shame (1 Pet. 3:16). Lastly, this manner of life is to be lived always in view of the End: the end of the individual Christian (Heb. 13:7), and the End of all things (2 Pet. 3:11).

The New Testament uses at least two other words for Christian conduct, though these two are less frequently found. When Paul in Acts 23:1 says, 'I have lived before God in all good conscience', he literally means, 'I have conducted myself as a *citizen* of God's kingdom'. He uses the same verb (*politeuō*) in Phil. 1:27; 'Let your manner of life be worthy of the gospel of Christ', where the R.V. margin tells us that the Greek literally means 'Behave worthily as citizens'. The word reaches its New Testament climax in Phil. 3:20; 'Our citizenship is in heaven'. Right conduct is one of the primary civic duties and we, as citizens of a heavenly kingdom, are due to conduct ourselves entirely according to its laws.

Finally there is the word *stoicheō*, which Paul uses four times, and which is usually translated 'walk' but means much more. It is a military word, meaning to march in line, not as an individual wandering at your own sweet will but keeping at one with your brethren. It is in this sense that we walk in the steps of the faith of Abraham (Rom. 4:12), going through the same experience as he did, whether we live in the first century or the twentieth. It is in this sense that we not only gain our new spiritual life from the Spirit, but learn to walk in Him regularly and steadily along with our fellow-Christians (Gal. 5:25). In walking by this rule we find God's peace (Gal. 6:16), and the rule is no mere new legalism. The previous verses show that it is crucifixion to the world and new creation. Lastly we are to walk in line with the truth that we have so far attained (Phil. 3:16). We do not yet know everything. We are still pressing on. But we must not lag behind what God in His goodness has already shown us.

This is Christian conduct as these New Testament words reveal it. May God give us vision to see — and power to walk!

V. WORSHIP

33. THANKSGIVING (i)

Worship without thanksgiving is impossible. Indeed, the Christian life as a whole without thanksgiving is unthinkable. It is therefore entirely to be expected that the New Testament should have a great deal to say about it.

Several words will need examination, but the chief one is *eucharistia* which, with its accompanying verb *eucharisteō*, comes fifty-four times, thirty-nine of them in St. Paul.

The word is at once recognisable as that by which our central act of worship is often described: The Eucharist. It is the word used in Mk. 14:23 and parallels, and in 1 Cor. 11:24; 'When He had *given thanks*'. It is also used with other meals which are kindred in nature: the feeding of the four thousand in Mk. 8:6 (Mt. 15:36) and of the five thousand in Jn. 6:11, 23, and when Paul gives thanks to God before joining in a meal with his fellow-passengers at the time when the terrible storm is abating (Acts 27:35).

Yet how frequently we fail to make our Eucharist a real eucharist of spirit. In fact how general is our failure in gratitude! That is the lesson of the miracle of the healing of the ten lepers. Only one of them returned to give thanks (Lk. 17:16). We are always better at importuning God for our needs than at thanking Him when He has supplied them. That is why three times over in the epistles thanksgiving is specially emphasised after prayer or supplication has been mentioned (Phil. 4:6; Col. 4:2; 1 Tim. 2:1). You don't get close to God if you limit yourself to asking Him for things. In fact the man who fails to give thanks to God for His gifts tends to go utterly astray in his reasoning and in his worship (Rom. 1:21 ff.). He is in danger of becoming a pagan and an idolater.

Yet even our acts of thanksgiving need watching, lest they be insincere and unhelpful. The Pharisee of Lk. 18:11 thanked God that he was not as the rest of men—and we have often done the same. The speaker with tongues in 1 Cor. 14:17 was genuine enough in his gratitude—but utterly unhelpful in the way he expressed it. One of the only two cases in the New Testament of gratitude to a man (Acts 24:3) is utter hypocrisy. The Jews had suffered greatly under the cruelty of Felix. Our thankfulness is sometimes perverted, as well as lacking.

This is why we need all the directions for gratitude that the New Testament gives us. 1 Thess. 5:18 says 'In *everything* give thanks,' and we find the whole sphere of thanksgiving covered: the material, the personal, the spiritual.

1. The material sphere: whether you are a vegetarian or a non-vegetarian, give thanks to God for what you eat (Rom. 14:6); even if you eat at a non-Christian table, God accepts your thanksgiving (1 Cor. 10:30). If God has blessed you with money, show your gratitude by sharing it with those in need (2 Cor. 9:11, 12). All God's gifts are good, and none are to be spurned as polluting, but accepted with thanksgiving (1 Tim. 4:3, 4).

2. The personal sphere: it is remarkable, though it should not be surprising, how often Paul gives thanks to God for his fellow-Christians. Eight of his letters have this as a very early note: 'I thank my God through Jesus Christ for you all' (Rom. 1:8). Compare 1 Cor. 1:4; Eph. 1:16; Phil. 1:3; Col. 1:3; 1 Thess. 1:2; 2 Thess. 1:3; Philemon 4. Nor is it only at the beginning of his letters, a mere conventional phrase soon forgotten. Look at the way he thanks Prisca and Aquila in Rom. 16:4 for the risk they took on his behalf, and at the renewed thanksgiving to God for the Thessalonians in 1 Thess. 3:9. We tend to be far too critical of our friends, and not nearly grateful enough for them.

3. The spiritual sphere: Paul gives thanks because God chose his converts (2 Thess. 2:13), because God delivers from sin through Christ (Rom. 7:25), because He translates us into the Kingdom of the Son of His love (Col. 1:12-13), because He delivers us from death through the prayers of others (2 Cor. 1:11), because of all the grace that we have in Jesus Christ (2 Cor. 4:15).

He thanks Him too for guidance in his pastoral work (1 Cor. 1:14), for the gift of tongues which he has learnt to keep under control (14:18), for the fact that when he preached his hearers took his message as gift from God, not as a wise utterance of his own (1 Thess. 2:13). Not all of us have that power of self-effacing gratitude.

Paul writes also of the place of thanksgiving in worship (1 Cor. 14:16; Eph. 5:20) and so, of course, does the book of Revelation (4:9; 7:12). Thanksgiving is also the cure for dirty language (Eph. 5:4). A man cannot foul his tongue with that, if he has acquired the habit of giving thanks to God. He has received

God's power over his tongue, the power for which, on the cosmic scale, the four and twenty elders thank God in Rev. 11:17.

Apart from the Last Supper and the two feedings, the word is used of Jesus in Jn. 11:41 only. There He thanks God for having heard Him, a thing we so often forget when our prayers have been answered. But Paul links Christ with thanksgiving in Col. 3:17: 'Do all things in the name of the Lord Jesus, giving thanks to God the Father through Him'. Our thanksgiving can never be adequate unless it is closely connected with the One for whom we have most cause of all to be grateful.

We round off the instances of this word with its use in Col. 2:7: '*Abounding* in thanksgiving'. True thanks must overflow. They are not just a measured part of our prayer routine. They come out of the fulness of hearts that cannot find words or time enough to express their gratitude for all that God has done for them.

Gratitude to God is closely associated with praising and blessing Him, so that we naturally go on to two of the words for this in the New Testament. The first is *aineo* which, in various forms, comes twenty-seven times. Seven of these refer to praise of human beings, but the remainder are concerned with God.

The simple form of the verb, as quoted above, is almost peculiar to Luke. He begins his gospel with the praise by the heavenly host in 2:13, and the praise by the shepherds in 2:20. He concludes it with the praise by the disciples at the Triumphal Entry (19:37) and after the Ascension (24:53), though many of our manuscripts have only the word 'blessing' in this place. He continues his theme of praise in Acts, where the first Christians are described as a community praising God (2:47), and the lame man as soon as he is healed joins in the chorus of praise (3:8-9). Paul brings the Gentiles into the chorus in Rom. 15:11, and Revelation makes the Hallelujah chorus full (19:5).

Heb. 13:15 uses a beautiful metaphor when it speaks of our praise as a sacrifice of the fruit of our lips — not just words that cost us nothing, but like a man offering the first fruits of his harvest, something over which he has toiled so that it may be perfect for giving.

The compound forms of the verb and the noun are used more frequently for praising men, but in ten instances they are concerned with praising God. The compound form in the second half of Rom. 15:11 reinforces the simple form in the first half. Phil. 1:11 emphasises that the righteousness which is ours through

Christ should turn us to praising God. But the chief use of the word in this sense is in Ephesians 1: 'God has made us His sons that we may praise Him' (v. 6); 'we have been destined and appointed to live for the praise of His glory' (v. 12, RSV); and our final possession of all that God has promised us will be the reason for our ultimate praise of Him (v. 14). The main purpose of our creation is for His praise. Not that He has made us in order to flatter Him, but that those whom He has made cannot help being full of boundless gratitude whenever they think truly on His goodness.

The remaining uses of the word concern not our praise of God, but His praise of us. St. Paul and St. Peter dare to use the same word in this opposite direction. The man whose circumcision is that of the heart is one who is praised by God (Rom. 2:29). The civil government is God-appointed, and one of its functions is to praise well-doers (Rom. 13:3; 1 Pet. 2:14). Whatever the problems of this statement, there is no doubt about the value of law and order, or of God's approval of those who live according to the law. But God's real praise of us will be at the End; when the hidden things of darkness are brought to light (1 Cor. 4:5), and when our faith has finally survived the test (1 Pet. 1:7). Till then encouragement will help us, but full praise will be suspended. Yet it will not be ultimately withheld, for He who demands that we should value Him at His true worth will value us at ours, the worth which comes only through our trust in Christ.

34. THANKSGIVING (ii)

Our next word is *Eulogeō*, I bless, which comes forty times in the New Testament. The words derived from it—'blessed' and 'blessing'—come eight and fourteen times respectively.

These words, both in English and in Greek, are used in two senses. God 'blesses' us in granting us His favours. But we also 'bless' Him, thanking Him for what He gives us.

Naturally in the New Testament the first sense is by far the more common, but the second, with which we are now concerned, is by no means rare, and it adds to our Christian vocabulary of thanksgiving.

The verb comes five times, three of them in St. Luke. At the beginning of the gospel, as soon as Zacharias's tongue is loosed the first thing he does with it is to bless God for His goodness (1:64). And when Jesus is taken for the first time to God's House, the old man Simeon takes Him in his arms and blesses God that before his end he has seen His salvation (2:28). That note of thanksgiving at the beginning of the incarnate life of our Lord returns, greatly enriched, in the last line of the gospel (24:53), where we leave the disciples again in the temple, blessing God for all that in that Life He has given them. Luke makes it clear that the greatest of all God's gifts is not one to be accepted without abundant and deep-felt gratitude.

The only two uses of the verb outside Luke warn us of two dangers. 1 Cor. 14:16 speaks of the man who blesses God unintelligibly, so that no one else can truly say Amen to his prayers. They do not know what he has been saying. A warning not only to Pentecostalists, but also to anyone who conducts worship with thoughts and vocabulary that his congregation cannot follow.

The other warning is in Jas. 3:9, regarding the tongue that is used both for blessing God and for cursing men, a tongue that can utter pious phrases in church, and then come out and say all sorts of things about other people.

Four of the fourteen uses of the noun 'blessing' refer to our thanksgiving to God. The first is in Jas. 3:10 and continues the thought of the previous verse. The other three are in Revelation, in three of the magnificent doxologies found in that book (5:12; 5:13; 7:12). The writer pulls out every stop on the organ, exhausting his vocabulary to find words adequate for the praise of God and of the Lamb. 5:12 concludes with blessing the Lamb. 5:13 goes on to bless Him that sits upon the throne and, with Him, the Lamb. 7:12, in the presence now of the great multitude which no man can number, begins with the angels saying 'Amen', solemnly confirming as their own the doxology of the martyrs in v. 10, and then goes on with the same word of blessing with which all creation had opened its doxology in 5:13. Whether at the beginning or the end, whether uttered by angels or martyrs or all created things, thanksgiving to God is something for which eternity itself is not too long.

In fact, when we come to the adjective 'blessed', we find that every use of this particular form is reserved for God. He is *The* Blessed One, the One whom we cannot name without thankfulness. It is the first word of Zacharias's song in Lk. 1:68, when the climax of God's blessed acts is beginning. It is the

word which the High Priest uses in Mk. 14:61, when he is forcing
Jesus to utter words by which He will be condemned.   To Caiaphas it has become a mere name, conventionally used and cruelly
misused; but this abuse makes use of the term of praise.   Paul
uses the tradition of his race as it was meant to be used.   The
Jew often broke into a sentence with it: 'The Holy One —
Blessed be he — said . . .'   This is what Paul does in Rom. 1:25;
9:5; 2 Cor. 11:31.   The phrase 'Blessed for ever' is not necessary
for either grammar or argument in any of these passages.   The
sentences read quite well without it.   But it is necessary for
Paul's own expression of his thankfulness.   He will not mention
Creation, Incarnation, God's love towards himself, without
turning aside to give thanks.

He carries the use of the word 'Blessed' a stage further in the
opening of two of his letters.   It was the conventional practice
of the time to begin a letter with a word of thanks to God, often
scribbled off as we tend to mutter grace before food.   Paul
turns this convention into a reality: 'Blessed be the God and Father
of our Lord Jesus Christ, the Father of mercies and God of all
comfort' (2 Cor. 1:3); 'Blessed be the God and Father of our
Lord Jesus Christ, who has blessed us with every spiritual blessing
in the heavenly sphere in Christ' (Eph. 1:3).   And Peter does the
same, blessing God for the new hope given in the resurrection
(1 Pet. 1:3).   Neither apostle could remain content with perfunctory custom when they thought of all that God had done for
them in Christ.

Another form of this word 'Blessed' (though translated by
the same word in English) is used in the New Testament to
ascribe praise to Christ.   It is used once of Mary (Lk. 1:42),
once of the righteous (Mt. 25:34), but the other eight uses all
refer to our Lord.   Twice, in Mt. 23:39 and Lk. 13:35, He
speaks of those who have turned away from Him and who will
not be able to get in touch with Him again until they are ready
to give Him the praise that shows their gratitude to Him.   The
word comes in all four accounts of the Triumphal Entry into
Jerusalem (Mt. 21:9; Mk. 11:9; Lk. 19:38; Jn. 12:13).   That
word, which was originally used by the priests as they blessed
the pilgrims coming to Jerusalem (Ps. 118:26), is now lifted out
of that human context into the praise of the One whose entry
into the Holy City will be a blessing not to Himself but to those
who follow in His train.   In Mk. 11:10 the praise is extended
from the King to the Kingdom that He will bring.   And all this

is the completion of the praise that Elizabeth had given Mary at the beginning, when she was not content with giving thanks for the mother but went beyond her to praise God for the fruit of her womb (Lk. 1:42).

Our last word, *Exomologeō*, is a word which literally means to 'confess out'. It is not always used for praise. Four times it is used for confession of sin (Mt. 3:6; Mk. 1:5; Acts 19:18; Jas. 5:16). Once it is used for confession of faith (Phil. 2:11). It is also used for the traitorous agreement that Judas made with the chief priests (Lk. 22:6). But four times it is used for the expression of thankful praise: 'I *thank* thee, O Father, Lord of heaven and earth, that thou didst hide these things from the wise and understanding, and didst reveal them unto babes' (Mt. 11:25; Lk. 10:21); 'Every tongue shall *give praise* to God' (Rom. 14:11, R.V. margin and R.S.V.); 'Therefore will I *give praise* to thee among the Gentiles' (15:9, R.V., R.S.V.).

The root idea behind the word is that of getting something out that would otherwise be concealed. It may be sin. It may be one's inward belief. It may be the treachery of one's heart. It may be the sense of gratitude to God. That sense of gratitude is not meant to be left unexpressed. Far too often we leave it like that. Jesus did not. He bursts out in praise to God for the way in which He works among men. Paul did not. He believed that 'every tongue' must give God praise, and he quoted in Rom. 15:9 the Psalmist (Ps. 18:49) who gave God praise among the Gentiles, turning that man's song of victory over his enemies into a glad rejoicing that God in Christ had called Jew and Gentile alike to praise Him. And so He still calls us today to give expression to what is due to Himself, so that our hearts may be set free by that utterance of gratitude for which He has made us.

35. CONFESSION

The end of the previous chapter dealt briefly with Confession in the sense of Praise. This chapter will look more fully at all the various meanings of the word, re-emphasising in the process some of the things that have been said already.

The Greek words concerned are the verb *homologeō*, with its strengthened form *exhomologeō*, the noun *homologia*, and an adverb *homologoumenōs*. The literal meaning of the verb is 'I speak or say together' with someone, I hold the same language with them, I agree with them. Hence it comes to mean 'I concede, confess, avow'. It involves making public what is inside oneself, so that all may share it. The varied content of such a declaration may, so far as the New Testament is concerned, be divided under four main heads: 1. A fairly general group of statements of a person's inward thoughts; 2. The declaration or confession of sins; 3. The declaration or confession of faith; 4. The pouring out in praise of a person's inward thoughts of God.

Homologeō and its associated forms occur forty-three times in the New Testament. We may put eight of these under the first head, only five under the second, as many as twenty-five under the third, and the remaining five under the fourth. The division between the different books is as follows: Matthew 6, Mark 1, Luke 4, John 4, Acts 4, Paul 6, Pastoral Epistles 5, Hebrews 5, James 1, Johannine Epistles 6, Revelation 1.

Since the word has so many shades of meaning, it is impossible to translate it always in the same way. In English it is normally 'confess' for the two main senses of declaration of faith and confession of sin, but in various contexts it is translated 'profess, promise, consent, praise'. The Revised Tamil New Testament uses twelve different expressions. These could be slightly reduced but most are necessary. The important point is to remember the root meaning of sharing something inside oneself with other people.

1. General Uses

In Mt. 7:23 Jesus answers those who claim unjustifiably that they belong to Him, by saying 'Then will I profess (literally "confess") unto them, I never knew you'. He will make His inward judgment of them perfectly clear. In Jn. 1:20 the word is used twice of John the Baptist: he makes it perfectly clear to his hearers that he is not the Messiah. Like all good words, it can be used hypocritically: Titus 1:16 speaks of those who profess that they know God; they want this to appear clear to others, though it is really not true. The word is also used twice in connection with a promise, something in a person's heart which he shares with the one to whom he makes the promise. The two instances are in sharp contrast: Herod promises to give Salome whatever she asks (Mt. 14:7), and God vouchsafes (literally 'confesses') to Abraham a promise about his posterity (Acts 7:17).

E

The two remaining instances under this general head are in the simple sense of agreement. Judas 'consents' to the arrangement to betray Jesus (Lk. 22:6), and 1 Tim. 3:16 says 'Without controversy (that is "by general agreement") great is the mystery of godliness'.

2. Confession of Sins

It is a little surprising how seldom the New Testament uses the word in this sense. The crowds who came to the Baptist came confessing their sins (Mk. 1:5; Mt. 3:6). The people who were influenced by Paul's ministry in Ephesus did the same (Acts 19:18). James (5:16) commands his readers to confess their sins to one another; and there is that best-known verse in 1 Jn. 1:9; 'If we confess our sins, he is faithful and righteous to forgive us our sins, and to cleanse us from all unrighteousness'.

That is all. It is enough New Testament evidence to establish confession of sin as an essential part of the Christian life. Yet why is there not more? Is it perhaps because mere confession of sin, however essential, is not enough, even when it is followed by personal cleansing and forgiveness? In itself it is in danger of being both negative and self-centred. Without it we cannot make a beginning of our Christian life, and we need to go on doing it, but the Christian life is not centred round confession of sin; it is centred round confession of faith in Christ. This is where the main New Testament emphasis lies, the emphasis to which we now turn.

3. Confession of Faith

In His own teaching Jesus made open avowal of faith in Himself central: 'Everyone who shall confess me before men, him will I also confess before my Father' (Mt. 10:32; Lk. 12:8) — public declaration of a man's faith in Jesus meant that He would acknowledge that man before God and confirm him in that eternal relationship. As glorified Christ He makes the same promise to the faithful in the church of Sardis (Rev. 3:5). The Jews on their side realized how fundamental this personal declaration of faith was. They made a regulation that if anyone confessed Him to be Christ, he should be excommunicated, and this scared many from making the public declaration that Jesus demanded (Jn. 12:42). John sees that open recognition of the fact that 'Jesus Christ is come in the flesh' (1 Jn. 4:2), that He is truly God made man, is at the heart of the Christian faith. Anyone who will not declare this 'is not of God' (1 Jn. 4:3), and if a man sets himself up as a teacher without being willing to make such a confession, he is a deceiver (2 Jn. 7).

Alongside this confession of the Incarnation John puts a parallel declaration of faith in Jesus as the Son of God: 'He who confesses that Jesus is the Son of God, God abides in him and he in God' (1 Jn. 4:15); 'He that confesseth the Son hath the Father also' (2:23). This follows up what Jesus Himself had said. When a man has the courage and faith to declare openly his belief in Christ, that puts him at once into right relationship with God.

Paul says the same thing in his own way in Rom. 10:9-10: 'If thou shalt confess with thy mouth Jesus as Lord . . . thou shalt be saved; for . . . with the mouth confession is made unto salvation'. Belief in the heart is essential, but it is incomplete without confession with the mouth. That is why, in our worship, we 'confess our faith' in the words of the Creeds. There are many who try to be secret Christians, and one can fully understand their problems, but inevitably their Christian faith is incomplete.

Paul's supreme use of the word is in Phil. 2:11, when he looks forward to the day when every tongue will 'confess that Jesus Christ is Lord', and we remember that this confession, and nothing more, was probably the earliest Christian creed. Elaborations came later, but the first Christians unerringly realized that if a man could make that declaration, he had done the vital thing.

Even in the New Testament, however, the confession already includes other things. Paul speaks of the Corinthians confessing (acknowledging, R.S.V.) the gospel of Christ as a whole (2 Cor. 9:13). He later made a general declaration or confession of his own faith to Felix, the governor (Acts 24:14). Hebrews three times uses the word 'confession' to describe a Christian's faith as a whole, though in each case it is centrally related to Jesus (3:1; 4:14; 10:23). The use is extended in 11:13 to the confession of the patriarchs that they did not really belong to this earth but to a better country. In 1 Tim. 6:12 the reference seems to be to the public confession of faith that Timothy made at his baptism, a confession that needed the same kind of courage and trust as Jesus Himself showed when He was before Pilate (6:13). The word is even used of Jewish faith: the Pharisees 'confess' belief in resurrection, angels and spirits (Acts 23:8).

4. The Praise of God

Yet there is still something more in confession than admission
of sin and declaration of faith. A man whose heart is set upon
God will declare himself also in praise. Jesus did. When
He thought of the wonder of God's revelation to the humble
through Himself, He turned to His Father and said: 'I thank
thee', and the R.V. margin has 'I praise thee' (Mt. 11:25; Lk.
10:21). But the original word is this same word 'confess':
'I declare the thought of my heart in praise and thanksgiving'.
Heb. 13:15 describes praise as the fruit of lips which make confession of God's name; and Paul in Rom. 14:11 and 15:9 looks
forward to the day when all men everywhere will 'confess'
and 'give praise' to God, the two expressions being again
interchangeable in text and margin. When any man in any part
of the world fully opens his heart to God, that opening must
include praise.

Let this word challenge us again: Are we willing to confess
our sin? Do we hide our faith under a bushel? To what extent
is there within us a spirit of praise?

36. INTERCESSION

No worship is complete without intercession, but intercession
is one of the hard things in prayer. What need is there to pray
for others when God knows all? How can our prayer help?
And what should we pray for?

This chapter will not attempt to answer these questions
fully. It will simply try to see what the New Testament has
to say about intercession. That is the surest starting point for
our answer.

We shall look in particular at two pairs of words which are used
for prayer, and at the instances of them which concern intercession:
Proseuchē (eleven times for intercession) and its verb *proseuchomai*
(ten times); *de-ēsis* (eleven times) and its verb *de-omai* (nine times).
There is no need to distinguish between the meanings of these
words, and they will be quoted interchangeably, though the first
pair are usually translated 'prayer' and 'pray', and the second
'supplication' and 'make supplication'.

1. In Jas. 5:16 we are commanded to pray for each other's
health. In Lk. 9:38, 40 the father of the epileptic boy beseeches

Jesus and His disciples on behalf of his son, and at the end of the
same incident in Mk. 9:29 Jesus says 'This kind can come out by
nothing save by prayer'. These are the only cases in the New
Testament of that commonest of all forms of intercession today:
prayer for others' physical well-being.

2. In Acts 12:5 the Jerusalem church prays for Peter's
release from prison. In Phil. 1:19 Paul may be asking the
Philippians to pray for his release, but probably he means
much more than that when he uses the word 'salvation'. In
1 Tim. 2:1-2 prayers are asked especially for kings and all in
high places, so that men may lead a tranquil and quiet life. These
seem to be the only cases in the New Testament of prayer for
bodily safety.

3. The only instance of that further common request for
intercession—that people may be saved from the consequences
of their own misdeeds—is that of Simon Magus in Acts 8:24.
Not an example that we should want to follow!

It would seem that instances of prayer for material benefit
are few and far between in the New Testament.

When we come to intercession for spiritual advantages, it is a
very different story.

4. It is surprising how often Paul and others ask for prayer
that they may be brought into their readers' company—and nearly
always there is associated with the request a declaration that
spiritual benefit will result from it. It is not simply the natural
human desire for reunion with friends. In Rom. 1:9-11, as
Paul remembers the Romans in his prayers, he asks that the way
may be opened for him to come to them 'that I may impart
unto you some spiritual gift'. In Rom. 15:30 he asks them to
strive with him in their prayers to God for him that the collection
which he is bringing to Jerusalem to unite the Gentile and
Jewish parts of the Church may be successful in its object and
that he may come on to Rome with a mind at rest. In 2 Cor.
1:11 he asks for prayer for deliverance from his great peril so
that what he gains may be passed on to many grateful hearers.
In 1 Thess. 3:10 he prays that he may see his readers' faces
so that he may perfect that which is lacking in their faith. 2 Tim.
1:3 ff. has the same longing for reunion, coupled with the
reminder that Timothy should stir up the gift of God bestowed
on him through Paul. Philemon's prayers are requested
(v. 22) so that Paul may be brought to him; and Hebrews
(13:18, 19) closes with the same request.

5. Then there are the prayers for the deepening of Christian character in others. They begin with Jesus' prayer for Peter in Lk. 22:32: 'that your faith may not fail'. Paul prays in Eph. 1:16 ff. (cp. Col. 1:9 ff.) that God will give his readers wisdom, and knowledge of Himself, and power. Col. 4:12 speaks of Epaphras striving for the Colossians in his prayers that they 'may stand perfect and fully assured in all the will of God'. In 2 Thess. 1:11-12 Paul prays for the Thessalonians, that God may make them worthy of their calling and that the name of Jesus may be glorified in them. And he prays for Philemon (vv. 4-6) that he may be able to share his faith effectively with other people.

6. A number of New Testament prayers for other people are prayers that spring out of gratitude. In 2 Cor. 9:14 Paul writes of the Jerusalem Christians praying for the Corinthians who have helped them, and reflecting thankfully on the glorious way that the grace of God has worked in their benefactors. In Col. 1:3ff. Paul says that he prays always for the Colossians, and goes on to give a long list of their spiritual qualities of which he has been told. In 1 Thess. 1:2 ff., while praying for that church which he knows so well, he lets his mind run back on the wonderful way in which they have been redeemed and the transformation he has seen in their spiritual condition.

7. But it is not only for good people that we are to pray. There is the Lord's word in Mt. 5:44; 'Pray for them that persecute you', and the other form of it in Lk. 6:28: 'Pray for them that despitefully use you'. Paul has learnt that lesson well. In Rom. 10:1 he writes: 'My heart's desire and my supplication to God is for Israel, that they may be saved'. Do not let us forget what lies behind those words, written in Corinth on the third missionary journey during the period Paul spent there in Acts 20:2, 3. He had been plotted against by the Jews in Damascus (Acts 9:23) and in Jerusalem (9:29). He had been driven out of Pisidian Antioch by them (13:50), and out of Iconium and Lystra (14:2 ff., 19). The same things had happened on his second journey in Thessalonica (17:5) and in Beroea (17:13) and in Corinth itself (18:12). And yet, with all this behind him, Paul can still go on praying that Israel may be saved.

8. Lastly, New Testament intercessions are frequently for the spread of the Gospel. Jesus Himself (Mt. 9:38; Lk. 10:2) says, 'Pray the Lord of the harvest that He send forth labourers

into His harvest'.   In Acts 4:31, when the early church had prayed, they were filled with the Holy Spirit and spoke the word of
God with boldness.   In Eph. 6:18 (cp. Col. 4:3) Paul asks for
prayer for all the saints and especially for himself that he may
be enabled to open his mouth boldly to preach the Gospel.
In Phil. 1:4, as he prays for that church, he rejoices in their
fellowship with him in the furtherance of the Gospel.   And in
2 Thess. 3:1 he asks for the prayers of the Thessalonians for
him that the word of the Lord may run and be glorified.

The prayers for material benefits under the first three heads
amount to eight at the most.   The prayers for spiritual benefits
under the last five come to twenty-nine.   Mere figures are not
everything, but they do show something of the proportions of
New Testament intercession.   Material things are not ruled out.
There is a place for them.   But a far greater place is given to
prayer for the things of the spirit, that they may develop and
grow as we pray for each other and for the Church.   Good for
us and for our friends if this is the proportion of our intercession!

VI. THE CHRISTIAN LIFE

37. GOD'S CALL

The Christian life begins not from man's side but from God's. Man's thinking and moral effort are important, but everything that we possess is God's gift, God's revelation, God's initiative. Our task is not to initiate but to respond.

One of the ways in which this truth is underlined in the New Testament is by its use of the word *Call*. This is, of course, a common word, used in many ways that we need not now consider, but it is specially used of the ways in which God and His Son call men, taking the initiative to summon and invite them, and to use them for divine purposes.

Four forms of the word are used: (1) the ordinary verb *kaleō*, 'call', of which we shall look at some fifty instances, spread fairly evenly through the New Testament, though about half are in St. Paul; (2) the strengthened verb 'call to oneself' of which we shall consider seventeen instances, all in the Gospels and Acts; (3) the noun 'calling' which occurs eleven times, all in the sense of God's calling of men, and never in the sense of 'profession' or 'occupation' in which we often use it; and (4) the participle 'called', which is found ten times referring to people called by God.

All these uses fall into three main classes. The first emphasises the fact that God's call is His own free act. He makes the first advance towards men; He does not wait for them to come to Him. The second class specifies the various people whom God and His Son call. The third shows the different purposes for which He calls them.

1. One of the remarkable things about the New Testament is the number of times it simply assumes that God has called us, and states the fact almost in passing, without any comment. For St. Paul and the other apostles it is an axiom that can be taken for granted. They have no doubt whatever that the first move comes, not from themselves but from God. Paul puts it very strongly in Rom. 8:30: 'Whom He foreordained, them He also called, and whom He called, them He also justified'. Those words have been overpressed into rigid theories of predestination. Paul did not mean them like that; he was simply expressing as confidently as he could the glorious fact that God wanted him

before he wanted God. It was not a reward for anything that he had done, but God's own choice (Rom. 9:11), a call that God would not retract (11:29). It did not depend upon a man's position in society, nor upon his intelligence (1 Cor. 1:26). It came entirely by God's grace (Gal. 1:6, 15), His own spontaneous love towards men. In fact this is the main message of Galatians. Look at 5:8 and the plain contrast between God's simple call and the complicated persuasions of men. We are called 'by His own glory and virtue' (2 Pet. 1:3), 'according to His purpose' (Rom. 8:28). In fact, Jude 1 describes Christians simply as 'them that are called', though that does not entitle us to any self-satisfaction. God has 'called us with a holy calling' (2 Tim. 1:9), and we shall see later what that implies.

2. But first let us see who they were whom God called. He began in early days by calling a nation, calling it through Abraham whose hope of posterity was non-existent (Rom. 4:17), Abraham who had already shown his readiness to obey God's call (Heb. 11:8). He went on to call that nation through Isaac, that son who was never expected and who was within an ace of being put to a premature death (Rom. 9:7; Heb. 11:18). God did not act in any way that might have led men to think that they had themselves been responsible for their national progress. The same was true of the call of His own Son. He was called out of Egypt where his parents had fled, and whence ordinary human intervention could not have brought Him back (Mt. 2:15). The same was true of Jesus's call of His disciples. James and John did not decide of their own accord to follow Him. He called them (Mt. 4:21; Mk. 1:20). Later He called the whole Twelve, selecting them from the general group of disciples and giving them their power and authority (Mt. 10:1; Mk. 3:13; 6:7). He called them too for special purposes such as feeding the four thousand (Mt. 15:32; Mk. 8:1), or driving home to them the meaning of the action of the poor widow (Mk. 12:43).

Nor is the call limited to a small, favoured circle. Jesus tells men that He came to call sinners (Mt. 9:13; Mk. 2:17; Lk. 5:32), and when the apostles go out on their missionary task, they go with the message that God calls not from the Jews only but also from the Gentiles (Rom. 9:24), calling as His people that which had not been His people (9:25), so that the contrast is no longer between Jew and Greek, but between those who are called (whether Jew or Greek) and those who are not (1 Cor. 1:24).

3. The largest number of references, however, is to the different purposes *for* which God calls men. He calls them in the first place simply to set them apart, not to make them aloof from others but that they may be dedicated. That was the command in the Law regarding first-born males (Lk. 2:23). It is the purpose for which all Christians are called: to be saints (Rom. 1:7; 1 Cor. 1:2); that is, not to be specially good in themselves, but to be distinctive because God has chosen them. There is privilege in that call, as the gospel parables show. It is like the invitation to a wedding feast (Mt. 22:3, 4, 9; Lk. 14:16, 17; cp. Rev. 19:9). But it is a call that can be ignored and refused to our shame and loss (Mt. 22:8; Lk. 14:24). Though the call is God's initiative, men are always free to refuse it.

The call may also be to create character. Simon was called, not just that he might be named Peter, but that he might become a man of rock (Jn. 1:42). We are called too that we may be men of peace, living in peace (1 Cor. 7:15; Col. 3:15). We are called also for holiness: 'Like as He who called you is holy, be ye yourselves also holy in all manner of living' (1 Pet. 1:15).

The call, further, is to be taught by Christ. Three times in the gospels He calls the people to Him that He may teach them (Mt. 15:10; Mk. 7:14; 8:34). And sometimes the call is in order to rebuke and condemn (Mt. 18:32; 20:25; Mk. 3:23; 10:42; Lk. 18:16). The call of Christ is always salutary, but not always pleasant.

The call is often for conduct: 'Walk worthily of the calling wherewith you were called' (Eph. 4:1); 'Walk worthily of the God who calls you' (1 Thess. 2:12); 'God did not call us for uncleanness' (4:7); 'We pray for you, that our God may count you worthy of your calling' (2 Thess. 1:11); 'Give diligence to make your calling and election sure; for if you do these things, you will never stumble' (2 Pet. 1:10). This calling and election come together again in Mt. 22:14. 'Many are called, but few chosen (elected)'. God's final selection of us depends on how we respond to His call.

He calls men too for responsibility. The man who was going away called his slaves and gave each his task (Mt. 25:14; Lk. 19:13). The apostles go out on their missionary journeys, knowing that they are accepting the responsibility of the divine call (Acts 13:2, 16:10). Paul is sure that he has been 'called to be an apostle' (Rom. 1:1; 1 Cor. 1:1). Neither the Jewish high priest nor the Great High Priest appoints himself to his responsible office; 'he is called of God' (Heb. 5:4).

Then we are even called for suffering: Peter says so in so many words (1 Pet. 2:21). And we are sometimes called to remain in the condition in which we are, not trying to change it, because it is not a handicap but a calling of God. Paul says this eight times over in different ways in the passage 1 Cor. 7:17-24. That may not always be God's will, but it is sometimes an essential part of it.

Yet we can thank Him that we are called for many brighter things: for salvation (Acts 2:39; Phil. 3:14; 2 Thess. 2:14; Heb. 3:1; 9:15); for life (1 Tim. 6:12); for fellowship with Christ and His Church (1 Cor. 1:9); for freedom (Gal. 5:13); for sanctification (1 Thess. 5:24); for hope (Eph. 1:18; 4:4); for light (1 Pet. 2:9); for sharing in God's glory (5:10).

But Paul has the best word when he says, in Rom. 1:6, that we are 'called to be Jesus Christ's' and Rev. 17:14 endorses that word with the vision of those who 'are *with* the Lamb, called and chosen and faithful'. The supreme object of our call is that we may belong to Christ. If we have accepted that call, so that we are truly His, then God's purpose has indeed been fulfilled in us and we are ready for all His will.

38. MINISTRY

When we speak of 'The Ministry', we are accustomed to think of the orders of Bishops, Presbyters and Deacons, with some hesitation as to whether Deacons are the junior rung on the ladder of the Ministry, or whether they are 'laymen' specially set apart for some particular office in the Church.

When we turn to the New Testament, however, we find that the word is normally used, not in this technical sense, but in its primary sense of Service, as in Mk. 10:45: 'The Son of Man came not to be *ministered* unto but to *minister*'. In fact the word Deacon, now used so technically, comes from the ordinary Greek word for Servant. It is good, especially for 'the ministry' (!) to keep on reminding ourselves of this. We are not ordained to an office; we are ordained for a task, the task of Service.

In this chapter, therefore, we examine the three Greek words *Diakonos*, servant or minister, *Diakoneō*, I serve or minister, and *Diakonia*, service or ministry. They occur twenty-nine, thirty-seven and thirty-four times respectively, exactly a hundred in all, and we shall treat them together. Matthew uses them nine times, Mark seven, Luke nine, John six, Acts ten, Paul forty-three (including twenty in 2 Corinthians, 'the epistle of ministry'), the Pastoral Epistles nine, Hebrews three, 1 Peter three and Revelation one.

The ordinary sense of 'servants' is found in Mt. 22:13; Jn. 2:5, 9: the servants of a king, and the servants at a feast. These references indicate the key meaning of the word. It is used to describe a rank or office in Phil. 1:1 ('the bishops and deacons'), and four times in 1 Tim. 3:8-13, where the character and duties of deacons are described: they must be grave, blameless, mono-gamous, and if they 'serve-well-as-deacons' ('serve-as-deacons' is the single word *Diakoneō*), they will earn a good standing. (The English Authorized Version says, 'They will purchase for themselves a good degree'—which shows how words change their meaning after three hundred and fifty years!) Acts 1:17, 25 also perhaps use the word 'ministry' in the sense of the office that the Twelve held as apostles.

All the other instances of the words, however, describe the task and not the position. We find the verb used frequently in the Gospels of those who minister to Christ. Angels do so after the Temptation (Mt. 4:11; Mk. 1:13). Peter's mother-in-law does after she has been cured (Mt. 8:15; Mk. 1:31; Lk. 4:39). So does Martha (Lk. 10:40; Jn. 12:2). So do other women (Lk. 8:3; Mt. 27:55; Mk. 15:41). In Jn. 12:26, Jesus three times speaks of the man who serves Him and is His servant. In Lk. 17:7-10, the noun 'servant' is a different word, the ordinary word for 'slave', but the verb in verse 8 is our word, and the reference is ultimately to serving Christ. Even those whom He condemns in the parable of the Sheep and the Goats made the claim that they had served Him (Mt. 25:44). Many people were eager to serve Him.

Yet it was not His aim to be served. 'The Son of Man came not to be served but to serve' (Mt. 20:28; Mk. 10:45). His own joy will be to serve His faithful servants (Lk. 12:37). His constant inculcation to His followers is that those who are first and greatest must be the servants of the rest (Mt. 20:26; 23:11; Mk. 9:35; 10:43). Lk. 22:26-27 links together their service and His: the chief man among them must be the server, because He Himself is in the midst of them as He that serves.

This is the teaching and the example that the workers in the early Church took as their model and inspiration. They spoke of themselves as 'in the Ministry of the Word' (Acts 6:4), as Ministers of the Gospel (Acts 20:24; Eph. 3:7; Col. 1:23; 1 Tim. 1:11-12), as Ministers of the New Covenant (2 Cor. 3:6). That is, they were Servants of the Word, with the task of proclaiming the Good News and declaring the new Covenant-relationship. The New Testament also speaks of them as Ministers of God (2 Cor. 6:4) and of Christ (2 Cor. 11:23; 1 Tim. 4:6), servants of the Divine will. It can even speak of the civil authorities as 'ministers of God' (Rom. 13:4), because it was their business to carry out God's will in the community.

The early Christians' ministry was largely carried out within the Church, though always as service rather than as office. Phoebe is a 'servant of the church in Cenchreae' (Rom. 16:1). Paul, as it were, 'robs other churches' that he may serve the church at Corinth (2 Cor. 11:8). In Col. 1:25 he describes himself as servant of the whole Church, Christ's body. He does for Christ's spiritual body what others had done for His physical body during His incarnation. There are many other places where the Church is not named as such, but where it is clearly implied. In Rom. 12:7 the context is of service within the Body of Christ. In 1 Cor. 3:5 Paul describes himself and Apollos as servants through whom the Corinthian church believed, and in 12:5 it is of the different kinds of service to the Church that he speaks. The services of Tychicus (Eph. 6:21; Col. 4:7), Archippus (Col. 4:17), Onesiphorus (2 Tim. 1:18), Timothy (2 Tim. 4:5) and the Thyatira church as a whole (Rev. 2:19) are services within the Church, even though the fact is not explicitly stated. The same is true of Heb. 1:14, where the angels themselves come to do service for those who inherit salvation. (N.B. It is the word 'service' in this verse which is our word. The word 'ministering' translates another word meaning 'performing a holy ritual act', the act of worship. The word 'liturgy' is derived from it).

Yet of course Christian service is not only service within the Church. It must go outwards as well. In Acts 21:19 Paul tells the Jerusalem church what God had wrought among the Gentiles by his ministry, and in Rom. 11:13, describing himself by that phrase which has so often been used of him since: 'the apostle of the Gentiles', he boasts of his service to them. Service is meant for everybody.

There are two kinds of service which the New Testament

especially emphasises: the material and the personal.   In Acts 6:4 the former is described as 'serving tables' a service for which the apostles appointed the best men they could find, though they did not feel that it was their own personal duty.   6:1 also speaks of this material help as a service.   11:29 and 12:25 use the same term for famine relief, and Heb. 6:10 also probably implies material service.   But the term is chiefly used by Paul to describe the collection for the poor in Jerusalem which he organised among the Gentile churches.   Eight times over he speaks of it in terms of service (Rom. 15:25, 31; 2 Cor. 8:4, 19, 20; 9:1, 12, 13).   We still know how practical service must be.

It also has to be practical in terms of personal help.   Paul is often glad to mention those who help him personally: Timothy and Erastus in Acts 19:22, Onesimus in Philemon 13, Mark in 2 Tim. 4:11.   Other mentions of personal service are of Stephanas and his family in 1 Cor. 16:15, Epaphras in Col. 1:7, and the Christians to whom Peter writes in 1 Pet. 4:10, 11.   Service must always be personal if it is to be truly Christian.

We have already referred to 2 Corinthians as 'the epistle of ministry', and have quoted a number of its twenty uses of the word.   We can group the remaining ones together.   Even the Law had a service to perform, though it was a service associated with the revelation of death and condemnation (2 Cor. 3:7, 9).   By contrast the Christian ministration reveals the Spirit and righteousness (3:8, 9).   This is the service entrusted to Paul, and in carrying it out he does not lose heart (4:1).   It is essentially a service of reconciliation (5:18), and he takes great care that in this service no one may need to blame him for any fault of his own (6:3).

Five other uses of the words do not quite fit into any of our categories and may be looked at separately.   In Rom. 15:8 Paul speaks of Christ as 'a minister of the circumcision'; that is, He performs the service of implementing God's promises to the Jews.   In 2 Cor. 3:3 Paul describes the Corinthians as 'a letter of Christ, ministered by us', meaning that their church is, as it were, a letter from Christ which Paul has performed the service of writing down and delivering.   2 Cor. 11:15 reminds us that there are those who are in the service of Satan, as well as those in the service of Christ.   Gal. 2:17 dismisses the idea that Christ is in the service of sin.   1 Pet. 1:12 speaks of the service of the prophets in foreshadowing the Gospel.

It was said at the beginning of the chapter that 'the Ministry' is not an office but a service, and the New Testament evidence fully bears this out. But our final reference shows that this is true not only for those whom we usually refer to as 'the Ministry', but for Christians as a whole. In Eph. 4:12 Paul, after mentioning five special types of ministry, goes on to indicate their task: it is 'the perfecting of the saints for the work of ministering'. The comma after 'saints' (which means simply 'Christians') found in the older translations must be dropped. This verse is not indicating a three-fold task ōf the special ministry. It is indicating that the ministry has the single task of equipping Christians for the work of service and of building up the Church. 'Ordained' or 'lay', it is to that task of service in all its forms that we are called—a task that will demand all our resources, and all the grace that we are willing to receive from God.

39. PREACHING THE GOSPEL

When a man knows what God has done for him and for all men in Jesus Christ, one of the things he most wants to do is to tell it as good news to other people. If he has no such desire, there is still something lacking in his Christian experience, something which the first Christians possessed abundantly. The noun *euangelion*, good news or gospel, comes seventy-six times in the New Testament, but it is with the verb derived from it, *euangelizomai*, the telling of the gospel to other people, that we shall be concerned in this chapter.

This verb comes fifty-four times, but unfortunately there is no corresponding single word in English. For some reason we do not happen to say 'to gospel'. This means that in the English New Testament the word is found under varying translations: preaching, bringing good tidings, preaching the gospel, bringing glad tidings—but all alike contain the idea of telling good news to other people.

This good news is not always the news of the full Christian Gospel. The word is used for the good news of the Thessalonian Christians which Timothy brought Paul in 1 Thess. 3:6. It is also used for the good news of a prospective son brought by Gabriel to Zacharias (Lk. 1:19). But normally it is used for the preaching of the Gospel as a whole, or of some essential part of it such as peace (Acts 10:36; Eph. 2:17).

Perhaps the most remarkable thing about the word is the astonishing variety with which it is used, and our study in this chapter will be mainly of that variety: variety of preachers, of people to whom they preach, of the circumstances in which they preach, and of the subjects of their preaching.   In the New Testament the passing on of the good news is not limited to certain specially qualified people under certain favourable conditions to restricted groups of hearers.   It is an activity that goes on boundlessly, with no restrictions.

1.   *The Variety of Preachers.*   The first preacher is, of course, Jesus Himself.   His own coming was proclaimed as good tidings by the angel at Bethlehem (Lk. 2:10), and He Himself continued to proclaim it as such (Mt. 11:5; Lk. 4:18,43; 7:22; 8:1; 16:16; 20:1).   But He was not content to proclaim it alone. Very soon He was sending out His disciples to try their prentice hand at the work (Lk. 9:6), so that later, when He had left them, they were able and eager to continue as He had begun and to stimulate others to join them.   Acts 5:42 speaks of their combined work of preaching .   Acts 8:25 probably refers to Peter and John. Acts 8 uses the word three times of Philip (vv. 12, 35, 40).   Acts 8:4 and 11:20 use it of those nameless Christians who were scattered abroad after the death of Stephen.   Acts 10:36 reminds us that the ultimate preacher of the Gospel is God Himself, and 1 Pet. 1:12 underlines the fact that all preaching of the Gospel is done by the help of the Holy Spirit.

St. Luke uses the word twenty-five times in his gospel and the Acts.   In fact the other gospels have it only once.   But the man with whom it is most closely associated is St. Paul.   He has it twenty-one times in his letters, and Luke associates it with him another five times in Acts.   He is above all the one who has been struck with the gladness of the news and with the necessity (1 Cor. 9:16) of passing it on.   Christ has sent him not to perform even such important and joyful acts as baptism, but to preach and preach and go on preaching (this is what the present continuous tense in 1 Cor. 1:17 implies).

2.   *The Variety of Hearers.*   Jesus Himself especially emphasises the poor (Mt. 11:5; Lk. 4:18; 7:22).   Philip begins with his bold and successful approach to the Ethiopian eunuch (Acts 8:35), but he is not content to rest on his laurels.   His contact with the eunuch stimulates him to go on and preach to all next the cities from Azotus to Caesarea (8:40). At the same time Peter and John were preaching to the Samaritans (8:25), and the

next step forward was about to be taken when, in 11:20, the men
of Cyprus and Cyrene preached Jesus to Greeks also in Antioch.
But again it is Paul who takes us the full way.   God was pleased
to reveal His Son in him that he might preach Him among the
Gentiles (Gal. 1:16), and this was the task that occupied the
rest of his life. Not that he neglected his own people. He sums
up the evangelistic work of Christ in Eph. 2:17, where he speaks
of Him as preaching peace both to the Gentiles who were far off
and to the Jews who were near.   1 Pet. 4:6 may even add one
word to Paul.   The reference there to the preaching of the Gospel
to the dead probably implies the descent of Christ into Hades,
though it may mean simply those who heard the Gospel when
alive but who are now dead.   In any case there is no limit whatever
to the hearers of the message.

3.   *The Variety of the Circumstances under which the Gospel is
preached.*   These circumstances are nearly always what we should
describe as unfavourable, times which we might consider needed
caution or relaxation.   Jesus in Lk. 20:1 preaches the Gospel
in the temple, just after the priests have begun plotting to destroy
Him, and just before they come challenging His authority.
The apostles, after they have been beaten and threatened,
continue in the very same temple to preach the good news that
Jesus is the expected Messiah (Acts 5:42).   Being driven out
never suppresses their zeal.   'Scattering abroad' only leads to
more preaching of the Word (8:4), and of the Lord Jesus (11:20).
When Paul and Barnabas are driven out of Iconium, they preach
in Lystra (14:7).   When Paul is ill and clearly in need of taking
rest, he regards his sanatorium in Galatia as a further opportunity
for preaching (Gal. 4:13).   Nor do financial circumstances ever
enter into his calculations.   In fact it is paradoxically a reward
to him to preach the Gospel without charge (1 Cor. 9:18).

Some of us when we preach prefer not to venture into new
places.   We like the familiar.   Not so with Paul.   It is his policy
to go to new places (Rom. 15:20; 2 Cor. 10:16).   He is ready to
preach in a new continent (Acts 16:10), to face a lot of rather
supercilious philosophers with his message (17:18), to go to the
heart of the empire itself (Rom. 1:15).   Yet he is not one of those
who can talk abroad but do nothing at home.   He does not fail
to preach in his own headquarters at Antioch (Acts 15:35).

4.   *The Variety of Good News that is preached.*   Jesus preached
the good news of the coming of the reign of God (Lk. 4:43, 8:1,
16:16).   Philip followed His example (Acts 8:12).   Lk. 3:18

speaks of the Baptist as preaching good tidings — with a mixture of good news and of very stern words. The Gospel is not always comfortable. Paul in Acts 13:32 tells the Jews that it means a reorientation of their understanding of the ancient promises, and in 14:15 he tells his Gentile audience that it means a similar reorientation in turning away from idols. Paul himself had had to learn to preach the faith of which he once made havoc (Gal. 1:23).

But the emphasis is mostly on the 'good things' (Rom. 10:15), especially on preaching Jesus (Acts 8:35; 17:18), His Word (15:35), His peace (10:36; Eph. 2:17), His resurrection (Acts 17:18; 1 Cor. 15:1, 2), His unsearchable riches (Eph. 3:8). This is the full Gospel as Paul preached it, beyond which he says there is nothing more (Gal. 1:8, 9). This is the Gospel which comes not from man but by revelation (1:11-12), the Word of the Lord that abideth for ever, the Word of good tidings which was preached to us (1 Pet. 1:25). And this is what it is our duty and joy to proclaim, even as it was proclaimed by those who first knew Christ.

40. TEACHING

Few activities have more far-reaching effects than teaching. For good or for ill it can sway a person's whole life. It is not surprising, therefore, that it has a large place in the New Testament. It is not to be compared unfavourably, as it sometimes is, with the message of salvation. The Christian needs the maximum of both. Either without the other falls short of the full Gospel.

The important place of Christian teaching could be illustrated, as it often has been, by a study of the actual teaching material in the gospels and epistles. It could be illustrated by a study of the number of times that Jesus is called Teacher or Rabbi. This chapter, however, will simply take the verb *Didaskō*, I teach. It occurs ninety-seven times in the New Testament, enough surely to emphasise the importance it places on teaching. Fourteen of these occurrences are in Matthew, seventeen in Mark, seventeen in Luke, ten in John, sixteen in Acts, eleven in Paul, five in the Pastoral Epistles, two in Hebrews, three in 1 John and two in Revelation. It is a little surprising to find that Matthew, the gospel which contains so much teaching, uses the word less often than Mark, which is less than two thirds of its length, but that warns us not to place our reliance too firmly upon vocabulary alone.

We begin, of course, with Jesus. It is remarkable what the gospels tell us about the variety of places in which He taught, the different people whom He taught, and the various subjects that he taught.

1. Right from the beginning of His ministry He taught in the synagogues, the places where Jews expected to receive their religious instruction. Even though there was often opposition to what He taught, men wanted to hear Him, because they knew that He had something to say. There are a dozen references to this synagogue teaching, including one or two parallel passages. See Mt. 4:23; 9:35; 13:54; Mk. 1:21, 22; 6:2; Lk. 4:15, 31; 6:6; 13:10; Jn. 6:59; 18:20.

He did not, however, limit His teaching to religious buildings. He went outside and taught in the cities (Mt. 11:1; Lk. 13:22), in the villages (Mk. 6:6; Lk. 13:22), by the sea side (Mk. 4:1), in the streets (Lk. 13:26), in a house (Lk. 5:17), throughout all Judaea (Lk. 23:5). John Wesley, who for a long time had a prejudice against preaching outside a religious building, had a true precedent in his Master, when he 'submitted to be more vile, and proclaimed in the highways the glad tidings of salvation, speaking from a little eminence in a ground adjoining to the city'.

Yet the final teaching of Jesus was done once more in a religious building. He went up to Jerusalem and challenged both the authorities and the crowds in the very Temple itself. See Mt. 21:23; 26:55; Mk. 11:17; 12:35; 14:49; Lk. 19:47; 20:1; 21:37. He had done this before—see Jn. 7:14, 28; 8:2, 20. Wherever His teaching was most needed, He went and gave it, regardless of personal danger to Himself.

2. The gospels mention two main classes of people whom He taught: the crowds and His disciples. Both needed what He had to say to them. The need of the crowd was immediate. The need of the disciples was not only immediate but also, as we shall see, for the teaching work that they themselves would be doing. The crowds are taught in Mk. 1:22; 2:13; 6:34; 10:1; Lk. 5:3. The actual word 'teach' is used with reference to the disciples only at the beginning of the Sermon on the Mount (Mt. 5:2), where they are linked with the crowds. At the end of the Sermon (7:29) it is the crowds who are astonished at the authority with

which He teaches. But the important verse in connection with the disciples is Acts 1:1. Luke speaks of 'all that Jesus began both to do and to teach' and immediately links this up with His commandment to the apostles who were going to continue that teaching.

3. The content of the teaching of Jesus has been the subject of many whole books. The actual word is used of His teaching 'the way of God in truth' (Mt. 22:16; cp. Mk. 12:14; Lk. 20:21), of His teaching in parables (Mk. 4:2), of His teaching about prayer (Lk. 11:1; Mk. 11:17), and of His teaching about the Cross (Mk. 8:31; 9:31)—a very short list on paper, but in fact one which covers almost all that He ever said.

This completes the list of references to Jesus teaching with His incalculable influence, but before we go on to the rest of the New Testament let us look at two instances where He Himself uses the word in criticism. In Mt. 5:19 He speaks of those who break the commandments and teach others to do the same. In Mk. 7:7 (cp. Mt. 15:9) He speaks of those who teach as their doctrines the mere precepts of men. Teaching can have a bad effect as well as a good one, and this is borne out in many places in the New Testament. The soldiers spread lies about the Resurrection of Jesus 'as they were taught' (Mt. 28:15). The Jewish Christians confused the new converts in Antioch by teaching them that they must be circumcised (Acts 15:1). Paul condemns the Jew who teaches others without teaching himself (Rom. 2:21). (Incidentally, shall we describe as not very good teaching Paul's own word that nature itself teaches that a man must not have long hair?! See 1 Cor. 11:14. And possibly the forbidding of a woman to teach might also be included in the description—1 Tim. 2:12). There is no doubt about the badness of those who teach for filthy lucre (Tit. 1:11), nor about the false prophetess in Rev. 2:20 who taught people to apostatise. Rev. 2:14, condemning the teaching of Balaam, shows that there were opinions about him which differed from the account in the book of Numbers.

But not all human teaching is bad. They are great in God's sight who do the commandments and teach them (Mt. 5:19). Apollos in Acts 18:25 is commended for his teaching, imperfect though it was. In Rom. 12:7 the teacher is urged to give himself to his teaching, and in Col. 3:16 Christians are urged to teach one another by singing. Yet finally the time will come when no teaching will be needed. We shall all know direct from God (Heb. 8:11; 1 Jn. 2:27).

That time, however, still lies in the future, and Jesus left His disciples with the task of teaching. Once they performed it even while He was with them (Mk. 6:30), but it was His last command to them in Mt. 28:20, and they obeyed it. They began by teaching in the Temple as He had done (Acts 4:2; 5:21, 25, 42). They taught in private houses as He had done (5:42, N.E.B.), and they taught in His name (4:18; 5:28). They and others, such as Paul and Barnabas, continued that teaching in Antioch (11:26; 15:35), in Corinth (18:11), in Ephesus (20:20), in Thessalonica (2 Thess. 2:15), everywhere (1 Cor. 4:17; Col. 1:28). As we leave Paul in Acts, we find him still teaching (28:31). When he himself has not done the teaching, he still reminds the Colossians (2:7) and those to whom he writes Ephesians (4:21) that they 'were taught'. Timothy is twice urged to teach (1 Tim. 4:11; 6:2). One of the qualifications of a faithful man is that he shall be able to teach others (2 Tim. 2:2). The defective Christian is one who has not become a teacher but still needs to be taught (Heb. 5:12). The opponents of the Faith are afraid of this teaching power and attack it: 'Will he go and teach the Greeks?' (Jn. 7:35), 'Do you teach us?' (9:34), 'You teach all the Jews to forsake Moses' . . . 'This is the man that teaches all men everywhere against the people' (Acts 21:21, 28). They had reason to be afraid.

Why? Because ultimately this teaching was not a code of instructions, nor was Jesus Himself an ordinary teacher, dependent on His own wisdom. He makes that very plain when He says, 'As the Father taught me, I speak these things' (Jn. 8:28). He tells His disciples that their teacher is to be the Holy Spirit (Lk. 12:12; Jn. 14:26). Paul confirms this when he says that the Gospel was not taught him; it came 'through revelation of Jesus Christ' (Gal. 1:12). And John's final word on the subject is that the anointing which we receive from Christ teaches us everything, most especially the lesson that we should abide in Him (1 Jn. 2:27). C. H. Dodd explains the 'anointing' as the Word of God, revealed in Christ and received into our hearts. When we are ready to let God's Word in Christ teach us, we have the full and perfect education.

41. BUILDING

The word *Building* is so often used as an ethical and spiritual metaphor that we have almost ceased to link it with the material action which it primarily signifies. In fact the English Bible frequently uses the word derived from the Latin equivalent, 'edify', which makes the connection still less obvious, particularly as this word has now become rather commonplace and second-class. When we read of someone delivering 'an edifying discourse', we pass by the phrase as mere jargon. It does not give us a vivid picture of talk that builds up knowledge and character.

But in the New Testament the word *oikodomeō* and its compounds are very living words. Altogether they come sixty-eight times, sometimes with simple reference to bricks and mortar, sometimes with equally plain reference to the building up of Christian character and fellowship, sometimes with a primary material sense but with underlying moral and spiritual implications.

Literal material references are about eleven, including several duplicates in the Synoptic Gospels. Lk. 4:29, for example, speaks of the position in which Nazareth was built. Mk. 13:1, 2 refer to the buildings of the Temple. The description in these places is of ordinary mason's work, and need not detain us, except to remind us to keep this word down to earth all the time. This is the simple action, one of the primary human actions, out of which our metaphor has sprung. We speak of food, clothing and shelter as our essential material needs; and since the day when people stopped living in caves, the builder has been a vital part of society.

Passing on from the literal significance of the word, there are far more places in the New Testament where physical building is described, but where the character of the builder is implied in his physical act. There are perhaps some twenty-one of these, though it is sometimes not easy to decide on which side of the border line any particular case should come. There are the wise and foolish men who build their houses on the rock and on the sand (Mt. 7:24, 26)—physical actions which show what kind of men they are. There are the builders who reject a stone which afterwards has a key place in the building (Ps. 118:22; Mk. 12:10). The Psalmist is describing the masons' misjudgement, but it is a parable of the nations' misjudgment of Israel, and the New Testament takes it as a parable of Israel's mis-judgment of Jesus. The scribes and Pharisees build the sepulch-res of the prophets (Mt. 23:29) as pieces of actual funereal masonry, but the work symbolises the hypocrisy of their minds. Jesus is accused in Mk. 14:58 of saying that He would destroy the Temple and build another in three days 'without hands'. His hearers had not understood Him, but at any rate they realized that here was something on the border line between the physical and the spiritual.

When we come into Luke's gospel, there is the man in 14:28-30 who begins to build a tower and cannot finish — another physical act depicting character. And the same is clear in Acts 7:47, 49: Solomon builds God a house, but only as a misguided illustration of man spending his labour on trying to do something that God does not really want, instead of concentrating on the obedience that He demands.

But the most interesting uses of the word in the New Testament are those where it has passed over into pure metaphor. There are thirty-six of these, all but five of them in Paul's letters. Paul regards the building up (or edifying — let us note the word but use it as little as possible) of the Church as one of his main tasks. Before he even uses the metaphor himself, Luke uses it about him. After describing Paul's conversion in Acts 9:1-30, Luke sums it all up in verse 31 with the words: 'So the Church . . . had peace, being built up'.

Our task as brethren is to build one another up. Time after time Paul emphasises that: 'Build each other up, even as ye also do' (1 Thess. 5:11); 'Let us follow after things . . . whereby we may build one another up' (Rom. 14:19); 'Let each one of us please his neighbour for that which is good, unto building up' (15:2); 'Let no corrupt speech proceed out of your mouth, but such as is good for the building up of the need' (Eph. 4:29). Speaking with tongues is deprecated primarily because it fails to build others up: 'He who speaks in a tongue builds himself up; but he who prophesies builds up the Church' (1 Cor. 14:4). The word comes five more times in the same passage (verses 3, 5, 12, 17, 26). And while asserting his apostolic authority in another letter to the Corinthians, Paul emphasises that that authority had been given him not for casting them down but for building them up (2 Cor. 10:8; 13:10).

We have to confess with shame how little we do towards building each other up. Criticism, personal ambition, lack of humility, all make us much more apt at casting down. Paul points to the reason for this several times. It is only love that builds another man up (1 Cor. 8:1). Even when he is criticising the Corinthians most severely in 2 Cor. 12:19, he says, 'All things, *beloved*, are for your building up'. And the last word of his great paragraph on the Body of Christ in Eph. 4 is that it builds itself up *in love* (v. 16). There are things that we might quite legitimately do, as Paul argues in 1 Cor. 10:23; our own conscience does not condemn us at all. But we refrain simply because they do not build our brother up. His conscience is likely to be offended, and we do not want to cause him to stumble. We love him too much for that.

Briefly note in passing that we must make sure that we build with the right object. It would be wrong to rebuild the Law, says Paul in Gal. 2:18; and our thoughtlessness may build our brother up ('embolden' is the English word in 1 Cor. 8:10) into bad habits from which he was previously free. A great deal of building springs from man's pride or perverseness.

But the true builder of the Church is not man but God. 'You are God's building', says Paul in 1 Cor. 3:9. Men may plant and water, but it is God who gives the increase. It is Christ who builds His Church (Mt. 16:18), though He needs the rock of men's faith in Him as a foundation. It is the word of *God's* grace to which Paul commits the Ephesian elders in Acts 20:32. *That* is able to build them up, whether Paul is there or not. And when Paul in Eph. 2:22 says, 'You *are builded together* for a habitation of God in the Spirit', and Peter in 1 Pet. 2:5 says, 'You also, as living stones, *are built up* a spiritual house', the passive voice, as so often in the New Testament, means that it is God's work: God has made them into a house for Him to dwell in. Or rather, He is still in the process of doing so, because both the verbs are 'present continuous', and the noun 'building' in Eph. 2:21 means not the completed structure but the whole process of the work.

Yet God's primary part does not absolve us from our task. In Mt. 16:18 Christ is the builder, but the foundation is Peter's faith in Him. In Jude 20 our faith is again the foundation, but we have to do the building. In 1 Cor. 3:10-14, Christ Himself is the foundation, and each man builds upon that foundation to the best of his capacity. So in Col. 2:7 Christ is the foundation upon which we are built, as well as the soil in which we grow; but in Eph. 2:20 the foundations are the apostles and the prophets upon whom God builds. Eph. 4:12 particularly stresses the part that *all* the saints have to play in the building. Almost certainly the comma should be removed in the translations that have one after 'saints', so that the meaning is that it is *they* who are perfected for the twofold task of ministering and of building up the Body of Christ. That task is not left to the specialists enumerated in verse 11; it is the work of all. The combination of metaphors in all these passages lights up the truth from many points of view. There is no contradiction, only many-sidedness.

Lastly, for our final, eternal habitation we have a building from God (2 Cor. 5:1), a heavenly body that will subsume this present temporary thing. God builds not only here and now. He builds for eternity—and our eternal privilege and joy is to live in that building that He has built for us.

42. THY WILL BE DONE

The noun *Will* is a common one, and we should expect to find it frequently in the New Testament. It occurs there sixty-three times: Matthew six, Mark one, Luke four, John eleven, Acts three, Paul twenty-two, Pastoral Epistles two, Hebrews six (including one use of the form *thelēsis* instead of the normal *thelēma*), 1 Peter four, 2 Peter one, 1 John two, Revelation one.

The outstanding result of a Concordance study of these occurrences is that nearly all of them refer to the will of *God*. Only seven, perhaps eight, speak of the will of *man*. In Lk. 23:25 Jesus is delivered up to the will of the Jews. In 1 Cor. 7:37 Paul speaks of a man having power over his own will, and in Eph. 2:3 of our doing the 'wills' of our flesh. In 1 Cor. 16:12, as the RV and RSV text and margin show, it is not clear from the Greek whether Paul is speaking of Apollos's will or God's will. There are four other mentions of man's will, but they are all used with negatives, laying the emphasis by contrast on God's will. In Jn. 1:13 the children of God are born 'not of the will of the flesh, nor of the will of man, but of God'. In 2 Pet. 1:21 'no prophecy ever came by the will of man, but men spoke from God'. And in Jn. 5:30 even Jesus says, 'I seek not my own will, but the will of Him that sent me'.

It is therefore with the will of *God* that the New Testament is essentially concerned. The creation itself was God's will: 'Thou didst create all things and by thy will they existed and were created' (Rev. 4:11).   The first business of man is to know God's will.   The Jew claimed to know it (Rom. 2:18).   Ananias told the newly converted Saul that God had appointed him to know His will (Acts 22:14), and Paul later tells the Ephesians that they must 'understand what the will of the Lord is' (Eph. 5:17), and prays that the Colossians 'may be filled with the knowledge of His will' (Col. 1:9) and 'fully assured in all the will of God' (4:12).   Jesus in a parable speaks of the 'servant who knew his master's will' (Lk. 12:47), even though he did not do it.   And this will is not something that God leaves us to discover for ourselves; 'He has made known to us the mystery of His will' (Eph. 1:9).

What is the purpose of God's will for us ?   The New Testament describes it under five heads:

(*a*) It is for our salvation and spiritual welfare.   'It is not the will of your Father that one of these little ones should perish' (Mt. 18:14).   'This is the will of Him that sent me, that I should lose nothing of all that He has given me . . . This is the will of my Father, that everyone who sees the Son and believes in Him should have eternal life' (Jn. 6:39, 40).   Christ rescues us 'according to the will of our God' (Gal. 1:4), our God who distributes the Spirit 'according to His own will' that we may receive His 'great salvation' (Heb. 2:4, 3).   God 'destined us in love to be His sons through Jesus Christ, according to the purpose of His will' (Eph. 1:5), that will through which He accomplishes all things (1:11).   And His will is for our sanctification (1 Thess. 4:3; Heb. 10:10), so that finally we prove what is His 'good and acceptable and perfect will' (Rom. 12:2).

(*b*) It is God's will to appoint men for His service.   Five times in the New Testament letters Paul is described as 'an apostle by the will of God' (1 Cor. 1:1; 2 Cor. 1:1; Eph. 1:1; Col. 1:1; 2 Tim. 1:1).   He did not do his missionary work of his own choice; he did it because he knew that he had been appointed by God's will.

(*c*) Twice Paul speaks of his missionary travels as being directed by the will of God.   In Rom. 1:10 he prays that he 'may be prospered by the will of God' to come to Rome, and he repeats the prayer in 15:32: 'so that by God's will I may come to you with joy'.   If in 1 Cor. 16:12 (see above) the reference is to God's will and not to that of Apollos, then Paul has it in mind that God has charge of Apollos's movements also.

(*d*) God's will is for men to live the Christian life. It was 'by the will of God' (2 Cor. 8:5) that the churches of Macedonia gave themselves to the Lord and to the apostles. The Thessalonians are commanded to rejoice, pray and give thanks, 'for this is the will of God' (1 Thess. 5:16-18). Persecuted Christians are told that 'It is God's will that by doing right you should put to silence the ignorance of foolish men' (1 Pet. 2:15), and that they should 'live ... no longer for human passions but for the will of God' (4:2). And John the Elder assures his readers 'that if we ask anything according to His will, He hears us' (1 Jn. 5:14).

(*e*) God's will is sometimes that we should suffer for doing right. 'It is better to suffer for doing right, if that should be God's will, than for doing wrong' (1 Pet. 3:17). 'Let those who suffer according to God's will do right and entrust their souls to a faithful Creator' (4:19).

And what is to be man's response to God's will? The New Testament has more to say about this than under any of the other heads. More than twenty times it speaks of *doing* God's will. 'Not everyone that says Lord, Lord, shall enter the kingdom of heaven, but he who does the will of my Father' (Mt. 7:21). 'Whoever does the will of my Father ... is my brother ...' (Mt. 12:50; Mk. 3:35). The two sons are judged by whether they did the will of their father or not (Mt. 21:31). So is the servant who did not according to his master's will (Lk. 12:47). We can understand Jesus' teaching only if we do God's will (Jn. 7:17), and even the man born blind knows that if we want God to listen to us we must do His will (9:31). When Paul at Antioch speaks of David, he quotes the Psalmist's description of him as 'a man after my heart, who shall do all my will' (Acts 13:22), and when later Paul is determined to go to Jerusalem to suffer and, if need be, die, the church in Caesarea sees even that as God's will (21:14).

The same emphasis on *doing* God's will continues in the epistles. The slaves in Eph. 6:6 are bidden to do God's will from the heart. 2 Tim. 2:26 speaks of men escaping from the snare of the devil to do God's will (though the Greek may refer to people ensnared by the devil to do his will). The 'Hebrews' are exhorted to endurance so as to do the will of God (Heb. 10:36), and are prayed for, that God may make them 'perfect in every good thing to do His will' (13:21). Finally John states that 'he who does the will of God abides for ever' (1 Jn. 2:17). 'Thy will be

done' (Mt. 6:10) is not a sigh of resignation, as on the tombstones;
it is a prayer for Christian action.

Yet we are still left with eight references that are the climax
of the matter. There is only One who has done God's will
perfectly on earth. He said, 'My meat is to do the will of Him
that sent me' (Jn. 4:34). He said, 'Lo, I am come to do Thy will,
O God' (Heb. 10:7, 9). He said, 'I seek not my own will, but
the will of Him that sent me' (Jn. 5:30), and 'I come down from
heaven, not to do my own will, but the will of Him that sent me'
(6:38). And when in Gethsemane He said, 'Nevertheless, not
my will but Thine be done' (Lk. 22:42, cp. Mt. 26:42), it led to
the Cross which has ever since made it possible for men to do
God's will. When we pray, 'Thy will be done', may we never
forget Him who did it perfectly and who promises that those
who trust in Him will be enabled to do it too.

43. FOR OTHERS' SAKE

Some of the most important words in the New Testament
are the smaller ones. The prepositions often have as much to
tell us as the great nouns. In this chapter we shall examine one
of them: the word *huper*, which is variously translated 'for',
'on the side of', 'on behalf of', 'for the sake of'. In its main
construction it used in connection with helping people, taking
their part. (We are not concerned now with the other, less
important construction.)

We have to look at no fewer than a hundred and thirty-two
occurrences of the word: six in the first three Gospels, thirteen
in John, seven in Acts, eighty-six in Paul (of which seventeen
are in Romans and thirty in 2 Corinthians), ten in Hebrews, and
ten in the remaining books.

In eight instances the word means nothing much more than
'concerning'. See, for example, 2 Cor. 8:23: 'If anyone enquires
concerning Titus', or 2 Cor. 12:8: 'I besought the Lord thrice
concerning this'. (The other examples are Rom. 9:27; 1 Cor.
10:30; 2 Cor. 1:7, 8; 1 Thess. 3:2; 2 Thess. 2:1).

The sense of being on someone's side is found in Mk. 9:40:
'He who is not against us is for us' (cp. Lk. 9:50); also in
Rom. 8:31: 'If God is for us, who is against us?', and in 1 Cor.
4:6: 'puffed up for the one against the other'.

A very similar use, where the best translation is 'on behalf of', occurs seven times. In Jn. 1:30 the Baptist says, 'This is He on behalf of whom I said. . . .' In 1 Cor. 15:29 there are two references to the strange custom of being 'baptized on behalf of the dead'. In 2 Cor. 5:20 and Eph. 6:20 Paul is an ambassador on behalf of Christ and the Gospel, and beseeches men on behalf of Christ (2 Cor. 5:20). In Col. 1:7 Epaphras serves the Colossians on Paul's behalf, and in Philemon 13 Onesimus serves Paul on Philemon's behalf.

The translation 'because of' is perhaps best in another four cases, all of them connected with thanksgiving and praise. In Rcm. 15:9 the Gentiles glorify God because of His mercy. In 2 Cor. 1:11 Paul wants his readers to thank God because of what He has done for him. In Eph. 1:16 Paul writes of his own thanksgiving because of his readers, and in 5:20 he urges them to give thanks because of everything that they have been given.

A special use that occurs eight times in 2 Corinthians and only once elsewhere is when Paul writes of glorying or boasting because of something that is worth praising in his readers. He can glory because they have listened to Titus and substantiated Paul's opinion of them (2 Cor. 7:4, 14). He can glory because of the effort they have put into raising the collection for Jerusalem (8:24; 9:2, 3). He can also glory because of the Thessalonians' patience and faith (2 Thess. 1:4). He will also let the Corinthians glory in his ministry (2 Cor. 5:12), but he will not glory in himself, only in what God has so wonderfully done for him (12:5, twice).

Most of the remaining instances of the word look forward rather than backward. They are concerned not with such things as the ground for thanksgiving or boasting, but with things that are done to help some person or cause.

A whole section of some twenty-six examples may be classified under the general heading of *purpose*. 'This sickness is for the glory of God' (Jn. 11:4). 'For their sakes I sanctify myself' (17:19). 'I could wish that I were anathema for my brethren's sake' (Rom. 9:3). 'Christ has been made a minister of the circumcision for the truth of God' (15:8). 'The members should have the same care one for another' (1 Cor. 12:25). 'We are afflicted—comforted—for your comfort' (2 Cor. 1:6). 'Your zeal for me' (7:7); 'your earnest care for us' (7:12); 'the same earnest care for you' (8:16). 'I take pleasure in weaknesses for Christ's sake', that is, for the purpose of relying upon Him

(12:10). 'I will most gladly spend and be spent for your souls'
(12:15). 'All things are for your edifying' (12:19). 'We can
do nothing against the truth, but for the truth' (13:8). What
a wealth of this use there is in 2 Corinthians!

The use goes on in Ephesians: 'prisoner for the sake of you
Gentiles' (3:1), 'my tribulations for you' (3:13); and in
Philippians: 'thus minded for the sake of you all' (1:7), 'granted
for the sake of Christ . . . to suffer for His sake' (1:29), 'to will and
to work for the sake of pleasing Him' (2:13), 'you have revived
your thought for me' (4:10). Colossians continues it: 'my
sufferings for your sake' (1:24), 'I fill up what is lacking of the
afflictions of Christ for His Body's sake' (1:24), 'I strive for you
and for those at Laodicea' (2:1), 'he has much labour for you
and for those in Laodicea' (4:13). The final example is in Heb.
13:17: 'they watch for the sake of your souls'.

A special instance of this purpose is with regard to *prayer*.
In sixteen places there is prayer or supplication for the sake of a
person or persons: 'pray for them that despitefully use you'
(Mt. 5:44); 'He makes intercession for the saints' (Rom. 8:27);
'with supplication on your behalf' (2 Cor. 9:14). There is no
need to quote the list in full. The other references are Rom.
8:34; 10:1; 15:30; 2 Cor. 1:11; Eph. 6:19; Phil. 1:4; Col. 1:3, 9;
4:12; 1 Tim. 2:1, 2; Heb. 7:25; Jas. 5:16.

Another special purpose is in connection with the *Name*
of Christ. In Rom. 1:5 Paul declares that he has received his
Gentile apostleship 'for His Name's sake', that is, so that Christ's
name and nature may be made known everywhere. In Acts that
evangelistic work is always linked with suffering: the apostles
rejoice that they are 'counted worthy to suffer dishonour for the
Name' (5:41). Immediately after his conversion Paul is shown
'how much he must suffer for my Name's sake' (9:16). In
15:26 the Jerusalem church describe Paul and Barnabas as 'men
that have hazarded their lives for the Name of our Lord Jesus
Christ', and in 21:13 Paul himself says that he is 'ready . . .
to die for the Name of the Lord Jesus'. 3 Jn. 7 completes the
list by telling of those who 'went forth for the sake of the Name',
taking nothing for their benefit or comfort.

This leads on to *sacrifice*, which is always something done for
the sake of helping people. That was true of Jewish sacrifice:
the offerings were offered for the four men in Acts 21:26. The
Jewish high priest was appointed for men, that he might offer
sacrifices for sins (Heb. 5:1), and he offered them first for his

own sins, but chiefly for those of the people (7:27; 9:7). Hebrews transfers the high priestly imagery to Christ, who entered within the veil for us (6:20), and who appears before the face of God for us (9:24).

And this brings us finally to the supreme use of this word in the New Testament: Christ died *for* our sins, and *for* our sakes. The word *huper* never means 'instead of'. It is always used in the sense of 'on behalf of'. He died to redeem us from our sins, to bring us back to God. Thirty-nine times in the New Testament in one way or another speaks of His dying 'for' us. His body, His flesh, was given for us (Lk. 22:19; Jn. 6:51; 1 Cor. 11:24), His blood was poured out (Mk. 14:24; Lk. 22:20). He laid down His life for His sheep (Jn. 10:11, 15), for His friends (15:13), for the ungodly (Rom. 5:6), for sinners (5:8), for the unrighteous (1 Pet. 3:18). He died 'for our sins', to redeem us from them (1 Cor. 15:3; Gal. 1:4; Heb. 10:12). He was made to be sin for us (2 Cor. 5:21), that is, to share our nature with all that sin can do to attack it. He 'became a curse for us', by sharing in the curse upon those who were crucified (Gal. 3:13). He delivered or gave Himself up for us of His own free will (Gal. 2:20; Eph. 5:2, 25; Tit. 2:14), He whom God delivered up for us as His Son (Rom. 8:32). He gave Himself for all to set us free, as a ransom gives a slave his freedom (1 Tim. 2:6). He died for all (2 Cor. 5:15; Heb. 2:9) — and there are other references in more general terms in Rom. 14:15; 2 Cor. 5:14, 15 (the word occurs a second time in the latter verse), 1 Thess. 5:10; 1 Pet. 2:21 and 1 Jn. 3:16. Even Caiaphas, speaking more truly than he knew, bore witness to this dying for others (Jn. 11:50, 51, 52; 18:14).

Can man do what Christ did? In one sense, no. Peter enthusiastically said that he would, but Jesus knew better (Jn. 13:37, 38). Even for a righteous man we would scarcely venture to die (Rom. 5:7). Paul denied that he had ever been crucified for anyone (1 Cor. 1:13). Yet there is a sphere in which even we may follow in His footsteps. Priscilla and Aquila laid down their necks for Paul (Rom. 16:4). The Thessalonians suffered for the kingdom of God (2 Thess. 1:5). And if Christ laid down His life for us, we are exhorted to lay down our lives for the brethren (1 Jn. 3:16).

There remain two unused references which underline by contrast the whole use of this word in the New Testament. In Acts 8:24 Simon Magus says 'Pray for me that none of these things come upon me', the only selfish request in the whole list.

And in Acts 26:1 Agrippa says to Paul, 'Thou art permitted to speak for thyself'. Paul never spoke for himself. He spoke only for Christ, and if he asked for prayer for himself, it was only that he might continue his ministry effectively (Rom. 15:30,31; Eph. 6:19). The world's motto is 'Every man for himself'. The New Testament knows nothing of that, because Christ died 'for us', and because He calls us to live and die for others and for Him.

44. FRUIT

The New Testament has a great deal to say about fruit-bearing. The noun *karpos*, fruit, occurs sixty-six times. The verb *karpophoreō*, bear fruit, is found eight times, and the adjective *karpophoros*, fruitful, once, making a total of seventy-five. Taking them all together, we find twenty instances in Matthew, seven in Mark, thirteen in Luke, ten in John, two in Acts, fourteen in Paul, one in the Pastorals, two in Hebrews, four in James and two in Revelation.

In a few cases the word is used in a physical sense. In Acts 14:17 Paul speaks of 'fruitful seasons'. In Lk. 1:42 we find the 'fruit' of Mary's womb, and Acts 2:30 the 'fruit' of David's loins.

In a few other cases the sense of the word is still physical, but it is introduced in order to make some deeper comparison. Just as the man who plants a vineyard has the right to eat its fruit, so the Christian minister has the right to be supported (1 Cor. 9:7; 2 Tim. 2:6). Just as the farmer waits patiently for his fruit, so we must wait patiently for the coming of the Lord (Jas. 5:7). Just as Elijah's prayer brought rain and the earth produced fruit, so we must pray with faith (5:18).

Again, in our Lord's parables there are several references to fruit which are circumstantial detail rather than spiritually significant. In the parable of the wheat and the tares, 'the blade sprang up and brought forth fruit' (Mt. 13:26). In the parable of the wicked husbandmen, 'the season of fruits drew near' (21:34). In the parable of the seed growing secretly, 'when the fruit is ripe', the farmer puts in the sickle (Mk. 4:29). And the rich fool in Lk. 12:17 says, 'I have not where to bestow my fruits'. Probably no spiritual significance should be attached to any of these instances.

In all the remaining cases, however, the spiritual significance is central. In all of them 'fruit' means 'result'. These results may be divided into three classes: results of action, results of character and results of conversion, though it is not always possible to be rigid in the classification.

1. *Action.* This type of result is stressed by John the Baptist: 'Bring forth fruit worthy of repentance' (Mt. 3:8; Lk. 3:8), do actions which show that your repentance is genuine. 'Every tree that bringeth not forth good fruit is hewn down' (Mt. 3:10; Lk. 3:9), every man who does not produce good actions comes under judgment.

Jesus stresses this even more. In Mt. 7:16-20 the word 'fruit' is repeated seven times. Mt. 12:33 reiterates the teaching in slightly different wording and uses the word three times. Lk. 6:43 has two parallels to Mt. 7:18 and a further parallel occurs between Lk. 6:44 and Mt. 12:33. Jesus wants to make it absolutely clear that men's natures are known from their actions. A good man's actions are good, and a bad man's actions are evil. Neither can act contrary to their nature. Jesus goes to the heart of things even more deeply than the Baptist. His word about a corrupt tree bringing forth evil fruit is matched by Paul's word in Rom. 7:5, where he speaks of sinful passions working in men to bring forth fruit unto death. There is no other fruit that sin can produce.

On the other hand there is a notable example of the fruit of good action in Rom. 15:28. The A.V. and R.V. have the rather obscure translation, 'When I have sealed to them this fruit', but behind this phrase lies the story of Paul's collection for the Jerusalem poor, which he raised among the Gentile churches. This collection was the fruit of their new faith, shown in a very tangible form by generous giving. The New English Bible translates, 'When I have delivered the proceeds under my own seal'. 'Proceeds' is perhaps a rather materialistic term, but these Gentile Christians are showing their faith in a materialistic, and therefore very obvious way. It is not mere words; it is action. Not that the New Testament despises words. Heb. 13:15 has the beautiful phrase 'the fruit of the lips', to describe the praise of God by those whose goodness of heart bears fruit in the thanksgiving which they offer to Him.

2. *Character.* This is what Paul speaks of in Rom. 6:22, when he says that his readers have their 'fruit unto sanctification';

F

in Christ they have become people with a new character. He
may also be thinking of this new character in Rom. 7:4, when he
speaks of bringing forth fruit unto God. Certainly he has
character in mind in Phil. 4:17; the fruit for which he seeks in
the Philippians is not primarily action, the gift of their generosity;
it is the new spirit that lies behind it. In Col. 1:10 fruit-bearing
is linked with action, but it is linked further with increase in the
knowledge of God, that is, with growth in character. Heb. 12:11
also refers to character, when it describes discipline as producing
'the fruit of righteousness', and Jas. 3:17-18 has a beautiful description of the Christian character as being, among other things,
full of good fruits and fruitful in righteousness. Perhaps also it is
of character that Jesus is thinking at the end of the parable of the
wicked husbandmen, when He speaks of those who will render,
or bring forth, fruit.

3. *Conversion.* 'Fruit' frequently designates those who are
won by the message of the Gospel. This is the fruit of the Word
in the parable of the sower (Mt. 13:8, 23; Mk. 4:8, 20; Lk. 8:8,
15), though in each case it is applied firstly to those who are
converted by the Word and then to the converts that they themselves make. The seed which fell among thorns bore no fruit
(Mk. 4:7); no conversion followed. In Jn. 4:36 Jesus uses the
term with regard to the Samaritan converts who are being won.
In 12:24 the reference is to the converts who are won through His
death. In 15:2, 8, 16 there may be more than one application,
but it could well be a warning that the only effective Christians
are those who win others for Christ. In Rom. 1:13 Paul is
certainly thinking of the new converts that he hopes to make in
Rome. The difficult phrase in Phil. 1:22; 'If to live in the flesh
is the fruit of my work' may have the same idea in mind. Kingsley Williams translates: 'If it is to be life in the flesh, this will mean
fruit from my work'. And in Col. 1:6 Paul describes the Gospel
as 'bearing fruit and increasing' in the growth of the Church.

Against all this, one great criticism that Jesus makes of the
Jews is for their barrenness. The parable of the barren fig tree
was aimed at them (Lk. 13:6, 7, 9). Whether the incident of the
barren fig tree in Matthew and Mark is a development of the
parable or an actual occurrence, its condemnation (Mt. 21:19;
Mk. 11:14) and its subsequent withering away must have been
intended as a lesson to the Jews. The wicked husbandmen also
are the Jews. They were asked for fruit (Mt. 21:34; Mk. 12:2;
Lk. 20:10) and they would not render what was due. Paul's

criticism of those who were servants of the Law and of sin is that they bore no fruit (Rom. 6:21).

But the fact of being a Christian does not enable a man to bear any fruit by his own power—only if he abides in Christ (Jn. 15:4, 5). God's earth bears fruit of itself, not by the farmer's efforts (Mk. 4:28). The heavenly tree of life yields its own fruits (Rev. 22:2). So the fruit of our righteousness comes through Jesus Christ (Phil. 1:11), and through being in the light of the Lord (Eph. 5:9). Love, joy, peace and all the Christian virtues are not self-achieved or self-grown; they are the fruit of the Spirit of God (Gal. 5:22).

45. CARE

The word *Care* is used in two senses. It may either mean anxiety and worry, or it may mean loving concern and attention. 'The cares of this age' mean its worries and anxieties; 'He cares for you' is the assurance of God's loving concern. In both cases there is fixed concentration upon an object, but in the first this leads to self-centred worry; in the second, self is forgotten because of the needs of the object of attention.

The Greek Testament has two words for *Care*, each used in both of the senses carried by the English word. (This double sense is of course found in many other languages; cp. the two senses of *kavalai* in Tamil). The first, in its verbal form, is *melō*, which in varying forms occurs fifteen times. The second is *merimnaō*, which in different forms is found thirty-one times. The two words are practically synonyms and will be treated together. Those of us, however, who use the English Authorised Version must remember that this is one of the cases where the meaning of the English language has changed in the course of the centuries; e.g. Mt. 6:34 there says 'Take no thought for the morrow', which would now mean 'Do not think about tomorrow', whereas Jesus means 'Do not be anxious about tomorrow'; and Phil. 4:6 there says 'Be careful for nothing', which would now mean 'You can be careless about everything', whereas Paul means 'Do not be anxious about anything'.

1. We look first at the New Testament references to the besetting sin of worry over things in the present. It is described in Mt. 13:22 (cp. Mk. 4:19) as the worry which belongs to this age when we are out of touch with the heavenly age, and it is

associated both in these places and in Lk. 8:14 with things like dependence on riches and pleasure in lust, as something that stifles God's word and prevents it from bearing fruit in us. Worry is not only an attitude for which we are to be pitied. It is a sin, because it separates us from God. Lk. 21:34 speaks of it along with drunkenness as something which weighs us down so that we are unable to respond to God's call. Mt. 6:25 and Lk. 12:22 bring it home personally: 'Be not anxious for your life'. The word here translated 'life', or sometimes 'soul', could perhaps better be rendered 'self': 'Be not anxious for your self, for anything associated with your personal needs or condition', and Mt. 6:28 applies it particularly to anxiety about a common matter such as our clothes. Both Mt. 6:25 and Lk. 12:22 also speak of anxiety about food. It was this that was Martha's concern. Jesus has to reprove her gently: 'Martha, Martha, thou art anxious and troubled about many things' (Lk. 10:41). It may be a simple rebuke to her for trying to provide too elaborate a meal: 'One course is enough'. We all know how easy it is to go wrong through anxiously trying to do more than necessary.

In 1 Cor. 7:21 Paul advises the Christian slave not to worry about his status; he can serve the Lord whatever his human condition. That is not approval of slavery, but it is a statement that our external situation is not the thing that matters most. Later in the chapter he applies the same advice in connection with marriage. Frankly he does not approve of marriage as the better state in the world as he knows it. He knows that husband and wife are often more anxious to please each other than to please the Lord (7:32-34), and he wants Christians to be free from such subordinate anxieties in the world which he believes is passing away (7:31-32). This ignores the fact that husband and wife can set each other free from anxiety so that they can the more freely serve Christ, but it is a true picture of what often happens. Paul's wisest word is in Phil. 4:6, when he bids his readers be anxious at no time, because always they can make their needs known to God. How different from the chief priests in Mt. 28:14, planning a lie with the soldiers and telling them not to be anxious, because they will talk the governor over if necessary!

2. We worry not only about the present but about the future. Nearly all of us worry about the length of our life. There is a word in Mt. 6:27 and Lk. 12:25 which is usually translated 'stature': 'Which of you by being anxious can add one cubit

unto his stature?' But in the Greek of the period the word more often means 'age' and, though we do not speak of a cubit in this connection, we do talk of the span of life. Probably, therefore, Jesus meant: 'Which of you can prolong his life by worrying?' Few of us want to be taller than we are; most of us want to live longer—but worry usually shortens life, not lengthens it.

Many Christians in the first century worried about the future in another connection. They were often in danger of persecution, and worried about what they should say when brought to trial. 'Don't be anxious in a situation like that', says Jesus; 'trust the Holy Spirit to tell you what to say' (Mk. 13:11; Lk. 12:11, 12; Mt. 10:19, 20). In fact the general principle is 'Don't worry about tomorrow; let tomorrow do its own worrying' (Mt. 6:34). This is not a command against planning; it is a command against lack of trust.

3. We are not to be anxious, but we are not to be indifferent. There were the men in Mt. 22:5 who were invited to the wedding feast, and simply did not care to accept. There is always the danger of our caring nothing about the great salvation offered us in Christ (Heb. 2:3). Even Timothy had to be warned not to be slack and indifferent about the divine gift that had been given him (1 Tim. 4:14). Judas is indifferent to the poor, whatever he may say (Jn. 12:6), and Gallio too is not concerned with the quarrels among the Jews (Acts 18:17); it was hardly his business to be. Worst of all is the man whose business is to look after the flock, but cares only for the money and his own safety (Jn. 10:13).

4. Our privilege as Christians is to care for one another. It was the word of Jesus in the parable of the Good Samaritan, who not only took care of the wounded man himself, but arranged for the innkeeper to continue the care (Lk. 10:34, 35). So the business of the bishop is to take care of the Church of God (1 Tim. 3:5), and Paul promises that Timothy will care truly for the Philippians (Phil. 2:20). Paul himself has the care of all the churches on his shoulders (2 Cor. 11:28), but he too, on his journey to Rome, receives the loving care and attention of the Christians at Sidon (Acts 27:3). If we are truly a body, then we are held together by care for one another (1 Cor. 12:25).

But any caring spirit in us is due to the central fact that God cares for us. As the woman sought caringly for the silver coin until it was found, because she valued it, so He seeks for us

(Lk. 15:8). We can cast all our care upon Him, because He cares for us (1 Pet. 5:7). The very fact that the disciples during the storm (Mk. 4:38) and Martha during her cooking (Lk. 10:40) can say to Jesus 'Carest Thou not?' is evidence, even by their misunderstanding, of how much they relied on His care.

And yet this care is not given indiscriminately. It puts first things first: Jesus's enemies can say to Him: 'Thou carest for no one' (Mt. 22:16; Mk. 12:14). He cares for truth and not for men's opinions of Him. God, says Paul, does not care particularly for animals, when His heart is set upon men (1 Cor. 9:9). And it can be forfeited: there is the solemn reminder in Heb. 8:9 that God had to transfer His care from the Jews when they ceased to obey His covenant.

But the true child of God may count on His care. There is an early inscription with a man's name: Amerimnos, 'Mr Carefree'. It has been suggested that he was given that name when he became a Christian. Coming to Christ had set him free from the cares of this world, and taught him to cast all his care upon God. What could be better than to be reminded of this every time anyone spoke to him?

46. GIVING (i)

The New Testament teaches that everything good which we possess is God's gift, and it is not surprising that the simple verb *didōmi*, I give, occurs four hundred and eleven times. This chapter will deal with its main uses in the gospels, leaving the rest of the New Testament for the next.

The total figures for each gospel are: Matthew fifty-six, Mark thirty-nine, Luke fifty-nine, John seventy-two. The main uses may be classified as follows: (1) God's gifts to His Son, (2) The gifts of God His Son to men, (3) The mis-giving of men and of Satan, (4) The true giving of men to God and to their fellow-men.

1. 'The Father loves the Son, and has given all things into His hand' (Jn. 3:35) is the heart and basis of all New Testament teaching on Giving. That story begins with Gabriel's promise that 'the Lord God shall give unto Him the throne of His father David' (Lk. 1:32). In His ministry He is given power to do miracles (Mt. 9:8; Jn. 11:22), power to judge (Jn. 5:22, 27), life in Himself (5:26), works to accomplish (5:36; 17:4), commandment as to what He is to say (12:49). Seven times over He

speaks of His disciples as having been given to Him by God
(Jn. 6:37; 10:29; 17:2, 6, 9, 24; 18:9), sometimes using the simple
phrase 'those whom Thou hast given me', sometimes (e.g.
17:24 in R.V.) speaking of them as a complete whole: 'that which
Thou hast given me'. And because they have been given to Him,
He will not lose any of them (6:39), but will give them eternal life
(17:2). In 17:7 He says 'All things whatsoever Thou hast given
me are from Thee', a statement that might seem a little obvious
until we remember that it is possible to give away that which is
not yours to give, or that you have not made your own. God
does not do that, and when Jesus speaks of His Father giving
Him His own Name (Jn. 17:11, 12), He is speaking of God's
very nature and character. So too when He speaks of the gift
of God's glory to Him in 17:22, 24. And the glory in John
includes the Cross, so that in 18:11 Jesus can speak also of the
cup which the Father has given Him, and in 13:3, 'knowing that
the Father had given all things into His hands' He can lay aside
His garments and perform the act of humility of which the Cross
is the ultimate symbol. Then in the end His final word can be:
'All authority has been given to me in heaven and on earth'
(Mt. 28:18).

2. God has given all things to His Son—and both Father
and Son give in abundance to us men. Jesus mentions few
material gifts. He asks men to pray for daily bread to be given
(Mt. 6:11). There is also the gift of bread at the feeding of the
five thousand (Mk. 6:41 and parallels), but that was not simply a
material gift. John, after telling the story of the miracle, links
it with the giving of Christ's flesh for the life of the world (6:51),
and Jesus at the Last Supper gives the bread and gives the cup
as His body and His blood (Mk. 14:22, 23). The divine gifts to
men are primarily spiritual: the disciples are given the mystery
of the Kingdom of God (Mk. 4:11); it is the Father's good
pleasure to give them the Kingdom (Lk. 12:32); they are given
authority over unclean spirits (Mk. 6:7), and the right word to
speak when they are brought to judgment (Mk. 13:11); God's
word, given by Him to Christ, is passed on to them (Jn. 17:8);
so also is the example of humility (13:15); and they are given
Christ's peace, not the world's (14:27)—in fact Christ did not
come to give peace in the earth (Lk. 12:51).

Supremely Christ's disciples are given the gift of His own
life, the ransom or 'costly deliverance' (to use Vincent Taylor's
phrase) which He announces in Mk. 10:45, the continuation of

what God did when He gave His only-begotten Son to the world
(Jn. 3:16). Christ gave His life, living and dying, so that He
might give life to men (6:27, 33; 10:28). And so that we may
be guided and strengthened in this given life, the Father gives us
another Paraclete, the Holy Spirit (14:16), the Spirit who was
not given until Jesus was glorified (7:39), but who is given without
measure both to Christ and to all believers (3:34—a difficult
verse, but this is its probable interpretation).

We cannot receive anything unless it is given to us (Mt. 19:11;
Jn. 3:27). We cannot even turn to Christ without its being a
drawing from God (6:65). But we can ask and it will be given
(Mt. 7:7, 11; Jn. 4:10), though we must ask in Christ's spirit
(Jn. 15:16; 16:23). We need too the capacity to receive. Jesus
gives nothing to those who cannot or will not receive (Mk. 8:12;
Jn. 19:9), though sometimes He gives something that is a stern
challenge, as He gave the sop to Judas (Jn. 13:26). And from
those to whom He gives, much is required (Lk. 12:48).

3. In contrast, however, with the divine giving, men often
refuse to give, or they give wrongly. Read the story of Herod
and Salome in Mk. 6, and note the word 'give' in verses 22, 23, 25
and 28. Look at the request of James and John in Mk. 10:37:
'Give unto us that we may sit. . . .'—and at the reply of Jesus in
verse 40: 'not mine to give'. Note the Pharisee in Lk. 7:44, 45:
'Thou gavest me no water . . . no kiss', and the man in bed in
Lk. 11:7, 8, who at first will not rise and give, and then does so
only reluctantly. Consider the four 'gives' in the parable of the
Prodigal Son in Lk. 15: 'Give me the portion' (12), 'No man gave
unto him' (16), 'You never gave me a kid' (29). And then by
contrast in verse 22 the father: 'Give a ring to his hand' (as
the literal translation is). When the Jews in Jn. 9:24 told the
man that was blind to 'give glory to God', they were using an
idiom that meant 'Tell the truth'—but really they were urging
him to deny it. And at the end of the gospel story Judas three
times drags the word still lower: the value of the ointment that
might have been 'given to the poor' (Jn. 12:5), the question to
the chief priests: 'What are ye willing to give me?' (Mt. 26:15),
and the final token of betrayal that he gave in Mk. 14:44. At
the beginning Satan had tempted the Lord with 'All these things
will I give thee, if thou wilt fall down and worship me' (Mt. 4:9).
Jesus resisted that temptation. Judas could not—and for him
would be the word: 'What shall a man give in exchange for his
soul?' (Mk. 8:37).

4. But there are men who have learnt how to give truly, giving to men as God has given to them — and, better still, giving back to God. Zacchaeus could say 'The half of my goods I give to the poor' (Lk. 19:8). The Good Samaritan completes his work of mercy by giving two pence to the innkeeper (Lk. 10:35). The Samaritan leper returns to give glory to God (17:18). After Bartimaeus has received his sight, all the people give praise to God (18:43).

The whole reason for our giving lies in the words: 'Freely ye received, freely give' (Mt. 10:8). Zacchaeus had received the forgiveness of God, the leper had been cleansed, the crowd had witnessed a gift to a blind man—and all made the right response, the one that God demands. 'Give, and it shall be given to you' (Lk. 6:38) is a true description of what often happens—generosity does beget generosity. But this must never be a motive. Jesus's word is 'Give to everyone who asks you' (Lk. 6:30). That, as we have seen, is God's practice. It does not mean that we should let ourselves be foolishly imposed upon. Jesus Himself laid down the restriction that all asking must be in His Name (Jn. 15:16), that is, in His spirit. But essentially we are to be as giving in our way as God is in His, even though we cannot approach His standard (Mt. 7:11). And when we are willing to receive God's gift of His Son, He gives us the right to become His children (Jn. 1:12), children who learn to give as He does.

47. GIVING (ii)

In the previous chapter we looked at the main uses of the verb *didōmi*, I give, in the gospels. We now look at its remaining occurrences in the rest of the New Testament. There are a hundred and eighty-five of these. Acts has the verb thirty-five times. Paul and the Pastoral Epistles have it seventy-two times. Revelation, which has some unique senses of the word, has it altogether no fewer than fifty-eight times. The remaining twenty uses are divided in small numbers between the other epistles. We shall take the same classification as for the gospels: (1) God's gifts to His Son, (2) The gifts of God or of His Son to men, (3) The misgiving of men and of Satan, (4) The true giving of men to God and to their fellow-men.

1. Naturally the first is not so freely illustrated as in the

gospels.   The gift of Resurrection Life (Acts 2:27; 13:35), 'the children whom God has given me' (Heb. 2:13), the gift of glory (1 Pet. 1:21) and the gift of revelation (Rev. 1:1) are the only examples.

2.   When we come to the gifts of God and of His Son to men, the instances are far more numerous.   (The translation is not always 'give'.   It may be 'grant', 'bestow', 'put', 'show'; but the Greek word is always the same).   There are a few material or physical gifts: rain (Acts 14:17; Jas. 5:18), life and breath (Acts 17:25), gifts to the poor in the Old Testament quotation in 2 Cor. 9:9; but, as in the gospels, God's main gifts are spiritual: signs of His power (Acts 2:19; 14:3), soundness that is spiritual as well as physical (3:16), boldness (4:29), repentance (5:31; 11:18; 2 Tim. 2:25), wisdom often (Acts 7:10; 1 Cor. 12:8; Eph. 1:17; Jas. 1:5; 2 Pet. 3:15), deliverance that is more than physical (Acts 7:25); an inheritance with the saints (20:32), unanimity (Rom. 15:5), the gift of ministry (1 Cor. 3:5), victory over death (1 Cor. 15:57), the ministry of reconciliation (2 Cor. 5:18), the power of caring (2 Cor. 8:16), authority for building up (2 Cor. 10:8; 13:10), the fulfilment of promise (Gal. 3:22), power (Eph. 3:16), the various ministers of the Church (4:11), utterance (6:19), peace (2 Thess. 3:16), power and love and discipline (2 Tim. 1:7), mercy (1:16, 18), understanding (2:7; 1 Jn. 5:20), the inward law in the heart (Heb. 8:10; 10:16), love (1 Jn. 3:1), life (5:11, 16), the rewards to him who overcomes (Rev. 2:7, 17, 26; 3:21), and the water of life (Rev. 21:6).   What a list of gifts it is, and how far we are from having accepted a fraction of what we are offered!

Yet even this is not the full list.   These are specific gifts, but behind them all is the gift of Christ Himself for our salvation (Acts 4:12), for manifestation to His chosen (10:40), for our deliverance (Gal. 1:4), to be our Head (Eph. 1:22), as our ransom (1 Tim. 2:6), to redeem and purify us (Tit. 2:14).

There is also the gift of the Holy Spirit, given to those who obey (Acts 5:32), given by the laying on of the apostles' hands (8:18), given to the Gentiles (11:17; 15:8) given to Paul and his Roman readers (Rom. 5:5), given for spiritual profit (1 Cor. 12:7), given as an earnest of what is to come (2 Cor. 1:22; 5:5), given to the Thessalonians (1 Thess. 4:8), given to John and his readers (1 Jn. 3:24), given for the assurance of abiding in God (4:13).

Then there is the gift of God's grace: given for humility (Rom. 12:3), for the exercise of spiritual gifts (12:6), for Paul's Gentile ministry (15:15; Gal. 2:9; Eph. 3:2, 7, 8; Col. 1:25), for the enrichment of the Corinthians (1 Cor. 1:4), for the foundation of a church (3:10), for generosity (2 Cor. 8:1), as God's gift to all (Eph. 4:7), for comfort and hope (2 Thess. 2:16), through Christ from eternity (2 Tim. 1:9), to the humble (Jas. 4:6; 1 Pet. 5:5). So much and more can grace perform.

But sometimes God's gifts are withheld, or are given for discipline or punishment. Abraham was not given inheritance in the promised land (Acts 7:5). Paul was given a thorn in the flesh (2 Cor. 12:7). Israel in Rom. 11:8 was given a spirit of stupor. In 2 Thess. 1:8 those who do not obey the gospel are given retribution. The church at Thyatira is given according to her works (Rev. 2:23). In fact so much of the giving in the book of Revelation is to angelic or demonic powers for purposes of punishment or evil-doing (Rev. 6:2, 4, 8; 7:2; 9:1, 3; 13:5, 7, 14, 15, 16). Whatever our interpretation of the detail, the broad effect is that God sometimes has to give hard things in order that His kingdom may come.

3. A few examples of men's failure to give, or of their wrong giving, can also be found in this second half of the New Testament. Simon Magus says 'Give me this power', and thinks that it can be purchased (Acts 8:19). Felix hopes that Paul will give him a bribe (24:26). Herod does not give glory to God (12:23). Paul knows the danger of giving occasion of stumbling (2 Cor. 6:3). He also warns the Ephesians not to give place to the devil (Eph. 4:27). A man may say fair words to the poor, but not give them what they need (Jas. 2:16). Men blaspheme God instead of giving Him the glory (Rev. 16:9) — and the dragon and the kings of the earth give their power to the beast for him to carry on his evil work (Rev. 13:2, 4; 17:13).

4. Nevertheless, many men have learnt from God the lesson of true giving. Peter can say to the lame man in Acts 3:6: 'What I have, that give I thee'. He holds nothing back. He has received freely; he gives freely. Moses does the same in 7:38: he has received God's oracles; he gives them to his people. Peter merely gives his hand to Tabitha in 9:41, but it is to raise her from death. Abraham both gives glory to God in Rom. 4:20 and a tithe of his spoils to Melchizedek in Heb. 7:4.

Paul in Rom. 14:12 speaks of another giving that is due to God: the giving account of oneself. As one who has learnt how to do that, he himself has sometimes in the light of it to give judgment to his readers: in 1 Cor. 7:25 he gives his judgment as one who has obtained mercy; in 2 Cor. 8:10 he gives it in connection with the performing of a Christian charity. By none of his actions does he want to give hindrance to the gospel (1 Cor. 9:12). He wants always to give his readers an occasion of glorying on his behalf (2 Cor. 5:12), to give himself as an example to them to imitate (2 Thess. 3:9). As his own speech has given grace to his hearers, he wants theirs to do the same (Eph. 4:29). And many of them do respond. The Macedonian churches, before giving any money, first gave their own selves to the Lord (2 Cor. 8:5), and the Galatians would, if possible, have plucked out their eyes and given them to Paul (Gal. 4:15).

And the New Testament finishes, where Abraham in bygone ages had begun (Rom. 4:20) with earth and heaven giving God the glory. The angel flying in mid heaven with the eternal gospel to proclaim cries 'Fear God and give Him glory' (Rev. 14:7). The great multitude in 19:6, 7 say 'Hallelujah: for the Lord our God, the Almighty reigns... Let us give the glory unto Him'. And the living creatures give glory and honour and thanks to Him that sits on the throne (4:9).

Why this emphasis in the New Testament on giving? It is summed up best in that word of the Lord which Paul quotes in Acts 20:35 — the only word of Jesus in the New Testament outside the gospels: 'It is more blessed to give than to receive'. That is true. God proved it true in giving His only Son (Jn. 3:16), and when men act upon it as true, then they can enter into His Kingdom.

48. RECEIVING

The counterpart of giving is receiving. Both are essential elements in our Christian life.

There are two main words so translated in the New Testament: *lambanō*, which means to *take* of one's own accord as well as to *receive* what is offered, and *dechomai*, which means only to *receive* or *accept* what is offered to one. The second word is therefore the more important of the two for our present purpose, and this chapter will limit itself to it.

In its simple form it occurs fifty-five times. Combined with various prepositions which modify its meaning to a greater or less extent, it occurs another fifty-three times, making a hundred and eight instances in all. Luke has forty-eight of these in his gospel and in Acts, Paul has twenty-four, Matthew has nine, Mark and Hebrews eight each. It occurs rarely in John's writings.

The instances may be divided into four classes: the receiving of 1. Some material object, 2. A truth, 3. A person or people, 4. God or Christ.

1. The material reception may be of something quite ordinary like the receiving of letters (Acts 22:5; 28:21). More important-ly, it may be the rain which the farmer depends on receiving for the growth of his crops (Jas. 5:7), or the moving of the water which the sick depend on receiving for their cure (Jn. 5:3). (In this verse the word is translated 'waiting for', but its full meaning is 'expecting to receive'). It may be the receiving and passing on of an heirloom such as the Tabernacle (Acts 7:45, where the translation in the R.V. is 'in their turn', the form of the word here literally meaning 'receiving as successors'). It may imply receiving as an act of fellowship, as Paul did when he received the gifts from Philippi (Phil. 4:18). The word is used in Luke 22:17, where the R.V. says that Jesus *received* a cup, and the A.V. that He *took* it. If the R.V. emphasis is right, it would mean that the cup was offered Him by a disciple, an element that is emphasised in the Church of S. India Liturgy when the elements are brought forward by members of the congregation. The parable of the Unrighteous Steward may almost be called a parable of receiving: the literal translation of what the steward says to the debtors is 'Receive your documents' (Lk. 16:6, 7). He makes them a generous offer, which they accept. His motive is that they in turn may *receive* him into their houses (v. 4), and the conclusion that Jesus draws is that, if we make right use of such a dangerous thing as money, God will receive us into the eternal home (v. 9). Two instances in Hebrews indicate by plays upon words the true Christian attitude to the material: the writer says that his readers received the plundering of their possessions with joy (10:34), and that others who were tortured would not receive their deliverance (11:35). Their minds were on something better, so that plunder and torture were things that they could accept as gifts.

2. The receiving of God's truth, God's message, God's salvation, God's kingdom, is a very frequent emphasis, of which there are some twenty-five instances. *Receiving God's Word* is a phrase used in Mk. 4:20; Lk. 8:13; Acts 8:14; 11:1; 17:11;

1 Thess. 1:6; 2:13; Jas. 1:21. In Acts 2:41 the direct reference is to Peter's word, but of course Peter would have stressed that it was not really his but God's. So in 7:38 it is Moses who gives the living oracles to Israel, but only because he himself has received them from God. In Mt. 11:14 it is a plain statement of fact that Jesus urges the multitudes to accept: 'If you are willing to *receive* it, this is Elijah who is to come'.

Other divine gifts which are offered for our acceptance are 'the things of the Spirit' (1 Cor. 2:14), the grace of God (2 Cor. 6:1), the Gospel (2 Cor. 11:4), the witness of Christians concerning Christ (Acts 22:18) and concerning Christian ethics (16:21), the promises of God (Heb. 11:17), and the love of truth, which can result in our salvation (2 Thess. 2:10). In connection with salvation, note especially Eph. 6:17, which should not be '*Take* the helmet of salvation', but '*Accept* or *receive* it'. Salvation is not something that we take for ourselves; it is a gift to be accepted from God.

Elsewhere the English translation is 'wait for' or 'look for', but the fundamental meaning is the same, though the time is transferred to the future. We are expecting to *receive*. In Rom. 8:19 creation waits expecting to receive God's revelation of the New Humanity. In 8:23 we wait, expecting to receive our adoption, and in 8:25 one of the essentials of hope is given as patient expectation of receiving. This note of receiving the fulfilment of our hope is also emphasised in Acts 24:15; Gal. 5:5 and in Tit. 2:13, where it is linked with the appearing of Jesus Christ. In 1 Cor. 1:7 Paul writes that the Corinthians also are expecting to receive this. Abraham, in Heb. 11:10, has the hope of receiving God's gift of the permanent home that He Himself has created. God's gifts may not come immediately, but they are worth waiting for.

3. The receiving of *people* is another frequent New Testament emphasis, with about twenty-seven references. *Dechomai* is sometimes translated *welcome* in such contexts. We do not always welcome people who come to us, and some of the New Testament references are to this negative attitude, but people can always be gifts from God, to be received either for our own benefit or for the help that we can give them. Jesus speaks of the benefit that comes to those who welcome a prophet or a righteous man because of what they are (Mt. 10:41) and of the loss that is suffered by those who reject His disciples when they come (Mt. 10:14; Mk. 6:11; Lk. 9:5; 10:10- by contrast note Lk. 10:8-9).

Paul often writes of this welcoming spirit. The Galatians had received him as an angel of God (Gal. 4:14). He was willing for the Corinthians to think him foolish, so long as they accepted him (2 Cor. 11:16). His companion, Luke, speaks several times of the way that Paul and his party were received and welcomed (Acts 15:4; 17:7; 21:17; 28:7). He himself writes to the Romans about receiving Phoebe and making her welcome (Rom. 16:2), to the Corinthians about Titus (2 Cor. 7:15), to the Philippians about Epaphroditus (Phil. 2:29), and to the Colossians about Mark (Col. 4:10). He was always eager to receive people himself. Almost the last verse of Acts (28:30) mentions that, and Acts 17:16 and 1 Cor. 16:11 have the same note of eager waiting for his friends. Nor was Paul the only welcoming spirit. In Acts 18:27 the Ephesians write to the Corinthians in the same way to ask them to welcome Apollos. The New Testament is critical of those who will not receive others. Diotrephes is twice condemned for this (3 Jn. 9:10), and the Corinthians are censured because they begin eating at the common meal without waiting to receive all who are joining in it (1 Cor. 11:33). Even Rahab the harlot is twice praised for her willingness to receive the spies (Heb. 11:31; Jas. 2:25).

This welcoming spirit springs from Him who received sinners and ate with them (Lk. 15:2), who welcomed the crowd and spoke to them of the Kingdom of God (9:11), and to whom Stephen could pray, 'Lord Jesus, receive my spirit' (Acts 7:59). His Father too promises 'I will receive you' (2 Cor. 6:17), and receives us as sons whom He disciplines as we need (Heb. 12:6).

4. Our response must therefore be the welcoming of God and Christ and all that they have to give. St. Luke in his early chapters gives the picture of those who were eager to receive (2:25, 38), and of Simeon who actually did receive the infant Christ into his arms (2:28). Others too welcomed Him: the crowd (8:40), Martha (10:38), Zacchaeus (19:6), the Galileans (Jn. 4:45). Some received or rejected Him through their attitudes to His followers (Mk. 9:37; Lk. 9:48), and those attitudes involved acceptance or rejection of God. The Samaritans would not receive Him on His way to Jerusalem (Lk. 9:53), but Joseph of Arimathaea was waiting to receive His Kingdom (Mk. 15:43; Lk. 23:51), and so are all those with the receptive, dependent spirit of a child (Mk. 10:15; Lk. 18:17). He has now been received back by God into the heavenly home (Acts 3:21), but we are to keep on being ready to receive Him (Phil. 3:20; Heb.

9:28) and to welcome His mercy (Jude 21). Indeed our whole attitude is to be that of men waiting to welcome their Lord (Lk. 12:36), not only at the End of all things but throughout our daily life. He wants us to be always receptive, because only then can He give.

49. THINKING

Psychology has analysed our mental processes. The Concordance shows how much more deeply the New Testament has done this in the spiritual sphere, showing the relation and reaction of the human mind to the great realities which Christ's coming makes clear. This chapter will examine four of the words that the New Testament uses for our thinking on the things of the spirit.

1. The first of these is *noeō*, fourteen times, and its intensive form *katanoeō*, also fourteen times. Not always, but most frequently, this means to *perceive*, to do what a mind should do: be quick at observing, and at seeing the significance of what you observe; not going round with your eyes half shut, and your mental processes in need of a good oiling. 'Do you not perceive that whatever goes into the man from outside cannot defile him?' (Mk. 7:18): are you so befogged with all this business of ceremonial law that your eyes cannot pierce through to realise the fact that the question of clean and unclean food is irrelevant in God's sight? 'Let him that reads *understand* (Mk. 13:14): let him see that Jesus is not just talking about some strange language in the book of Daniel. He has got contemporary history in mind. 'The invisible things of Him since the creation of the world are clearly seen, being perceived through the things that are made' (Rom. 1:20): you can look at the world around, it should be obvious to any pagan with his eyes open that it is *God's* creation (cp. Heb. 11:3). 'Whereby, when you read, ye can perceive my understanding in the mystery of Christ' (Eph. 3:4): can you really see the thing as I see it—that the Gentiles *are* fellow-heirs along with the Jews? or are your mental spectacles so dirty with prejudice that you see only what is on them, and not the truth beyond?

And then using the intensive form of the word: *Consider*, Jesus invites us to follow the process of perception to the end. Don't just see the crows squawking away near your house, but realise that God cares even for those impudent creatures (Lk.

12:24). Don't just cut the wild flowers indifferently along with the grass, to dry for fuel, but realise the creative work of God in them (12:27). When Moses tries to see into the heart of the mystery of the burning bush (Acts 7:31, 32), he is checked. He must not presume too far. But when we come to Christian times, Heb. 3:1 invites us to 'consider' the Apostle and High Priest of our calling — to come to Him with the inward perceptive eye, not just glancing Him over familiarly and perfunctorily, but setting our eyes on Him, saying 'What does this coming of God into our midst really mean?', thinking the matter through to the end.

That is the kind of thinking which is rewarded. In Acts 27:27 the sailors *surmised* (and Luke uses a form of our verb that goes only half way) that land was near, but they were groping in the dark. When day came, they *perceived* it (v. 39). They still had adventures ahead, but their troubles were over. And so it is when, with open eyes and clear minds, we can perceive Christ.

2. Our second word is *logizomai*, which comes forty times in the New Testament. Thirty-four of these are in Paul, who is especially fond of it in Romans and Corinthians. This is thinking in the sense of 'reckoning it out', 'calculating', getting all the implications clear. It implies putting it all down in the accounts so that they balance; not paying out something here, something there, without being sure how it has been spent. It is used in the papyri by a careful man who had a camel foal which grew up, and so he had to change it over and 'reckon' it among the full-grown camels, to make his lists tally.

That is the kind of Christian accuracy which we need in our thinking. We are not to leave things all jumbled up and unsorted out; we are to have them straight, so that we know where we are. 'Reckonest thou this, O man', says Paul in Rom. 2:3: '*Work it out*, you critical man. Do you really calculate that you are likely to be free from condemnation yourself?' Paul himself always calculates carefully: 'I have *worked it out* that our present sufferings are a mere trifle compared with the glory which Christ has in store for us' (Rom. 8:18). 'Looking carefully at my past life, I cannot *soberly calculate* that I have any achievements to boast of' (Phil. 3:13). In Heb. 11:19 you find Abraham, faced with the greatest test of his life, quietly reckoning up that he can trust God. And Peter, at the end of his first letter (5:12), is glad to 'account' Silvanus as faithful, sure that he has expressed Peter's mind truly in the Greek which Peter does not feel quite competent to use himself.

But the surprising thing about this word for careful calculation is how often it is used in connection with *Faith*, the one sphere where we should expect to be out of the realm of debit and credit. One third of Paul's uses come in Rom. 4, in connection with the faith of Abraham: 'Abraham believed God, and it was *reckoned* to him for righteousness' (4:3). God does reckon—more carefully than we ever can—but not on the plus and minus basis that is usually the height of our achievement. He calculates, not on the pros and cons of man's character and actions, but first and chiefly on man's trust in Him. If that is there, we need not try to add up the sum of good deeds required for salvation. The one all-inclusive reckoning is made. Good works will spring out of faith. They must. If they do not, any claim to faith is hood-winking oneself. But faith alone 'counts'—and that means '*Nothing* in my hand I bring'. Not even faith saves us—only grace. But when faith is there, the way is open for God to do that reckoning which brings us home to Him.

And if good deeds do not go into the reckoning, neither (thank God) do bad ones: 'Blessed is the man whose sin the Lord does not reckon against him' (Rom. 4:8). God wants us too to be like that: 'Love does not put evil into the account book' (1 Cor. 13:5). Most church quarrels would disappear if people really accepted that. Let us have all our thinking far more clearly reckoned out than we usually have—and let us never forget that God's calculations are so often the other way up from ours, and be ready always to calculate things His way.

3. The third word, *nomizō*, comes fifteen times in the New Testament. The interesting thing about this word for thinking is that in most cases it means *wrong* thinking, or if not, at any rate *doubt*. Perhaps it is best translated 'suppose'. 'Don't suppose that I came to destroy the law' (Mt. 5:17). 'Don't suppose that I came to bring peace' (10:34). 'The first supposed that they would receive more' (Mt. 20:10)—but they didn't! 'His parents supposed Jesus to be in the company' (Lk. 2:44)—but He wasn't! 'Being, as was supposed, the son of Joseph' (3:23)—but that was far less than the truth! 'He supposed that his brethren understood' (Acts 7:25)—but they didn't! 'Thou hast thought to obtain the gift of God with money' (8:20)—what a supposition! The people of Lystra dragged Paul out of the city, 'supposing that he was dead' (14:19)—but he was still very

much alive! The Philippian jailor 'supposed that the prisoners had escaped' (16:27) — but fortunately for him he was wrong! 'We ought not to suppose that the Godhead is like unto gold or silver or stone' (17:29) — what a false way of thought! 'Trophimus whom they supposed that Paul had brought into the temple' (21:29) — what a tragic mistake! 'Supposing that godliness is a way of gain' (1 Tim. 6:5) — what supposition could be worse!

Or you find hesitation in Acts 16:13 — the apostles are not quite sure about the place of prayer; and in 1 Cor. 7:26 — Paul is not wanting to be dogmatic in his advice about celibacy; and in 7:36 — a man may be in some uncertainty about the right line of conduct towards his virgin.

All these examples point to the danger of jumping to hasty conclusions. Realise the harm it did in the cases of Jesus's parents, of Moses, of Simon Magus, of Trophimus. Realise the harm it does on wider lines if we hastily try to cut out the Old Testament (Mt. 5:17), to use Christianity as something purely inoffensive (10:34), to expect preferential treatment above others (20:10), to use our religion for profit (1 Tim. 6:5). Caution can be overdone, but it has its very important place.

We so often rush into false judgments. We judge people by hearsay, on the basis of a single meeting, on their different approach to one of our problems or pet projects, on differences that are due simply to custom and background. The New Testament makes a point of warning us against this dangerous practice. The conclusions drawn from this word for thinking may be mainly negative, but are none the less valuable. 'Judge not according to appearance, but judge righteous judgment' (Jn. 7:24) is our standard. It is a high one, but nothing less is truly Christian.

4. Our fourth word, *phroneō*, occurs twenty-seven times in the New Testament. This is the word which brings us to our very inmost thoughts. It comes from the noun which designates your 'middle' or a little higher up, your heart. This kind of thinking is not just the remote pure intellect, but that which affects the whole being, warming your heart or making it go pit-a-pat, satisfying you or perturbing you in the pit of your stomach. It is the kind that we mean when we speak of 'the thoughts of our hearts'.

Like *logizomai*, this is mainly a Pauline word. Twenty-four out of the twenty-seven uses are his, dealing with man's thought-life, bad and good. Rom. 8:5 says 'They that are after the flesh do *mind* the things of the flesh'—'fix their thoughts on' them, says Kingsley Williams. Rom. 11:20; 12:3, 16; 1 Tim. 6:17 speak in different ways of being 'high-minded' — going round with too big an opinion of yourself, letting your thoughts of yourself get up on to the level where only God should be. Phil. 3:19, on the other hand, gives the other extreme: letting your thought-life get down in the dirt—'whose god is the belly, whose glory is in their shame, who *mind* earthly things'. And in 1 Cor. 13:11 Paul talks of another danger to thought-life: the continuation by the adult of the immature thinking of the child.

By contrast with all these he writes of the thought-life that the true Christian ought to have. Five times over (Rom. 12:16; 15:5; 2 Cor. 13:11; Phil. 2:2; 4:2) he exhorts churches or individuals to 'be of the same mind' to let their thinking harmonise with that of their fellow-Christians. This does not mean regimented uniformity. It does mean putting aside merely individualistic thinking and being determined to reach a truly common mind.

Paul writes too of the mind that instinctively thinks of others because it loves. He has it himself: 'It is right of me to be thus minded on behalf of you all, because I have you in my heart' (Phil. 1:7). He is grateful for it in others: 'I rejoice in the Lord greatly, that now at length you have revived your thought for me' (4:10).

And then there is the mind that thinks upwards: '*Set your mind* on the things that are above' (Col. 3:2). Contrast that with the mind that is satisfied with a high opinion of its owner.

Centrally the Christian mind is the mind of Christ: 'Have this mind in you which was also in Christ Jesus' (Phil. 2:5). Whatever the exact exposition of this verse, its meaning is clear from the context: the disposition of Christ is a disposition that is utterly self-emptying in order that others may be saved. This was what Peter could not grasp when he rebuked the Lord for talking about His death. So Jesus had to tell him: 'Thou mindest not the things of God, but the things of men' (Mk. 8:33). 'Your way of thinking is not God's but man's' (Kingsley Williams). Peter's mental attitudes could not adjust themselves to the idea of Christ deliberately throwing Himself away. If he thought that way about his Master, he would think the same way about himself—as most of us do. That meant that Jesus had to go on and say 'If any man would come after me, let him deny himself'.

That is the mind of Christ, the mind by which alone He can bring the world to Himself.

50. TRUTH

'What is truth?' said Pilate (Jn. 18:38), but he was not capable of receiving the answer, the answer that is available in the New Testament for all who will study it.

The noun *Truth* occurs a hundred and nine times. There is a verb, to act or speak truly, which comes twice. Then two adjectives, with slightly different meanings, come twenty-six and twenty-seven times respectively, and an adverb *truly* eighteen times. This makes a total of a hundred and eighty-two, of which eighty-two are in John's Gospel and Epistles, forty in Paul, eighteen in the Synoptic gospels, and the remaining forty-two elsewhere. The figures alone show what a tremendous emphasis the New Testament, and particularly St. John, places upon truth.

A number of the uses describe what we may call simply 'the plain facts of the case', with no special religious or moral emphasis. The woman in Mk. 5:33 just comes and tells Jesus the facts. The man in the high priest's court says of Peter: 'It is a fact that this man also was with Him' (Lk. 22:59). But most of the uses of the word in the New Testament are either statements about God or about conduct, often a combination of the two. And they are nearly always concrete, not abstract, personal rather than philosophical. Perhaps the only abstract use is Pilate's. If so, the New Testament does not give him the answer he wants. It will be convenient to divide this chapter, as far as possible, to deal on the one hand with statements about God, His Son and His Spirit, and on the other with statements about human conduct, always remembering that the two can never be finally separated.

1. God Himself is true (Jn. 3:33; 8:26; Rom. 3:4). That is the axiom with which we begin. If it were not so, then the New Testament and anything written about it would be valueless. God is Reality, self-consistent, truthful in all that He says and does. And this truth is manifested in the revelation of His Son, coming among us full of grace and truth (Jn. 1:14, 17). In fact, He too *is* Truth (Jn. 14:6). Truth is in Him (2 Cor. 11:10; Eph. 4:21). He speaks Truth (Jn. 8:40, 45, 46; 16:7). The Spirit also *is* the Truth (1 Jn. 5:6; in some Bibles 5:7) and is the Spirit of Truth (Jn. 14:17; 15:26; 16:13; 1 Jn. 4:6). God's

word is truth (Jn. 17:17). His judgment is according to truth (Rom. 2:2). The Gospel too is truth (Gal. 2:5, 14; Eph. 1:13; Col. 1:5).

On the other hand, one of the descriptions of the devil is that there is no truth in him (Jn. 8:44); and people who go wrong 'hold down the truth in unrighteousness' (Rom. 1:18), exchange the truth for a lie (1:25), disobey the truth (Rom. 2:8; Gal. 5:7), are bereft of the truth (1 Tim. 6:5), miss the mark of the truth (2 Tim. 2:18), withstand the truth (3:8), turn away from the truth (Tit. 1:14), lie against the truth (Jas. 3:14), wander from the truth (5:19). Being linked with the devil automatically means turning one's back on truth.

The truth of God, however (to use the phrase of Rom. 3:7; 15:8), makes men free (Jn. 8:32). It is that into which the Spirit guides us (16:13). It is that in which God sanctifies us (17:17, 19). It is one of the fruits of His light (Eph. 5:9). It is that which is *with* us and *in* us (2 Pet. 1:12; 2 Jn. 2).

2.   This means that the whole of our conduct is to be related to truth. Often we limit truth to speaking, and the New Testament frequently emphasises this. As Jesus Himself spoke truth, so did Paul (Acts 26:25; Rom. 9:1; 2 Cor. 6:7; 7:14; 12:6; Gal. 4:16; cp. 1 Tim. 2:7), and he commanded the Ephesians to do the same (Eph. 4:25) because truth is the foundation on which society is built.

But speaking the truth involves *knowing* it too: 'You shall know the truth, and the truth shall make you free' (Jn. 8:32). Those very practical books, the Pastoral Epistles, lay considerable emphasis on knowledge of the truth, and they are thinking of knowledge of God and of right conduct together. See 1 Tim. 2:4; 4:3; 2 Tim. 2:25; 3:7; Tit. 1:1. That very different letter, the epistle to the Hebrews (10:26), uses the same phrase, and we meet it again in St. John (1 Jn. 2:21; 2 Jn. 1).

This leads on to *doing* it. Note the striking phrase 'He that does the truth' in Jn. 3:21, echoed in 1 Jn. 1:6. And translate Eph. 4:15 according to the R.V. margin: '*dealing truly* in love'. This includes speaking truly, but makes it a much wider thing than just speech. In 2 Cor. 13:8 Paul dares to say of himself that he can do nothing against the truth, but only for the truth.

Knowing the truth also involves *witnessing* to it. Jesus said that He had come into the world for this (Jn. 18:37). John the

Baptist bore his witness to it (5:33), and we are to bear witness to it as we find it in our fellow men (3 Jn. 3). The truth itself will bear witness along with us (3 Jn. 12).

The New Testament inspires us to be obedient to the truth (1 Pet. 1:22), to put on the new nature of truth which God has created for us to wear (Eph. 4:24), to let truth gird our loins for action (6:14), to believe truth (2 Thess. 2:12, 13), to teach in truth (1 Tim. 2:7), to walk in truth (2 Jn. 4; 3 Jn. 3, 4) to be fellow-workers with the truth (3 Jn. 8). Most of all, it inspires us to *love* truth (2 Thess. 2:10). Bare truth can be cold and forbidding, but not in the New Testament. Love rejoices with the truth (1 Cor. 13:6). Three times over in his letters St. John links love and truth (1 Jn. 3:18; 2 Jn. 1; 3 Jn. 1). 'Whom I love in truth'—that is how he thinks of his dear readers, and he speaks of God's grace, mercy and peace being given to us in truth and love (2 Jn. 3). And so Paul when he bids the Ephesians deal truly (4:15), says that this must be in love, for only so will the Body be truly built up, that Church of God which is the pillar and the ground of the truth (1 Tim. 3:15). John describes the true Christian as being 'of the truth' (1 Jn. 3:19), and the test whereby we can prove that we are of the truth is that we have learnt how to love both in deed and in truth (3:18).

Of the two *adjectives* for true, one (*alēthēs*) has mostly the straightforward meaning of true as opposed to false and may be passed over for the present, through its analysis is interesting. The other (*alēthinos*) means 'genuine' as opposed to 'imitation', the real thing as opposed to something that does not necessarily try to deceive, but that does not come up to the standard. Jesus in Lk. 16:11 speaks of the genuine riches as opposed to those which may be hard cash, but which are really only imitations of true wealth. He Himself is the genuine light (Jn. 1:9; 1 Jn. 2:8) as opposed to the artificial lights of the world, the genuine bread that feeds in a way that even manna could not (Jn. 6:32), the genuine vine as distinct from the merely natural one (Jn. 15:1). He twice describes God in this way (Jn. 7:28; 17:3), and the apostles contrast the only real God with idols (1 Thess. 1:9; 1 Jn. 5: 20-21). This God, who provides the real means of worship in place of what the tabernacle could do only by imitation (Heb. 8:2; 9:24) demands of us that we draw near to Him with a genuine heart (Heb. 10:22) as His genuine worshippers, worshipping in spirit and in truth (Jn. 4:23). When we can do this, then will the purposes of His truth be fulfilled.

51. HEARING

'Let every man be swift to hear, slow to speak', says St. James (1:19). It is wise advice, seldom obeyed! It may therefore be good for us to see what the New Testament has to tell us about hearing. The Greek verb, *akouō*, occurs there over four hundred times, but it will be enough to look at its sixty-two uses in the Epistles: twenty-nine in Paul's letters, sixteen in John's, and seventeen in the remainder.

Hearing must first of all include understanding. That is what St. Paul means when in 1 Cor. 14:2 he says that no one 'hears' words spoken in a 'tongue'. We have to translate 'No one understands'. Similarly in Gal. 4:21, when Paul says 'Do you not hear the law?', he means 'Do you not understand it?'

Understanding is essential when we are doing the most important hearing of all: listening to Christ and to the proclamation of His Gospel. The simple act of physical hearing is the first step: 'How shall they believe in Him whom they have not heard? and how shall they hear without a preacher?' (Rom. 10:14), but the next step is that of understanding and accepting. Israel certainly heard, but their hearing did not go on to belief (Rom. 10:18). The Gentiles on the other hand, though they had not previously heard, went on gladly to understand (15:21). Paul was sure that the Lord specially stood by him so that 'all the Gentiles might hear' (2 Tim. 4:17), and he records of the Ephesians with joy that they had heard Christ (Eph. 4:21), and of the Colossians that they had not moved away from the hope of the Gospel which they heard (Col. 1:23). (The 'if' which introduces these last two instances in the A.V. and R.V. would be better translated 'since' or 'because'. Paul has no doubts in his mind). The New Testament urges Christians to give earnest heed to what they hear (Heb. 2:1), especially as the message of the Gospel goes back in the first place to what was actually heard from the Lord Himself (2:3). St. John in particular emphasises that he is not declaring a message of his own: 'That which we have heard ... that which we have seen and heard declare we unto you' (1 Jn. 1:1, 3); 'this is the message which we have heard from *Him*' (1:5). Since the Christian message comes directly or indirectly from Christ Himself, we must surely be willing to hear it.

There is also the joy of hearing good news about our fellow-Christians. Paul is often grateful for that. He is not so wrapped up in himself that he has no power to be thankful for the good in others. He gives thanks, having heard of the Ephesians' faith in the Lord Jesus (Eph. 1:15). He does the same, having heard of the Colossians' faith and love (Col. 1:4). He uses almost the same words in writing to Philemon (v. 5). He hears of the Colossians' growth in Christ, and this leads him on to pray for its even greater extension (Col. 1:9). His love for the Philippians makes him long to hear that they are standing fast (Phil. 1:27). Nothing will give him greater satisfaction. John has the same longing to hear good news of his spiritual children: 'Greater joy have I none than this: to hear of my children walking in the truth' (3 Jn. 4). Nor is this joyful hearing limited to the apostles. The Christians of Judaea hear that their persecutor is now a preacher, and they glorify God (Gal. 1:23-24). The Ephesian Christians hear of the stewardship of God's grace given to Paul, and their profit from that gift is immeasurable. And the power to endure persecution to the end can be strengthened by hearing of the patience of Job (Jas. 5:11).

Hearing is by no means always the hearing of something sensational. It is far more often the plain hearing of the wise and true words of a teacher: 'The things you heard and saw in me, do' (Phil. 4:9); 'the pattern of sound words which you have heard from me' (2 Tim. 1:13); John's oft repeated, slightly varied 'message, command, word, which you heard from the beginning' (1 Jn. 2:7, 24; 3:11; 2 Jn. 6). James uses the word in particular for his teaching about riches and poverty: 'Hear, my beloved brethren' (Jas. 2:5). Paul tells the Corinthians that he is resisting the temptation to boast because he wants them to judge him only by what they hear from him of the truth (2 Cor. 12:6).

But the New Testament goes on with the corollary that those who are taught must themselves teach: 'What you have heard from me . . . commit to faithful men' (2 Tim. 2:2); 'take heed to your teaching, for in doing this you will save both yourself and those who hear you' (1 Tim. 4:16); let your speech 'give grace to them that hear' (Eph. 4:29). We are never to hear for ourselves alone, but always for what we may pass on to others.

Hearing must also be sympathetic hearing. The Philippians had heard that their friend Ephaphroditus was sick and were deeply concerned, so much so that, when Ephaphroditus heard of their concern, he was equally troubled (Phil. 2:26). There was no indifference there. Paul prays that in their own sufferings the fact that they hear of his suffering also may be an encouragement to them (1:30). The sense of sharing in the same persecution for Christ's sake can be a very strengthening experience.

Hearing must also involve obedience. The letter to the Hebrews has much to say about this. Three times (3:7, 15; 4:7) it quotes Psalm 95: 'O that today you would hearken to his voice' (R.S.V.), and the context makes it clear that hearkening means obeying. The ancient Israelites had heard but had disobeyed (3:16). 'They were not united by faith with them that heard' and obeyed (4:2). The world hears and obeys teachers of falsehood (1 Jn. 4:5). Obedience and disobedience depend upon willingness or unwillingness to know God (4:6). There are those who are so unwilling to hear and obey that Paul feels that God has given them 'a spirit of stupor' (Rom. 11:8), and there are those teachers who only ruin their hearers (2 Tim. 2:14); but the true hearer is the one who hears the word of the truth (Eph. 1:13), believes it, and obeys.

We must not ignore the half-dozen references to the hearing of bad news. If we listen carefully, we cannot always expect to hear what is good. Paul hears of fornication and of divisions in the Corinthian church (1 Cor. 5:1; 11:18), and of disorderly conduct in Thessalonica (2 Thess. 3:11). His converts had heard of his own misguided past (Gal. 1:13). John's readers had heard of the coming of Antichrist (1 Jn. 2:18; 4:3).

Yet far more momentous is the hearing of the voice of God. It may bring dread: when the Israelites in the wilderness heard it, they intreated that no word more should be spoken (Heb. 12:19). It may bring assurance, as when the disciples heard it on the Mount of Transfiguration (2 Pet. 1:18). It may bring the knowledge of God's grace, as it did to the Colossians (1:6). It may bring revelation of God's deepest mysteries, as it did to St. Paul (2 Cor. 12:4), and as it can do to all who love Him (1 Cor. 2:9). God does speak.

And His final word to us is that He hears also. 'If we ask anything according to His will, He hears us ' (1 Jn. 5:14). We know that our requests are heard (5:15).

So let us keep our ears open in love, as God's ears are always open. Let us listen to one another in gladness and in sympathy, and to God in understanding and obedience, so that as we listen we may receive and may give.

52. BELIEVING

This is one of the great New Testament words, far too great to be dealt with in one chapter. We shall therefore limit ourselves to its use in St. John's Gospel and First Epistle. It is also a word that is so familiar that we sometimes take it too much for granted. We shall therefore look at its fresh treatment in the New English Bible, in the hope that this will open our eyes to some fresh insights.

We are concerned now only with the verb *pisteuō*, I believe, trust, have faith, and not with the noun *pistis*, faith, though in the English translation of the verb the noun faith is often used, because English unfortunately lacks a verb formed from 'faith'.

There are three main constructions of the verb in John's writings: 1. the construction normally used to indicate belief in a fact or in a person's word. This is found twenty-one times; 2. the construction where the verb occurs without any expressed object and is normally translated by the simple word 'believe', as in Jn. 1:50. This is found thirty times; 3. the construction where the preposition 'in' follows the verb. The Greek word literally means 'into', and the phrase often expresses what Bishop Westcott called 'faith-union with Christ', belief *into* Him. This construction occurs thirty-seven times.

The Revised Version translates each of these constructions as uniformly as possible. The first is 'believe'; 'they believed the scripture' (2:22). The second is also 'believe': 'that all might believe through Him' (1:7). The third is 'believe on': 'that whosoever believeth on Him should not perish' (3:16).

The New English Bible however, allows itself considerable variation, taking each particular passage as it comes and not seeking primarily for consistency. A few of the variations hardly seem necessary, but many of them are particularly happy, and all of them set us thinking again.

1. Most of the places where John is speaking of simple belief in a person's word or in a fact are translated in the New English by the ordinary word 'believe'. Nothing more is needed. For example, 'the man believed what Jesus said' (4:50); 'If what I say is true, why do you not believe me?' (8:46). The other straightforward instances are to be found at 2:22; 4:21; 5:38, 46, 47, 6:30; 8:31, 45; 10:37, 38 ('even if you do not believe me'), 12:38; 14:11.

There are, however, one or two striking variations. In 1 Jn.
5:10 the R.V. has quite literally 'He that believeth not God hath
made him a liar'. The N.E.B. has 'He who disbelieves God
makes Him out to be a liar', thereby giving just that slightly
added emphasis that brings the sentence to life. In Jn. 10:38
the N.E.B., instead of 'believe the works', has 'accept the evidence of my deeds'. So also in 14:11, though the Greek construction is slightly different: 'accept the evidence of the deeds
themselves', and in 1 Jn. 5:10, translating our third construction,
'refusing to accept God's own witness', instead of 'hath not believed in the witness that God hath borne'. This surely lights
up the meaning.

There are two places where the N.E.B. translators have evidently
felt that our first construction means more than just believing
a person and have used the word 'trust'. In Jn. 5:24 we have
'Anyone who . . . puts his trust in Him who sent me', and in 1 Jn.
4:1 'do not trust any and every spirit'. These overtones seem
entirely justifiable. The same word 'trust' is also used to translate our third construction: 'While you have the light, trust to the
light' (Jn. 12:36), and 'Set your troubled hearts at rest. Trust
in God always; trust also in me' (14:1). I would venture to
predict that this new translation of this familiar verse will be
treasured by many to their comfort.

2. Our second construction is often translated, as in the
older versions, by the single word 'believe': 'Lord, I believe'
(9:38). The other instances are at 3:12; 4:42, 48; 6:36; 10:25, 26;
12:39; 16:31; 19:35; 20:8. Sometimes, however, a phrase that
is both stronger and more natural is used. In 6:47, instead of 'he
that believeth hath eternal life', we have 'the believer possesses
eternal life'. In 3:18 'he that believeth not' becomes 'the
unbeliever'. In 1:7 the phrase 'that all might become believers
through Him' is used. Compare also 4:41, 53.

Sometimes it is felt desirable to use the word 'faith'. 'Because
I said unto thee, I saw thee under the fig tree, believest thou?'
becomes 'Is this the ground of your faith, that I told you I saw you
under the fig tree?' (Jn. 1:50). 'To the intent ye may believe'
becomes 'for the good of your faith' (11:15). 'That you may
believe that Jesus is the Christ' becomes 'that you may hold the
faith that Jesus is the Christ' (20:31). See also 3:15; 5:44;
6:64, 69; 11:40; 14:29; 20:29.

3. The third construction is translated most simply by 'believe
in' or 'believers in': 'This deed at Cana-in-Galilee . . . led His

disciples to believe in Him' (2:11); 'the Spirit which believers in Him would receive' (7:39). Compare also 4:39; 6:29, 35; 7:5, 31, 38, 48; 10:42; 11:48; 12: 42, 44; 16:9; 1 Jn. 5:10.

Sometimes, however, the word 'faith is again used. Jn. 3:16 becomes 'every one who has faith in Him' and 3:18 continues: 'The man who puts his faith in Him'. In fact this phrase, 'putting one's faith in Christ', an act of trust and fidelity, occurs eight times in all. 'He who puts his faith in the Son has hold of eternal life' (3:36). 'Everyone who puts his faith in Him shall possess eternal life' (6:40). 'Many put their faith in Him' (8:30). The blind man, in answer to Jesus' question 'Have you faith in the Son of Man?' replies 'Tell me who he is sir, that I should put my faith in him' (9:36). In 11:45 'many of the Jews . . . put their faith in Him'. See also 12:11. And lastly, in the high priestly prayer (17:20), Jesus prays for those who put their faith in Him as a result of the words of His followers.

The remaining places where the phrase 'has faith in me' are used are 11:25, 26 (where 'in me' is not repeated), 12:46; 14:12.

Perhaps the most interesting translation of all is that of the phrase which the A.V. translates 'believe in (or on) the name' of Christ, and the R.V. 'believe on the name', except in 1 Jn. 3:23, where it takes careful account of the slightly different construction there. The 'name' in the Bible stands for the nature or character of God or of Christ, so that believing in that name means putting one's faith and trust in the character of God and His Son. For this the N.E.B. boldly uses the word 'allegiance': 'those who have yielded Him their allegiance' (Jn. 1:12), 'many gave their allegiance to Him' (2:23), 'the unbeliever has not given his allegiance to God's only Son' (3:18), 'those who give their allegiance to the Son of God' (1 Jn. 5:13), and 'This is His command: to give our allegiance to His Son' (3:23).

This is not only a challenge in translation. It is a personal challenge for deeper loyalty. A new translation is not only a landmark in scholarship or a stimulus to new interest. It is a demand for new devotion. May this New English Bible increase our belief, our faith, our trust, and help to make our allegiance complete!

53. TURNING

The verb *epistrephō* is found thirty-six times in the New Testament. It means literally 'turn towards', 'turn round', 'turn back'. In addition, there is one occurrence of the noun derived from it.

The word comes four times in Matthew and four in Mark. Luke has it seven times in his gospel and twelve (including the single use of the noun) in Acts; it is a favourite word of his. It comes only once in John, and only three times in Paul; they express the same idea in other language. The remaining figures are: James twice, 1 Peter once, 2 Peter once, Revelation twice.

Epistrephō is used twice of simple physical turning. The Holy Family returned to Galilee from Jerusalem after they had taken Jesus up to the Temple (Lk. 2:39). Peter turned and saw the Beloved Disciple in Jn. 21:20. In this category we may also include the return of the spirit of Jairus' daughter (Lk. 8:55), and the 'return' of the unaccepted peaceable greeting of the disciples when they entered an unworthy house (Mt. 10:13).

2. More often, however, the New Testament uses the word to describe turning for some definite good purpose. Jesus turns in the crowd to see how He can fully restore the woman who has touched His garment (Mk. 5:30). He later turns to look at His disciples and rebuke Peter for suggesting that the way of the Cross was the wrong way (8:33). The angel's prophecy about John the Baptist was that he would turn the hearts of the fathers towards their children (Lk. 1:17), and Jesus' teaching about forgiveness involved a man who turned to his brother and said, 'I repent' (17:4). In Acts 9:40 Peter, as so often, copied his Master, in turning to a woman and meeting her need. In 15:36 Paul and Barnabas turn back to visit the cities where they have worked, and stablish them in the faith. In the course of their journey Paul has occasion to turn to a devil-possessed girl and cure her (16:18). The list is completed in the book of Revelation, when John turns to see the voice which is speaking to him, and when he turns he sees the seven golden candlesticks which are the beginning of the great series of visions (Rev. 1:12).

3. Yet turning is not always physical, and not always for a good purpose. The unclean spirit seeks to turn back to the man from whom he has been driven out (Mt. 12:44). The unstable Galatians turn back to the weak and beggarly elements of the creeds that they have forsaken (Gal. 4:9). Those who through Christ have escaped the defilements of the world and then have become entangled in them again are like dogs which

turn to back their own vomit (2 Pet. 2:22). Turning back may be dangerous under many circumstances, as Jesus knew when He warned His disciples not to turn back for their material possessions at the time of imminent catastrophe (Mt. 24:18; Mk. 13:16; Lk. 17:31). Lot's wife turned back and was lost.

4. So far, however, we have dealt only with the subsidiary uses of the word. Its main use in the New Testament is with regard to that fundamental turning back to God which we call Conversion. The word is in bad odour among many people who think of it as a mere external change from one form of religion to another. That is not the New Testament sense of the word. There it always means the whole-hearted turning of the personality from ignorance and sin to right living and to God. It occurs in this sense eighteen times, nearly half of the total number of uses. It was prophesied of the infant John that he would turn many of the children of Israel to the Lord their God (Lk. 1:16). Conversion is the constant message of the apostles in the book of Acts. Peter addresses the crowd in the Temple, saying, 'Repent and turn again, that your sins may be blotted out' (3:19). On the Damascus road the Lord tells Paul that He will send him to open men's eyes, 'that they may turn from darkness to light' (26:18), and immediately Paul begins to declare to men 'that they should repent and turn to God, doing works worthy of repentance' (26:20). Peter's message bore fruit, confirmed as it was by the continuance of the healing work of Christ: 'All that dwelt at Lydda and in Sharon saw him (Aeneas), and they turned to the Lord (9:35). So did the message of other unnamed early Christians: 'The hand of the Lord was with them, and a great number of them that believed turned unto the Lord' (11:21). So did the message of Paul and Barnabas. After the first missionary journey they were able to travel through their own country 'declaring the conversion (turning) of the Gentiles' (15:3). And James, the leader of the conservative church in Jerusalem which was perhaps not very eager to include non-Jews in the new Christian fellowship, set the seal of his approval on what had been done through the two missionaries. He refers to the new converts as 'those who from among the Gentiles turn to God' (15:19).

As has been said, Paul does not often use the word in his letters, but he rejoices in the fact that the Thessalonians had made a deep impression on people all over Greece when they 'turned unto God from idols' (1 Thess. 1:9). This was just what he and Barnabas had besought the people of Lystra to do when they tried to associate the two apostles with idolatry (Acts 14:15). A man who does not turn to the Lord has, as it were, a veil over his face, obscuring his proper vision, but when he does so turn, 'the veil is taken away' (2 Cor. 3:16), and he can see the truth clearly.

This turning of the heart to the true God was what Jesus longed for in men. The longing underlies the irony of the passage which He quotes from Isaiah: 'lest haply they should turn again, and it should be forgiven them' (Mk. 4:12; cp. Mt. 13:15 and Acts 28:27). Our actual words are sometimes the opposite of what we really mean. Strangely enough, to speak in this way expresses the intensity of our desire.

Yet Jesus is not content simply to turn men back to God and let that be enough. Those who have so turned must themselves turn others. He looks at Peter when Peter is about to fail, and He says, 'When once you have turned again, stablish your brethren' (Lk. 22:32). It was not enough for Peter to repent alone; he must bring others with him. Peter learnt that lesson. We have seen how he carried it out in his own land, but we find him re-iterating it long afterwards to readers scattered in distant parts of the world: 'You were going astray like sheep, but are now returned unto the Shepherd and Guardian of your souls' (1 Pet. 2:25).

Let James have the last word. In Acts 15:19 he had approved of what Paul and Barnabas had done. In the final words of his own letter he commends true conversion of his own accord: 'If any among you do err from the truth, and one convert him, let him know that he who converts a sinner from the error of his way shall save a soul from death, and shall cover a multitude of sins' (Jas. 5:19, 20). Everyone must be glad to see a soul brought back from error and from death, and every truly converted Christian must rejoice to share in that work.

54. CLEANSING AND PURITY

Personal conversion is not complete until it goes on to the conversion of others, but neither is it complete without personal purity. Everyone needs that God should make him truly clean, and purity is the outcome of putting oneself fully in God's hands. We should therefore naturally expect to find words for cleansing and purity frequently in the New Testament.

The verb *katharizō*, 'cleanse, make clean', occurs in its different forms thirty-six times. The adjective *katharos*, 'clean, pure', is found twenty-five times; and the nouns *katharismos*, *katharotēs*, 'cleansing, cleanness', come eight times, making a total of sixty-nine uses of this centrally important word.

Sometimes the primary meaning is that of physical cleanliness: the clean linen cloth in which Jesus was buried (Mt. 27:59), the pure water of baptism in which the Christian is bathed (Heb. 10:22), the clean linen in which the Lamb's Bride and His armies are clad in heaven (Rev. 19:8, 14). In each of these cases there is also an underlying thought of spiritual purity.

Similar to this is the sense of 'unadulterated', unmixed with anything inferior or evil, which is found three times in Revelation: of the pure jewels which the angels wore (15:6), and of the pure gold of the heavenly city (21:18) and of its street (21:21).

There is always a danger, however, that religious people will lay more emphasis on external cleanliness and freedom from contamination than on purity of heart. It is the easier way. The Jews were especially prone to this error. Jesus criticised them for cleansing the outside of the cup and the platter, while being inwardly full of evil (Mt. 23:25; Lk. 11:39). They were keen to discuss the merits of purification (Jn. 3:25). The blood of goats and bulls was considered adequate to sanctify unto cleanness of the flesh (Heb. 9:13). In fact, according to the Law, almost everything could be cleansed by blood (Heb. 9:22), though Hebrews demonstrates its ineffectiveness (10:2).

Jesus waged a constant struggle against this attitude. 'First cleanse the inside', He said (Mt. 23:26); and His pronouncement in Mk. 7:19 made all food equally clean. Peter had that underlined by the vision in Acts 10, and by the words 'What God has cleansed make thou not common' (10:15). At the Council of Jerusalem he declared that God cleanses men's heart by faith, not by ritual observance (15:9). To those who are inwardly pure all things are pure (Tit. 1:15), though one must not on that basis cause one's brother to stumble (Rom. 14:20). External attempts at cleansing of men's spirits work only in the realm of copies, not of realities (Heb. 9:23).

When Jesus worked, He dealt with reality, even on the physical level. It is remarkable that the verb 'cleanse' is used no fewer than fourteen times in the gospels in connection with the cleansing of lepers. There is the appeal of the leper in Mk. 1:40 and the response of Jesus in the following verses (cp. Mt. 8:2 and Lk.

5:12-14). There are the ten lepers in Lk. 17:14-17. There is Jesus' reference to Naaman in Lk. 4:27, and His description of His own work to John's disciples (Mt. 11:5; Lk. 7:22). And there is the command to His own disciples to continue His practice (Mt. 10:8).

Yet the deeper uses of the word are not physical. They concern the mind and the spirit. Cleanness can mean innocence, as in Paul's protestation to the Jews in Corinth that, after they had rejected his message, he was cleared of responsibility for them (Acts 18:6). He makes a similar declaration to the Ephesian elders in 20:26.

The word can also be used of a pure conscience, which knows nothing that can be reckoned against it, as it holds the mystery of the faith (1 Tim. 3:9) or serves God (2 Tim. 1:3). Yet in order to be in possession of such a conscience tremendous moral effort is demanded. 'Cleanse your hands, ye sinners', cries James (4:8). Only by cleansing (purging) ourselves from what is ignoble shall we be vessels for noble use by the master of the house (2 Tim. 2:21). And this moral effort is not merely individual. The purging of the Church is demanded too. The Corinthians are to remove the contaminating member of their community as the Jewish household cleanses out all contaminating leaven at Passover time (1 Cor. 5:7).

Purity of spirit alone can bring men to see and know God (Mt. 5:8). Jesus longs that His disciples shall be like this, and mourns over the traitor who is not (Jn. 13:10, 11). That is why Paul urges the Corinthians to cleanse themselves from every defilement of flesh and spirit (2 Cor. 7:1). 1 Tim. 1:5 underlines the demand, saying that 'the aim of our charge is love out of a pure heart' (R.S.V.); and 2 Tim. 2:22 speaks of those who call on the Lord out of a pure heart, because that is the kind of heart that He wants in us. In fact, religion in its various manifestations of worship, thought and service is not acceptable to God unless it is what James (1:27) calls 'pure'.

Yet of course in the New Testament moral effort is neither the last nor the first word. We are to do our utmost to be clean and pure, but it is God in Christ who makes purity possible and who gives us the power for all moral effort. The Baptist, in his own stern way, realized that his moral message would be inadequate in itself, and the One who came after Him would have the means in His hand of purifying His domain from the worthless chaff that encumbered it (Mt. 3:12; Lk. 3:17). Jesus Himself speaks more positively but equally sternly when He talks of God cleansing us as a vinedresser prunes his branches (Jn. 15:2). He does it not for destruction but so that the branch may be free from weakening encumbrances to bear more fruit, the fruit not only of personal goodness but of bringing others into Christ. The quickening word of life spoken by Jesus can give that cleansing power (15:3).

In fact the central work of Christ is a cleansing work. His blood cleanses from all sin (1 Jn. 1:7). We ought not to be satisfied here to speak of being 'washed' in Christ's blood. That is nowhere New Testament language, because Rev. 1:5 in our best manuscripts reads '*loosed* us from our sins by His blood', and Rev. 7:14 is the linking of Christian martyrdom with the Cross. When the Jew thought of blood, he thought of life poured out in sacrifice. It is Christ's life, freely given for us, that makes our purity possible. It is when, looking at that life poured out, we confess our sinfulness, He comes to cleanse us from all unrighteousness (1 Jn. 1:9). The initial symbol of that cleansing is Baptism. Eph. 5:26 speaks of Christ as the bridegroom who sanctifies His Church, cleansing it by the washing of water. The thought behind this verse may be the bathing of a bride before her wedding, but the immediate reference is to God's act of purifying grace which all Paul's Ephesian readers had received as the symbol of their new, clean start in Christ.

The New Testament takes one Old Testament idea after another to bring home the truth of the divine cleansing power. Tit. 2:14 speaks of Christ purifying unto Himself a people for His own possession, taking up the words of Ezek. 37:23, where God says 'I will cleanse them; so shall they be my people, and I will be their God'. Heb. 1:3, at the very beginning of that great epistle of priesthood, speaks of Christ's high priestly work of purification of our sins. How immeasurably superior that work is to the work of the Jewish high priest is shown in 9:14: Christ does not offer the blood of unwilling ignorant animals. He, as high priest, offers His own life willingly, that our conscience may be cleansed from the struggle against sin in which legalism is of no help.

How unready we are to accept this cleansing power and, even if we have once accepted it, to forget the cleansing from our old sins (2 Pet. 1:9). The New Testament keeps on reminding us that Christ can cleanse from all sins—of the flesh, of the temperament, of the will. Every time we turn to Him, He can purify—and keep us pure.

55. OPENING AND SHUTTING

Opening and shutting are two of the common activities of daily life. We open doors, mouths, hearts for communication; we close them, rightly or wrongly, for privacy and secrecy. We would therefore expect to find the two verbs commonly in the New Testament, both for man's activity and for God's.

The verb *anoigō*, I open, and its compound *dianoigō*, I open fully, occur together eighty-six times in the New Testament. They are favourite words of St. Luke, who uses them thirty times in his two books. Revelation has them twenty-seven times, Matthew and John eleven times each, Paul five times and Mark twice.

1. Many of the uses are merely physical: the fish's mouth in Mt. 17:27; Jesus' opening of the Book in Lk. 4:17, the blind man's eyes in John 9 from the point of view of the sceptics, the prison doors in Acts 5:23, Paul's physical eyes in 9:8, the door of John Mark's mother's house in 12:14, 16, the prison doors in 16:27, the opening of the pit in Rev. 9:2, and the quotation in Lk. 2:23: 'every male that openeth the womb'.

The remainder, however, are much more than that.

2. Many are associated with the miraculous restoration of communication, through opening of eyes or ears or prison doors: blind men in Mt. 9:30, 20:33, John 9 and the two later references in 10:21 and 11:37 from the believers' point of view, Acts 9:40 with the recovery from the blindness of death: the deaf man's ears in Mk. 7:34-35; the prisons in Acts 5:19; 12:10 and (from the believer's viewpoint) 16:26.

3. Many more are the opening of communication with God. Seven times the opening of heaven is mentioned. There is the baptism of Jesus (Mt. 3:16; Lk. 3:21) when God communicates to Him the assurance of His Sonship. There is the word of Jesus to Nathanael (Jn. 1:51) when He tells him that He will see heaven open and God's messengers communicating with man upon Himself as the ladder linking them with God. There is Peter in Acts 10:11 with the heaven open for God to communicate His message about the equality of the Gentiles. There is Stephen at his end (7:56), given an open view into heaven and seeing his Saviour at God's right hand. There is St. John the

Divine, framing his vision with 'a door opened in heaven' (Rev. 4:1) and 'I saw the heaven opened' (19:11).

There is 'Knock and it shall be opened unto you' (Mt. 7:7-8; Lk. 11:9-10). So often in the New Testament a passive voice such as 'It shall be opened' really implies 'God will open'. There are the tombs opened in Mt. 27:52; and whatever we make of this difficult verse, suggesting that these saints were raised before the great Firstfruit from the dead Himself, there is no doubt that Matthew is thinking of a divine opening. There is the parable of Lk. 12:36 when the servants open to admit their lord—and the parable is of Christ's own coming. He Himself is the one to whom 'the porter opens' (Jn. 10:3); He is always in communication with His flock. It is He who still opens to us the Scriptures as He opened them to the disciples on the Emmaus road (Lk. 24:32), and opens our minds to understand them, as He opened the minds of the larger group later that same Easter Day (24:45). Right to the end of time it is He who 'opens and none shall shut' (Rev. 3:7, 8), He who alone is worthy to open the book of destiny (5:2, 3, 4, 5) and its seals (5:9; 6:1, 3, 5, 7, 9, 12; 8:1). And whatever else is opened in Revelation, whether it is the little book in the hand of the angel (10:2, 8), or the Temple of God in heaven (11:19; 15:5), or the earth intervening to help the woman attacked by the dragon (the Church attacked by persecution—12:16), or the books on the Judgment Day (20:12)—all are, at heart, communication from God Himself and from His Son. The only people with whom Christ refuses to open communication are those who have had their opportunities and carelessly neglected them, such as the foolish virgins in Mt. 25:11 and His own fellow-countrymen on earth in Lk. 13:25.

4. Next comes a phrase that occurs nine times: the opening of the mouth. It is an obvious phrase. How else can you speak? Once (Acts 18:14) it is simply a synonym for 'speak'. In Lk. 1:64 it is used for the restoration of speech to Zacharias. Elsewhere, however, it marks utterance that is outstanding for solemnity or in some other way. At the beginning of the Sermon on the Mount, Jesus 'opened His mouth and taught them' (Mt. 5:2). Later Matthew sums up the Lord's parabolic teaching with the quotation from the Psalms: 'I will open my mouth in parables' (13:35). Philip, taking the plunge and appealing to the high Ethiopian official, 'opened his mouth and . . . preached to him Jesus' (Acts 8:35). Peter, at an equally momentous conversation with Cornelius and his friends, 'opened his mouth and

said, Of a truth I perceive that God is no respecter of persons' (10:34). Paul, yearning over the Corinthians, exclaims 'Our mouth is open unto you', always ready to share the thoughts of his heart (2 Cor. 6:11). Even the beast's momentous denial is characterised by this phrase: 'He opened his mouth for blasphemies against God' (Rev. 13:6). By contrast, most telling is the portion of Isaiah which the Ethiopian eunuch was reading, telling of Him who, despite all they did to Him, opened not His mouth (Acts 8:32).

5. Lastly, there are the openings that man makes, or that he accepts from God: the wise men open their treasures to give (Mt. 2:11); the Gentiles go through the 'door into faith' (Acts 14:27, Moffatt) that God opens for them on Paul's first missionary journey, those Gentiles to whom Paul had been sent to 'open their eyes' (26:18), as the Lord Himself had opened His disciples' eyes (Lk. 24:31). There is the open door for evangelism, for which Paul is always looking (1 Cor. 16:9; 2 Cor. 2:12; Col. 4:3). There is the opening up of discussion as one of the ways by which he might win people (Acts 17:3). Since we are all under sin, Paul uses the Psalmist's words to describe our throats as 'open sepulchres' (Rom. 3:13). Yet if any man hears His voice and opens the door, He promises to come in (Rev. 3:20), and still today there are those like Lydia 'whose heart the Lord opened' (Acts 16:14).

The word *kleiō*, I shut, and its compounds occur twenty-five times, many of them in the same passages as the verb 'open'.

1. There are the shuttings of God: the shutting off of rain in Lk. 4:25 and Rev. 11:6; the shutting out of all human boasting by His grace (Rom. 3:27); the shutting up of all in disobedience and sin so that they are compelled to rely by faith on His mercy alone (Rom. 11:32; Gal. 3:22, 23); the final shutting out of those who will not take their opportunity (Mt. 25:10; Lk. 13:25), because He is the One who shuts and none opens (Rev. 3:7), who shuts up even the Devil at His pleasure (20:3). Yet that is not the last word about God, because John in his final vision of the New Jerusalem see the gates of the city never shut (21:25).

2. And there are the shuttings of men. These are sometimes good: there are the fishermen shutting in (enclosing) their miraculous catch (Lk. 5:6) and the men of prayer shutting their doors (Mt. 6:6)—both, be it noted, by divine command. But more often our shutting is evil: Herod shut up John in prison (Lk. 3:20), as the high priest did the apostles (Acts 5:23), as

Saul did many of the saints (26:10); Jews shut out those who were seeking to enter on God's way (Mt. 23:13; Gal. 4:17); men shut their hearts against their fellows' need (Lk. 11:7; 1 Jn. 3:17); others shut doors through fear (Jn. 20:19; Acts 21:30). But still Jesus can come, though the doors are shut (Jn. 20:26), because it is always He who opens and none shall shut (Rev. 3:7) and sets before us too an open door which none can shut (3:8), so that always there may be perfect openness for us, towards Him and towards our fellow men.

56. PERSEVERANCE

There is a group of words surprisingly common in the New Testament, which are part of the essential spiritual equipment of every Christian but which are not brought to our attention as often as they ought to be.

To give just one translation of each for the moment, they are: (1) Not growing weary (*enkakeō*), (2) Longsuffering (*makrothumia*), (3) Endurance (*hupomonē*), (4) Perseverance (*proskarterēsis*). Put together, they are an element in Christian life and character that we all deeply need.

1. The first word is variously translated 'fainting', 'losing heart', slackening', 'growing discouraged'. It come six times altogether in the New Testament. Paul has it in Gal. 6:9 and in 2 Thess. 3:13 with an identical message: 'Don't grow weary in well-doing'. Notice the preposition. He is not warning them against growing weary *of* well-doing, giving it up completely. Their temptation will be to continue their good works but to do them wearily, without zest. He foresaw the danger of a church consisting of perfunctory Christians, weary well-doers. And remember that the Galatians and Thessalonians were new Christians, not people who have had nineteen hundred years more in which to grow stale.

Eph. 3:13 shows this word from another angle: 'Faint not at my tribulations for you, which are your glory'. Paul's imprisonment is a blow to the church, but they mustn't let it get them down. The loss of their leader must be for their glory, leading them on to renewed boldness. Our Greek word really means 'going to the bad', and Paul here speaks of loss of courage as the essential badness.

But to keep up our courage we need persistent faith and prayer. And so we come to the only New Testament use of the word outside Paul: 'He spake a parable . . . that they ought always to pray and not to faint' (Lk. 18:1). Jesus could see the merit in that annoying old widow, pestering the judge till he gave in out of sheer fatigue. We don't need to pester God like that, but we do need that kind of persistence in prayer. We are slacker there than anywhere else.

And the last two uses give us the secret of all persistence and courage. Both come in 2 Cor. 4—verses 1 and 16: 'Even as we have obtained mercy we faint not'; 'The grace being multiplied . . . wherefore we faint not'. We have this power in so far as we are certain of the received mercy of God and of His abundant grace. Like everything worth having, it is His gift — to be desired and aimed at, but primarily to be *accepted*. Tiredness, strain, worry? The divine courage is available to those who accept, giving us new heart for everything.

2. Our second word, translated 'long-suffering' or 'patience', comes twenty-five times as noun, verb or adjective. It is the opposite of being quick-tempered, hasty, over-impetuous. It does not imply laziness, sluggishness, indifference, but it means not jumping to conclusions too quickly, nor trying to hurry things along that should be left to mature. It is the farmer's word in Jas. 5:7: 'patient' over his crops.

That is the way God treats us. 2 Pet. 3:9 speaks of Him as 'long-suffering to you-ward, not wishing that any should perish'. Even at the time of the Flood He was very very patient (1 Pet. 3:20). Rom. 2:4 speaks of the *richness* of His long-suffering. 1 Tim. 1:16 tells us of Christ showing forth all His long-suffering to sinners. God and His Son do this because it is the way of love: 'Love suffers long' (1 Cor. 13:4).

The most frequent uses of the word in the New Testament are therefore in laying down the way of life for the new Christian community. We have to learn to be long-suffering with one another. Long-suffering is one of the fruits of the Spirit (Gal. 5:22). It is one of the articles of the new, heavenly raiment to be put on by God's elect (Col. 3:12). Eph. 4:2 speaks of how we must learn to put up with one another. Doubtless we could all improve one another considerably, but we must forbear! And this spirit of patience will carry us through persecution (Jas. 5:10), through injustice (2 Cor. 6:6), through our relations with dull, perverse people (2 Tim. 4:2), through periods of delay and disappointment (Heb. 6:12, 15). The ultimate waiting is for the Presence of the Lord, that which will accomplish everything, that which of all things is most worth waiting for (Jas. 5:7, 8).

This is a hard lesson for us impatient people who see only part of the picture, and of course it is a lesson that may be misused. But remember the only time that Jesus uses the word in this sense (Mt. 18:26, 29). Here is a man unforgiving because impatient, and because he could not see himself as he really was. How much do we, undeserving recipients of the patience of God, need to do to others as He has so abundantly done to us!

3. The third word, translated 'patience' or 'endurance', comes forty-nine times as noun or verb. The primary meaning of the word is simply 'staying behind', the sense in which we find it in Lk. 2:43 and Acts 17:14. Hence spiritually it comes to mean 'sticking it out', staying the course which others have given up.

Hence 'endurance' is a better translation than 'patience'. Patience may be just letting blows rain down on your head without resistance. Endurance is a stronger quality: going through with things in continuous consciousness of the end. Lk. 8:15 speaks of those who 'bring forth fruit with endurance', like a seed which bravely survives all the perils of drought and storm. Jas. 1:12 blesses the man who similarly endures the storm of temptation. He passes its test, and the crown of life is his. All the seven instances of the word in the book of Revelation deal with the enduring of persecution (1:9; 2:2, 3, 19; 3:10; 13:10; 14:12). Persecution can be the making of a man. Paul is speaking out of his own experience when he says: 'Suffering produces endurance, and endurance produces character' (Rom. 5:3, 4, R.S.V.). A man who has come through a hard time successfully is always the better for it. That was what the Hebrews needed (10:36). They gave in too easily: they had 'need of endurance', to let it 'have its perfect work' (Jas. 1:4).

The word is more common in the epistles than on the lips of Jesus. In fact He uses it only in Mk. 13:13 (cp. Mt. 10:22; 24:13) and in Lk. 21:19, which gives the same challenge. 'He who endures *to the end* shall be saved'. It is no good swimming nine tenths of the way across a river; you will be as surely drowned as if you had swum only one tenth. It is no good waiting hours for a person if you go five minutes before he arrives; you miss him just as surely as if you had not waited at all.

But endurance is not just something grim and determined, with never a smile on its face. Three times in the Pastoral Epistles (1 Tim. 6:11; 2 Tim. 3:10; Tit. 2:2) it is coupled with the greatest of Christian words. The only perfect endurance is the endurance of love, love that will wait to the end for another's salvation as well as for a man's own, because he cares enough to go on waiting. That what the 'God of patience and comfort' (Rom. 15:5) does with us, and what He longs for us to learn from Him to do for one another.

4. Lastly we come to Perseverance, which is found twelve times in varying forms. In sense it is not unlike our third word, but it has the word 'strength' in its root: 'going strong'. It has quite ordinary uses: the little boat firmly anchored waiting for Jesus in Mk. 3:9, Simon Magus attaching himself to Philip after his baptism (Acts 8:13), the soldiers in constant attendance on Cornelius (10:7). It is also used several times of the regular performance of secular or Christian duty, as of government officials in Rom. 13:6, or of the infant Church in Acts 2:42, 46.

But it is used five times in the New Testament of Prayer: in Acts 1:14 of the waiting Church, in 6:4 of the apostles, in Rom. 12:12 where it is the only word on prayer in this long exhortation on Christian duty, in Col. 4:2 with the same message to another church, and also in Eph. 6:18. As our first word showed us, perseverance is one of the main New Testament emphases on prayer. Our prayers are such butterfly things, light-hearted and intermittent, with little constancy behind them. One great thing that the New Testament says is: keep at them, not merely in time, but in continued earnestness and caring.

I like the way this word is lit up by the normal uses of the New Testament times: the village munsiff in Egypt taking office and swearing that he will stick to his job and not always be wandering off; the petition of two brothers employed on a royal farm, that one of them might be released to return to their own farm — it needed someone to 'stay there regularly' or it would revert to jungle; the poor people who wrote a letter home saying that they were going to attend court until their case was decided, squatting patiently in the compound till they saw the thing through; the family who had been waiting day after day till the butcher came — they were determined to have their mutton! If only we were as persistent in prayer as these people were in the different necessities of daily life!

But why persist in prayer? Only because we know that God is at the other end. That alone makes persistence worth while. That is how Heb. 11:27 speaks of Moses in the last use of this word: 'He *endured* as seeing Him who is invisible'. Things will come right because God *is*. There is a secular use of a farmer 'holding on' to his barley. The price is bad now, so he won't sell. But he has faith that it will improve. He doesn't panic. All will be well. Moses 'held on', and we are to hold on, because of God. The king's wrath and the perils of the wilderness are things that we can literally 'overlook' when we have our eyes on Him who is invisible.

57. A STEADFAST FAITH

One of St. Paul's most difficult tasks was that of keeping his new churches firm in their faith. They were so young and inexperienced, and were so easily led astray by people who came to them preaching perversions of Christian truth with every possible type of persuasiveness.

We cannot altogether blame the new Christians for listening to them. Their teaching sounded good, and there was no long tradition to hold the converts steadily to it. Paul has therefore to keep on exhorting them to be constant to what he had taught them. One verse in which he tries to drive home his message with a remarkable variety of expression is Col. 1:23. The relevant part of the verse, in the Revised Version, is: '*Continue* in the faith, *grounded* (stable, R.S.V.) and *steadfast* (settled, A.V.), and *not moved away* (not shifting, R.S.V.) from the hope of the gospel which you heard'. These four words in italics, pleading under different metaphors for steadfastness, will be the theme of this chapter.

Continue. The word is the ordinary word for making a stay of some length in a place, as contrasted with a quick passing through. In Acts 10:48 Cornelius asks Peter to remain with him for some time in order to consolidate the wonderful Pentecost that had come to him and his household. The word is often used also of Paul's stays in different places on his journeys (21:4, 10; 28:12, 14; 1 Cor. 16:7, 8; Gal. 1:18). Paul also uses it when he speaks of continuing alive (Phil. 1:24), and of continuing in God's goodness (Rom. 11:22). 1 Tim. 4:16 is an appeal to Timothy to continue without fail in the commissions that have been entrusted to him. And of course it is equally possible to continue in sin (Rom. 6:1) and in unbelief (11:23). 'Persist' would often be a good translation: the Pharisees persist in questioning Jesus (Jn. 8:7), Peter persists in knocking until he is admitted (Acts 12:16). All of this is background to the verse

in Colossians. The readers are to continue in their faith as a
man makes a long stay in a place, and does not just halt for an
hour or two. They are to continue as a man continues in life
itself, letting their faith be as much a part of them as their very
life. They are to persist and persevere in it, as Peter persisted
until he attained the entrance he desperately needed.

Grounded. The metaphor is not immediately clear in English,
though it is, for instance, in Tamil. The word is the normal
Greek word for the foundations of a building, firmly built into
the ground. Our Lord used it of the man who bases his action on
the firm rock of His teaching (Mt. 7:25; Lk. 6:48). Heb. 1:10
quote Ps. 102:25 where the Psalmist speaks of God's having laid
the foundation of the earth, firm and sure. Eph. 3:17 has the
beautiful phrase 'founded on love', the firmest of all foundations.
1 Pet. 5:10 (A.V.) has the promise that God will 'settle' those
new Christian readers. It is the same word: He will give them
fixed foundations for their faith.

The noun 'foundation' is even more frequent than the verb.
Lk. 6:49 speaks of the man who does not do what Jesus says as
being like a house built on earth without a foundation. Paul
talks of his work in Corinth as that of laying a foundation (1 Cor.
3:10), the only possible foundation, Jesus Christ (3:11). It is
left to each man to build wisely or unwisely on the foundation
that has been laid for him, and God Himself will test which it
is (3:12f.). In Eph. 2:20 the foundation is the apostles and
prophets (the order of words implies Christian prophets rather
than Old Testament ones), but this is simply a change of metaphor. Christ Jesus is here the chief corner stone, and the
apostles and prophets are thought of as the beginning of the
Church on its human side. 2 Tim. 2:19 speaks of the 'firm
foundation of God' in contrast with the profane babblings of
false teachers. It is a double foundation, based firstly on the
fact that God knows His own, and secondly on the need for
righteousness in ourselves. (A great text to preach from!)
And of course this foundation is concerned not only with the
present but with the future. We need to lay a good foundation
for the life eternal which is life indeed (1 Tim. 6:19). The
foundations of the heavenly city are themselves firm and permanent, as Abraham knew (Heb. 11:10), and precious in every way,
as Revelation shows in its beautiful symbolism (21:14, 19).

In Eph. 3:17, along with the word 'founded' goes the word
Rooted, which is also used in Col. 2:7: '*Rooted* and builded up

in Him'. Therefore, although the word does not occur in our text, it may be looked at here. Roots and foundations go equally into the ground, though in one case the metaphor is a plant and in the other a building. The New Testament frequently emphasises our need of roots. Christians whose spiritual life is shallow soon wither away (Mt. 13:6, 21; Mk. 4:6, 17; Lk. 8:13). Only a Church that is rooted in love can apprehend the fulness of God (Eph. 3:17ff.). And here again the metaphor can be varied. The root may be God's chosen people, the community into which we must be grafted in order to partake of His goodness, and essentially it is that community on which we depend, rather than it on us (Rom. 11:16-18). Deepest of all, Christ Himself is the Root (Rom. 15:12; Rev. 5:5; 22:16), the Source of all life and strength for the tree.

Yet if a root can go deep for good, it can go deep also for evil. 'The love of money is a root of all kinds of evil' (1 Tim. 6:10) —note, not money itself, but too great an attachment to it. Bitterness can be a root that goes very deep (Heb. 12:15), 'poisoning the lives of many others' (Phillips). The gospels twice indicate that sometimes the only remedy may be extirpation (the Latin word means 'taking up by the roots'). The Baptist says 'The axe is laid at the root of the trees' (Mt. 3:10; Lk. 3:9); and in Mk. 11:20 the fig tree is 'withered away from the roots'. Whether that was an actual incident or not, it was clearly meant to apply to the nation that had produced no fruit, and that deserved to be rooted out entirely.

But to come back to Col. 1:23. The next word is *steadfast*, firm. The metaphor this time is that of being firmly seated in a fixed position, not wandering about from place to place. It is used of a firm, unshakable resolve in 1 Cor. 7:37. In 15:58 it describes the steadiness of Christian life that comes from sure belief in the Resurrection. In 1 Tim. 3:15 the corresponding noun is translated 'ground', with 'stay' in the R.V. margin. The picture is of the Church as something that gives support and steadiness to the truth, so that it may not be rocked about by those who try to upset it.

The last expression *Not moved away* occurs elsewhere only as an adjective in 1 Cor. 15:58: 'immovable'. The metaphor is straightforward. Paul is thinking of things that cannnot be easily picked up and put down in a different place, so that you do not know where to find them.

What a picture this verse builds up! Christians are to be as firm in their faith as people who have a fixed home and are not perpetually roaming around. They are to be as little liable to cracks as a building whose foundations have gone down to the rock. They are to have deep roots so that no wind can blow them down. They are to be firmly supported like a building with its buttresses. They are always to be found in the same place, not shifting their view with every new opinion.

It need not be said that all this is not an argument for stagnation, for failing to move forward. No one can imagine St. Paul arguing for that! It is, however, a plea for knowing our faith, for holding it fast, for not taking up strange views that do not belong to the Gospel, and for being utterly dependable and reliable both in our faith and in our practice. The Colossians needed that plea — and we still need it today.

58. ABIDING

The Greek verb *menō* has a rich variety of meanings. It is translated in English by *stay, tarry, remain, last, stand, abide* and other synonyms. It is also used with various prepositions prefixed to it which increase the variety, but the simple verb will be enough for this chapter.

It occurs a hundred and nineteen times in the New Testament: twelve times in the Synoptic gospels, forty times in John, fourteen in Acts, thirteen in Paul, four in the Pastorals, six in Hebrews, two in 1 Peter, twenty-seven in the first and second epistles of John, and once in Revelation. The figures make clear that it is a particularly Johannine word, though it spreads through most of the New Testament.

Quite often, especially in the narratives of the gospels and Acts, it has no significance beyond that of simply staying in a place. This is the force in Lk. 8:27; Jn. 2:12; 10:40; 11:54; Acts 9:43; 18:20; 21:7, 8; 27:31; 28:16; 2 Tim. 4:20. Legion, for example, did not stay in a house but in tombs (Lk. 8:27); Paul and his companions stayed with Philip in Caesarea (Acts 21:8).

In another nineteen places, nearly all of them in the gospels, the word has the same essential meaning, but with a spiritual overtone that adds significance. Jesus tells His disciples that on their preaching tours they are not to move from house to house but are to remain in the first house to which they go (Mt. 10:11;

Mk. 6:10; Lk. 9:4; 10:7). There is an underlying spiritual purpose here which goes beyond mere lodging arrangements. The same thing is true when He tells His three disciples to remain and watch with Him in Gethsemane (Mt. 26:38; Mk. 14:34), and when He says to Zacchaeus that He is going to stay in his house (Lk. 19:5). The Emmaus story, with its 'Abide with us ... and He went in to abide with them' (Lk. 24:29), is also far more than the mere staying in a house; and there is a purpose too in Jesus' remaining in Galilee in Jn. 7:9, and in His staying on in the place where He was when He first heard of Lazarus' illness (11:6). An examination of Lk. 1:56; Jn. 1:38, 39 (twice), 4:40 (twice), 14:25 and Acts 16:15 may also reveal a fuller meaning beyond the word itself, though the dividing line is often far from rigid.

The word *menō* implies not only remaining in a place, but remaining in a condition. This use occurs some twenty-six times, mostly in the epistles. 'If the mighty works had been done in Sodom ... it would have remained in its flourishing condition' (Mt. 11:23). 'Unless a grain of wheat dies, it remains in its lonely condition' (Jn. 12:24). 'If I want him to remain alive till I come, what is that to you?' (Jn. 21:22, 23). 'Let each man remain in the calling in which he was called' (1 Cor. 7:20, 24). 'Let brotherly love continue' (Heb. 13:1). 'He who does the will of God lasts on for ever' (1 Jn. 2:17). Other examples of this use can be seen at Jn. 15:16; 19:31; Acts 5:4 (twice); 27:41; 1 Cor. 3:14; 7:8, 11, 40; 13:13; 15:6; Phil. 1:25; 1 Tim. 2:15; 2 Tim. 3:14; Heb. 10:34; 13:14; 1 Jn. 2:19; Rev. 17:10.

An occasional use is that of waiting for someone or something. It occurs only in Acts 20:5: 'They went ahead and waited for us in Troas', and in Acts 20:23: 'Bonds and tribulations await me'.

And now we come to the uses of the word which give it its particularly Christian value. First of all, it emphasises the abiding nature of God and of His attributes. The word is used in this connection some thirteen times: the abiding wrath of God (Jn. 3:36), His word that abides (5:38), the divine food that abides to eternal life (6:27), the abiding Christ (12:34), the abiding purpose of God (Rom. 9:11), the ministration of the Spirit that remains all glorious (2 Cor. 3:11), God's righteousness that lasts for ever (9:9), His abiding faithfulness (2 Tim. 2:13), Jesus our abiding High Priest (Heb. 7:24), His prototype Melchizedek (7:3), God's unshaken kingdom (12:27), and finally

God's word once again, living and abiding for ever (1 Pet. 1:23, 25). What a rich list of permanences!

On the other hand, sin also may be something permanent. That fact is emphasised four times: 'Your sin remains', says Jesus to the Jews who were under the impression that their spiritual sight was perfect (Jn. 9:41); those who do not believe in Him are in danger of remaining permanently in the darkness (12:46); the Jews have the veil of ignorance permanently remaining on them because they have not accepted God's revelation in Christ (2 Cor. 3:14); and the man who does not love has made his permanent abode in death (1 Jn. 3:14).

Finally we reach the two great Johannine themes of God and His Son and His Spirit abiding in us, and of our abiding in them—the two uses of the word that give us its central Christian purpose. John speaks eighteen times of the Divine Abiding in us, with a further three of the Spirit or the Father abiding in the Son (Jn. 1:32, 33; 14:10). He speaks a further twenty-two times of our abiding in God or in Christ, and once of Christ abiding in the Father (15:10). In six of these instances the two sides are matched with each other in the mutual abiding of God in us and we in Him (Jn. 15:4, 5, 7; 1 Jn. 4:13, 15, 16).

This is the spiritual union on which our Christian life depends. On the one side God's Spirit abides with us so that we can know Him (Jn. 14:17); God's word abides in us so that we are strong (1 Jn. 2:14); God's anointing abides in us and teaches us all that we need (1 Jn. 2:27); God's life-giving seed abides in us and keeps us from sin (3:9); God's eternal life abides in us and keeps us from hate (3:15); God's love abides in us and makes us compassionate (3:17); God's Spirit abides in us, making us recognise that He Himself abides in us (3:24); God's truth abides in us, and will be with us for ever (2 Jn. 2). No wonder that John urges his readers to let what they had heard from the beginning remain in them (1 Jn. 2:24), so that none of this may be lost, and that he stresses the need for mutual love, so that God may abide in them (4:12).

Then on the other side there is our abiding in God and in Christ: abiding in Him by taking the benefits of His incarnation into ourselves (Jn. 6:56), abiding in His word and so being His true disciples (8:31), abiding in Him as sons (8:35), remaining in living contact with Him like a branch in a vine (15:4, 6), abiding in His love (15:9, 10), proving our claim to abide by following Christ's example (1 Jn. 2:6), abiding in the light by living in love (2:10), abiding in the Son and in the Father by remaining in what we have heard (2:24), abiding as He taught us (2:27), abiding in Him till the End (2:28), abiding so that we may be free from sin (3:6), abiding by keeping His commandments (3:24), abiding in the teaching, and making sure that as we go forward we do not go away from the things in which we are commanded to abide (2 Jn. 9).

And the gospel message will not allow these two abidings to be kept separate in our thought. We abide in Him and He in us at the same time, like a vine and its branches (Jn. 15:4). Then alone can there be fruit-bearing (15:5). Then alone can our prayer be truly fulfilled (15:7). If we are sure that Jesus is the Son of God, then we abide in God and He in us (1 Jn. 4:15). If we abide in love, then we abide in Him and He in us (4:16). And the power to know all this, to be certain of it in our hearts, is ours because He gives us His Spirit (4:13).

How poor we are in thought, in life, in power, if we do not accept the offer of this mutual relationship with God! How abundantly rich we are if we do!

59. OBEDIENCE

There are four main New Testament words for that prime requisite for the Christian life: Obedience.

1. The first, hupakouō, means literally 'hear under', that is, 'hear and submit yourself to what you hear'. It may be just the answering of a knock on the door (Acts 12:13). It may be the obedience due from children to parents (Eph. 6:1), or from servants to masters (6:5), or the natural obedience of a friend to the wishes of a friend (Philemon 21). It may be the obedience of Satanic powers to One stronger than themselves (Mk. 1:27), or the obedience of nature to nature's Lord (4:41).

But nearly all the New Testament uses refer to the essential Christian obedience. This is expressed in various ways: obedience to the Faith (Acts 6:7), obedience to the Gospel (Rom. 10:16), obedience to the Teaching (6:17), obedience to Christ Himself (Heb. 5:9). A man cannot avoid obedience by saying that any one particular line of approach does not appeal to him. He has the choice of obedience to a Creed, to a Message, to specific Instruction, to a Person — and if none of those suit him, he cannot be very much in earnest!

In fact, still worse, he can turn his obedience in entirely the wrong direction. Instead of being obedient unto righteousness (Rom. 6:16), he can be obedient to his lusts (6:12), and so the slave of sin unto death (6:16).

And how can he escape from such slavery? Not by anything that he can do himself, but by the power of the obedience with which Christ obeyed (Rom. 5:19), by which He broke down the continuity of evil from which we cannot shake ourselves free, and established a new continuity of good. Just because He became obedient unto death (Phil. 2:8), and because He learned obedience from the things that He suffered (Heb. 5:8), He was able to become to all who obey Him the author of eternal salvation (5:9), so that 1 Peter 1:2 can link our obedience with the sprinkling of the blood of Christ.

Then we can have the obedience that springs from faith in Him (Rom. 1:15; 16:26; note how obedience is linked with faith both at the beginning and the end of the great epistle of faith). Then we can bring every thought into captivity unto the obedience of Christ (2 Cor. 10:5), and our obedience can be perfected (10:6), so that we have the power to go out and do that work for which Christ has called us: winning 'the obedience of the Gentiles, by word and by deed' (Rom. 15:18).

2.   The second word, *hupotassō*, means 'range or rank under'. It is used frequently in the same sense as the first word. Wives are to be 'subject' to husbands (Eph. 5:22; Col. 3:18; Tit. 2:5; 1 Pet. 3:1, 5). This is not to defend the injunction; it is merely to state the apostolic vocabulary, and to point out the qualification in Eph. 5:24 that this subjection is to be only in the sense in which the Church is subject to Christ. Slaves are to be subject to their masters (Tit. 2:9) and younger people to their elders (1 Pet. 5:5), with the beautiful example of the boy Jesus in Lk. 2:51. The demons too are subject to the disciples in Christ's name (Lk. 10:17, 20 — the only other uses of the word in the gospels). And the term is used of subjection to civil authority in Rom. 13:1.

But its main use in the New Testament is not on the human plane. It is in the realm of the divine cosmic order. No less than ten times is it associated with the word *all*, and in all these cases it is connected directly or indirectly with Christ. 'He subjected all things under His feet' (1 Cor. 15:27; Eph. 1:22); 'He is able to subject all things unto Himself' (Phil. 3:21). This is God's dispensation of His universe: that everything in it

shall be ranked in its order below Christ, that 'angels and authorities and powers' (1 Pet. 3:22) also shall be subject to Him.
There is mention of subjection to *God* too: to His law (Rom. 8:7),
to His righteousness (Rom. 10:3), to Him as Father (Heb. 12:9),
to His grace (Jas. 4:7). But for now He has put His Son in the
centre of the picture to receive all submission until He Himself
is finally subjected to His Father (1 Cor. 15:28). New Testament
obedience is ultimately related to the supremacy of Christ,
so that men are to be subject to one another in the fear of Christ
(Eph. 5:21), and though we do not yet see all things subjected,
we do see Jesus (Heb. 2:8), and all our obedience is related to
His sufferings and His glory.

But that subjection is not really to be described in terms
of fear. It is the glad subjection of love. The Church is subject
to Christ (Eph. 5:24), but He exercises no despotism over
her, over us who belong to her. Instead, He loves her and gives
Himself for her, and is united with her. And that which elsewhere is tyranny is here saving and cleansing power, because
she has surrendered herself into the hands of One who makes
her not a subject, but the Body of which He is the Head.

3. Our third word, *peithomai*, and its negative *apeitheō*, and
their derivatives, mean to obey in the sense of being inwardly
persuaded, or to disobey in the opposite sense. It is used often
enough in terms of ordinary human obedience: the followers of
Theudas and Judas (Acts 5:36, 37), were sufficiently convinced
by these men's claims to put themselves under their orders;
Paul's nephew suggested to the chief captain (23:21) that he
should not let himself be persuaded to follow the instructions
of the Jews, designed to result in Paul's death in their ambush.
James (3:3) even uses it of putting a bit into a horse's mouth to
persuade it to obey us. Anyone who has watched a horse fighting
against its bit knows that persuasion is needed even more than
force here. And so it is used at the end of Hebrews (13:17)
in the injunction to 'obey them that have the rule over you'—
not give in to superior force, but let yourself be persuaded that
they are really watching on behalf of your soul, and therefore
accept what they say and do.

Paul uses the word twice with abstract nouns in striking phrases:
obeying the truth (Gal. 5:7) — it is very certain that you cannot do
that unless you are inwardly persuaded that it is true; and obeying
unrighteousness (Rom. 2:8) — again you will not do that unless
you have been fatally persuaded.

But it is the negative forms, the ones that deal with *dis*-obedience, that are really the more remarkable: the times when men will not allow themselves to be persuaded by what is good, but deliberately turn against it. In Rom. 10:21 God stretches out appealing hands all day to Israel, and yet they will not be persuaded to turn to Him; they are the same disobedient people to whom He has to swear in Heb. 3:18 that they shall not enter into His rest. If a man can obey the Word, he can also disobey it: 1 Pet. 2:8 speaks of those who stumble at it, not allowing themselves to be persuaded into accepting its truth. A man can also disobey the Gospel (1 Pet. 4:17), refusing to let himself be convinced that the name of Christian and the suffering that name may involve is a value beyond all other values.

In fact a man can become what Paul three times (Eph. 2:2; 5:6; Col. 3:6) calls a '*son* of disobedience', not just a casual offender, but one whose very nature is closed against the persuasions of the Gospel and so is in the direct line of that inevitable retribution which Paul calls the wrath of God. The opposite of the man who 'believes in the Son and has eternal life' is not the man who *dis*believes. The English Authorised Version translated Jn. 3:36 that way, but it has been well and truly disproved by the papyri. The opposite of a man who believes is a man who dis*obeys*, who will not let Christ persuade him into goodness. That, rather than unbelief, is the cardinal rejection.

But we do not end on this negative note. Paul, in his speech in front of Agrippa, puts a negative before the negative which cancels it out: 'I was not disobedient to the heavenly vision' (Acts 26:19). Paul let himself be fully persuaded by Christ, and in that obedience he lived the rest of his days — and was usable because of it. That spirit of convinced obedience can make us usable too.

4. The last word, *tēreō*, means primarily 'watch, guard, keep safe'. When therefore we use it in the sphere of obedience, it means holding on firmly to the word or commandment of God, so that nothing gets lost in understanding or execution. Just as a prisoner is kept safe so that he cannot escape (e.g. Acts 24:23), or as the Jews most carefully kept the Sabbath (Jn. 9:16), the New Testament speaks of *keeping* the word and commandment of God. Jesus says to the rich young ruler in Mt. 19:17: 'Be scrupulous in your observance of what God has told you to do'. 1 Tim. 6:14 says, 'Keep the commandment without spot',

until the Lord's Coming, letting nothing stain it, as you would try to keep your clothes spotless that you had put on for an interview with a great man.

But nearly all the uses of the word in this sense come in the Johannine writings; twenty-four out of the twenty-seven are found in the Gospel, the First Epistle and in Revelation. Here we have the three sources and results of obedience, the three things that make it possible and that spring from it.

(*a*) The first is the Knowledge of God. See 1 Jn. 2:3, 4 for the dependence of knowledge on obedience, and 3:24 for the dependence of communion with God on obedience also. Our constant temptation is to reverse the order of these things.

(*b*) The second thing that springs from obedience is endurance. This is the main emphasis in Revelation. See, for example, 3:8: 'Thou didst keep my word and didst not deny' in the time of persecution. 3:10 actually speaks of keeping 'the word of my endurance', the endurance that springs from God and is used for Him. 12:17; 14:12; and 22:7 make the same link between obedience and endurance. The first is one of the strongest incentives to the second. A man who knows that he is obeying God can go beyond human limits, because obedience is always given power.

(*c*) But the incentive to obedience is Love — and the best way of showing love is by obedience (1 Jn. 5:3). This link between the two comes most frequently and clearly in the words of Jesus Himself, those reiterated words at the Last Supper: Jn. 14:15, 21, 23, 24; 15:10; 17:6 (His 'name' is love). The repetition is almost monotonous, but in these last hours one of the things Jesus wants to bring permanently home to His disciples is that love and obedience go together: that we cannot talk of love without obeying, or obey truly and richly unless we love. Here is the heart of it all.

But there is one more word: obedience is not just something personal for ourselves alone. We are commanded to bring it home to others as we have learnt it ourselves. Look at the final words in Matthew: 'teaching *them* to keep all the commands which I have given *you*'—and at the parallel in Jn. 15:20: 'If they kept my words, they will keep yours also'. This is the word meant for *all*, slave or free, married or single, Jew or Gentile. For 'Circumcision is nothing, uncircumcision is nothing—but the keeping of the commandments of God' (1 Cor. 7:19).

60. WORKS

Jesus and Paul were constantly facing people who thought that good conduct and character were the essential things for man's salvation. Thus one of the chief New Testament emphases is on the fact that we are saved not by our own good acts but only through that humble acceptance of God's grace which we call faith. Romans, chapters 3 and 4, and Galatians, chapters 2 and 3, make that especially clear, e.g. 'a man is justified by faith apart from the works of the law' (Rom. 3:28).

Yet this must not blind us to the fact that the New Testament has a great deal to say about the importance of works in the Christian life. Their true place is basically stated in Eph. 2:8-10: 'By grace have ye been saved through faith . . . not of works . . . we are created in Christ Jesus *for* good works'. That is to say, God's saving power puts us in a position to live a life of good works, and if we do not do so, our so-called faith is 'barren', as Jas. 2:20 says, and as the whole of that chapter argues.

This study will therefore examine the Greek verb *ergazomai*, I work, which occurs fifty-one times in the New Testament, and its noun *ergon*, work or deed, which comes one hundred and seventy times, and attempt to see the true place of works in our Christian thought and practice.

1. In contrast with faith the words occur some thirty-seven times. When the Jews ask Jesus, 'What must we do that we may work the works of God?', the unexpected answer is, 'This is the *work* of God, that ye *believe* (have faith) in Him whom He has sent' (Jn. 6:28-29). Abraham was justified by his trust in God's promises, rather than by anything that he did (Rom. 4:2-3). It is not 'the works of the law' that do anything for us, but 'faith in Jesus Christ' (Gal. 2:16).

Yet James, even in this context, puts in the necessary corrective. There were people even in those early days who talked a great deal about faith, but whose works did not substantiate their talk. He points out that Abraham's great act of faith in offering up Isaac on the altar was itself a 'work' (Jas. 2:21). He even brings in Rahab the harlot as a person brought into right relationship with God by what she *did* (2:25). Faith that does not issue in works is meaningless.

2. So, with the underlying understanding that a personal trust in God and not in ourselves is essential, the New Testament

says a great deal to commend good works. The servant who received the five talents and went and traded (literally 'worked') with them is the one who is praised, as against the lazy man who did nothing (Mt. 25:16). The woman who anointed Jesus is defended and praised by Him: 'She has worked a good work upon me' (Mt. 26:10; Mk. 14:6). Tabitha is 'full of good works' (Acts 9:36). The first missionary journey is a 'work' to which the Holy Spirit calls and which the apostles complete by the grace of God (13:2; 14:26). Even Romans very naturally approves of good work (2:7; 13:3,10; 15:18). Paul constantly speaks of his own work: the Corinthians are his work in the Lord (1 Cor. 9:1); he is as effective in action when present as in his letters when absent (2 Cor. 10:11); he realises that continuing to live in the flesh may be the fruit of his work (Phil. 1:22); he often works with his own hands (1 Cor. 4:12). Timothy (1 Cor. 16:10) and Epaphroditus (Phil. 2:30) also do the work of Christ. So it must be with Paul's churches: the Corinthians must abound in the work of the Lord (1 Cor. 15:58); the reminder comes again in the second letter that they must abound unto every good work (2 Cor. 9:8); the Ephesians are told that the saints are perfected for the work of ministering (Eph. 4:12); Paul's prayer for the Colossians is that they may bear fruit in every good work (Col. 1:10); the Thessalonians must esteem their leaders for their works' sake (1 Thess. 5:13), and Paul's prayer for them is that they may be stablished in every good work (2 Thess. 2:17).

Yet the reminder keeps on coming that good works are not independent of God. When men see our good works, they are to glorify our Father in heaven (Mt. 5:16). These works are to be made manifest that they have been worked in God (Jn. 3:21). 1 Thess. 1:3 speaks of a 'work of faith', and Heb. 11:33 of working righteousness through faith. Our goodness is never our own unaided product.

3. Just as good deeds are urged and commended, so evil works are condemned. Christ exposes our evil deeds (Jn. 3:19, 20). They are condemned as 'unfruitful' (Eph. 5:11), as alienating us from God (Col. 1:21), as denying God (Tit. 1:16), as 'dead' in themselves (Heb. 6:1; 9:14), as belonging to the devil (1 Jn. 3:8), as the product of defective churches (Rev. 3:1 — Sardis; 3:15 — Laodicea), as the worship of false gods (9:20).

4. And so by our works we are judged. 'In that day', Christ will say, 'Depart from me, you that work iniquity' (Mt. 7:23).

Nine times comes the phrase that God will judge, or render, or give to us, according to our works (Rom. 2:6; 2 Tim. 4:14; 1 Pet. 1:17; Jude 15; Rev. 2:23; 18:6; 20:12, 13; 22:12). Four times over in 1 Cor. 3:13-15 comes the declaration that on 'the day' men's work will be tested as fire tests materials to see whether they can endure or not.

5. But the importance of good work and the seriousness of evil work is particularly emphasised by the fact that God and Christ themselves are workers. 'My Father works even until now, and I work', says Jesus in Jn. 5:17. God was the Creator in the beginning. 'The heavens are the work of His hands' (Heb. 1:10). He has set man over His works on earth (2:7). He worked in creation before He rested (4:3, 4, 10). The present tense: 'works' in Jn. 5:17 means that God did not cease His creative activity even when He had finished making the worlds, but He continues it throughout, so that Philo could say, 'As it is the property of fire to burn and of snow to chill, so it is the property of God to *make*'.

When Jesus does His miracles, He is continuing the work of God: 'We must work the works of Him that sent me while it is day' (Jn. 9:4). John the Baptist in prison hears of these works (Mt. 11:2), and Jesus declares that the Divine wisdom is justified by them (11:19). The works that Jesus does bear witness of Him (Jn. 10:25), because He is doing the works of the Father (10:37-38), and because the Father, abiding in Him, is doing His works (14:10). At the end He can say that He has finished the work that God has given Him (17:4), and His followers can describe Him as a prophet mighty in work and word (Lk. 24:19).

Yet the Divine working continues even further. When Paul in Rom. 14:20 says, 'Overthrow not for food's sake the work of God', he is really repeating in other words what he has just said in 14:15, 'Destroy not with your food him for whom Christ died'. The death of Christ is God's work for us. Paul reminds the Philippians how Christ had begun a good work among them which He will go on perfecting till His own day comes (Phil. 1:6). And at the end the victorious in heaven will sing of His works that they are great and marvellous (Rev. 15:3).

The most marvellous work of all is that He quickens the dead (Jn. 5:20-21), not just by physical resurrection but by that life with God, here and hereafter, which He calls 'eternal'. This means that the works that He does we can do also, and greater works still because He has gone where He can help us more

effectively (Jn. 14:12). As the angel said to the church in
Thyatira (Rev. 2:26), we 'can keep His works to the end', doing
them because they are His, and because the power to do them
comes from Him, and because His is the glory. That is true
Christian work.

61. RICHES

Riches! How many want them, openly or secretly! How
many feel it their duty to condemn them in principle! How
few trouble to examine what the New Testament has to say
about them!

The Greek noun *ploutos*, wealth, comes twenty-two times
in the New Testament. Its adjective, rich, comes twenty-eight
times; its adverb, richly, four times; and two verbs, I am rich,
I make rich, fifteen times between them, making a total of sixty-
nine occurrences which may be considered together.

Of these, rather more than half, thirty-nine in all, refer to
material wealth. Twenty such references are in the Synoptic
Gospels, ten in Revelation, none in Paul, and nine in the other
epistles.

Eighteen of the references definitely condemn wealth. In
Luke's account of the Beatitudes (6:24), Jesus says 'Woe unto you
that are rich!' The parable of the Sower (Mk. 4:19 and parallels)
speaks of riches choking the Word. The rich man in Lk.
12:16 ff. is condemned because he could not think beyond
his riches. The parable of Dives and Lazarus ('Dives' is simply
the Latin word for a rich man — Lk. 16:19, 21, 22) is even
more severe. 'He has sent the rich empty away', says the Magnificat (Lk. 1:53). James continues the condemnation: 'Do not
the rich oppress you?' (2:6); 'Come now, you rich, weep and
howl' (5:1); 'Your riches have rotted away' (5:2). Revelation
completes the list: there are the Laodiceans with their false
pride, saying 'I am rich; I have gotten riches' (3:17); there are
the rich who hide from the wrath of the Lamb (6:15); there are the
merchants of doomed Babylon (18:3, 15, 17).

But material wealth is not automatically condemned. Twice
it is praised: Joseph of Arimathea was a rich man (Mt. 27:57),
and riches are something that may be offered to the Lamb
(Rev. 5:12). Three times they are mentioned without praise
or blame: the rich neighbours in Lk. 14:12, the rich man in
the parable of the unrighteous steward (16:1), and the rich who,

along with the poor, come under the domination of the beast in Rev. 13:16.

The central attitude of the New Testament towards riches, however, is one of warning. They are not wrong absolutely, but they are very dangerous. As the Bible Reading Fellowship Notes once put it: 'the ministry of wealth is scheduled in the New Testament as one of the "dangerous trades", in which there is a high rate of spiritual mortality'. So Jesus says, 'It is hard for a rich man to enter the kingdom of heaven ... It is easier for a camel to go through the eye of a needle than for a rich man to enter the kingdom of God' (Mt. 19:23, 24; cp. Mk. 10:24, 25; Lk. 18:24, 25). Jesus does not say that it is impossible. He points out the great obstacle that wealth may be. The ruler refused to respond to the challenge of Jesus for the simple reason that he was very rich (Lk. 18:23). The same note of warning is implied in the incident where the poor widow is contrasted with the rich men who are casting their gifts into the treasury (Mk. 12:41; Lk. 21:1). It is there also in the story of Zacchaeus (Lk. 19:2), who did accept the challenge to realise where his corrupt use of wealth had led him. 1 Timothy utters the same note again: those who desire to be rich fall into temptation (6:9); they need charging not to be proud (6:17), not to set their hopes on uncertain riches (6:17), but to be rich in good deeds (6:18). James too sees the danger: let the rich man 'find his pride in being brought low' (1:10, N.E.B.); otherwise he will fade away like the grass (1:10). Revelation adds to the list with the picture of those who had lost their wealth by the fall of Babylon (18:19), and the advice to gain true wealth from God in the place of their boasted material prosperity (3:18).

But the New Testament does not leave this word to be monopolised by material possessions. *Ploutos* comes from the same root as the Greek verb *pimplemi*, I fill, and is connected etymologically with the Latin word from which 'plenty' comes, with the Sanskrit *purnam*, and with the English 'fill'. And it is true that we are made far more rich, full, complete (another word from the same root) on the spiritual level than we can ever be on the material. The New Testament therefore uses our series of words for riches thirty times in a spiritual sense.

We find it in this sense only once in the Gospels: of the man who is not 'rich towards God' (Lk. 12:21). It is used twice in the Pastoral Epistles of God's bounty: He provides all things richly for our enjoyment (1 Tim. 6:17); He pours out the Spirit richly on us through Christ (Tit. 3:6). Heb. 11:26 speaks of Moses as regarding even the abuse that he suffered in Israel's cause as greater riches than the treasures of Egypt. James describes the materially poor as called to be rich in faith (2:5). 2 Pet. 1:11 promises the rich provision that God makes for us in the right of entry into His kingdom. Rev. 2:9 follows James when it tells the poor of Smyrna that they are really rich.

But the man who most fully takes hold of the words in their spiritual sense is St. Paul. He will not use them for material wealth. He has them twenty-three times, and every use of them is to describe spiritual riches. Ten times over he speaks of the richness of God. He is rich in mercy (Eph. 2:4). He is rich in kindness (Rom. 2:4). He is rich in grace (Eph. 1:7; 2:7). Four times Paul mentions the riches of His glory, which we are to know or share (Rom. 9:23; Eph. 1:18; 3:16; Phil. 4:19). No wonder that Paul is led to declare that He is rich unto all that call upon Him (Rom. 10:12), and to exclaim in ecstasy: 'O the depth of the riches both of the wisdom and the knowledge of God' (11:33).

These riches he finds equally in Christ. His riches are unsearchable (Eph. 3:8), but Paul always links them with the Incarnation. The essential thing about them is that they are shared with men. 'Though He was rich, yet for your sakes He became poor' (2 Cor. 8:9). God was delighted to make known the riches of this glorious mystery which is 'Christ in you' (Col. 1:27). So the word of Christ is to dwell in us richly (3:16), and the richness of full understanding in us leads to the knowledge of God's secrets in Christ (2:2). In fact Paul can thank God as he writes to the Corinthians that in *everything* they were enriched in Christ (1 Cor. 1:5).

God means us to share His richness. When the Jews refuse it, 'their fall is the riches of the world, and their loss the riches of the Gentiles' (Rom. 11:12). God must find those to whom He can give it. Paul is expressing in his own way what Jesus had already said in the parable of the Great Supper (Lk. 14:15-24). His ironical word to some of the Corinthians: 'Already ye are become rich' (1 Cor. 4:8) is another commentary on the parable. There are always people who think that they can get on very satisfactorily without God.

But the true response to God's generosity is to accept it, and then as far as possible to imitate it. Paul is following in his Master's footsteps in his own ministry which he describes in 2 Cor. 6:10: he is 'poor, yet making many rich'. The Corinthians have become rich through Christ's impoverishment of Himself (2 Cor. 8:9), and Paul urges them to imitate the Macedonian churches. Materially those churches in Philippi and Thessalonica were poor, but in generosity they were wealthy indeed (2 Cor. 8:2). That is the purpose for which God enriches us, whether materially or spiritually: that we may be divinely generous with what we have received, and that those who receive from us may thank, not us, but God (2 Cor. 9:11).

Material possessions—evil? The New Testament does not say so. Dangerous, 'to be handled with care'? Yes, indeed. Spiritual wealth? It is there with God in all its fulness, for us to receive and pass on without limit. God forgive us that we live in such wilful poverty.

62. BOASTING

Boasting is neither a nice word nor a nice action. In its most commonly used sense it is defined by the dictionary as 'speaking with vanity, with a view to self-commendation'. Most of us are guilty of it in one form or another. Even if we are not ostentatious in our boasting, we like to make our worth clear to other people in more indirect ways. Boasting in this sense is certainly one of the things that we should give up—at any rate during Lent!

Yet the word has other uses and senses. The Psalmist can say, 'My soul shall make her boast in the Lord' (34:2). There is no vanity there, nor self-commendation. Instead there is commendation of God, and a pride in Him. Pride in other men's qualities and achievements can also be justifiable, and so even can pride in oneself, provided it is pride about the right things in the right spirit.

The Greek verb *kauchaomai*, I boast, with its two nouns, *kauchēma*, a boast, and *kauchēsis*, boasting, can be used in all these senses, though the English Bible tends to conceal the fact that there is only one Greek root by translating it as 'boast' when the meaning is bad, and as 'glory' or 'rejoice' when it is good. The three Greek forms come altogether fifty-eight times in the New Testament. Fifty-four of these occurrences are in Paul. It is a word that he frequently feels the need to use, especially in 2 Corinthians, where he has it twenty-nine times. 1 Corinthians has nine occurrences and Romans eight.

We may divide boasting under the four heads indicated below:
1. boasting that is entirely bad; 2. boasting that is a legitimate
pride in oneself though, as Paul always notes, one has to be very
careful about this kind of boasting; 3. boasting that is a pride in
others' achievements, and that can usually be commendable;
and 4. the only entirely justifiable boasting: magnifying God's
goodness and love.

1. There is boasting about the merits of the Jewish Law
(Rom. 2:23), a boasting that we have learnt to condemn in the
Jews, but that we do not recognise so easily in our own case
when we boast of some system of which we happen to approve,
even if it is a good system such as the Constitution of the Church
of South India. Then there is boasting about works (Rom.
3:27; 4:2; Eph. 2:9; Jas. 4:16)—again a fault that we readily
condemn in the Jews, while forgetting how often we pat ourselves on the back for our own achievements. Then there is
pride in our status or position—see 1 Cor. 1:29; 4:7; 5:6; 2 Cor.
5:12; 11:12, 18). We have no difficulty in finding parallels to
that in ourselves. Like the Corinthians, we continually forget
that we have nothing that we have not received from God
(1 Cor. 4:7). Then there is boasting of what we have made of
other people (Gal. 6:13); we still boast of our converts, if any.
And there is boasting about our leaders (1 Cor. 3:21), as though
we deserved any credit for them. Whether Nehru or Churchill
take any credit for their own achievements or not, we are not
justified in claiming any of their merit for ourselves. The last
kind of bad boasting of which Paul writes is the boasting that
takes the credit even more directly for other people's work.
In 2 Cor. 10:13, 15, 16 he declares strongly that his practice has
always been to evangelize in new areas and not to go where
others have been—the principle of comity right from the beginning! He is not going to glory in other men's labours, as though
he had done them all himself. Dare we claim that we have
never tried to take the credit for what has really been done by
someone else?

2. There are, however, some things that may be legitimate
ground for personal pride. Paul has quite a bit to say about
these, though often he does so rather reluctantly, and only
because he is compelled by his opponents. These opponents
gave him a particularly bad time in Corinth, and he had to take
action to prevent himself from being misrepresented. One

thing of which he felt that he could legitimately boast was that he was no expense to them when he came preaching the Gospel (1 Cor. 9:15; 2 Cor. 11:10). Another fair ground for boasting was the labour that he had put into his work of evangelism (2 Cor. 11:16, 17, 18). He felt too that he might boast of a good conscience (2 Cor. 1:12), of the authority given to him by God for building up the Church (10:8), and of the revelations which he had received (12:1, 5, 6). But he still has considerable reluctance. The only thing about which he really wants to boast is his weakness (11:30; 12:9), because that weakness throws him back on Christ. He will not even boast about his preaching of the Gospel; that is a 'must' which is no personal credit to him (1 Cor. 9:16).

The other instances of legitimate boasting are few and far between. The Jew may boast of his relationship to God (Rom. 2:17). A man may perhaps boast a little when he has tested his work and found it worthwhile (Gal. 6:4). The only two other places may be classed with Paul's boasting in his weakness: we are to boast when we are being tried and troubled (Rom. 5:3), and the brother of low degree is to boast of his high estate (Jas. 1:9). Nothing in this section gives any ground for the kind of boasting in which we are tempted to indulge.

3. But there is room for pride in the spiritual development of other people, especially those who have come out of paganism into a true Christian experience and life. Paul tells the Thessalonians that they are the crown of his boasting, at the top of the list of those of whom he is proud (1 Thess. 2:19). He would like also to be proud of the effects of his work among the Philippians (2:16), and he asks them in their turn to be proud of him because of what his work among them has done for them (1:26). He could even boast about those difficult Corinthians whose attitude had compelled him to boast about himself: in the middle of his great resurrection chapter he mentions (irrelevantly, it seems) his pride in them as he writes to them (1 Cor. 15:31), and in 2 Cor. 9:2, 3 he says that he has boasted to the Macedonians that the Corinthians are ready with their gifts for the Jerusalem church. That was partly to stimulate the Macedonians, and Paul takes steps to see that the Corinthians do not let him down! but he has ground for his boast. And at the end of the terrible trouble with Corinth, when Paul is filled to the brim with relief and joy, he boasts over and over again of the new spirit that has been born in them (2 Cor. 7:4, 14 (twice); 8:24). He claims

too that they ought to be proud of him (5:12). In fact this feeling should be mutual throughout (1:14).

4. Yet in the last analysis the only true ground for boasting is in God and in His Son. 'He that boasts, let him boast of the Lord', says Paul twice over to the Corinthians (1 Cor. 1:31; 2 Cor. 10:17). 'Far be it from me to boast, save in the cross of our Lord Jesus Christ', he says to the Galatians (6:14). If he has any reason to be proud of his own work, it is only 'in Christ Jesus' (Rom. 15:17). In fact, Christians can be described as those who 'boast of God through our Lord Jesus Christ' because of the new relationship with God which has come to them through Him (Rom. 5:11), or simply as those who 'boast of Christ Jesus' (Phil. 3:3). And, finally, this boasting is not only for the present. We can 'boast of our hope of the glory of God' (Rom. 5:2), and we are bidden to hold that boasting of our hope fast, and never let it go (Heb. 3:6).

Let us examine our boasting again in the light of the New Testament. Our boasting in ourselves, of which there is so much, receives frequent condemnation and little support. Our pride in other people is encouraged. But pre-eminently we are bidden to be proud of our God and to let other people share in our pride. We have a great God who has done great things. Perhaps He has done great things for us. Are we as proud of Him as we are of even our own smallest achievements? and are we willing to let that pride be seen?

63. CAUSES OF STUMBLING

The New Testament has a good deal to say about causes of stumbling, both of the ways in which men are themselves caused to stumble and of the ways in which they cause others to stumble.

'Causes of stumbling' is a somewhat clumsy translation, though it is perhaps the only one that will cover all our instances. Older English could use the words 'offence', 'offend', which come from the Latin word meaning a cause of stumbling, but in modern English 'offence' means an affront or a crime, rather than a cause of stumbling. That is why, in the Revised Standard Version, we find such translations as 'obstacle, hindrance, pitfall, temptation, difficulty, falling away', and in the New English Bible 'downfall, leading astray, undoing, falling foul, losing faith'.

There are two series of Greek words included within our subject. The first—*proskoptō*, I knock against, stumble, *proskomma*, *proskopē*, knocking against, stumbling—has fifteen occurrences, five in the gospels, eight in Paul, and two in 1 Peter. The second series—*skandalizō*, I ensnare, entrap, *skandalon*, a snare or trap—has forty-four occurrences, thirty-two in the gospels (of which nineteen are in Matthew), nine in Paul, and three other single instances. (N.B. ´ The English word 'scandal', which comes from this, has—like 'offence'—changed its meaning. It now means causing offence by bad behaviour or by gossip.) All the Greek words have the same fundamental meaning of moral or spiritual stumbling or falling, or of causing others to stumble or fall, and we shall consider them all as a whole.

In five instances the words are used in their literal sense, though each case has a metaphorical meaning behind it. In Mt. 4:6 (Lk. 4:11) Satan tempts Jesus with the Scriptural promise that angels would save Him from *striking* His foot against a stone if He threw Himself down from the temple. In Mt. 7:27 the word is used of winds *beating* against a house. In Jn. 11:9, 10 Jesus speaks of a man not stumbling in the daytime, but stumbling if he walks at night.

In all other instances, however, the words are used in a direct moral or spiritual sense. They may be divided into two main classes: 1. when the man concerned is caused to stumble by some outside person or circumstance and is warned or criticised in consequence; 2. when the man concerned has caused someone else to stumble and is likewise warned or criticised. There is no case where a man is ever excused for falling himself, or for causing others to fall.

1. The first outside circumstance which causes a man to stumble may be no further away than his own body. 'If your right eye or hand causes you to stumble', get rid of it, to avoid worse evils that may come (Mt. 5:29, 30). Self-discipline in sex may save a man from utter downfall. Or the discipline may be needed with regard to food. Those rather obscure words in Rom. 11:9: 'Let their table be made a snare' refer in the Psalm (69:22), though not in the Romans context, to people who were so occupied with feasting that their enemies attacked them unnoticed. Stumbling may also be caused by persecution: 'When tribulation or persecution arises because of the word, straightway he stumbles' (Mt. 13:21; Mk. 4:17). 'They shall deliver you up unto tribulation . . . and then shall many stumble'

(Mt. 24:9, 10). Some people cannot remain loyal to Christ unless everything is going easily. Stumbling may also be caused by a straight word from Christ: 'The Pharisees were offended' (Mt. 15:12) because of what Jesus had to say about the Jewish food laws. The disciples were caused to stumble because of what He said about Himself as the Living Bread (Jn. 6:61). And Peter notes how this attitude continues: 'They stumble at the word' (1 Pet. 2:8).

Most of all, the New Testament underlines the way in which men are made to stumble by the fact of Christ Himself and by their refusal to accept Him. He is 'a stone of stumbling and a rock of offence' over which men constantly stumble. One word or the other comes six times in Rom. 9:32, 33 and 1 Pet. 2:8. His own people in Nazareth took offence at Him (Mt. 13:57; Mk. 6:3). His death was a stumbling-block to His disciples, as He Himself told them that it would be (Mt. 26:31; Mk. 14:27); and Peter, even though he assured his Master that it would not make him fall away (Mt. 26:33; Mk. 14:29), was the one who disgraced himself most openly. Paul twice describes the Cross as a stumbling-block, with special reference to the Jews. It was a stumbling-block to them, just as it was foolishness to the Gentiles (1 Cor. 1:23). It was a stumbling-block just because it stood for the exact opposite of all that circumcision implied (Gal. 5:11). Only the true follower of Christ—and how few there are!—can accept without stumbling all that His Cross entails.

2. The second of the two classes covers the instances when we cause others to stumble. The New Testament often emphasises this with regard to the weak. We noted in Mt. 5:29, 30 the reference to the eye or the hand causing a man to stumble in matters of self-discipline. In Mk. 9:42-47 this is put in the context of causing the 'little ones' who believe in Christ to stumble, upsetting those who are weak in their faith and who need all possible help. Lk. 17:1, 2 has it in the same context, and Matthew, who had it in the other context in chapter 5, has it in Mark's context in 18:6-9. In the parable of the tares, when Jesus speaks of the angels gathering out of His kingdom all things that cause stumbling, He is probably referring to all the 'causes of sin' (R.S.V.) that lead weak men astray (Mt. 13:41). Paul twice uses the word in connection with the weak: 'Beware lest your liberty become a stumbling-block to the weak' (1 Cor. 8:9). And he goes on in 2 Cor. 11:29 to speak of how he himself

H

is made to burn with anger when the weak are caused to stumble. He cannot bear to see them tripped up. The rather strange reference to Balak and Balaam in Rev. 2:14 at any rate indicates that the Israelites were weak in their faith and were tripped up deliberately.

Seven times Paul makes his appeal not on grounds of weakness but of brotherhood. The words come four times in Rom. 14:13, 20, 21: 'Let no man put a stumbling-block or occasion of falling in his *brother's* way'; 'Everything is pure in itself, but anything is bad for the man who by his eating causes another to fall'; 'It is a fine thing to abstain from eating meat or drinking wine or doing anything which causes your *brother's* downfall' (N.E.B.) In 1 Cor. 8:13 the same appeal is made twice. In Rom. 16:17, with a slightly different emphasis, Paul appeals to his readers, as *brethren*, to turn away from those who cause offence.

Mt. 16:23 is unique. Jesus tells Peter that, by his attempting to turn Him from the Cross, he is a stumbling-block to Him.

Finally, by contrast, there are those who are neither caused to stumble nor cause others to do so. Jesus Himself took care not to cause offence to the collectors of the temple tax (Mt. 17:27). He was delighted to find some who were not caused to stumble by His ministry (Mt. 11:6; Lk. 7:23). He spoke to His disciples at the Last Supper to guard them against the breakdown of their faith (Jn. 16:1, N.E.B.). And the man who loves his brother and walks in the light is the man in whom 'there is no occasion of stumbling' (1 Jn. 2:10). That is how Christ would have us all be, so that His Church may truly fulfil His purposes.

64. ENMITY

The words 'enemy' and 'enmity' normally bring to our minds individuals or nations who are hostile to us, and whom it is our business to resist and overcome.

What a different attitude the New Testament presents! It uses the abstract noun *enmity* six times, and the personal noun *enemy* thirty-two times. Out of these thirty-eight instances seventeen are in the Synoptic Gospels, thirteen in Paul, and eight in the rest of the New Testament.

Seven of the uses are in the ordinary worldly sense. Herod and Pilate were at enmity with each other (Lk. 23:12). Enmities are in the list of the 'works of the flesh' in Gal. 5:20. The old Jewish law was 'Love your neighbour and hate your enemy' (Mt. 5:43). A personal enemy comes into the parable of the wheat and the tares (Mt. 13:25, 28). The parable of the pounds also includes personal enemies of the nobleman who is its central figure (Lk. 19:27). Finally Jesus prophesies the time when the enemies of Jerusalem will bring about its destruction (Lk. 19:43). The New Testament knows the normal use of the word.

These instances, however, are almost incidental. The New Testament takes the meaning of enmity very much deeper. It does this in two distinct ways. Firstly it indicates that the ultimate enmity is enmity against God and against all that is connected with Him. This aspect of the word is found in twenty-two places. And secondly it tells us the true Christian attitude to our enemies and to the spirit of enmity as a whole. This aspect occurs nine times.

1. 'The mind of the flesh', says St. Paul in Rom. 8:7, 'is enmity against God'. 'The outlook of the lower nature' (as the New English Bible translates it) is not to be thought of simply as selfishness, self-indulgence, a passion for carnal pleasures. It is more than that. It is hostility to God Himself, opposition to His purposes. James, so often contrasted with Paul, says almost the same thing: 'The friendship of the world is enmity with God. Whosoever would be a friend of the world makes himself an enemy of God' (4:4). If we live according to the standards of the *kosmos* (the world organised without reference to God), then however pleasant our life, however free from gross vices, we are ultimately God's enemies. We are failing to fulfil His purposes, and he that is not for Him is against Him. In Col. 1:21 Paul talks of our being alienated and enemies in our mind in our evil works. That takes the matter a stage further. A life of wickedness inevitably turns a man against God. He usually knows that what he is doing is displeasing to God, and if that knowledge does not make him repent, it makes him all the more hostile, attacking God in order to justify his own practices. Paul uses the phrase 'Thou enemy of all righteousness' in addressing Elymas the sorcerer in Acts 13:10. Paul had been interesting the proconsul in Cyprus, getting him to listen to God's word; and Elymas had tried to turn aside the proconsul's interest, knowing that he would lose his influence with him if he became a Christian. Paul saw that that

was not just a matter of rival human interests. It was direct opposition to the righteousness of God.

In Gal. 4:16 this opposition to God is described in terms of opposition to the truth. Paul has been telling the truth to the Galatians, and because of that has come to be regarded by some as an enemy. In Phil. 3:18 he speaks of those who are 'enemies of the cross of Christ', saying the same thing in even more specifically Christian terms. This kind of opposition is often aroused when a man such as Paul commits himself to Christ. Jesus had foretold this: 'a man's enemies shall be they of his own household' (Mt. 10:36).

But God promises ultimate victory over such hostility. Zacharias realised this. There would be 'salvation from our enemies', and we should expect to be 'delivered out of the hands of our enemies and serve God without fear' (Lk. 1:71, 74). The vision in the Book of Revelation speaks of the Two Witnesses (probably meaning Moses and Elijah, the Law and the Prophets), persecuted and killed, but rising again and triumphing over their enemies (Rev. 11:5, 12). The same triumph of Christ is emphasised in an oft-repeated quotation from Ps. 110:1: 'Sit thou on my right hand, till I put thine enemies under thy feet' or, in some passages, 'till I make thine enemies the footstool of thy feet' (see Mt. 22:44; Mk. 12:36; Lk. 20:43; Acts 2:35; Heb. 1:13; 10:13, and compare 1 Cor. 15:25). This phraseology is not to be taken literally in terms of human warfare. The real enemy, who inspires all opposition to Christ and to His followers, is not a human one, to be opposed with material weapons. He is the Devil. It is he who is the enemy who sows all the tares among the wheat of God's goodness (Mt. 13:39). It is of him that Jesus was thinking when He said to His disciples, 'I have given you the power to tread underfoot . . . all the forces of the enemy' (Lk. 10:19, N.E.B.). It is he who is associated with Death, the last enemy of all to be overcome (1 Cor. 15:26). He is the supreme enemy in all our spiritual warfare.

2. The second New Testament aspect of the word *enemy* would seem to contradict the first, but it does not. We are to oppose evil and the Devil with all our power, but we are to love our enemies in themselves and try to win them over by doing them all the good we can. This is one of the most striking elements in the whole teaching of Jesus (Mt. 5:44; Lk. 6:27, 35). In fact it is the teaching of parts of the Old Testament as well. The book of Proverbs says, 'If your enemy hunger, feed him'

(25:21), and Paul passed that word on to the Romans (12:20), having learnt its message no doubt from the Old Testament, but even more truly from his Master. He gives a similar message to the Thessalonians (2 Thess. 3:15) when he is speaking about those who will not obey what he says. They are not to be counted as enemies, but admonished as brothers.

Loving your enemies in order to win them back is the essential Christian message because it is what God Himself did in Christ: 'While we were enemies, we were reconciled to Him through the death of His Son' (Rom. 5:10). The old law of commandments could be described as 'the enmity' (Eph. 2:15), and Israel could be spoken of as 'enemies' for the sake of the Gentiles (Rom. 11:28), because they were in such a state of enmity against God that He turned from them to save the Gentiles. But on His Cross Christ slew 'the enmity' (Eph. 2:16). He brought it about so that men who accept the meaning of that Cross can no longer be at enmity either with God or with one another. All enmity is abolished in love.

These New Testament words were spoken to people like ourselves, who always believe that we are in the right and others in the wrong, so that we think of them as our enemies. Think of one single person in your church or institution whom you regard in that way. And what does the New Testament tell you to do — not in general, but to him?

65. FEAR AND FEAR NOT

The verb *phobeomai*, I fear, I am afraid, occurs ninety-five times in the New Testament: eighteen times in Matthew, twelve in Mark, twenty-three in Luke, only five in John, fourteen in Acts, and more rarely in Paul (nine), Hebrews (four), 1 Peter (three), 1 John (one) and Revelation (six). (The noun 'fear' occurs forty-six times, but we limit ourselves here to the verb.)

1. Ten of the ninety-five occurrences describe natural human fear. Joseph was afraid to return to Judaea because Herod's son was reigning there (Mt. 2:22). Peter was afraid of the wind when he was walking on the water (14:30). The woman with the issue of blood was afraid when her secret action was recognised (Mk. 5:33). The parents of the blind man feared the Jews (Jn. 9:22). The temple police were afraid of being stoned by the crowd (Acts 5:26). The Jerusalem Christians were naturally afraid of Paul, their former persecutor, even when he returned

a converted man (9:26).   The sailors were twice afraid of the risks of the sea (27:17, 29).   Peter was for a while afraid of the narrow-minded Jewish Christians (Gal. 2:12).   And John says that a man with fear in his heart instead of love cannot be a perfect Christian (1 Jn. 4:18).

2.   Fifteen of the instances are more than just natural fear; they are guilty fear.   Antipas feared the Baptist because he had condemned his conduct (Mk. 6:20).   The priests and the scribes feared Jesus because of His cleansing of the temple and the popular approval of His act (11:18).   Herod once (Mt. 14:5) and the Jewish authorities six times (Mt. 21:26; Mk. 11:32; Mt. 21:46; Mk. 12:12; Lk. 20:19; Lk. 22:2) are spoken of as fearing the multitudes.   That may be partly fear of civil commotion, but it also indicates a guilty conscience.   Twice even the Roman authorities have a guilty fear when they realise that they have acted unlawfully against Roman citizens (Acts 16:38; 22:29).   There is also a guilty fear in the mind of the man who hid his talent in the earth (Mt. 25:25; Lk. 19:21).   Yet sometimes a guilty fear may be salutary, as when a wrongdoer is afraid of the law (Rom. 13:3, 4).

3.   Five times fear is altruistic fear for the physical or spiritual welfare of others.   The chief captain is afraid lest Paul should be torn in pieces (Acts 23:10).   Paul is afraid lest his readers' minds should be corrupted (2 Cor. 11:3), lest he should not find them the kind of people they ought to be (12:20), lest he should have worked among them to no purpose (Gal. 4:11).   The writer to the Hebrews is similarly afraid lest his readers should have missed their chance with God (4:1).   This is a good kind of fear.

4.   So is the next division of the subject, when the word means awe or reverence of God or Christ.   (We may note in passing the one place where it means reverence or respect for a human being—Eph. 5:33.)   References to the fear of God or Christ occur no fewer than thirty-five times.   During Christ's earthly ministry, men or women often stood in awe of what He did or said: when He healed the paralytic (Mt. 9:8), when He stilled the storm (Mk. 4:41; Lk. 8:25), when He walked on the water (Jn. 6:19), when He cured the demoniac (Mk. 5:15; Lk. 8:35), when He was transfigured (Mt. 17:6; Lk. 9:34), when He spoke of His death and moved towards it (Mk. 9:32; 10:32; Lk. 9:45), when they heard His claim to be Son of God (Jn. 19:8), when the truth of that claim struck them (Mt. 27:54).

when finally He rose from the dead (Mk. 16:8). He Himself bade men fear God; that is the meaning of Mt. 10:28 and the thrice repeated word in Lk. 12:5. It does not refer to the devil. Paul continues the exhortation in Rom. 11:20, though he does not actually mention God's name. 1 Pet. 2:17 puts 'Fear God' as one of the four basic commandments. Rev. 14:7 repeats the same terse command, and in three other places Revelation speaks of fearing God and His name (11:18; 15:4; 19:5). In Acts the Gentiles who have become attached to Judaism are five times almost technically described as God-fearers (10:2; 10:22, 35; 13:16, 26). The term is not so technical in Lk. 1:50 ('His mercy is on them that fear Him'), or in 23:40 ('Do you not even fear God?'), but it describes the same religious attitude. Even the unjust judge accepts the negative description of himeslf as one who does not fear God (Lk. 18:2, 4). The phrase is carried right over into the Christian sphere in Col. 3:22, where 'in singleness of heart fearing *the Lord*' almost certainly refers to Christ rather than to God. And even the shepherds who heard the great announcement of the Incarnation 'were sore afraid' (Lk. 2:9). They could not but be in awe of the glory of God accompanying that announcement, though its message was one of deliverance from fear.

5. This brings us to our final and most striking section. God's greatest word to man is not 'Fear', but 'Fear not'. Twenty-nine times the word occurs with a negative, either as a direct command from God or Christ, or indicating a fearlessness that is due to trust in God. The Gospels fourteen times record the words on the lips of Jesus. When Peter is overcome by the miraculous draught of fishes and his own unworthiness, the Lord bids him 'Fear not'. There are great tasks awaiting him (Lk. 5:10). When the disciples are troubled at the sight of Jesus walking on the water, His immediate response is 'Fear not' (Mt. 14:27; Mk. 6:50; Jn. 6:20). The same kind of fear at the Transfiguration evokes the same encouraging reply (Mt. 17:7). And Jairus, when he comes full of anxiety for his little daughter, is bidden 'Fear not, only believe' (Mk. 5:36; Lk. 8:50). The command particularly underlines the right Christian attitude to persecution: 'Fear them not' (Mt. 10:26); 'Fear not them which kill the body, but are not able to kill the soul' (Mt. 10:28; Lk. 12:4); 'The very hairs of your head are numbered. Fear not therefore' (Mt. 10:31; Lk. 12:7). Christ's continued word to His Church is 'Fear not, little flock; for it is your Father's good

pleasure to give you the kingdom' (Lk. 12:32). The message extends on to the Triumphal Entry. Because the King comes, Jerusalem can get rid of her fear (Jn. 12:15). And after the awesome event of the Resurrection, first the angel, and then the Lord Himself, say to the women, 'Fear not' (Mt. 28:5, 10).

The Church did not forget the message. Paul, perhaps hesitating to go on preaching in Corinth, saw the Lord in a vision saying 'Fear not' (Acts 18:9), and when he was in imminent danger of shipwreck, the same calming word came to him (27:24). In each case a commission accompanied the command: 'I have much people in this city', 'Thou must stand before Caesar'. The promise was not just for Paul's own safety. Hebrews twice reminds its readers of earlier fearlessness: Moses' parents were not afraid of Pharaoh (11:23), nor was Moses himself (11:27). And the writer can go on to say with the Psalmist, 'The Lord is my helper; I will not fear' (13:6). Peter, writing to persecuted people, twice bids them not to be afraid (1 Pet. 3:6, 14). So does St. John the Divine (Rev. 2:10). He himself had had Christ's hand laid upon him, saying 'Fear not' (Rev. 1:17).

Our last four instances are in connection with the Incarnation. 'Fear not, Zacharias', says the angel when he announces the birth of Christ's forerunner (Lk. 1:13). 'Fear not', says Gabriel again to Mary, when he announces Christ's birth (1:30). 'Fear not to take Mary thy wife', says the angel to Joseph (Mt. 1:20), and 'Fear not, there is born to you this day a Saviour', says the angel to the shepherds at Bethlehem (Lk. 2:10). From the very beginning, right up to the end, Christ is the victor over all fear.

66. CHRISTIAN TOGETHERNESS

There is a small Greek preposition, *sun*, meaning 'with' or 'together with', which is often prefixed to a noun or adjective in the same sense that English prefixes the word 'fellow'. There are seventeen of these compound words in the New Testament, nearly all of them in the Epistles. Some of them occur only once; one of them occurs thirteen times. The sum total of uses is forty-nine, of which thirty-two are in St. Paul. Taken together they have a great deal to show us about Christian unity and colleagueship. No Christian can be an individualist, either in what he receives from God or in what he does for God.

1. We look first at the words that stress our fellowship in receiving from God. Four times the New Testament uses the word *fellow-heir*. There is no one who selfishly inherits all his father's property. We share it. Isaac and Jacob began this joint inheritance by being fellow-heirs with Abraham (Heb. 11:9) of God's promises. The Gentiles are fellow-heirs with the Jews through Christ (Eph. 3:6). Wives, in that age that gave no equality to women, are fellow-heirs with their husbands of the grace of life (1 Pet. 3:7). Greatest privilege of all, we are fellow-heirs with Christ, sharing in His sufferings and in His glory (Rom. 8:17).

Then we are *fellow-partakers*. A partaker means literally 'one who takes a part' and does not seek to grab the whole. So Gentile and Jew together take their part of God's promise in Christ Jesus (Eph. 3:6), though the Gentiles are later warned against a different kind of sharing; they are not to be fellow-partakers with those who disobey God's will (5:7).

Paul even speaks of *fellow-partners*. One would have thought that the word 'partner' was enough in itself, but there are those who have been partners in name only and who have worked selfishly for their own interests. The prefix 'fellow' is intended to rule out that kind of partner. The Gentiles are grafted, like the branch of a wild tree, into a good stock, and so become fellow-partners in all its fatness (Rom. 11:17). The Philippians and Paul are together fellow-partners of God's grace (Phil. 1:7). That involves not only privilege but responsibility: Paul is ready to go to any length in order that he may be a fellow-partner with his Master and his brethren in the work of the Gospel (1 Cor. 9:23). In fact, this is a partnership both in hardship and in joy: John describes himself as 'your fellow-partner in the tribulation and the kingdom and the endurance which are in Jesus' (Rev. 1:9).

The metaphor changes yet again when St. Paul speaks of the Gentiles as *fellow-citizens* of the saints (Eph. 2:19), sharing equally in the duties and privileges that belong to those who owe loyalty to a common country. He changes it once more when he speaks of the same Gentiles as *fellow-members-of-the-body* (Eph. 3:6 —a single word in Greek); there is no greater physical unity than that of the human body, with all its parts instinctively co-operating for the good of the whole.

St. Peter has one more word. The church in Babylon (by which he probably means Rome) is *fellow-elect* with the churches to whom Peter is writing (1 Pet. 5:13). All are on the same basis, equally chosen by God. That is why they can support each other in times of trial.

2.   There are two adjectives which express this spirit of fellowship between Christians. There is the word translated 'of one accord' in Phil. 2:2, but which is literally 'fellow-souled'. There is also the word translated 'compassionate' in 1 Pet. 3:8 which, as the R.V. margin shows, is literally 'sympathetic', *fellow-feeling*, sharing fully in each others' feelings.

When we thus share in God's gifts and share each others' feelings, we can then go on to work together. The New Testament uses no fewer than nine 'fellow' words to describe the different aspects of our colleagueship. First of all we must be *fellow-disciples* (Jn. 11:16), learning together how to work together. Then we can go on to be *fellow-workers*. Paul loves to describe his companions by this word: in Romans 16, first Prisca and Aquila (3), then Urbanus (9), and then Timothy (21) are his comrades in action. Titus is so described in 2 Cor. 8:23, with all the more appropriateness after the difficult and delicate task he has just performed in restoring right relationships in the Corinthian church. Then Epaphroditus, Paul's link with the Philippian church, is given the same title (Phil. 2:25). So are Clement and others in Phil. 4:3, and the longer list in Col. 4:10-11: Aristarchus, Mark, Jesus Justus, Paul's fellow-workers for the kingdom of God. Philemon, in the first verse of the letter to him, is included in the same category, and at the end of the letter (24) comes the longest list of all: Mark, Aristarchus, Demas, Luke. Paul may be in prison, but he and his friends are still on the job.

Nor do the names of people exhaust the uses of this word. In 2 Cor. 1:24 Paul uses the same word, though it is translated '*helpers* of your joy'. Paul thinks of himself and others as being not superiors over the Corinthians but as joining in the work of creating Christian joy in the church. 3 Jn. 8 speaks of being *fellow-workers* with the truth, co-operating with it so that it is victorious everywhere. But the two most interesting uses of the word remain. 1 Cor. 3:9 speaks of Paul and Apollos as 'God's fellow-workers'. This may mean that they worked together, belonging to God, or it may mean that they were fellow-workers with God, actually being allowed to co-operate with Him. In the same way, if we take the reading in 1 Thess. 3:2 which is given in the R.V. margin, Paul describes Timothy as a 'fellow-worker with God', the greatest privilege that any man could be given.

A word that goes even a little deeper is the word that is translated *fellow-servant* (better *fellow-slave*) in Mt. 18:28, 29, 31, 33 and 24:49. There it has no spiritual significance, but in Col. 1:7 and 4:7 Epaphras and Tychicus are described as Paul's fellow-slaves. They do not simply work together with him. They are together with him in being the property of Christ, completely at His disposal. The book of Revelation (6:11) speaks of all faithful Christians as being in that condition, and even the angels in 19:10 and 22:9 place themselves in the same category. Along with human beings they belong to God.

A further compound is the word *fellow-traveller*, a word with a somewhat sinister significance these days, but meaning quite simply those who shared Paul's arduous journeys: Gaius and Aristarchus in Acts 19:29, and Titus in 2 Cor. 8:19, where the English translation is 'to travel with us'. Even more arduous is the task of being a *fellow-soldier*, as Epaphroditus is in Phil. 2:25 and Archippus in Philemon 2, fighting the Christian fight along with Paul. And a soldier runs the risk of capture, so that in Rom. 16:7 Andronicus and Junias are Paul's *fellow-prisoners*, as are Aristarchus in Col. 4:10 and Epaphras in Philemon 23. Yet they are still in the fight, with cheerful greetings passing between them and those outside.

Three words remain, with one striking use each. Peter (1 Pet. 5:1) echoes Paul's note of humility in 2 Cor. 1:24 when he speaks of himself to the elders not as a superior but as a *fellow-elder*. Paul in Phil. 4:3 asks for the help of a friend to settle a quarrel. He addresses him as 'True *yoke-fellow*'. It may well be that the Greek word, *Synzygus*, meaning yoke-fellow, was actually the friend's name, and that Paul is appealing to him to live up to it by sharing this awkward task. And lastly, in Phil. 3:17 there is the exhortation: 'Be *fellow-imitators* of me'. The Philippians are to be united in copying Paul. That is not egoism on his part, since in 1 Cor. 11:1 he goes on to say 'as I imitate Christ'. A Church united in the Imitation of Christ would indeed be a Church that was perfectly one.

67. PARTNERSHIP

Man can do very little without the help of his fellow-men. This is true in daily living, and in business. It is true also in religion, and that is the reason for the Church. And if it is true that man can do little apart from his fellow-men, it is far more true that he can do little without the help of God.

We should therefore expect to find words for partnership, fellowship and sharing in a prominent place in the New Testament—and so we do. There are two which, in their varying forms, are outstanding. The first, *koinōnia*, has as its basis the word meaning 'common', and is translated by 'communion', 'fellowship' and similar words. The personal noun allied with it is translated 'partner', 'partaker' etc. The cognate verb is 'share', 'partake', 'contribute'; and there is also an adjective, translated 'willing to communicate', that is, 'willing to share'. The second word, *metochē*, means 'having a share or part in', 'partnership', and has a verb 'partake', and a personal noun 'partner' or 'partaker'.

Taken altogether these words occur sixty-two times: three times in the Synoptic Gospels, once in Acts, thirty-five times in Paul, twice in the Pastorals, eleven times in Hebrews, twice in 1 Peter, once in 2 Peter, five times in the epistles of John, and twice in Revelation.

As is the case with most words in the New Testament, they are used on a number of occasions in no specially religious sense. Peter, James and John were business-partners in fishing (Lk. 5:7, 10). Both the Greek nouns are used here with the same meaning, the meaning that we often find in the business correspondence of the period.

Other general uses are found in 2 Cor. 6:14: 'What common interest can there be between goodness and evil? How can light and darkness share life together?' (J. B. Phillips), and in Heb. 2:14, where the writer speaks of us men and of Jesus in His incarnation all having a share of the flesh and blood of which human bodies are made. In Heb. 5:13 the reference is to a baby's share in the supply of milk, and in 7:13 it is to participation in a common racial heritage. (The Greek word is our word, though the English translations are 'pertains', 'belongs'; see R.V. margin).

The main usage of the words in the New Testament is, however, in a directly spiritual context. The Christian is called to have *fellowship with God* (1 Jn. 1:3, 6), that is, to share in His life and in His purposes. He is to be a sharer in the divine nature (2 Pet. 1:4). He is a sharer in God's grace (Phil. 1:7), and in God's calling (Heb. 3:1). He is a sharer too in God's discipline (12:8), a sharing that we are usually very unwilling to accept. And finally he will be a sharer in God's glory (1 Pet. 5:1).

The Christian is also called to have *fellowship with Christ*, though to say 'the Christian' in the singular is to give only part of the truth, because the New Testament, when it speaks of fellowship either with God or with Christ, nearly always does so in the plural. This fellowship must be personal. We cannot depend upon others' relationship with God without making it our own. But it must never be merely individual. It is always linked with that of other Christians in the Church. In 1 Cor. 1:9 Paul says 'You were called into the fellowship of His Son', and the phrase has a twofold meaning: personal relationship with Christ, within the fellowship created by Him. So in 1 Cor. 10:16, 'communion of the body of Christ' means being linked personally to Christ Himself and linked equally strongly to His Body, the Church. The following verse underlines this: '*we all* partake of the one bread'. The corporate nature of this personal fellowship with Christ is taken for granted in most of the other passages which speak of fellowship with Him. We *share* in the benefits of the death of Christ (1 Cor. 10:16). *Our* fellowship is with Him (1 Jn. 1:3). *We* can participate in all that He has to give us (Heb. 3:14). We even have the privilege of sharing in His sufferings (1 Pet. 4:13; 2 Cor. 1:7). Paul on one occasion speaks of that privilege as his own personal experience, but John comes back to the participation with the Church as a whole: 'partaker *with you* in the tribulation and kingdom and patience which are in Jesus' (Rev. 1:9).

The same is true with regard to *fellowship with the Holy Spirit*. We are 'partakers of the Holy Spirit' (Heb. 6:4), but not simply as individuals. Paul appeals to the Philippians to be united with one another, saying 'If there is any fellowship of the Spirit' (Phil. 2:1), by which he means both personal fellowship with the Spirit and also the fellowship in the Church which the Spirit creates. And so too the familiar phrase with which our worship often closes, 'the fellowship of the Holy Spirit' (2 Cor. 13:14), is a prayer for the personal presence of the Spirit in each member's heart, and also for the binding together of the whole Church in fellowship by the Spirit's action.

This leads us on to a large number of instances of participation, partnership, sharing, fellowship in various ways in the life of the Church. And if God's name is not always mentioned in these instances, it is always implied that this fellowship is in Him. Right from the beginning, one of the practices of the Church was fellowship (Acts 2:42). They grew because they lived in close association with the apostles and with one another. Next, the battle was won whereby the Gentiles became sharers with Jewish Christians of the rich inheritance of Israel (Rom. 11:17), and shared in their spiritual things (15:27), and became 'fellow-partakers of the promise' (Eph. 3:6), so that Paul could write to the largely Gentile church at Philippi: 'You are all my fellow-partakers of grace' (Phil. 1:7). James and the leaders of the Jerusalem church gave Paul the right hand of fellowship to confirm that spiritual partnership (Gal. 2:9).

This partnership is not only between Jew and Gentile. It is also between men engaged in the same Christian task. Paul calls both Titus and Philemon his partners (2 Cor. 8:23; Phm. 17). Philemon's own faith spreads out to the whole group of Christians in his house, so that there is an effective fellowship of faith (Phm. 6). Nor is the partnership under easy conditions only. The Philippians have fellowship with Paul's affliction (4:14), helping him in time of need. The Hebrew Christians became partakers with others undergoing persecution (Heb. 10: 33). Fellowship in the Church rounds off our fellowship with the Father and the Son, as the four successive uses of the word in 1 Jn. 1:3-7 show.

In the New Testament this fellowship is often very practical. There are eight places where the word is used of an act of material giving. The translation is variously 'fellowship', 'contribution', 'communicating', but the original word is the same: an act of fellowship expressed in material form. In Rom. 15:26; 2 Cor. 8:4; 9:13, it is connected with the collection that Paul took among the Gentile churches for the poor in Jerusalem. In Rom. 12:13; Gal. 6:6; 1 Tim. 6:18 and Heb. 13:16, where the word 'communicate' is used, the meaning is 'share your possessions with those in need'. (It has nothing to do with partaking of Holy Communion.) In Phil. 4:15 Paul writes of the real fellowship involved in loving financial giving. Money has often done much harm. It is a joy to remember how much good it can do when given and received in Christian partnership.

Yet not all partnerships are good. There is partnership with evil, against which the New Testament eight times warns us. Jesus condemns the Pharisees for their hypocrisy in asserting that they would not have been partners in murder (Mt. 23:30). Paul speaks of the danger of being in fellowship with devils (1 Cor. 10:20, 21). 'Do not be a partner in other men's sins' says 1 Tim. 5:22. And the same thought is expressed in Eph. 5:7, 11, 2 Jn. 11 and Rev. 18:4. Messrs Evil and Partners are a bad firm to work for.

The ideal partnership is that in which we can be joint partners of the Gospel (1 Cor. 9:23), and when we can have fellowship with other Christians in its furtherance (Phil. 1:5). That is a partnership which will never fail to be productive, because it is organised by Christ and run in fellowship with Him.

68. FOUR NOTES OF THE EARLY CHURCH

(a) Boldness and Fellowship

1. *Boldness.* The Greek word *parrēsia* comes five times in Acts, and its corresponding verb, 'to speak boldly', seven times. The words were originally used of the right of every Greek citizen to address his city assembly. To take advantage of that right needed courage; he might have to face jeers and worse. But the possession of the right gave him confidence. It was a 'fundamental right', which no one could take from him.

So it was with the apostles. To speak as they did to the variety of audiences we find in Acts must have taken greater courage than we sometimes stop to realise — but they could do it because they knew their rights as citizens of the Kingdom, and because they were called to do it by God.

We see Peter first (Acts 2:29), daring to stand up in the Mecca of the Jews and say that the true interpretation of their Scriptures was that this Galilean teacher was the Messiah. It took courage based on certainty to make such a claim in that place — the sort of courage which might be expected only from an outstanding leader such as Peter. But it was not limited to him. After he and John had been arrested and threatened by the Sanhedrin, they returned to their own company, and the immediate reaction of the infant church was not fear but a prayer for boldness (4:29). That prayer was answered immediately (4:31).

The quality comes next in apostolic succession to Paul, the man with whom we associate it most closely. There is no delay before he begins. Right from the start in Damascus (9:27) Barnabas can testify to him—and on his very first return to the city which he had left on his errand of persecution he starts his bold preaching in the name of the Lord (9:29). The next momentous step forward, the turning to the Gentiles at Antioch, is made with the same boldness (13:46), and followed up in the same spirit in Iconium (14:3). Not that the Jews ceased to benefit. He continues his bold speaking in the synagogue at Ephesus (19:8); he talks equally freely before Agrippa (26:26) at a time when he might well have been inhibited by a public enquiry; and it is his manner towards all, right up to the end, almost the last word in the book. Even though in prison, he teaches the things concerning Jesus Christ 'with all boldness'. We cannot be sure where the letter to the Ephesians was written, here or during an earlier imprisonment, but it is revealing that one of the few personal notes in that letter which is mainly concerned with his apostleship to the Gentiles is a request for prayer that he may be given boldness to preach the Gospel (6:20).

What was the secret of this boldness? Acts makes that perfectly clear. In 4:13 the Sanhedrin notes the boldness of the two uneducated Galilean peasants, and the only explanation seems to be that they had been with Jesus. And in 4:31 the answer to the prayer for boldness is the gift of the Holy Spirit. That gives them what they have prayed for.

We still have frightening, inhibiting circumstances to face. The Church always has had, and always will, till the end. Just as then, there are individuals who make trouble, officials who are hostile, people with utterly different ways of religious thought, new spheres hitherto unentered. We still need this boldness, and know how sorely we lack it. But it still comes on the same terms: as the result of companionship with Jesus and the giving, in answer to prayer, of His Spirit of power and love.

2. *Fellowship*. The actual word comes only once in Acts (2:42), though it is common in the epistles; but many other words express its meaning in the apostolic history. The phrase 'with one accord' (one word, *homothumadon*, in Greek) is used five times of the Church: in 1:14 they are praying with one accord, in 2:46 the phrase describes their joyous common life, in 4:24 it comes again in connection with prayer, in 5:12 it is in relation

to their gathering in God's house, and in 15:25 they use it to describe their agreement with regard to the unity of Jew and Gentile in Christ.

Then there is the unusual phrase *epi to auto*, usually translated 'together', which probably has the special meaning 'in Church fellowship'. If we look up Acts 1:15, 2:44, 2:47 (where the R.V. margin shows that 'to them' is really this same phrase), and also 1 Cor. 11:20 and 14:23, and translate each occurrence in this way, we shall find the meaning greatly enriched.

Nor are we limited to particular phrases. The sense of togetherness is expressed in Acts with great variety. In 2:14 Peter stands up 'with the eleven' to speak. In 4:32 the multitude of them that believe are 'of one heart and soul'. The story of Dorcas (9:36 ff.) introduces the fellowship of the women. The church is 'gathered together' in John Mark's house (12:12) to pray for Peter in prison. Paul's speech to the Ephesian elders (20:18-35) is the most moving expression of fellowship in the book, but his willingness to accommodate himself to the practices of the Jerusalem church (21:17-26) shows a triumph in an even greater test: the test of living together in unity with people from whom you differ. The final instance of fellowship in Acts is the long journey made by the Italian Christians in 28:15 to welcome a shipwrecked prisoner to their soil and give him fresh courage.

It is not only, however, in detailed examples but in the whole spirit of Acts that we find the proof of fellowship. The early Church could never have accomplished what it did if its strength had been sapped by inward dissensions, if its work had been the work of individuals, if it had not preached the Gospel out of a spirit of glad unity.

The Church has never lost sight of the need for vital fellowship. The Franciscans, the early Methodists, the Church of South India—these are only a few examples, yet so often we ignore fellowship, or work against it to further the aims of a party or of our own selfishness. Men divide the Church, and especially the local congregation, because they have no sense of the team and do not understand what it means 'each to count other better than himself' (Phil. 2:3). Committees meet and deal painstakingly, though not always without friction, with the business before them, yet seldom rise to the sense of fellowship in a crusade. Individuals work with devotion at their teaching, their medical work, their preaching, their administration, without

the uplift and power that team-work can give. The most assi-
duous workers are so wrapped up in their own job that they have
no time or thought for their fellow-labourers. We are sometimes so sure that we ourselves can do the job best, that we never
think of sharing it with anyone else, like the common sight
of the clever dribbler on the football field who has never learnt
the spiritual lesson of passing.

All of us have the capacity for fellowship, and many seize on
it eagerly when it is offered. But the condition for fellowship
is always openness. Ananias and Sapphira damaged the fellowship of the early Church because they 'kept back part' (Acts 5:2).
If people are not willing, under the .guidance of God, to open
their hearts to each other in words of gratitude, of confession,
of challenge, of guidance, of comfort, then fellowship cannot
grow. But when men learn costly openness with each other,
then they can come into each others' hearts and become a unity
which God can use, as He used the unity of the Church of the
Acts.

69. FOUR NOTES OF THE EARLY CHURCH

(b) Joy and Witness

Joy and Witness are two more of the characteristic notes of
the early Church as depicted in the Acts of the Apostles.

3. *Joy.* There are two Greek words for Joy: *Chara* and its
corresponding verb *chairō*, which together come eleven times in
Acts, and *agalliasis* which, with its verb, comes another three
times. There is little difference in the use of the two words,
but the second is somewhat stronger: exultation, exuberant joy.

Acts gives us no fewer than five different types of joy. There
is *firstly* the joy that comes because of the discovery that God
is fulfilling His promises. At Pentecost Peter quotes the words
of the sixteenth Psalm to express his joy that Christ had risen
from the dead as David said He would (Acts 2:26-28). At
Antioch the Gentiles are glad that the words spoken through
Isaiah (49:6) are now taking effect and that Jesus has in truth
become 'for a light of the Gentiles' (Acts 13:47, 48). Nothing
gives more delight than the realisation that the Scriptures are
not just beautiful words, but are guarantees which God will
fulfil.

Secondly, Acts shows us the joy of men over their own conversion. The Ethiopean eunuch 'went on his way rejoicing' (8:39). The Philippian jailor (16:34) was 'overjoyed' (Moffatt) at having believed in God. This is the stronger word: 'bubbling over with joy'. As Charles Wesley puts it: 'In the heavenly Lamb Thrice happy I am, And my heart it doth dance at the sound of His name'. How can you help rejoicing when for the first time it comes home to you that God loves you and that His power can set you free from sin?

But, *thirdly*, to rejoice over one's own conversion alone is not enough. People in Acts are big enough to rejoice over the conversion of others, even though they are utterly different from themselves. When great numbers of Greeks began to turn to the Lord in Antioch (11:20-21), Barnabas was sent by the Jerusalem church to investigate. This event seemed rather strange and disturbing. But Barnabas was able to recognise it for what it was: the working of the grace of God, and he was glad (11:23). And when later he joined Paul in his visit to Jerusalem to discuss the problems raised by the entry of the Gentiles into the Church, as they went on their way through Phoenicia and Samaria, they told the churches there what had happened and 'caused great joy to all the brethren' (15:3). There is no selfish individualism in such an experience.

This is borne out, *fourthly*, by the references to joy in fellowship. The beautiful description of the common life of the early Church in 2:46 speaks of their sharing their meals with unaffected joy (N.E.B.). And when the problems of the relationship between Jewish and Gentile Christians have been dealt with at the Council of Jerusalem, and the Gentile Christians are reading the sympathetic letter which has been sent to them, they rejoice for the consolation (15:31). Joy in fellowship did indeed lead Rhoda astray: 'When she knew Peter's voice, she opened not the gate for joy' (12:14), but at any rate there was the right feeling in her heart, a better feeling than we often have today in the company of our fellow-Christians.

But, *fifthly*, Acts speaks of a deeper joy than joy in happy circumstances. It speaks of a joy that still remains constant in trouble. In 5:41 the apostles, after being threatened and beaten, depart 'rejoicing that they have been counted worthy to suffer dishonour for the Name'. In 13:52, though Paul and Barnabas have been cast out of Antioch, yet the new disciples, left to stand on their own, are 'filled with joy and with the Holy

Ghost'. This is what has carried the Church through the centuries: a joy that does not depend upon mere outward happiness, but upon the power of the Spirit of God.

4. *Witness.* This, as one would expect, is a very prominent word in Acts. The verb *martureō* comes eleven times, the abstract nouns *marturion, marturia* three times, and the personal noun *martus* thirteen times.

The verb is not used in any outstanding sense. Five times it comes with regard to the testimony given to men's good character, usually with the translation 'report': The Seven (6:3), Cornelius (10:22), David (13:22), Timothy (16:2), Ananias (22:12). Twice Paul calls on the Jewish authorities to testify to his zeal for his original faith (22:5; 26:5). Once it is the witness of the prophets to Christ (10:43). Twice it is God bearing witness, by signs and wonders (14:3) and by the gift of the Holy Spirit (15:8), to the preaching of His word. Finally it is the Lord's command to Paul (23:11) to go and witness to Him in Rome itself. Nothing outstanding unless you consider the whole Christian witness as outstanding in itself.

The abstract nouns refer once to the Tabernacle as the evidence of God's presence (7:44), once to general Christian witness (22:18), and once (4:33) to special witness to the Resurrection. It is this which leads us to the most remarkable use of the idea in Acts, because the personal noun, 'a witness' is used almost entirely in the context of the Resurrection.

Two of its thirteen uses are not Christian (6:13; 7:58). But look at the other eleven in order: 1:8 'Ye shall be my witnesses', and it is the Risen Christ who is speaking; 1:22—the twelfth apostle is to be specifically a 'witness with us of His resurrection'; 2:32—'This Jesus did God raise up, whereof we all are witnesses'; 5:32—'we are witnesses of these things', and these things include other elements in Christ's ministry, but the Resurrection is prominent; 10:39—'we are witnesses of all things which He did', the reference being mainly to the earthly ministry; 10:41 —'Him God raised up . . . and gave Him to be made manifest . . . unto witnesses': 13:31—'God raised Him from the dead . . . and He was seen for many days of them . . . who are now His witnesses'; 22:15—'You shall be a witness . . . of what you have seen and heard', and the reference is to Paul's vision of the Risen Christ; 22:20—'Stephen thy witness', and again it was of the Risen Christ, standing at the right hand of God, that Stephen

had borne witness; 26:16 — 'a witness of the things which you
have seen', this being a repetition of 22:15.

Thus, out of the eleven uses, only one has nothing special
to do with the Resurrection (10:39). Of the other ten, five are
concerned exclusively with it, and the other five more or less
directly. Above all things the early Church wanted, and were
commanded, to make it known that Jesus was alive. They
were not living on their recollections of a dead teacher, however
great. They were the servants, joyful and confident, of a living
Lord. They were speaking not in the language of idealism but
of fact.

This is the message which we remember and try to proclaim
not only at Easter but at all seasons. The early Church preached
it at all times, because at all times it was the certainty of their
experience. It was because the Lord was risen that they could
face even persecution with joy. It was because the Lord was
risen that their work went always forward. And in so far as we
too are sure of a Risen Lord and witness to Him, He will continue
to prosper His work in our hands today.

70. GOD'S SOVEREIGNTY AND MAN'S DUTY

This is a long title for a chapter dealing with a very short
word, the Greek word *dei*, which is variously translated 'must',
'ought', 'must needs', 'it is necessary'.

It is a word which comes a hundred and two times in the New
Testament: eight times in Matthew, six in Mark, eighteen in
Luke, ten in John, twenty-two in Acts, sixteen in Paul, nine in
the Pastoral Letters, three in Hebrews, once each in 1 and 2 Peter,
and eight in Revelation.

1. It is often used of God's sovereign government of the
affairs of the world and of men, of the things that 'must' happen
because they are according to His will. 2. In this sense Jesus
uses it with regard to His own divine destiny. 3. Occasionally
also it is used with regard to the inevitability of evil.

On the human side it is used 4. with reference to legal obligation, 5. in connection with human disobedience, the things that
people 'ought not' to do and yet so often do, and 6. with regard
to moral and spiritual duty, the things that Christians especially
'must' do because of their obedience to Christ. This last is the

most frequent sense, accounting for nearly half of the total uses.

1. There is always controversy with regard to the extent of God's control of men and of history. The extremist on the one hand would say that this control was absolute. The extremist on the other would deny it altogether. What the New Testament does is to remind us very strongly of God's direction of affairs, though it equally assumes man's free will throughout. Three times the Book of Revelation speaks of 'the things which *must* shortly come to pass' (1:1; 4:1; 22:6), signifying the writer's certainty that the course of history is in God's hands. The symbolism of this book ought not to be taken literally, but the writer's confidence in God's ultimate control of all things is one that we must share. This same belief in God's direction is shown by 'Elijah *must* first come' (Mt. 17:10; Mk. 9:11), 'Thou *must* stand before Caesar' (Acts 27:24), 'we *must* be cast upon an island' (27:26), 'that recompense of their error which was *necessary*' by the laws of God (Rom. 1:27), 'this corruptible *must* put on incorruption' (1 Cor. 15:53), 'we *must* all be made manifest before the judgment seat of Christ' (2 Cor. 5:10). Whether in general or in particular, God's will is to be carried out.

2. Jesus Himself felt this very strongly with regard to His own life. He begins by saying to His parents, 'Did you not know that I *must* be in my Father's house?' (Lk. 2:49). He begins His ministry with 'I *must* preach the good tidings' (4:43). He sums up His mission with 'We *must* work the works of Him that sent me' (Jn. 9:4) and 'Other sheep I have . . .; them also I *must* bring' (10:16). The implication of this second necessity is twice illustrated: 'He *must needs* pass through Samaria' (Jn. 4:4); that was no geographical necessity but a spiritual one. And to Zacchaeus He says, 'Today I *must* abide at your house' (Lk. 19:5). The result in both cases is the salvation of those to whom He goes.

And because the Cross is the heart of His saving work, it also is associated with the word *must;* 'The Son of man *must* suffer many things' (Mk. 8:31; Lk. 9:22; 17:25); 'I *must* go on my way today and tomorrow and the day following' (Lk. 13:33); 'I *must* go unto Jerusalem' (Mt. 16:21). All takes place within this *must* of God's purpose: 'Thus it *must* be' (Mt. 26:54); 'This which is written *must* be fulfilled in me' (Lk. 22:37); '*Must* not the Christ have suffered these things and enter into His glory?'

(24:26); 'The Son of man *must* be lifted up' (Jn. 3:14; 12:34). Yet it is not only the Cross that is a *must*.   So is the Resurrection: 'the Scripture that He *must* rise again from the dead' (Jn. 20:9). In fact they are both bound together as a whole: 'The Son of man *must* be delivered up . . . be crucified . . . rise' (Lk. 24:7); '*all* things *must needs* be fulfilled which are written' (24:44).

His disciples preached the same message: 'The Christ *must* suffer and rise' (Acts 17:3); 'else *must* He often have suffered' (Heb. 9:26, where the argument denies the word 'often', but does not deny the word 'must'); 'He *must* reign till He has put all His enemies under His feet' (1 Cor. 15:25); 'whom heaven *must* receive till the times of restoration' (Acts 3:21).   And they all would have echoed the words of the Baptist: 'He *must* increase, but I *must* decrease' (Jn. 3:30).   It was the certainty of *His* triumph, not their own, that they proclaimed.

3.   Along with the certainty of the fulfilment of God's will comes also an element of the inevitability of evil.   'These things *must* come to pass' (Mt. 24:6; Mk. 13:7; Lk. 21:9), says Jesus, looking ahead to the troubles that will meet His disciples before the End.   'For a little while, since it is *necessary*, you have had to suffer', says Peter (1 Pet. 1:6) according to the most probable translation of the sentence.   Revelation has the same *must* of trouble and evil before the final triumph (13:10; 17:10; 20:3). The Scripture had to be fulfilled with regard to the fate of Judas, said the apostles (Acts 1:16), and in lesser degrees inevitability is associated with evil when Peter says 'If I *must* die with you' (Mt. 26:35; Mk. 14:31), when the Jews cry out that Paul *must* not live any longer (Acts 25:24), and when Paul says that there *must needs* be divisions among the Corinthians (1 Cor. 11:19). God is in control, but the New Testament makes it clear that our path will not be soft and easy.   There will inevitably be hardship and struggle, to purge and purify.

4.   Turning now to the *musts* of human obligation, there are a few legal instances: 'the day on which the Passover *must* be sacrificed' (Lk. 22:7); 'it is *needful* to circumcise them' (Acts 15:5); 'the husbandman *must* be the first to partake of the fruits' (2 Tim. 2:6).   The most significant are in Lk. 13:14, 16, when the ruler of the synagogue says 'There are six days in which men *ought* to work', and Jesus picks up his word in replying '*Ought* not this woman . . . to have been loosed . . . on the sabbath?'

5.   Then there are the obligations which are disobeyed: the abomination of desolation stands 'where he *ought not*' (Mk.

13:14); the young widows in 1 Tim. 5:13 speak 'things which they *ought not*'; the teachers in Tit. 1:11 teach 'things which they *ought not*, for filthy lucre's sake'. Twice over Paul, though he says that he '*must* boast' (2 Cor. 11:30; 12:1), has an uneasy feeling that it is an act of disobedience.

6.   But the glory of human obligation in the New Testament lies in the positive Christian *must*. See what God and His Son tell us we *must* be and do: we *must* have mercy (Mt. 18:33), and combine with it justice and faith (23:23); we *must* be good stewards of what is entrusted to us (25:27); we *must* be ready to preach the Gospel universally (Mk. 13:10; Rev. 10:11), to be witnesses to the Risen Christ (Acts 1:22), to say what we *ought* to say even under persecution (Lk. 12:12). We *ought* to be glad when sinners return to God (Lk. 15:32). We *ought* always to pray (Lk. 18:1), and to accept the Spirit's help because we do not know 'how to pray as we *ought*' (Rom. 8:26). We *ought* to worship, not in some special locality (Jn. 4:20), but 'in spirit and truth' (4:24). We *ought* to obey God rather than men (Acts 5:29). We *ought* to be ready to suffer for Christ's name (9:16) and for His kingdom (14:22). We *ought* to be eager to go to key places and bear witness there (19:21; 23:11). We *ought* to be ready to speak boldly about the Gospel (Eph. 6:20) and to make it manifest (Col. 4:4), but never to think of ourselves more highly than we *ought* (Rom. 12:3). If we are conceited, we do not yet know as we *ought* (1 Cor. 8:2).

If we are in positions of responsibility, we *must* be without reproach (1 Tim. 3:2), blameless (Tit. 1:7), gentle (2 Tim. 2:24), of a good reputation among non-Christians (1 Tim. 3:7), conscious of our responsibility to help the weak (Acts 20:35). Whoever we are, our ears *must* be open to God's commands (9:6), giving earnest heed to the Gospel message (Heb. 2:1), so that in turn we may know how we *ought* to answer any enquiry or argument (Col. 4:6). Within the Christian fellowship we have a duty of personal conduct (1 Tim. 3:15), a duty which can be learnt from men such as Paul, either by hearing how we *ought* to walk (1 Thess. 4:1), or by obeying the command 'Ye *ought* to imitate us' (2 Thess. 3:7). The whole of the Christian obligation is summed up in 2 Pet. 3:11: 'What manner of persons *ought* you to be in all holy living and godliness!'

(For the complete record the reader may look up Acts 19:36; 24:19; 25:10; 26:9; 27:21; 2 Cor. 2:3; Tit. 1:11; Rev. 11:5, but these verses need no special comment here).

We cannot, however, end on the note of mere moral obligation, important though that is. Underneath it lies something more fundamental. The primary *must* is that of faith in God: 'He that cometh to God *must* believe that He is' (Heb. 11:6). And he must believe not only in God's existence but in His saving power. Peter uses the word *must* very unexpectedly in Acts 4:12 when he speaks of the Name 'wherein we *must* be saved'. He may mean that salvation is God's determined plan for us, or that it is something that we cannot do without. Both are true. The Philippian jailor thought only in terms of his own obligation when he said: 'What *must* I do to be saved?' (Acts 16:30). Paul's reply was like that of Heb. 11:6: 'Believe'. The Lord Himself sums it up finally in His word to Nicodemus. Human performance of duty is both inadequate and impossible. 'You *must* be born again' (Jn. 3:7). When new life has been accepted from God, then all the *musts* of duty become possible in His power.

71. IMITATION

We do not always use the word Imitation in a good sense. We very often contrast it with what is real and genuine. And the word Mimic, which is derived from the Greek word for Imitating is a word that is used contemptuously, if it is not used humorously.

Yet, surprisingly enough, the New Testament when it uses the word always does so in a favourable sense, and one of the most popular books of Christian devotion is, after all, called The Imitation of Christ. Clearly the word and the thought behind it are worth consideration.

The verb *imitate* (*mimeomai*) occurs four times, and the noun *imitator* (*mimētēs*) seven. Of these eleven instances no fewer than eight are in St. Paul. In his dealing with new believers he knew the value of simple imitation. How often the teacher, especially of young children, has to say 'Now look at me and do it as I do'. Paul quite unashamedly tells his new converts to imitate him. This is not egoism. Paul has no personal vanity. But he knows what a difference his own conversion has made to him, and that the new converts in Thessalonica, Corinth and elsewhere have had no previous opportunity to see what a Christian man is like. The simplest and most unaffected thing, therefore, is to tell them to imitate him.

The Thessalonians, his simplest church, are told that they ought to imitate him (he says 'us'; perhaps he includes his companions, Silvanus and Timothy) in living disciplined lives, and not being lazy and thus a burden to others. Paul's own life among them was deliberately organised so that he would be a true pattern for them in this respect (2 Thess. 3:7, 9). It is still true that we say of certain people that their industry shames us out of our laziness, and it is good that there should be people like that for us to imitate.

Most of us form a great part of our character by imitating our parents. Sometimes this is for our good, sometimes it is not; but the fact remains that we do it. We have an old letter, written on papyrus at the end of the second century A.D., in which the young man to whom the letter is written is given the advice: 'Imitate your father, the lover of office, the brave old man'. The advice to imitate his bravery is all right. We would like to know, however, whether the old man was just ambitious for office, or whether he was willing to take responsibility. It makes rather a difference as to whether he should be imitated or not! Anyhow St. Paul appeals to the practice of imitating parents when he is writing to the Corinthians. He tells them that in Christ Jesus he has begotten them through the Gospel; that is to say, under Christ his preaching has been the cause of their new birth. And so he goes on to appeal to them to imitate him (1 Cor. 4:16), as children would naturally copy their father.

His word to the Philippians (3:17) adds a further point. He says to them, 'Be ye imitators-together of me', using a compound word which we have already looked at (p. 219), which means 'fellow-imitators'. There is always the danger of individualism, even in the best life. The Philippians are to learn to work out *together* the method of following Paul as their pattern.

Yet Paul is far from holding himself up as the only person to be imitated. The Thessalonians are praised because they became imitators of the churches in Judaea, suffering for their faith at the hands of their own countrymen as the Jewish Christians had suffered at the hands of the Jews (1 Thess. 2:14). This is a particularly generous reference, because the Jewish Christians had not always given Paul an easy time. They had criticised him, but he did not overlook their merits.

The epistle to the Hebrews also exhorts its readers to imitate other Christians. The letter is written to Christians who are not new in the faith and who have lost their first enthusiasm. They have become lazy and sluggish (and we know that we ought often to apply that description to ourselves). Their need is to imitate their fellow-Christians who really do have faith in Christ and long-suffering in adversity, and who thus are in actual possession of God's promises. The verb 'inherit' in Heb. 6:12 is a present tense, indicating not a general principle but a present fact. We too know the people whose certainty of God is not just a piece of wishful thinking but an obvious reality, and we long to imitate them in their certainty. Heb. 13:7 repeats the emphasis on the imitation of others' faith in a rather different context. The reference here is to past leaders of the church. The readers are urged to think about 'the issue of their manner of life' (R.V. margin). The word 'issue' may mean the *result* of their Christian life, or it may mean the *ending* of it, perhaps by martyrdom. Whichever it is, both their life as they had lived it and the way in which they had met their death showed their dependence in faith on things unseen. Their successors could have nothing better to copy.

But we are not to be content with imitation of other Christians alone, however fine examples they may be. Paul takes the matter of imitation back to its ultimate example. When he writes to the Corinthians (1 Cor. 11:1), 'Be imitators of me', he at once goes on to add, 'even as I also am of Christ'. To copy a mere human being, however outstanding, can be very dangerous, unless the man himself is copying the only ultimate pattern. Paul humbly claims that here he is so doing, and that in Christ's most essential work. In the previous verse he has spoken of seeking the profit of the many that they may be *saved*. It is Christ as Saviour whom he is here trying to imitate, and he wants his readers also to have the same saving desire towards all men.

In 1 Thess. 1:6 he puts the same thing a little differently. He praises the Thessalonians because they are imitators both of him *and* of the Lord. Both in their readiness to suffer and in their joy they imitate the Lord directly, not simply through Paul. Their experience of the Lord is first-hand, not just second-hand, however valuable that also may be.

This leads on to Paul's boldest word. In Eph. 5:1 he actually urges his readers to be 'imitators of God, as beloved children'. It is the same principle of children imitating parents, as in 1 Cor.

4:16, but here the parent is not human but divine. Yet we ought not really to be astonished. The context here is of imitation in kindness and love, and what is that but the word of Jesus in Mt. 5:48 when, after speaking of God's love, He says, 'You shall be perfect as your heavenly Father is perfect'? Paul's exhortation to imitate God is one that the Lord Himself says can be made possible.

Even on the pagan level there was a physician of whom it was said that 'he imitated the god', Asclepius the god of medicine whose servant he was — a happy testimonial for anyone to receive. But let St. John bring us back to the Christian context: 'Beloved imitate not that which is evil, but that which is good. He who does good is of God' (3 Jn. 11). In other words, the imitation of good brings a man into unity with God, the source of all good, so that imitating good is really imitating God.

Yet, lest we tend to think too highly of ourselves and our possibilities, let St. Ignatius in his letter to the Magnesians bring us back to sobering reality: 'If *He* should imitate *us* according to our deeds, we are lost'. We humbly thank God that He never seeks to pay us back in our own coin, but that He continues to hold Himself before us as our Example, and to provide the grace by which alone we can imitate Him.

VII. CHRISTIAN CHARACTER

72. THE DISCIPLE

We frequently use the words 'disciples' and 'apostles' more or less interchangeably. We tend to refer to the Twelve by either term as it happens to come to our tongue. A study of the Concordance very quickly shows that the New Testament does not do this. The word 'disciples' occurs two hundred and thirty times in the gospels. Most, though not all, of the references are to the Twelve, or to one or more of them. They are very rarely called 'apostles' in the gospels: once each in Matthew and Mark, six times in Luke, never in John. In Acts they are never called 'disciples'. That word is used twenty-eight times for other Christians, but the inner band (possibly not always the exact Twelve) are referred to (again twenty-eight times) as 'apostles', and this term is frequently used in the epistles, though the word 'disciple' does not occur in the New Testament after Acts 21:16.

The reason for this distinction is very clear when we look at the exact meaning of the Greek words. A disciple, *mathētēs*, is a *learner*; an apostle, *apostolos*, is *one who is sent*, a missionary. In the gospels the Twelve are still learning; it is only after the Holy Spirit has come upon them that they are really fit to be sent out on Christ's service.

Yet the true Christian is always learning, and a study of the verb *manthanō*, I learn, has perhaps more to tell us than the noun. The verb occurs twenty-five times, spread fairly evenly through the New Testament. The things that we are told to learn give us the best idea of what the 'disciple' ought to be, in the exact sense of the word.

Before we begin to examine the instances, however, let us note the way in which we are to learn. The late Dr. T. W. Manson in his magnificent book 'The Teaching of Jesus' (pages 237-240) has wise words to say about this. He points out that with Jesus the emphasis was far more on learning by watching the Master, and trying to obey and imitate Him, than by the study of books. Manson suggests that the word 'apprentice' gives the right description — the man who learns by working alongside the craftsman, rather than the one who learns it all out of books. This is a warning to the merely academic student, and men like Manson,

who know the proper value of books, have the right to utter it.
It is not a justification to the lazy for avoiding all reading!

In this chapter, instead of classifying, we will follow the word
manthanō in order through the New Testament.   It occurs first
in Mt. 9:13: 'Go and *learn* what this means: I desire mercy
and not sacrifice'.   The Christian disciple must first of all learn
the lesson of sympathy with those whom he dislikes, as the
Pharisees are here commanded to learn to love the taxgatherers
and sinners.   Then comes the best-known of all the 'learn'
verses, Mt. 11:29: 'Take My yoke upon you and learn of Me'.
When the Jew took the yoke of the Law upon him, that meant
obedience to the Law, and he learnt its meaning from a Rabbi.
How complicated this obedience was, every Jew learnt by hard
experience.   Jesus, by contrast, demands an obedience to Himself that is not complicated, though it must be complete, and
offers Himself as the perfect and tender Teacher.

Mk. 13:28, with its parallel in Mt. 24:32, appeals to common-
sense learning by observation: when you see the new leaves on
the trees, you know the time of year; surely you can keep your
eyes as wide open in looking for the things of God!

Jn. 6:45 repeats the invitation of Mt. 11:29 to 'come unto Me',
and takes it a stage further by adding that if men are ready to
listen to God and learn from Him, they will inevitably come to
Christ.   Does not this imply that any non-Christian who is truly
ready to learn from God will be led on to come to His Son?
The only other instance in John (7:15) is a remark of the Jews:
'How does this man know letters when he has never learned?'
This is the narrow idea of learning that limits it to book-learning
at the feet of a religious teacher.

The one use of the word in Acts (23:27) is when the Roman
military officer writes of his having learnt that Paul was a Roman.
Claudius Lysias uses the ordinary sense of the word, with a touch
of dishonesty — he did not learn that Paul was a Roman before
he rescued him, but afterwards!

Paul in his letters takes us back to the Christian meaning of
the word.   Rom. 16:17 speaks of those who are causing divisions
in the church, contrary to that teaching of unity which his readers
have learned.   1 Cor. 4:6 is also in the context of unity: the
Corinthians must learn the maxim 'Not beyond what is written'.
That rather cryptic verse may well mean: 'Learn not to form
parties, contrary to all that Scripture says'.   1 Cor. 14:31 is

again concerned with the fellowship of the church: 'Speak one at once and don't interrupt one another. Then all can learn something from each other'. 1 Cor. 14:35 reflects Paul's attitude to women's conduct in church: if they want to learn anything, let them ask their own husbands at home! This command may have been necessitated by local conditions. It is certainly not of universal application. Many women can teach both their husbands and the church more than they can learn from them!

Gal. 3:2 is very personal. Paul wants to learn if the Galatians gained their Christian experience by faith or by adherence to the Law. Their whole standing with God turns on that. Eph. 4:20 has that beautiful phrase: 'But you did not so learn Christ'. Christ was the subject of their lesson, and the next verse continues the metaphor: they heard Him as their teacher, and were taught 'in Him' as their school. In Phil. 4:9 Paul speaks of his readers having learnt from his personal example, and in 4:11 he goes on to name one great thing that he himself has learnt: contentment with his state, whatever it is. Paul, however, is not the only teacher. The Colossians (1:7) have learnt from Epaphras 'the grace of God in truth', another spiritual lesson that is not acquired chiefly by academic methods, however much these may help.

1 Tim. 2:11, like 1 Cor. 14:35, forbids a woman to do anything but learn; she must not teach. But 1 Tim. 5:4 is on happier ground in requiring that one of the first lessons for children to learn is the sense of family life. That comes even before the alphabet. The foolish women in 5:13 have been learning a much less profitable lesson—they have simply been learning to be idle. In 2 Tim. 3:7 there is an even worse form of the disease—continuing to learn and never getting anywhere near the truth. By contrast Timothy (3:14) is to remain firm in the real truth that he has learned, remembering the teachers from whom he has learned it. Titus 3:14 once more hammers home the practical aspect: 'Our people should learn to earn what they require by leading an honest life' (Phillips).

In Heb. 5:8 we come back to Jesus: 'He learnt obedience by the things that He suffered'. Learning the most important things is not done cheaply and easily. It is costly, and even the Lord learnt that way.

Lastly there is the new song in heaven (Rev. 14:3) that none could learn except those whom the Lamb had redeemed. We do not learn by our own cleverness. We have the power only through what Christ does for us and there is never any place for boasting of our knowledge.

The total picture here is rather different from our ordinary idea of learning. It is never merely theoretical. It concerns the practical life, the Christian society, the things of God, and the One who alone can teach them to us. Luke tells us in Acts 11:26 that at Antioch the two names, disciple (learner) and Christian, were first equated with one another. They must never be separated. They never will be, so long as the learner himself is never separated from the Teacher and His ways.

73. HOPE

Hope is one of the great Christian words, though not the greatest. According to its finest definition it is 'the joyful expectation of good things to come'. Yet it is often used with neither assurance nor joy. We may say 'I hope he will come', implying 'but I very much doubt it'. A student even once said to me 'I hope you are not very well today', not wishing me any ill, but meaning simply that he thought I looked unwell! For the true Christian sense the Revised Tamil New Testament has had to coin a new word: *Nannambikkai*. No existing word was adequate.

The New Testament uses the verb thirty-three times and the noun fifty-three, making a total of eighty-six. The verb comes only six times in the gospels, and only once there in the full Christian sense; the noun does not occur at all. Neither noun nor verb occurs in Revelation. Acts has them ten times, the non-Pauline epistles twenty-two times. Far the most frequent user is therefore Paul, who has them no less than forty-eight times. Of these uses seventeen are in Romans and fourteen in the two Corinthian letters.

1. Even the New Testament often uses the words in the natural human sense; for example, Herod hoped to see a sign done by Jesus (Lk. 23:8), all hope of being saved was gradually taken away from Paul's storm-tossed ship (Acts 27:20), 'Who hopes for what he sees?' (Rom. 8:24).

Paul also often expresses his hopes to his readers — hoping to come to them (Rom. 15:24; 1 Cor. 16:7; Phm. 22; cp. 2 Jn. 12; 3 Jn. 14), hoping to send Timothy (Phil. 2:19, 23), hoping that they understand him (2 Cor. 1:13; 5:11; 13:6), hoping for their true welfare (2 Cor. 1:7; 1 Thess. 2:19), hoping that he himself may remain faithful (Phil. 1:20). There are altogether some twenty-four natural human uses of the word in the New Testament.

2. There are also some cases where hope has gone wrong. There are the Philippian owners of the mad slave girl who hoped for nothing but money out of her (Acts 16:19), and all those whose hope is set on the uncertainty of riches (1 Tim. 6:17). There are the Jews who cannot set their hope beyond Moses (Jn. 5:45). There is Christianity without the Resurrection, when Christ is only a hope and nothing more (1 Cor. 15:19). (This would seem to be the better interpretation of this ambiguous verse.) Perhaps worst of all there are those with no hope (Eph. 2:12; 1 Thess. 4:13).

3. But we pass from these uses to the remaining two-thirds which show us the different aspects of the Christian hope. That hope has its roots in the Jewish Messianic hope. The disciples on the Emmaus road felt deeply disappointed in that hope (Lk. 24:21). The twelve tribes struggled earnestly to attain to it (Acts 26:7a). But Paul knew that it had been fulfilled in Jesus (26:6, 7b)—and note the implication in that last instance: 'Concerning which hope I am being accused by Jews of all people!' It was an astonishing thing that he was actually in chains for the sake of the hope of Israel (28:20).

4. But the centre of the New Testament message here is that of Christ as *the* hope of men. Mt. 12:21 and Rom. 15:12 quote the Septuagint of Is. 42:4: 'On His name shall the Gentiles hope', and apply it directly to Jesus. Jewish Christians such as Paul were the first to hope in Christ (Eph. 1:12), and then the Gentiles followed: the Thessalonians with 'endurance of hope' in Jesus (1 Thess. 1:3), the readers of 1 Peter with 'a reason for their hope' in Him whom they acknowledge as Lord (3:15), the writer to the Hebrews who, whenever he mentions hope, appears to have Jesus directly or indirectly in mind (3:6; 6:18; 7:19; 10:23, and 11:1 with its completion in 12:2). In fact 1 Tim. 1:1 can make the identification 'Christ Jesus our hope'.

5. Closely linked with hope in Christ goes hope in God. Indeed the two can never be separated. God is 'the God of hope', believing in whom we 'abound in hope' (Rom. 15:13). He 'begat us again to a living hope' (1 Pet. 1:3), and raised Christ from the dead so that our faith and hope are in God (1:21) Paul therefore hopes in God that there will be a resurrection (Acts 24:15). 1 Tim. 4:10 speaks of our having our hope set

I

on the living God.   Hope is a gift from God 'who gave us good
hope through grace' (2 Thess. 2:16).   It is God on whom Paul
has set his hope that he will deliver him (2 Cor. 1:10).   And this
hope is not confined to the one sex: there is the widow who 'has set
her hope on God' (1 Tim. 5:5), and the holy women who have
'hoped in God' (1 Pet. 3:5).   Nor is it confined to the New
Testament: far away in the past is Abraham who 'in hope believed
against hope' that God's promise would be fulfilled (Rom. 4:18).

6.   This hope in Christ and in God is often defined more
specifically.   There is hope in Christ's resurrection (Acts 2:26),
and in ours (23:6).   There is hope of eternal life (Tit. 1:2), of
which we are 'heirs according to hope' (Tit. 3:7), and which is
laid up for us in heaven (Col. 1:5).

There is the hope of glory.   In fact Paul describes Christ
as 'the hope of glory' (Col. 1:27).   Because of Him we can boast
in our hope of sharing the glory of God (Rom. 5:2).   Paul had
to go through the process by which suffering produced the power
to endure, and endurance developed character, before character
produced hope (5:4), but when that hope came he knew that
God would not disappoint it (5:5).   In fact God has tied down
the whole of creation in a state of present hope from which one
day it will be released by fulfilment, and obtain God's glorious
liberty (8:20).   It was in this state of hope that Paul and his
readers received their salvation (8:24), while they looked for glory
yet to come.   They could hope for a glory far greater than was
granted to Moses on Sinai (2 Cor. 3:12).   The consummation
of this hope will be 'the appearing of the glory of our great God
and Saviour Jesus Christ' (Tit. 2:13).   We are to set our hope
on the grace that will come to us when He is revealed (1 Pet. 1:13).
And that means that everyone who has this hope must purify
himself even as Christ is pure (1 Jn. 3:3).

7.   The remainder of the list shows how hope is linked with
so many other of the great New Testament words.   It is one of
the qualities of love, which 'hopes all things' (1 Cor. 13:7).
It is a ground for rejoicing (Rom. 12:12).   It is one of the results
of the study of the Scriptures (15:4).   We are to hope, in the
power of the Spirit through faith, for a right relationship with
God (Gal. 5:5).   Our common hope is one of the things that
holds Christians together and makes them one (Eph. 4:4).   The
Gospel itself is a gospel of hope (Col. 1:23).   We are to continue
hoping for our final salvation (1 Thess. 5:8).   We are to be in
earnest in *fully* grasping the hope that is in us (Heb. 6:11), not

leaving any part of it unaccepted, so that we live on only a part of what God offers us.

The time will come when hope, like faith, will no longer be needed. They will be fulfilled, and only love will need to remain. But now, in this present time, hope is one of the abiding things (1 Cor. 13:13), and as long as any of us live on this earth it must be part and parcel of the substance of our faith.

74. WONDER

No man is as he ought to be if he has no sense of wonder. If he lacks that, he is satisfied with his present knowledge of the world around him and his present knowledge of God. He is neither questing for more, nor humble in the presence of the unknown immensities.

Wonder may be at many different levels. It may be puzzlement; it may be surprise; it may be admiration; it may be worship. In each case it is a realization that there is something that we do not understand. If this leaves us frustrated, resigned or angry, it has not done us much good. If it leads us on to explore, to marvel, to worship, then it has served the purpose for which God has given it to us.

The New Testament uses the word in most of these senses. Actually it uses more than one word, but only one will now be considered: the verb *thaumazō* and its associated forms. In the English Bible it is translated 'I wonder', 'I marvel', 'I admire' etc., according to context. The verb occurs forty-three times, and nouns and adjectives another nine times, making fifty-two in all. These instances are distributed as follows: Matthew nine, Mark six, Luke twelve, John seven, Acts five, Paul three, other epistles three, Revelation seven. The theme therefore runs right through the New Testament, though it is strongest in the gospels.

Its usages separate themselves under five heads: 1. cases where people are simply puzzled, 2. cases where they are surprised, 3. times when they are told not to be surprised, 4. admiration, 5. worship. In many places rigid distinctions cannot be made, or two elements may be present together.

1. In some ten places people are frankly puzzled at what they see or hear. For example, the crowd are puzzled at the long delay of Zacharias in the sanctuary (Lk. 1:21). The Jews are puzzled at Jesus' ability to teach when they know that He has never

received academic instruction (Jn. 7:15). They have the same feeling about Peter and John, and they associate them with Jesus (Acts 4:13). The disciples are puzzled about the withering of the fig-tree (Mt. 21:20). Pilate is very puzzled that Jesus keeps silence at His trial (Mt. 27:14; Mk. 15:5). At Antioch in Pisidia Paul quotes the prophet Habakkuk's description of those who despise God's message: that they are puzzled and vanish (Acts 13:41). And, not surprisingly, St. John the Divine is puzzled at the vision of the scarlet woman seated upon the beast (Rev. 17:7).

2. In another six places the emotion is the kindred, but slightly different, one of surprise. The disciples are surprised to find Jesus talking with a woman (Jn. 4:27), and His Pharisee host is surprised that He does not go through the ritual washing before a meal (Lk. 11:38). The man cured of blindness ironically pretends surprise at the Jews' ignorance of Jesus' origin, despite His miraculous power (Jn. 9:30). Pilate is surprised at the quick death of Jesus on the cross (Mk. 15:44). Prisoners usually lingered longer. Paul is very surprised at the quick change of mind in his Galatian churches (Gal. 1:6). Even Jesus is surprised at the lack of faith that He finds in Nazareth (Mk. 6:6). In all these cases the reasons for the surprise are significant: the refusal of Jesus to be bound by convention, the refusal of the Jews to admit His power, the uniqueness of His death, Paul's battle for faith as against Jewish legalism, the rejection of Jesus by those who knew Him best.

3. In four cases we are told *not* to be surprised at something that may seem naturally surprising. We are not to be surprised that we need to be born again (Jn. 3:7). Nor are we to be surprised if the world hates us (1 Jn. 3:13), nor if Satan disguises himself as an angel of light (2 Cor. 11:14), nor that the final judgment is in the hands of the Son and that the dead will hear His voice (Jn. 5:28). All this, as Christians, we expect and accept without question.

4. When wonder passes from puzzlement and surprise to admiration, the New Testament instances become more numerous. There are some twenty-six under this head, though in a number of them there is still an element of puzzlement, and in some there is a moving on towards worship. Wonder that is both admiring and puzzled is much in evidence at the beginning of the gospel story. Here is something new, and naturally people's sense of wonder is stirred. They marvel at dumb Zacharias's certainty

of the name to be given to his son (Lk. 1:63). The shepherds'
account of the angelic vision is marvelled at by those who hear
it (2:18). Joseph and Mary marvel at Simeon's prophecy
(2:33), and Jesus' first sermon at Nazareth produces similar
astonishment (4:22).

Admiration and amazement at His miracles is perhaps the
most frequent. His disciples marvel at the stilling of the storm
(Mt. 8:27; Lk. 8:25). People marvel at the curing of the dumb
(Mt. 9:33; 15:31 — with other healings — and Lk. 11:14). They
marvel at His healing of the impotent man at the pool of Bethesda
(Jn. 7:21), at His curing of Legion (Mk. 5:20), at His healings
in the Temple (Mt. 21:15). Jesus, however, did not want men
to be satisfied with admiration of Him as a miracle-worker.
When they marvelled at Him for healing the epileptic boy after
the Transfiguration (Lk. 9:43), He turned at once to speak of
His death that lay ahead. That was more significant, though
they would not realize it. There were to be greater works than
miracles of healing; there was to be His own resurrection and
the quickening of spirit given to those who believe in Him
(Jn. 5:20 ff.). The rejected stone will be made the head of the
corner; whatever men do to Him now, after His resurrection He
will be supreme. That is the thing that is to be 'marvellous in
our eyes' (Mt. 21:42). Even on the first Easter evening, though
the disciples disbelieved for joy ('too good to be true', as we say),
yet they marvelled (Lk. 24:41) — and marvelled at the central
point.

Even during Jesus' ministry people did marvel at other things
than His miracles. All the Synoptic gospels record His critics'
admiration at His reply to the question about rendering tribute
to Caesar (Mt. 22:22; Mk. 12:17; Lk. 20:26). There is also
one recorded instance of His own admiration of another character.
He finds in the centurion the faith that He has failed to find
elsewhere, and He marvels (Mt. 8:10; Lk. 7:9).

The Acts of the Apostles begin with the marvelling of the
crowd at the gift of tongues (2:7), but Peter, like his Master,
discourages mere marvelling at miracles. In 3:12 he says, 'Why
do you marvel at this man (or thing)?' Far more important is
belief in Jesus as the Christ. Any miraculous power comes only
from Him, and is in any case only part of His Person and work.
Moses is right in marvelling at the Bush (7:31); it was the way
by which God got in touch with him to show him His will for
him. Jude completes the list with an example of the wrong

type of admiration: admiring people for the sake of what you can get out of them (Jude 16). That was far from Moses' intention and experience. No material advantage came from his marvelling — only the supreme satisfaction of being used throughout his life as the instrument of God's purposes.

5. Finally there are six cases where marvelling includes worship. There is the false worship of the beast (Rev. 13:3; 17:8), the emperor-worship of John's time. But there is the true worship of God in His working (Rev. 15:1, 3). There is the worship of Christ at His coming again (2 Thess. 1:10), and there is the fact that God has called us out of darkness into His marvellous light (1 Pet. 2:9), a fact for which we give praise to Him for ever and ever. Whatever else is beyond our comprehension, we give thanks that His riches are unsearchable and that yet He has called us — and because of this we are 'lost in wonder, love and praise'.

75. SEEING

Seeing is one of the senses that link us up with the outside physical world, and the New Testament uses the word fairly frequently with this physical meaning. But often when we say 'I see', we mean 'I understand', and when we describe a man as having vision, we are referring not to his eyesight but to a spiritual capacity within him which links him up with unseen reality.

As we should expect, the New Testament very often uses the verb 'to see' in this way. This chapter will take the common verb *horaō*, and attempt to study the uses of certain of its tenses which the Concordance groups together. These, to use technical grammatical language, are the present, the future, the perfect, and the aorist passive. The aorist active, which is in most instances a simple past tense, comes from a different root and is placed elsewhere in the Concordance. This will not be dealt with here. The reason is that it is mostly used to describe ordinary physical sight. It is the other group which is particularly interesting because most of its uses go beyond the physical to the spiritual — which is the function of true Christian vision.

The various tenses of this group occur a hundred and thirteen times in all. The English translation is usually 'see', but is sometimes 'appear', e.g. in the Transfiguration (Mk. 9:4 and parallels) 'there *appeared* unto them Elijah with Moses' is literally 'there *was seen* to them'. The purely physical uses would seem to be only twelve, though there are a few borderline cases. Sometimes the physical emphasis is underlined, as in 1 Pet. 1:8 (the second use, the first being the normal physical form), 1 Jn. 1:1 and 4:20.

But these uses are the small minority, and we pass on to the large majority of non-physical and 'physical plus' uses, where eyesight may be involved but not as the most important element. The first step up from the physical is when the word is used in the sense of 'beware' or 'take care'. There are twelve instances of this, e.g. Mk. 1:44, 8:15 (take heed), Heb. 8:5. A similar meaning is that of 'attend to', the three New Testament examples being all cases of disclaiming responsibility: Gallio in Acts 18:15 says 'Look to it yourselves', and in Mt. 27:4 and 27:24 the priests and Pilate both seek to lay the blame elsewhere: 'See thou to it', 'See ye to it'.

Three times the word is used of mental perception: Peter says to Simon Magus, 'I *perceive* that you are in the gall of bitterness' (Acts 8:23). Heb. 2:8 and Jas. 2:24 are the other instances.

The next class of uses is in connection with what we often call visions, either of angels or of some other supernatural visitors. Angelic appearances are referred to in Lk. 1:11 (Zacharias), Lk. 22:43 (Gethsemane), Lk. 24:23 (the women after the Resurrection), Acts 7:30, 35 (to Moses at the Bush)—and then there is the man of Macedonia, whoever he was, who appeared to Paul in Acts 16:9. Moses and Elijah at the Transfiguration (Mt. 17:3; Mk. 9:4; Lk. 9:31, 36) have already been mentioned. In this category too come the tongues like as of fire (Acts 2:3) and Joel's prophecy of the young men with their visions (Acts 2:17) in the narrative of the day of Pentecost. Moses' vision of the model tabernacle (Acts 7:44) would not be out of place in this section.

Interestingly our verb is used four times in connection with Abraham: the physical reference in Jn. 8:57, the appearance of God to him in Acts 7:2, and the two Lucan mentions of people seeing him in God's realm (13:28; 16:23).

But we come to our highest plane when the word is used of Christ and of God. It occurs nineteen times in connection with the Resurrection. In the Easter Day narratives it comes in Mt. 28:7, 10; Mk. 16:7; Lk. 24:34; Jn. 20:18, 25, and also in Jn. 20:29 a week later. Paul refers to these appearances in Acts 13:31 and in 1 Cor. 15:5, 6, 7. Then there is the appearance of the Risen Christ to Paul himself on the Damascus road (Acts

9:17; 26:16) to which he is probably referring in 1 Cor. 9:1 and
15:8. This is in accordance with Christ's own promise that His
disciples would see Him, and He them, again (Jn. 16:16, 17, 19,
22). That vision would culminate in the vision of the Son of
Man coming in power and glory (Mt. 24:30; 26:64; Mk. 13:26;
14:62; Lk. 21:27), a vision that is described in varying language
in Heb. 9:28, 1 Jn. 3:2 and Rev. 1:7. At the very beginning of
His earthly ministry Jesus had said that His followers would see
greater things than they could see then (Jn. 1:50) and that they
would see the heaven opened (1:51). Here is the ultimate
fulfilment of that promise.

When we turn to the vision of God, the New Testament
emphasis is threefold. In the first place, no *man* has seen God
(Jn. 1:18; 5:37; 6:46; 1 Jn. 4:20); only Christ has seen Him (Jn.
6:46; 8:38). Secondly, He who has seen Christ has seen the Father
(Jn. 14:7, 9). Thirdly, it is promised that we shall see God, but
only if we are pure in heart (Mt. 5:8). Whosoever sins has
not seen Him (1 Jn. 3:6); he that does evil has not seen God
(3 Jn. 11). There is that sanctification without which no man
shall see the Lord (Heb. 12:14). When the Fourth Gospel
says 'He who does not obey the Son shall not see *life*', it is expressing very much the same thought (Jn. 3:36). As against that,
God's true servants 'shall see His face' (Rev. 22:4).

But seeing Christ and God is not simply for personal pleasure
or benefit. Those who see are to *bear witness*. John the Baptist
does this: 'I have seen and have borne witness that this is the
Son of God' (Jn. 1:34). Jesus Himself also bears witness of
what He has seen (Jn. 3:11, 32). The evangelist (if it be he)
who has seen the events on the Cross bears witness to them (Jn.
19:35), and the opening paragraph of the first epistle of John,
which contains this word 'seen' three times over, emphasises an
equal number of times that what has been seen is to be witnessed
to and declared. Paul too has the same link in his speech in the
Temple: it is the Lord's word to him that he shall be a witness
of what he has seen (Acts 22:15). And the consequence of all
this witness from the Baptist onwards is to be that 'all flesh shall
see the salvation of God' (Lk. 3:6). Or to put it in the words
of another quotation from Isaiah in Rom. 15:21: 'They shall
see, to whom no tidings of him came' before Paul and others fully
preached the gospel of Christ.

It is not what we see with our physical eyes that matters most.
When Lazarus was raised, many people saw him alive (Jn. 12:9);

but Jesus promised Martha that through the miracle she should see more than a living brother — she should see the glory of God (11:40). When the blind man had his sight restored, it meant more to him than physical sight; it meant his conversion (9:37, 38). Many people saw the things that Jesus did in Jerusalem at the feast, but the Galileans who were there not only saw — they 'received Him' as a result (4:45).

We endure 'as seeing Him who is invisible' (Heb. 11:27), and we not only look back to the New Testament for this spiritual vision. We look forward for its constant possession. In the words of Acts 26:16, when the Lord spoke to Paul on the Damascus road, he appointed him to be a witness not only of what he had already seen but of what he would continue to see of Himself in the days ahead. And to us too the promise holds good, because He is the same Risen Lord.

76. KNOWLEDGE

There are various words for knowledge in the New Testament, with various shades of meaning. In this chapter we shall look at one noun and its accompanying verb which have a special interest of their own. The verb is *epi-ginōskō* and its noun is *epi-gnōsis*. The preposition *epi* at the beginning has been the subject of much discussion. It has sometimes been maintained that it indicates fuller knowledge. Probably, however, it means knowledge aimed in some particular, definite direction; directed knowledge; and it is this meaning that we shall be noticing, though we shall remember that many instances of the word have no special directive force.

The verb occurs forty-four times: seventeen in the Synoptic gospels, never in John, thirteen times in Acts, eleven in Paul, once in the Pastoral Epistles, and twice in 2 Peter. The noun is found twenty times: never in the gospels, eleven times in Paul, four in the Pastoral Epistles, once in Hebrews and four in 2 Peter.

The verb is used ten times simply in connection with knowledge directed to finding out or learning the facts. Luke writes his gospel that Theophilus may be able to turn his attention to learning the facts of the life and teaching of Jesus. The happy phrase in the New English Bible is 'to give you authentic knowledge' (Lk. 1:4). In 7:37 the woman finds out that Jesus is in a particular house. In 23:7 Pilate finds out that Jesus comes under Herod's authority. In Acts 9:30 the brethren discover that

Paul's life is in danger in Damascus. Acts 22:24, 23:28, 24:8, 11 and 25:10 are all concerned with the Roman authorities directing their attention to finding out the real facts of the charge against Paul. The final example under this head is the knowledge of a spiritual fact: in Rom. 1:32 Paul asserts that the Gentiles know very well the fact of God's decree against evil, though they do not act according to what they know.

Another class of instances of directed knowledge is best translated in English by the word 'recognise', knowledge directed towards the identification of a particular person or place. There are twelve examples of this in the New Testament. The crowds recognise Jesus when He comes among them unexpectedly (Mt. 14:35; Mk. 6:33, 54). Jesus Himself grieves that, when the prophetic work of Elijah was done again by John the Baptist, the people did not recognise him (Mt. 17:12). The most moving uses of this sense of the word in the gospels are in the Emmaus story: the two disciples did not recognise Jesus (Lk. 24:16)—and then they did (24:31)! In Acts there is directed attention leading to recognition in the story of the lame man at the Beautiful Gate of the Temple (3:10), when the apostles are recognised as the companions of Jesus (4:13), when Rhoda recognises Peter's voice outside the door (12:14), and when the shipwrecked sailors at first do not know where they are (27:39), but later identify the land as Malta (28:1). All these instances make the one in Rom. 1:28 the more striking: here are men who refuse to recognise God when they meet Him, and who have to suffer the consequences.

In Mt. 7:16, 20 the recognition is not simply identification. It is recognition of character. By what the false prophet or the bad man produces in his way of life you recognise him for what he is.

In Lk. 1:22 the directed knowledge involved is best translated by 'realised': 'they realised that he had seen a vision'. So also in Acts 19:34 the crowd realise that Alexander is a Jew, and in 22:29 the chief captain realises that Paul is a Roman.

We go on to a deeper use of the word, that of inward awareness and perception. In Mk. 2:8 (cp. Lk. 5:22) Jesus is aware in Himself of the scribes' criticism of His word of forgiveness. In Mk. 5:30 He is aware of the power that has gone out of Him to cure the ailing woman. Similarly Paul wants the Corinthians to be aware that what he is writing has the Lord's authority (1 Cor. 14:37), and to be spiritually aware of their own condition so as to know that Jesus Christ is in them (2 Cor. 13:5). He uses the word again in this sense when he says that one thing that the Law does is to give men a sense of awareness of sin (Rom. 3:20).

This passes on to the meaning 'understand'. The Jews have a zeal for God, but not with real understanding (Rom. 10:2). But the Christian, however imperfect he is, may be expected to understand Paul's words to him (2 Cor. 1:13 — twice) and to understand Paul himself (1:14), just as he may be expected to understand 'all the blessings that our union with Christ brings us' (Philemon 6, N.E.B.).

The New Testament uses this sense nine times with one special object: knowledge and understanding directed towards *the truth*. The Colossians have come to know the grace of God in truth (Col. 1:6). Understanding of the truth is the result of salvation (1 Tim. 2:4), of belief (4:3), and of repentance (2 Tim. 2:25). It is 'according to godliness' (Tit. 1:1), that is, an essential part of our religion. There are those who are always dallying with the truth and are never able to come to a true understanding of it (2 Tim. 3:7), but the severest strictures are reserved for those who sin after they have been given an understanding of the truth (Heb. 10:26). It would have been better for them never to have understood the way of righteousness than, after understanding it, to turn back (2 Pet. 2:21 — twice).

The application of these words which goes deepest, however, is in the sense of knowledge directed towards the understanding of a person in himself. Twice this sense is applied to human beings. Paul describes himself as being 'well-known', at any rate to those who want to know him (2 Cor. 6:9), and he commends his friends to the Corinthian church and bids it get to know them well (1 Cor. 16:18).

But far more often the New Testament bids us direct our attention towards God and His Son, that we may know them. Nearly a quarter of its uses of our noun and verb are in this sense. 'Grace to you and peace be multiplied in the knowledge of God and of Jesus our Lord', says 2 Pet. 1:2. And Paul prays that the Ephesians may be granted wisdom to know God (Eph. 1:17), and that the Colossians may be filled with the knowledge of God's will (Col. 1:9) and may increase in the knowledge of God (1:10). Their new nature has been given them for the very purpose of knowing God (3:10, see N.E.B.). In fact everything that pertains to life and godliness comes to us through our knowledge of God (2 Pet 1:3).

The New Testament urges us to know Christ in the same way. Paul strives for the Colossians and Laodiceans 'that they may know the mystery of God, even Christ' (Col. 2:2). 2 Pet. 1:8 lays before its readers the things that will keep them from being idle or unfruitful in the knowledge of Christ. Through knowledge of Him we can escape the defilements of the world (2:20), and the full-grown Christian man is one who has knowledge of the Son of God (Eph. 4:13). Phil. 1:9 speaks of love abounding in knowledge, without actually saying who is the object of the knowledge, but our Reference Bibles link this verse with Col. 1:9, and there is no doubt that Paul is thinking of the knowledge of God and of His Son.

The height of this personally directed knowledge is given in Mt. 11:27, where Jesus speaks of the way in which His Father knows Him and He knows His Father. We cannot yet know God like that, but Paul assures us in 1 Cor. 13:12 that God knows us, and that one day we shall know Him in the same way. However imperfect our efforts may be, the New Testament bids us direct our knowledge supremely towards God, and promises that ultimately the Unknowable will let us know Him in His fulness.

77. MEEKNESS AND LOWLINESS

There are three New Testament words that must be taken together under this head:

1. *Praus*, meek, which comes four times, and its noun, meekness which comes eleven times;

2. *Tapeinos*, humble, which comes eight times, together with the noun humble-mindedness (7), the adjective humble-minded (1), the verb to humble (14), and the noun humbling (4);

3. *Epieikēs*, reasonable or open-minded, which comes five times, and its noun twice.

In ordinary speech these were not words of deep moral content. *Praus* was used for such things as a mild climate, a slight illness, a tame animal. *Tapeinos* could describe a low-lying place, or a person of low caste. *Epieikēs* need mean nothing more than fair-minded. This ordinary speech is sometimes reflected in the New Testament. In the Magnificat, Mary is thinking chiefly of her own and others' humble position (Lk. 1:48, 52). The quotation from Isaiah in Lk. 3:5 refers to the levelling of hills. The further quotation in Acts 8:33 is applied to the deeds that brought Jesus to the Cross: 'In his humiliation justice was denied him' (R.S.V.). In Rom. 12:16 Paul is speaking in secular language: 'Take a real interest in ordinary people' (Phillips). He also uses the word when writing to his opponents in Corinth: he seems insignificant in their presence (2 Cor.10:1), he does not want to be humiliated before God by their misconduct (12:21). There are those in Colossae who have a false humility which is no more than external asceticism (2:18, 23). He himself knows how to live in humble circumstances (Phil. 4:12). He knows that God comforts those who are depressed (2 Cor. 7:6), and believes that one day He will transform this body of ours that is now in such poor estate and that so often humiliates us (Phil. 3:21).

So much for the 'ordinary' uses of the words. But Christ had given a new meaning to them. He had made them into Christian virtues, the nature that God means us to have. He said, '*I* am meek and lowly' (Mt. 11:29), and 'Your King comes to you meek' was applied to Him (Mt. 21:5). 'Being found in fashion as a man He humbled Himself' (Phil. 2:8), so that Paul could appeal to his readers 'by the meekness and gentleness of Christ' (2 Cor. 10:1). Gladstone once said, 'Humility as a sovereign grace is a creation of Christianity'. It was Christ who made it so. He gives us a complete reversal of human values. It is the meek, not the grasping, who will inherit the earth (Mt. 5:5). He who tries to push himself forward will be humiliated; he who deliberately suppresses himself is the one who will be on top in the end (Mt. 23:12; Lk. 14:11; 18:14). Of course we are not to humble ourselves with that aim in view. The reason for humility lies in the words of Mt. 18:4: he who brings himself down to the utterly dependent state of a little child is the one who will be greatest in God's kingdom, because he will be the one who has learnt to be dependent on God's power and not on his own pushfulness.

Paul claims that he has served the Lord in this spirit of humble dependence (Acts 20:19). He longs to be able to visit the Corinthians in a spirit of meekness, not driven by them to self-assertion (1 Cor. 4:21). He has deliberately taken less than his rights in preaching the Gospel to them free (2 Cor. 11:7). Meekness is one of the fruits of the Spirit of God within us (Gal. 5:23), so he can tell the Galatians that they must restore an erring brother in a spirit of meekness and not with any self-righteousness (6:1). He can emphasise to the Ephesians that real unity depends on lowliness and meekness (4:2). The Philippians can be shown that the example of Christ means that they too must, in lowliness of mind, each reckon the other man better than himself (2:3). The Colossians are bidden, since God has chosen them, to put on humility and meekness as their daily dress. They must no more think of forgetting them than they would forget their clothes (3:12). Timothy is reminded that in dealing with quarrelsome persons he must not be tempted into the same attitude of self-assertion (2 Tim. 2:25), and the congregation equally is told to 'show all meekness to all men' (Tit. 3:2).

It is remarkable how often the lesson of meekness and lowliness is enforced in the two short letters of James and 1 Peter. In James there is the reminiscence of the Lord's teaching: that the lowly brother should glory in his exaltation and the rich in his humiliation (1:9, 10). God gives grace to the humble (4:6), and so we are to receive with meekness His implanted word (1:21), and humble ourselves in His sight (4:10). Dependence once more is the only true attitude, and the truly wise man is the one who knows it. That beautiful phrase in 3:13, 'the meekness of wisdom', reminds us that genuine wisdom is always humble.

1 Peter also has a beautiful reminiscence of the Lord: 'All of you, gird yourselves with humility' (5:5), as He did when He took a towel. And Peter has two of James' phrases: 'He gives grace to the humble' (5:5), and 'Humble yourselves under the mighty hand of God' (5:6), a strengthened form of Jas. 4:10. Women are asked to 'adorn themselves' (and the word is the word from which 'cosmetic' is derived) with a meek and quiet spirit (3:4), but this spirit is not limited to one sex. Peter goes on: 'Be ye *all* . . . humble-minded' (3:8), and this is to extend to the times when they are doing battle for their faith: 'Be ready always to give a defence of the hope that is in you . . . but with meekness (3:15). Sometimes we are too truculent in our witness.

We have taken the two words 'meek and lowly' together because the Lord did. Before we come to our third word, it is interesting to note how often they are either paired or come in lists of Christian virtues. See Gal. 5:23, Eph. 4:2, Col. 3:12, 1 Pet. 3:4, 8, and the pairing of meekness with our third word in 2 Cor. 10:1. The whole idea of meekness and humility is embedded deep in Christian character.

Our third word comes in a secular sense in Acts 24:4. Tertullus asks Felix to hear him with an open mind. But we soon come to the divine source of the Christian virtue with the open-mindedness of Christ that Paul wants to see in the Corinthians (2 Cor. 10:1), and with the description of the wisdom that comes from above as free from all intellectual pride (Jas. 3:17 — 'gentle' is an inadequate translation). The bishop must be open-minded (1 Tim. 3:3); so must the people (Tit. 3:2). That spirit of gentle, forbearing open-mindedness is something that we must show to all men. In view of the Judgment Day, how can we be narrow and opinionated? (Phil. 4:5). There may be some who are open and reasonable towards us; there may be others who are crookedness itself (1 Pet. 2:18). This ought to make no difference at all to the conduct of a true servant of Christ.

Self-denial must go to the root of the matter. It must be the acceptance of the fact that the true follower of Christ has no rights to insist upon, in church politics, in litigation, anywhere. He must follow Him who freely gave up all His rights, and live in dependence upon Him alone. That is the only self-denial — and let no one think that it is an easy thing.

78. WEAKNESS

A study of the New Testament uses of this word shows very clearly the difference between the ordinary human attitude towards it and the attitude which Jesus and His apostles taught, and which they encourage us to adopt.

The Greek word is *astheneia*, which occurs twenty-four times. It is sometimes translated *infirmity*. Derived from it are the verb *astheneō, I am weak* or *sick* (thirty-three times), another noun *asthenēma, weakness* or *infirmity* (once only), and the adjective *asthenēs, weak* or *sick* (twenty-five times), making a total of eighty-three. These can all be examined together, but it is interesting to note their distribution in the New Testament. Matthew has them seven times, Mark two, Luke six, John ten, Acts seven, Paul forty-two, the remaining letters nine. Paul thus accounts for just over half the total.

The words, like most New Testament words, occur a number of times in the ordinary sense without any special Christian emphasis. They are used eight times to describe ordinary physical weakness. In Gal. 4:13 Paul refers to some normal illness that he had had. Timothy is told to treat himself for his stomach's sake and his frequent illnesses (1 Tim. 5:23). In Heb. 7:28 the Jewish high priests are described as having the usual physical weakness. Trophimus was left sick in Miletus (2 Tim. 4:20). Paul's own bodily presence was described by his opponents as weak (2 Cor. 10:10). He is sure that many of the Corinthians are physically ill because they have broken the fellowship of the church (1 Cor. 11:30). And our Lord puts the sleepiness of the disciples down to physical weakness (Mt. 26:41; Mk. 14:38).

Paul's opponents describe him as being weak in action (2 Cor. 11:21). He replies a little later (13:3) by pointing out that Christ is not weak in *His* action. He also writes to the Romans of the weakness of human nature (6:19) and of the weakness of the Old Testament Law just because of this weak human nature of ours (8:3). Heb. 7:18 also refers to the weakness of the Law, and Gal. 4:9 has that rather difficult reference to the 'weak and beggarly elements', the forces of nature which wrongly impressed people of that time as they continue to do many today.

All the other New Testament references to weakness, however, are not content simply to describe or to condemn it. They all of them underline in one way or another the Christian response to weakness, which is always one of *helpfulness*. The most frequent response is that of healing. Twenty-seven times the New Testament speaks of healing the sick. Seventeen of these instances concern Jesus Himself. Whenever He saw sick people, He healed, and throughout His ministry they were constantly brought to Him. It will be enough to give the references, as they all follow the same general pattern: Mt. 8:17; Mk. 6:56; Lk. 4:40; 5:15; 8:2; 13:11, 12; Jn. 4:46; 5:3, 5, 7; 6:2; 11:1, 2, 3, 4, 6. Even while He was still on earth, He commanded His disciples to heal the sick (Mt. 10:8; Lk. 10:9), and that work was continued in the Acts of the Apostles: in Jerusalem (4:9; 5:15, 16), in Joppa (9:37), in Ephesus (19:12) and in Malta (28:9). Paul speaks of God showing His healing mercy on Epaphroditus (Phil. 2:27), and James bids prayer be made for the recovery of the sick (5:14).

Some people are a little too eager for physical recovery in itself, and hanker too much for direct miracles, but there is no doubt that the Church has often failed to make use of the faith and prayer enjoined in the Scriptures. At the same time we might look a little more closely at the wording of Acts 28:9, 10. Luke says that when those who had sicknesses were cured, the islanders honoured *us*. They included Luke, the doctor, as well as Paul, the miracle-worker! But whatever the method of healing, the normal New Testament response to physical weakness is help.

The response to weakness does not always include healing. In fact there may be no need for healing. It does, however, always include sympathy. There are eighteen more instances where this is brought home to us. Jesus Himself lists sympathy or lack of sympathy for the sick among the things that will be taken into account at the Last Judgment (Mt. 25:36, 39, 43, 44). Understanding fellowship with the weak is one of the mainsprings of Paul's ministry: 'To the weak I became weak that I might gain the weak' (1 Cor. 9:22); 'Who is weak and I am not weak?' (2 Cor. 11:29). The same spirit underlies even the ironical words in 2 Cor. 13:9: 'We rejoice when we are weak and you are strong'. Poor Corinthians! They are not really strong, but Paul is willing to seem weak in their eyes, if only he can build them up in the faith.

What he practises himself he urges upon others. The Ephesian elders are reminded: 'I gave you an example, how that so labouring you ought to help the weak' (Acts 20:35). 'We that are strong ought to bear the infirmities of the weak' (Rom. 15:1). 'Support the weak' (1 Thess. 5:14). We are all one body, and even the weak parts of it are necessary (1 Cor. 12:22). The Philippians evidently learnt the lesson. They must have been very distressed at the sickness of Epaphroditus if he was so concerned at their hearing of his illness (Phil. 2:26).

This concern for the weak is not limited to Paul. 1 Pet. 3:7 has the command to honour woman as being the weaker vessel, but its origin is in Jesus Himself. The Jewish high priest was appointed to deal gently with men because he also was compassed with infirmity (Heb. 5:2); Jesus too is ever touched with the feeling of our infirmities, tested as He has been in all points like as we are (4:15). Sympathy is not just a human virtue; it is part of the nature of God.

Paul makes a special point of urging the need for sympathy with those who are weak in faith. He describes the vegetarian as being weak in faith (Rom. 14:2)! He does not personally agree with him, but he begins the chapter with the command, 'Receive him who is weak in faith' (14:1). And when, in 1 Cor. 8, he is discussing the problem of eating food offered to idols, he himself does not think that it matters, but five times over he mentions those whose conscience is weak (verses 7, 9, 10, 11, 12),

K

and swears that he will do nothing to offend the brother for whom Christ died. He rejoices in the example of Abraham, who was not weakened in faith (Rom. 4:19), but he must sympathise with those who are.

But there is another aspect of weakness which Paul, in the midst of his sympathy for other weak human beings, does not forget. By contrast with God we are all weak, and we must never forget our weakness because only so can God help us. Independently we get nowhere, because even the weakness of God is stronger than men (1 Cor. 1:25), but when we admit our weakness, then the way is open for us to receive the divine strength (2 Cor. 12:10). Fifteen times the New Testament tries to make us realise this, particularly in this passage in 2 Corinthians. Paul has been tempted to boast of his achievements, but he very soon declares that he would much rather boast of his weakness (11:30; 12:5, 9). God's power is made perfect *in* weakness (12:9), not necessarily by removing it. Paul can therefore take pleasure in his weakness (12:10), because then the strength of Christ rests upon him. He does not mind the Corinthians thinking of him as weak and themselves as strong (1 Cor. 4:10), because he knows how God works through weakness. God sometimes turns weakness into strength (Heb. 11:34), but He chose the weak things of the world to put to shame the things that are strong (1 Cor. 1:27). The great instance of that was the Cross, where Christ was crucified through weakness (2 Cor. 13:4), and Paul is glad to be weak in Him because only so will he find life and power (13:4). Christ came to meet our weakness; while we were yet weak He died for us (Rom. 5:6) and was raised so that our body, sown in weakness, may be raised in power (1 Cor. 15:43). When Paul preached in Corinth, he did so in utter human weakness, but he relied on Christ's Cross and on the power of the Spirit (1 Cor. 2:2-4), and all was well. On that Spirit he can rely. He declares that in prayer the Spirit helps our weakness (Rom. 8:26), but He helps not only in prayer but in everything, provided we never forget our weakness and always rely on the strength of God.

79. COMPASSION AND MERCY

We should expect these two words to occur frequently in the New Testament—and they do. They represent three groups of Greek words. There is the noun *eleos*, mercy or pity, and the verb and the adjective derived from it, which together occur sixty-one times. There is the noun *oiktirmos*, pity or compassion, and the verb and adjective derived from it, which altogether occur ten times. And there is the noun *splanchna*, which literally means 'bowels' and hence 'feelings of compassion'. In this sense it occurs seven times, and the verb derived from it twelve times. These three groups of words are used almost interchangeably, except that the last group is not used of God. The New Testament has a rich vocabulary to show the place of compassion and mercy in Christian belief and practice.

1. Those who met Jesus in the flesh saw the depth of this compassion in Him. Five times the gospels record His seeing a crowd of people in need and being moved with compassion for them (Mt. 9:36; 14:14; 15:32; Mk. 6:34; 8:2). On three other occasions, when He is performing a physical miracle, not only the miracle but also the compassion is emphasised. He is moved with compassion and touches the eyes of the blind men (Mt. 20:34), He is moved with compassion (so most of our manuscripts) and touches the leper (Mk. 1:41). He has compassion on the widow and raises her son (Lk. 7:13). No wonder that people kept on coming to Him expecting that compassion: blind men (Mt. 9:27; 20:30, 31; Mk. 10:47, 48; Lk. 18:38, 39), lepers (Lk. 17:13), parents with children in need (Mt. 15:22; 17:15; Mk. 9:22). No wonder that even after He had returned to heaven, that most human epistle, the Letter to the Hebrews, continues to speak of Him as a merciful high priest (2:17), from whom we may still receive mercy for help in time of need (4:16). We are never to stop looking for the mercy of the Lord Jesus Christ, because in the end that will bring us to eternal life (Jude 21).

2. The New Testament goes on to say that this mercy which is part of the nature of Christ is part of the nature of God also. The word keeps on occurring in the first chapter of Luke. The coming of Jesus was in line with God's mercy through the ages (verses 50, 54, 72, 78). The coming of the Baptist was also a part of that mercy (v. 58). Jesus, when He came, did not simply show compassion Himself. He said to the man who had had the Legion: 'Tell them how great things *the Lord* (i.e. God) has done for you' (Mk. 5:19), and when He told the parable of the Prodigal Son, He underlined this with the description of the father 'moved with compassion' as he ran to welcome the sinner (Lk. 15:20). God is always ready to do this. In the beautiful

words of 2 Cor. 1:3, He is 'the Father of mercies'.   When Paul
in the ninth and eleventh chapters of Romans, is grappling with
the tremendous problem of God's sovereignty and its relationship
to the falling away of the Chosen People and the acceptance of
the Gentiles, that word 'mercy' comes no fewer than nine times,
and its synonym twice more.   Mercy is a quality entirely at
God's disposal: 'He has mercy on whom He will' (9:18; cp.
9:15, 16).   The Jews have rejected that mercy, but it is struggling
to get through to men, and so the Gentiles obtain the mercy from
which the Jews in their disobedience have turned away (11:30).
Yet even the Jews' disobedience was only in order that they might
obtain the same mercy as the previously disobedient Gentiles
(11:31).   If Jew and Gentile alike are willing to trust, not in
themselves, but in God's mercy, that mercy will always be there.
God's expressed aim is to 'have mercy upon all' (11:32).   All
men, Jew and Gentile alike, are objects of His mercy (9:23,
N.E.B.).   And so, later on in the letter, Paul can speak of Christ
as confirming God's promises given to the Jews, and coming
so that the Gentiles also 'might glorify God for His mercy'
(15:8, 9).   Peter confirms Paul's message when he himself is
writing to Gentile Christians.   Once, he says, they were not God's
people at all, but now they are.   And then he expresses the same
truth in terms of mercy: 'outside His mercy once, you have now
received His mercy' (1 Pet. 2:10, N.E.B.).

But God's mercy is not limited to the Jew-Gentile issue.
'The Lord is full-of-pity (James here invents a strong adjective
from the noun "bowels") and merciful', as He showed in the case
of Job (Jas. 5:11).   He showed that mercy to Epaphroditus in
restoring him to health (Phil. 2:27).   Onesiphorus could count
on God's mercy because of the way in which he helped Paul
when he was a prisoner (2 Tim. 1:16, 18).   But centrally God's
mercy is concerned with personal salvation.   'According to
His mercy He saved us' (Tit. 3:5).   'I obtained mercy because
I did it ignorantly in unbelief (1 Tim. 1:13).   'According to
His great mercy He begat us again unto a living hope' (1 Pet. 1:3).

This means that one of the chief elements in the preaching of
the Gospel is the proclamation of God's mercy.   Since Paul
had himself obtained the mercy of God, he could not faint in
his ministry (2 Cor. 4:1).   He had obtained it that Jesus might
use him as an example of all the patience that He shows towards
sinners (1 Tim. 1:16).   He can give judgment on difficult
problems 'as one who by God's mercy is fit to be trusted' (1 Cor.

7:25, N.E.B.). Thus very naturally mercy becomes part of the greeting in Christian letters: 'Grace, mercy, peace, from God the Father and Christ Jesus our Lord' (1 Tim. 1:2; 2 Tim. 1:2; cp. 2 Jn. 3); 'Mercy unto you and peace and love be multiplied' (Jude 2); and it is the farewell in Gal. 6:16; 'As many as shall walk by this rule, peace be upon them, and mercy'. The Church which has experienced that God is 'rich in mercy' (Eph. 2:4) must spread the message of that mercy everywhere.

Yet since God is so merciful to us, we must, within our sphere, be merciful to one another. Sometimes human mercy is enjoined without direct emphasis on its relationship with the divine mercy. The Good Samaritan (see Lk. 10:33, 37) is primarily, if not entirely, a parable of human 'neighbourliness'. 'Tender mercies and compassions' (Phil. 2:1) are part of the Christian recipe for living together. Two verses in 2 Corinthians show the contrast between a warm, open-hearted man such as Titus (7:15), and the shut-in attitude of the Corinthians towards Paul (6:12) — the Greek word translated 'affections' in both verses is the same word as is translated 'compassion' elsewhere. Whether we show mercy with cheerfulness (Rom. 12:8) or with a certain fear of contamination (Jude 23), we are still to show it. Jesus' great indictment against the Pharisees was that they had 'left undone . . . judgment and mercy and faith' (Mt. 23:23).

Essentially, however, the New Testament links together divine and human mercy as parts of one whole. It is God who desires a spirit of mercy in men rather than mere ritual observance (Mt. 9:13; 12:7). It is because He has had mercy on us and forgiven us that we are to forgive others *even as* He has acted towards us (Mt. 18:27, 33). It is the merciful who can themselves expect God's mercy (Mt. 5:7). The man who has not shown it on earth will cry out in vain for it later (Lk. 16:24). He who shuts up his compassion from his brother in need knows nothing of the nature of God's love (1 Jn. 3:17). And God's judgment is merciless against those who show no mercy; only the mercy that we have shown to others will be evidence in our favour on the Judgment Day (Jas. 2:13). So Jude pleads with his readers to have mercy on doubters, because even those who do not doubt have to rely on the mercy of Christ for eternal life (Jude 21, 22). And Paul, who longs for the Philippians with a longing that is not his own but is part of the 'tender mercies of Christ' (Phil. 1:8), tells the Colossians that the reason that they must 'put on . . . a heart of compassion' is that they are 'God's elect', His chosen ones, selected to act as He does (Col. 3:12). The basis of his appeal to the Romans is the same. He has been arguing that by God's mercy Jew and Gentile are alike His people. 'By the mercies of God', therefore, they are besought to present themselves to Him for the doing of His perfect will (Rom. 12:1, 2). 'The wisdom that is from above . . . is full of mercy', says James (3:17). This is *God's* wisdom, and it is also to be *our* wisdom for living. When we have learnt to be merciful, even as our Father is merciful (Lk. 6:36), then the world can become nearer to being in truth His world.

80. CHRISTIAN GREATNESS

We are always taught that the man who humbles himself is the greatest in the kingdom of heaven (see Mt. 18:4), though we do not always understand what it means, or live according to the teaching. Perhaps we do not always realise how fully the words of our Lord are borne out by the New Testament uses of the word that challenges us in this chapter.

That word is the Greek word *meizōn*, which as the R.V. text and margin show us in Mt. 18:4 and many other places may be translated 'greater' or 'greatest', according to the context. It occurs altogether forty-seven times: nine in Matthew, three in Mark, seven in Luke, thirteen in John, four in Paul, four in Hebrews, two in James, one in 2 Peter, and four in the Johannine Epistles.

There are plenty of instances which show the ordinary human use of the word. When the disciples ask the question, 'Who then is greatest in the kingdom of heaven?' (Mt. 18:1), they are thinking in terms of selfish human pre-eminence. Sad to say, the question arose more than once. Mk. 9:34 and Lk. 9:46 refer to the same occasion as Mt. 18:1, but the dispute in Lk. 22:24 came on the very eve of the Crucifixion itself. Even at that moment they could not stop arguing as to whether Peter, or someone else, was to be the captain of the team when Jesus had gone. And are any of us in a position to criticise them? Jesus first answers them in their own terms: 'Which is the greater, he who sits at table, or he who serves' (Lk. 22:27). There is no doubt about the human answer to that question, and Jesus gives it: 'Is not he who sits at table?' He then goes on to add the paradox that must have pierced home at last: 'But I' (whom you have taken as your Lord and Master) 'am in the midst of you as one who serves'.

The disciples were, of course, echoing the thoughts of their time and ours. The rich fool said, 'I will pull down my barns, and build greater ' (Lk. 12:18), and Jesus goes on to show what a fool he was. The Samaritan woman thought that Jacob's action in providing a well was greater than anything that Jesus could do (Jn. 4:12), and she had to be shown that she was wrong. The Jews would not accept that Jesus could give men eternal life and show Himself to be greater than Abraham, who had died like other men (Jn. 8:53). They could not be convinced of the wrongness of their ideas about greatness.

Not that all human ideas of greatness are wrong. Some are plain recognition of natural facts. The mustard tree is physically greater than other herbs (Mt. 13:32; Mk. 4:32). Men do swear by the greatest thing they can think of (Heb. 6:16), and people with great responsibility — such as teachers — deserve greater condemnation if they fail than those with little (Jas. 3:1). These natural instances, however, are few, and we pass on to the places where Jesus gives us His own teaching about greatness.

Some of this teaching is at the more general level, without the element of paradox that makes His teaching what it is. 'Among them that are born of women there has not arisen a greater than John the Baptist' (Mt. 11:11; cp. Lk. 7:28) is a straightforward tribute to a fine man. 'Which is greater, the gold or the sanctuary . . . the gift or the altar ?' (Mt. 23:17, 19) is a challenge to the Jews to come back to obvious fact. In the same class comes Paul's Old Testament quotation about the older (literally greater) son Esau serving the younger (literally lesser) son Jacob (Rom. 9:12, from Gen. 25:23), though perhaps there is something of paradox here.

Most of the New Testament teaching about greatness is, however, entirely contrary to the usual sense of the word. Some twenty uses of 'greater' or 'greatest'—nearly half the total number—come into this paradoxical category. 'He is that is but little in the kingdom of heaven is greater than (John)' (Mt. 11:11, cp. Lk. 7:28). This is the first of the many astonishing statements. By ordinary standards the Baptist was a man of the highest spiritual stature, but because the kingdom of heaven is the sphere where God's power is at work, anyone who accepts that power is at once in possession of something that man by himself can never gain. Jesus makes the same point with reference to the temple and the kingdom in Mt. 12:6. The temple was the supreme spiritual centre for the Jews, 'but a greater thing than the temple is here'. This is the translation of our best manuscripts. Others have 'one greater than the temple'. But whether the reference is to the kingdom or to Jesus Himself, the fact remains that when God gives His power even the least of us is lifted on to a plane higher than all those without it. The most daring word about this is the word of Jesus Himself when He said that those who believe on Him will do greater works than He Himself has done (Jn. 14:12), not of course in their own strength, but only because He by His Ascension will make the Father's power more fully available.

But these statements and promises are no incentive to spiritual pride. The emphasis is always the other way. No one can be considered great unless, with no thought of self at all, he gladly takes inferior positions. Jesus keeps on ramming that home: 'Whosoever shall humble himself ... the same is the greatest' (Mt. 18:4), 'He that is greatest among you shall be your servant' (23:11), 'He that is the greater among you, let him become as the younger' (Lk. 22:26), 'A slave is not greater than his master, neither one that is sent greater than he that sent him' (Jn. 13:16, cp. 15:20).

Yet there is no virtue in humility for its own sake. True greatness comes only when we have learned to love. There is no commandment greater than the commandment to love (Mk. 12:31). Love is greater than even faith or hope (1 Cor. 13:13), and it was in terms of the greatest possible act of love that Jesus laid down His life (Jn. 15:13).

By the time the apostles wrote their letters they had learnt something of this paradoxical reversal of ordinary values. Paul can include a number of things among 'the greater gifts' (1 Cor. 12:31), but he knows that 'prophesying', or straightforward declaration of God's truth, is greater than sensational speaking with tongues (14:5), and he knows that love is the greatest of all (13:13). Hebrews (9:11) can speak of the heavenly tabernacle the spiritual reality, as greater than the earthly material one, and of suffering for Christ as greater treasure than a king's wealth (11:26). 2 Pet. 2:11 can write of the humility even of angels despite their greatness, and the Elder John can describe as his greatest joy his satisfaction that his converts are true to their faith (3 Jn. 4).

Yet there is still one further, final stage. This paradox is true because it is *God's* way, and the New Testament never

forgets that God is greater than all, even than the most faithful
Christian. It is God who is the source of even the greatness of
Christ (Jn. 1:50-51; 5:20, 36; 14:28; 1 Jn. 5:9). It is God who
gives authority at the other end of the scale to a human ruler
such as Pilate, so that Caiaphas, who delivered Jesus to Pilate, had
'greater sin' because it was a sin against God-given authority
(Jn. 19:11). There is none greater than God (Heb. 6:13).
He is greater than our hearts and knows us utterly (1 Jn. 3:20).
He is greater than any spiritual enemy that can assail us (4:4).
He gives grace greater than the power of any temptation (Jas.
4:6) — if only men will acknowledge His greatness, and follow
that way of His which appears humiliating, but which alone is
truly great.

81. SELF

One of the hardest words in the New Testament to translate
adequately is the word *Psychē*. Sometimes it is translated *soul*,
but it does not mean what we normally mean by *soul*: that part of
us which God can take for eternal life with Himself. The
New Testament word for that is *pneuma*, spirit. Sometimes it is
translated *life*, physical life, as for example in Acts 20:10, where
Paul says of Eutychus: 'His life is in him'; that is, he is not dead.
Often a translation feels compelled to give two alternatives, as the
Revised Version does in Mt. 10:39: 'He that findeth his life
(margin, soul) shall lose it'. The first syllable of the word
'psychology' is derived from it, and how should we define that
word? Is it the science of the soul? Not in the purely religious
sense. Yet it is certainly not the science of physical life either.

Perhaps we should explain psychology as the science of the
personality, and that word may give us the clue to the heart of
the meaning of the word *psychē*. It is that part of a man which
makes him most truly what he is. It need not be religious. In
fact it may often be bad; but it is the core of what he is — his
self. We cannot always translate *psychē* by *self*, but very often
we can and should, and in this chapter we shall look at the occasions when this is a good translation, and see what they have to
teach us.

We shall examine some thirty-two uses, and in addition six
uses of the adjective formed from *psychē*, which may often be
translated *self-centred*. Eight of these thirty-eight instances are
in Matthew, five in Mark, eight in Luke, two in John, three in

Acts, eight in Paul, and one each in Hebrews, James, 1 Peter and Jude. We shall find that most of the cases (perhaps twenty-eight) use the word in a neutral sense, not necessarily either bad or good in itself, but depending upon a man's attitude to it. Sometimes it is definitely a bad self and sometimes a good one. It all depends upon what we make it.

In Mt. 6:25 and Lk. 12:22 Jesus says, 'Be not anxious for your *self* what ye shall eat . . .' He is of course thinking of the physical life here, but also of more than that. He is thinking of our whole personality, which is affected so much by our attitude to material things. It would be dreadful if we were to be shown a time chart indicating the hours of thought that we give to food and to clothes — and that applies to both rich and poor, if for different reasons. Jesus says, 'Don't let these things be a central part of your personality'. He gives an outstanding example of the man who concentrates on food and drink in the parable of the Rich Fool (Lk. 12:19, 20). That self-centred man holds a conversation with his self: 'Self, you have much goods laid up . . . eat, drink, be merry'. But he is checkmated in the next verse: his self, the core of his being, is going to be taken away, and then there will be no one to enjoy all these things. The same point is made in Mt. 16:26 and Mk. 8:36, 37; 'What shall a man be profited if he shall gain the whole world and forfeit his self? or what shall a man give in exchange for his self?' The word translated 'forfeit' is the word for a legal penalty. If a man is fined a few rupees, that is only a part of his possessions. If all his goods are confiscated, he himself still remains. But if the fine is his *self*, what is left to possess anything? In all commercial transactions, we exchange goods for money, or goods for goods. The one thing that we cannot exchange is our self. If we could, there would be no one left to do any exchanging. It is interesting that Luke in his parallel passage here (9:25) uses the normal word for 'himself'. This was almost interchangeable with *psyche*.

Yet, though the self is so fundamentally important, the great paradox of the gospels is that when you try to find it and save it you lose it (Mt. 10:39; 16:25; Mk. 8:35; Lk. 9:24; 17:33; Jn. 12:25), but when you are willing to lose it or 'hate' it (Mt. 10:39; 16:25; Mk. 8:35; Lk. 9:24; 14:26; Jn. 12:25), then you really find it and keep it. The self-centred man, who concentrates on getting his own way and securing his own comfort, becomes a man with a personality valueless to God and man alike. The self-forgetful man, the man who truly forgets himself and does not make self-denial a form of self-advertisement, is the man who is of real value both to God and to man.   Jesus gives one special instance of this self-forgetfulness in Lk. 21:19: 'By your steadfastness you shall win your selves'.   These words were spoken with regard to steadfastness in persecution.   When the outlook is black, when the easiest thing would be to give in, don't think of your self.   Hold on, for Christ's sake, and your personality at the end will be one that God can approve.   The writer to the Hebrews (12:3) has remembered these words when he writes to those undergoing some lesser persecution: 'Wax not weary, fainting in your selves'.

The chief thing therefore for a true Christian to do with his self is to hand it over to God and his fellow men.   This is what the ancient commandment had already said: 'Thou shalt love the Lord thy God . . . with all thy self'.   No wonder that Jesus took up that commandment as central for His own teaching (Mt. 22:37; Mk. 12:30), and that He approved the lawyer's use of it in Lk. 10:27.   And St. Paul learnt the lesson well.   After the Council of Jerusalem, the other apostles described him and Barnabas as men who had devoted their selves to the cause of Jesus Christ (Acts 15:26—a more accurate translation than 'hazarded their lives').   He himself says later to the Ephesian elders (20:24) that he does not hold his self to be of any account; and in that beautiful word to the Thessalonians which is not pondered over as much as it should be, he tells them that he has come not simply to share a message with them, however true it may be, but to share his very self (1 Thess. 2:8).

Paul had to learn that lesson.   He knew the other side of the picture.   In 1 Cor. 2:14 he speaks of the *psychikos*, the 'natural man', by nature self-centred.   A man such as that cannot understand God's Spirit.   It is outside his realm of thought.   That is how we all begin.   In 1 Cor. 15:44, 46 Paul is thinking partly about our physical body when he three times uses the word 'natural'; but he is thinking also of our self-centred nature which needs redeeming by God.   Jude 19 makes this same contrast, though the word is there translated 'sensual'—here are men who are sensual because they are fundamentally self-centred.   And so too in Jas. 3:15, where this self-centredness is put in very bad company.

Yet a man may purify his self of 'self' by submission to God and by outgoing love (1 Pet. 1:22).   Then he will have the only kind of self of which the New Testament speaks with approval. It will be a self that is entirely united with fellow-Christians: the early Jerusalem church was 'of one heart and self' (Acts 4:32), living with a single corporate personality: the Philippians were urged by Paul to strive 'with one self' for the faith of the Gospel and abandon all division (1:27). It will also be a self that is completely devoted to God's will. Such a man will do the will of God 'out of the self', as the Greek of Eph. 6:6 says, with the whole of his personality. He will do his daily work 'out of the self', as unto the Lord (Col. 3:23), losing his self-centredness in Christ-centredness.

Let us be sure of what we mean by self-denial. It is not some small sacrifice, though that may be truly symbolic. It is the deliberate rejection of our entire self-centredness, the surrender of our whole self to God and to our fellow men. The New Testament lets us off with nothing less than that.

82. TRUSTING AND TRUSTWORTHY

The Greek word *pistos* has a double sense which cannot be represented by any single English word. On the one hand it means 'trustworthy, reliable, dependable', and can be used in this sense with regard to men, facts or God. On the other it means 'trusting, relying, depending, believing', and applies only to man's attitude to God. In some contexts it includes something of both meanings. It is, of course, the adjective connected with the noun *pistis*, 'faith', and is often translated either by 'faithful' on the one hand, or 'believing, having faith in' on the other. Both aspects of its meaning are Christian essentials.

The word occurs sixty-seven times in the New Testament: five times in Matthew, six in Luke, once in John, four times in Acts, sixteen in Paul, seventeen in the Pastoral Epistles (the highest proportion in the New Testament), five times in Hebrews, thrice in 1 Peter, twice in the Johannine letters, and eight times in Revelation.

1. We look first at its uses in the sense of 'trustworthy, reliable, dependable'. With one exception, this is its only meaning on the lips of Jesus. He speaks of the trustworthy, dependable steward whom his master can count on to give his servants their rations at the appointed time (Mt. 24:45; Lk. 12:42). In His parable, the servants who had made good use of the money

entrusted to them are praised for being trustworthy and reliable
(Mt. 25:21, 23; Lk. 19:17). That other, very difficult, parable
about the unrighteous steward is given three possible applications
at the end, but all of them deal with faithfulness: the man who
can be trusted in a small matter can be trusted also in a bigger
one (Lk. 16:10); the man who cannot be trusted on the material
level cannot be trusted spiritually (16:11); and the man who
cannot be trusted with someone else's property cannot be trusted
with his own (16:12).

Paul twice emphasises that one of the chief qualities of a
minister of Christ is trustworthiness, reliability (1 Cor. 4:2;
7:25). In the second of these instances he describes reliability
as a gift from God. And when he speaks of his colleagues and
friends, he singles out their reliability. Timothy is a 'beloved
and faithful child in the Lord', who can be trusted to carry out
a mission on Paul's behalf (1 Cor. 4:17). Tychicus too is a
'faithful minister in the Lord', equally to be trusted with a commission (Eph. 6:21; Col. 4:7). Epaphras wins the same commendation; he has done his job faithfully (Col. 1:7). Even
Onesimus wins the appellation in the end (Col. 4:9). He had
been far from trustworthy when Paul first met him, but his new
start made it possible for Paul to count him as dependable.

In the Pastoral Epistles the writer gives thanks to God for
relying on him, counting him faithful (1 Tim. 1:12), and goes
on to speak of reliability as one of the qualities needed in the
women of the church (3:11). In 2 Tim. 2:2, Timothy is urged
to pass on what he has learnt to men who can be relied on to
teach others with the same faithfulness.

Hebrews speaks of Moses as 'faithful in all his duties in God's
household' (3:5, J. B. Phillips), and then daringly goes on in the
next verse to link Jesus with the word. He has already been
described as 'a merciful and faithful high priest' (2:17), One
who can be depended on for bringing men into a right relationship
with God. God knew that He could count on Him, and that
He would be 'faithful to Him that appointed Him' (3:2). The
book of Revelation also boldly uses the word of Jesus: He is
'Faithful and True' (19:11), 'the faithful witness' (1:5; 3:14),
who can be relied upon to declare the mind of God.

1 Peter 5:12 and 3 John 5 follow Paul in speaking of the reliability of Christian disciples: Silvanus is regarded by Peter as a
brother who can be trusted, and Gaius is praised for his dependable
hospitality.

2. The word is not limited to the dependability of persons. It occurs five times in the Pastoral Epistles in the phrase 'Faithful is the saying'. There are certain Christian statements upon which we can rely absolutely: That Christ came to save sinners (1 Tim. 1:15), that godliness is profitable both for the present and for the future (4:9), that if we die with Christ, we shall also live with Him (2 Tim. 2:11), that God sent Christ and saved us, justifying us and making us heirs of eternal life (Tit. 3:8), and even that it is a good thing to seek the position of being a bishop (1 Tim. 3:1). Perhaps the writer wants to hint that only men willing to devote themselves fully to the service of the Church should seek to be bishops.

3. The other sense of the word: 'trusting, believing, having faith in' is found only once in the gospels, when Jesus says to Thomas, 'Be not faithless but believing ' (Jn. 20:27). In Greek the second word is simply the positive form of the first, but in English it is not quite the same if we say 'Be not faithless but faithful'. Acts has it three times to describe those who put their faith and trust in Christ and believe in Him: the Jewish Christians in Caesarea (10:45), Timothy's mother (16:1), and Lydia (16:15). Paul uses it four times in this sense: of the believer in Christ as contrasted with the unbeliever (2 Cor. 6:15), of Abraham and his faith in God (Gal. 3:9), and of the whole community of the faithful in Ephesus and in Colossae (Eph. 1:1; Col. 1:2) who have put their trust in Christ. The Pastoral Epistles use the word seven times in this last sense (1 Tim. 4:3, 10, 12; 5:16; 6:2 twice; Tit. 1:6). Peter also speaks of those who through Christ 'are believers in God' (1 Pet. 1:21), and Revelation three times uses the word primarily in the sense of trusting, but with perhaps an additional hint of trustworthiness: 'Be thou faithful unto death' (2:10) means both 'trusting in God to the end' and also 'utterly dependable as a Christian'. The same may be said of Antipas, the 'faithful one' in 2:13, and of the 'called and chosen and faithful' in 17:14.

4. When the word is used of God (or once of Christ), it is of course in the earlier sense of 'absolutely reliable and trustworthy'. Acts 13:34 refers to God's sure and dependable promises, once made to David and now fulfilled for the Church. Five times Paul writes of God's faithfulness, his complete trustworthiness: He has called us, and His call can be trusted (1 Cor. 1:9; 1 Thess. 5:24). He will not suffer us to be tempted beyond bearing, and we can rely on Him (1 Cor. 10:13). He will stablish us, that is,

give us all the stability we need, and we can count on Him for that (2 Thess. 3:3). And the standard of His trustworthiness is the guarantee of His ministers' reliability (2 Cor. 1:18).

'He is faithful that promised' says Hebrews (10:23); He will not break His word. Sarah relied on that promise for the son that seemed impossible (11:11). Whatever the degree of persecution a Christian may suffer, he can commit his soul to a faithful Creator (1 Pet. 4:19). His faithfulness does not depend upon ours: 'He is faithful and righteous to forgive us our sins' (1 Jn. 1:9), and 'if we are faithless, he abides faithful' (2 Tim. 2:13). The word that He speaks is always a 'faithful word' (Tit. 1:9), an assurance which the last book of the New Testament twice repeats: 'These words are faithful and true' (Rev. 21:5; 22:6). Knowing God's nature, we can count on His word.

God's nature is the heart of the New Testament meaning of *pistos*. Because God is utterly reliable and trustworthy, men can put their whole faith and trust in Him. And because they rely upon Him, they can themselves be reliable — men and women upon whom others can count never to let them down, because they have become like Him in whom they have put their whole trust.

83. PUTTING OFF AND ON

Dressing and undressing are among the commonest actions of our lives. We put off what is dirty, or unsuitable, or worn-out. We put on what is clean, or effective for our next task, or dignified. Clothes symbolise our condition: the rags of a beggar, the simplicity of a workman, the majesty of a king.

It is not surprising, therefore, that the New Testament often uses words for these actions, either literally or symbolically. The word *duō* and its various combinations, signifying putting on and putting off, come forty-nine times. The word *apotithemai*, meaning to lay aside, comes another nine times, and its simple form *tithēmi* once in this sense, making a total of fifty-nine times in all.

Literal uses are such as are to be found in the Sermon on the Mount: 'Be not anxious ... what you shall put on' (Mt. 6:25), in the Good Samaritan: 'They stripped him and beat him' (Lk. 10:30), in the story of the Passion where they put the purple robe on our Lord and later took it off (e.g. Mk. 15:17, 20), and when those who stoned Stephen 'laid down their garments at the feet of a young man named Saul' (Acts 7:58).

It is not easy to decide where this literal sense shades over into the symbolical. 'John was clothed with camel's hair' (Mk. 1:6) is more than a mere fashion detail; it is a symbol of his way of life. Similarly, 'Do not put on two coats' (Mk. 6:9) is more than a baggage instruction; it is a command for simplicity. Legion's lack of clothes (Lk. 8:27) is a sign of his mental condition and the 'best robe' for the Prodigal (15:22) symbolises the Father's forgiveness. So also in Revelation the 'garment down to the foot' (1:13), the angels 'robed in pure bright linen' (15:6), and the armies 'clothed in fine linen' (19:14) are not simply description but demand interpretation. Nor, perhaps, will it be forcing the meaning if we put the only two uses of one of our forms into this class: *endidusko* describes both Dives clothed in purple in Lk. 16:19, and Jesus clothed in purple in Mk. 15:17.

The chief uses in the New Testament, however, are ethical. The Christian life includes as a most essential element the putting off of things that are evil, like the putting off of dirty clothes, and the putting on of the clean newness of Christian life and character. We are to put off the works of darkness (Rom. 13:12), falsehood (Eph. 4:25), anger, wrath, malice, shameful speaking (Col. 3:8), all filthiness (Jas. 1:21), all wickedness (1 Pet. 2:1). We are to lay aside (it is the same word in Greek) every weight (Heb. 12:1), everything that hampers us in the race. And instead of these we are to put on the armour of light (the weapons 'for the fight of the Day', as J. B. Phillips translates it—Rom. 13:12), the whole armour of God, as Eph. 6:11 has it, with special mention of putting on the breastplate of righteousness (Eph. 6:14) or of faith and love (1 Thess. 5:8). Col. 3:12 gets down beneath the breastplate to the 'heart of compassion, kindness, humility, meekness, longsuffering', which has to be put on within. Mt. 22:11 tells of the wedding guest who had not put on his wedding garment as he ought to have done. Does this mean that he had spurned the king's gift? or that he refused to identify himself with the fellowship of the wedding company? In either case it was a failure in Christian putting on.

But we all know how we fail to obey even Christ's commands to put off or to put on. We therefore need to go deeper, behind the action into the inward nature. And so St. Paul tells people yet more radically to put off 'the old man', the old nature (Eph. 4:22; Col. 3:9), and to put on the new man (Eph. 4:24;

Col. 3:10). Indeed, in the Colossian references he says that they have actually done this. The change in their nature has been effected.

And how? Again we have to go yet deeper. Putting off vices and putting on virtues, still more putting off one nature and putting on another, is impossible unless we have One who can do it for us. And so Paul's next word is 'Put on the Lord Jesus Christ' (Rom. 13:14), and again what is a command in one place he states as an accomplished fact elsewhere: 'As many of you as were baptized into Christ did put on Christ' (Gal. 3:27). This followed a setting-free from the past life of the flesh that Paul describes in terms of circumcision. All that was bad before was cut away, the body of the flesh was put off (Col. 2:11), so that the new life in Christ could begin. That was the new life in the Spirit that Jesus promises in His final words in St. Luke's Gospel (24:49): 'Tarry in the city until you are clothed with power from on high'.

Yet even this promise of power does not complete the matter. How did Christ Himself obtain the victory over evil of which He makes us partakers? Paul has a profound saying about that in Col. 2:15. It is not one that is easy to translate or expound, and there have been many views expressed on it. Yet each one lights up the word 'putting off' from a different angle. The King James Version says, 'Having spoiled principalities and powers', i.e. 'having made them put off their effectiveness for evil'. The Revised Version text says, 'Having put off from Himself the principalities and the powers', i.e. 'having taken off Himself those evil forces which, like a dirty garment, were clinging to Him on the Cross'. The New English Bible follows this rendering, saying that He discarded them like a garment. The Revised Version margin boldly says, 'Having put off from Himself *His body*, He made a show of the principalities and powers', i.e. having put off that on to which they could fasten, so that there was no longer any means by which they could do Him harm. The Revised Standard Version has, 'He disarmed the principalities and powers', thus in effect going back to the King James, i.e. making them drop their weapons of offence. And J. B. Phillips has the same idea with another metaphor, 'Having drawn the sting of all the powers. . . .' But whether it is the powers of evil who are made to put off their ability to hurt, or whether it is Christ Himself who slips out of their polluting sphere and so leaves them impotent, in either case the Cross has left evil essentially ineffective, and so has rescued us from the peril of its attack.

The final group of uses of the idea of unclothing and clothing is found in two passages in 1 Cor. 15:53-54 and 2 Cor. 5:2-4. Paul is thinking here of the soul as having the body as its clothing. What will happen at death, when the soul will have finished with this poor, worn-out garment of the flesh? Will it have to wander about naked throughout eternity? The thought makes Paul shiver a little. But the answer to his fear is there. We shall not be left exposed to the elements. We shall be 'clothed upon'. A far more satisfying heavenly garment will be wrapped round us: 'This mortal must put on immortality'. In both passages Paul uses the word 'swallowed up' to complete his picture. What is mortal is swallowed up by life; Death is swallowed up in victory. Swallowing up and clothing are really the same idea under two different metaphors. In each case there is the disappearance of something beneath something else that surrounds it and takes it into itself.

Metaphors must never be pressed too far, but of the essential truth behind them here there is no doubt. We do not lose our personality, our identity, when we move from this world to another. We retain it in a far more adequate vehicle. And that new vehicle is not anything that we have to struggle to acquire for ourselves, and perhaps fail, or anything that is due to mere metaphysical permanence. It is the gift of God who gives us everything from our earthly clothing here to our permanent heavenly habitation. That is the note on which Paul closes both these passages: 'He that wrought for us this very thing is God' (2 Cor. 5:5); 'Thanks be to God who giveth us the victory through our Lord Jesus Christ (1 Cor. 15:57).

84. PERFECTION

How can man ever become perfect? Is it not dangerous that he should even think of being so? Ought we not to put the thought far from our minds? We should naturally say yes, except for the fact that the New Testament so insistently talks about being perfect — and that not in heaven alone, but here and now on this earth. The adjective *teleios*, perfect, comes nineteen times; the corresponding verb twenty-three times; and other forms six times, making a total of forty-eight — no inconsiderable number.

A few of these times relate to the absolute perfection of God — e.g. 'as your heavenly Father is perfect' in Mt. 5:48, 'the perfect will of God' in Rom. 12:2, 'the perfect boon that comes from above' in Jas. 1:17, and the 'perfect law' in 1:25.

A few seem to mean no more than the finishing or ending of something. The rich young ruler thought that he had done everything that was required to merit eternal life, but Jesus challenges him with a far deeper idea of perfection (Mt. 19:21). In 1 Cor. 2:6 Paul says that he speaks to men who are mature, who have finished their childhood, physically and mentally. In Lk. 2:43 the 'fulfilling' of the days probably means no more than the finishing of the period in Jerusalem.

Other instances go beyond the idea of mere finishing to the idea of Fulfilment — e.g. 'that the Scripture might be fulfilled' (Jn. 19:28), and the two verses in Hebrews (11:40; 12:23) which refer to man's perfect fulfilment in the heavenly sphere. Elizabeth in Lk. 1:45 speaks of a fulfilment of God's plans in the birth of Christ, and Heb. 7:11 points out that there was no such fulfilment in the Levitical priesthood. 1 Pet. 1:13 speaks of the perfect hope which believes that there will be a complete future fulfilment.

The great majority of New Testament references, however, are in a further category — the perfection of Christian character in this life. Paul, John and Hebrews in particular are deeply concerned with this, not allowing their readers to stop short with any lower ideal. Yet it is never of static perfection that they write. It is remarkable that they normally link perfection with the purpose for which it is desired, and that most of all they link it with love, the most purposeful of all the God-given elements in our character. The rest of this chapter will be concerned with this regular connection in the New Testament between perfection and purpose, and especially between perfection and love.

Perfection for purpose is a frequent idea in the ordinary language of New Testament times: a man buys a 'perfect' mill, i.e. one in good working order; another advertises a 'perfect' lampstand, i.e. one that will function properly; another sells eight laying hens in perfect condition, and the 'perfection' chiefly consists in their ability to lay well. The verb is often used for the execution of a legal deed, i.e. bringing it out of the paper on which it is written into actual operation in life.

In 1 Cor. 14:20, the literal translation is 'In mind be *perfect*', i.e. full-grown, mature. But the context shows that Paul is not thinking simply of individual perfection; he wants them to be mature in order that they may take a proper part in the life of the Church. In Phil. 3:15 the 'perfect' are urged to be 'thus minded', and the previous verse shows that that means pressing on with a purpose: the goal of the upward calling of God in Christ Jesus. In Col. 1:28 Paul speaks of presenting every man perfect in Christ; and that aim is in the context of his own never-failing purposefulness. In 4:12 Epaphras is working with exactly the same aim. In Heb. 5:14 the full-grown (perfect) men are given the solid food of advanced teaching in order that they themselves may become teachers. Hebrews particularly emphasises this idea of perfection for a purpose: in 2:10 and 5:9 Jesus is made perfect (a daring conception) in order that He may be able to save. In 7:19 it is noted that the Law makes nothing perfect, but by contrast in 7:28 the Son is perfected for evermore, and this follows on the declaration that He is able to save to the uttermost (7:25). Perfection for the purpose of true worship is stressed in 9:9, 11 and 10:1, and for the whole life of Christian worship and conduct in 10:14, the theme of which is explained and developed in 10:22-24. Finally, in Heb. 12:2 Jesus is the perfecter of our *faith*, and in Hebrews faith is essentially forward-looking and purposeful.

James has six references to perfection in various contexts (1:4 twice, 17, 25; 2:22; 3:2), and that essentially practical writer is certainly not concerned with a static quality. What he wants is that which will provide perfect Christian living.

The gospels do not use the adjective often, but they use the verb five times in the sense of fulfilment and perfection for a task lying ahead. In Lk. 13:32 Jesus speaks of Himself as to be perfected on the third day. But the Resurrection was not the end; it was a new beginning. Jn. 4:34, 5:36 and 17:4 speak of His 'accomplishing' God's work. This was not finalised during His time on earth. The purpose of His coming was that the disciples, in unity with His Father and Himself, might be perfected into one; and they were to be perfected with a very clear purpose: that the world might realise the truth of the Incarnation and the fact of God's love (17:23). So Paul, in speaking to the Ephesian elders (Acts 20:24), talks of accomplishing his course, but the accomplishment consists in his witness to the never-ending Gospel of the grace of God.

Yet the ultimate New Testament perfection is the perfection of Love. Mt. 5:48 is spoken in the context of loving our enemies.

Perhaps in no other way can we approach God's perfection, but the quality of our love can be the quality of His. The 'full-grown man', the perfect humanity, of Eph. 4:13 depends for its realisation on 'speaking the truth in love' (4:15), so that it may finally be built up in love (4:16). Paul again links love with perfectness in Col. 3:14: it is only love which binds men perfectly together.

It is, of course, in 1 John that the connection is made most strongly. Learning to keep God's word leads to the perfection of His love in us (2:5). The perfecting of love in us takes away the need for fear, both now and hereafter (4:17, 18). The perfection of love fulfils the purpose of the Incarnation. Compare John 1:18 and 1 John 4:12. Both verses begin with the same words: 'No man has beheld God at any time'. The Gospel goes on to say that it is the Son who has declared Him. The Epistle adds that if we have learned to love·one another, then God abides in us and the purpose for which Christ came is fulfilled.

Yet we finish with two warnings. In Phil. 3:12 Paul says, 'Not that I am already made perfect. . . .' He knows that perfection is the ideal and that it is possible, but he shrinks from claiming it as his present possession. And in 1 Cor. 13:10 he speaks of that which is perfect as being yet to come, even though love abides now.

We dare not have a lower standard than perfection. We dare not, in the light of the New Testament, say that it is impossible. We dare not boastfully claim that we have attained it. But we do believe that we can be in God's hands for Him to equip us *fully* for the tasks which He entrusts to us. To come back to those prosaic hens in the Egyptian market, the question asked of every Christian regarding perfection is (as a beloved colleague once put it to me): 'Do you lay?'

VIII. THE SCRIPTURES

85. TRANSLATION: CONSISTENCY OR VARIETY?

The New English Bible is a wonderful stimulus to Bible study. Some of its readers are uncritically enthusiastic. Others are prejudiced against it from the start. The wise and humble are glad to study it for the new light that they can find in it, ready to accept what is good and to try to understand where they feel unable to agree.

One important question which it raises, not by any means for the first time, is the problem of consistency in translation. When the Greek Concordance gives us a single word, such as in this book we have attempted to follow through all its uses in the New Testament, should translation into another language use the same word always to render the Greek word? Should it use the same word whenever possible, varying it only when absolutely necessary? Should it use any word that will give the sense, regardless of consistency? Or should it pay some regard to consistency, but allow itself considerable freedom in order to make the result more idiomatic, more vivid, or more true to the spirit of the original?

The first of these four courses is impossible. A very large number of words in any language have shades of meaning that by no means correspond exactly with the shades of meaning of apparently similar words in another language. The second is the method of the English Revised Version. It aims at the maximum possible consistency, departing from it only when compelled by the sense. This helps a Bible student unfamiliar with Greek to be sure of his ground, and to get as close to the literal meaning of the original as he can. It sometimes has the disadvantage of being insufficiently flexible. The third is the practice of the Authorised Version. Consistency was not regarded by the translators of 1611 as being of any importance. In fact they made it their aim to introduce as much variety as possible, in order to preserve and increase the vocabulary of the English language. The fourth is the method of the New English New Testament, and it is the main purpose of this chapter to examine how the method is worked out.

We shall take a word that has already been studied—in chapter 58. It is the verb *menō*, which may be variously translated 'abide, stay, dwell, remain' etc. It is a word of which St. John is especially fond. He uses it with various shades of meaning forty times in his gospel and twenty-seven times in his epistles. An examination of the various translations of these sixty-seven uses will illustrate the different methods of the three characteristic English translations referred to above.

The Revised Version chooses the word 'abide' and adheres to it for sixty-one out of the sixty-seven instances, whether it means staying in a place, remaining in a condition, or indwelling spiritually. It uses 'remain' in Jn. 9:41 and 19:31, 'continue' in 1 Jn. 2:19, and 'tarry' in Jn. 11:54; 21:22, 23. In these places 'abide' would have been unidiomatic, except perhaps in 11:54.

The Authorised Version has seven variants: 'abide' (36), 'dwell' (13), 'remain' (6), 'continue' (6), 'tarry' (3), 'endure' (Jn. 6:27), 'be present' (14:25). In 1 Jn. 4:16 it leaves the last of three occurrences of the word to be understood. There is no attempt at uniformity. Sometimes the Christian is spoken of as 'abiding' in Christ (e.g. 1 Jn. 2:28), sometimes as 'dwelling' in Him (e.g. Jn. 6:56). Five times the word is actually changed when it is used in the same sense in consecutive sentences. In Jn. 1:32 the Spirit *abides* upon Christ; in 1:33 it *remains* on Him. In 1:39 the two disciples saw where Jesus *dwelt* and they *abode* with Him that day. In 4:40 the Samaritans besought Him to *tarry* with them, and He *abode* there two days. 1 Jn. 2:24 begins: 'Let that *abide* in you which ye have heard from the beginning', and goes on immediately: 'If that which ye have heard from the beginning shall *remain* in you, ye also shall *continue* in the Son'. In 3:24 the believer *dwells* in Christ, but Christ *abides* in us. This perhaps does not matter for the general reader, but it is most misleading for the student or the translator.

The New English Bible is an interesting blend of consistency and freedom. When *meno* means to remain physically in a place, the translation is regularly *stay*. The Samaritans 'pressed Him to stay with them; and He stayed there two days' (Jn. 4:40). See also 1:38, 39; 2:12; 7:9; 10:40; 11:54; 1 Jn. 2:19. When it means to continue in a particular state or condition, the translation is *remain*. 'Your guilt remains' (Jn. 9:41). 'A grain of wheat remains a solitary grain unless it falls into the ground and dies' (12:24). See also 12:46; 15:4 (twice), 19:31; 1 Jn. 3:9.

When it refers to the Spirit of God or the wrath of God coming upon a person, the translation is *rest*. The Spirit rested upon Jesus (Jn. 1:32,33). The wrath of God rests upon the disobedient (Jn. 3:36). In Jn. 12:34 'the Messiah *continues* for ever'—this is the nearest idiomatic word in the context, as also is the word *wait* in 11:6; 21:22, 23.

The great Johannine use of *menō*, however, is in connection with personal, spiritual union, when the believer is *in* God and in Christ, and they in him. Along with these may be placed the passages where the believer abides in the words, the light, or the love of God or Christ, or when these things abide in him. For this relationship the N.E.B. consistently uses the word *dwell*, as it does also for the personal relationship between God and Christ. 'Dwell in me, as I in you' (Jn. 15:4). 'Dwell in my love' (15:9). 'Only the man who loves his brother dwells in light' (1 Jn. 2:10). 'How can it be said that the divine love dwells iu him?' (3:17). 'It is the Father who dwells in me, doing His own work' (Jn. 14:10). See also Jn. 6:56; 8:31; 14:17; 15:5, 6, 7 (twice), 10; 1 Jn. 2:6, 24 (twice), 27, 28; 3:6, 24 (twice); 4:12, 13, 15, 16 (twice); 2 Jn. 2. This gives a total of twenty-eight uses in all, contained both in the words of Jesus in the gospel, and in John's later personal letters.

So much for the carefully thought out consistency of the N.E.B. Perhaps even more interesting are the places where the translation is entirely free and idiomatic, attempting primarily to bring out vividly the force of the particular context. There are fifteen such instances. It will be enough to quote them. They may profitably be compared with the more literal older translations. 'They *spent* the rest of the day with Him' (Jn. 1:39). 'His word has *found no home* in you' (5:38). 'Work ... for the food that *lasts*' (6:27). 'The slave *has no permanent standing* in the household, but the son *belongs to it* for ever' (8:35). 'I have told you all this while I *am still here* with you' (14:25). 'I appointed you to go on and bear fruit, fruit that shall *last*' (15:16). 'God's word *is* in you' (1 Jn. 2:14). 'He who does God's will *stands* for evermore' (2:17). 'You must *keep in your hearts* that which you heard' (2:24). 'The initiation which you received from Him *stays* with you' (2:27). 'The man who does not love God *is still* in the realm of death' (3:14). 'No murderer has eternal life *within* him' (3:15—here the word is not actually translated, but *in* is strengthened to *within*). 'Anyone who runs ahead too far, and does not *stand by* the doctrine of Christ, is without God.

he who *stands by* that doctrine possesses both the Father and the Son' (2 Jn. 9).

The reader may think that any or all of these verses might have been expressed differently. That is always true of any translation, but it is not the relevant point here. The important question is: 'When we compare these words with the words of previous translations, do they help us to see a little more deeply into the full meaning of God's word?' That is the purpose of all Bible study, and there is little doubt that this New English version will, if studied with care and prayer, play its part in revealing to us more of God's truth and of His will.

86. THE SCRIPTURES

It is fitting that the final chapter of this book, which was also the final article in the South India Churchman series, should be on The Scriptures. All the previous chapters have arisen out of Scripture. They have sought, not to accommodate Scripture to what I have wanted to say, but to let Scripture say what it contains, and do nothing more than try to make its content a little plainer. The only proper concluding word, therefore, is the word Scripture itself, the sum total of what we have been considering part by part.

The Greek plural *graphai*, writings, usually referring to the Scriptures in general, and its singular *graphē*, writing, usually indicating a particular passage of Scripture, together occur fifty-one times in the New Testament. In addition there is the plural form *grammata*, which occurs twice in the sense of Scriptures. We shall not include consideration of the corresponding verb *graphō*, I write, which, especially in the form 'It is written', refers to Scripture. Besides making the chapter too long, the verb would teach us no more than the nouns can by themselves.

Our fifty-three occurrences are very generally distributed: Matthew four, Mark four, Luke four, John thirteen, Acts seven, Paul twelve, Pastoral Epistles three, James three, 1 Peter one, 2 Peter two. It will be noted that three books in particular which quote a great deal of Scripture, Matthew, Hebrews and Revelation, use the words seldom or never (though Matthew frequently uses the expression 'it is written'), but that will not affect what the words as a whole have to tell us. It must also be remembered that, in the New Testament, 'Scripture' means the Old Testament but what the New Testament has to say about the Old can be said equally in nearly every way about itself.

1.   The most frequent use that the New Testament makes of the Old Testament Scriptures is to emphasise how they point forward to Jesus.   His ministry was in fulfilment of the Scriptures (Lk. 4:21).   So was His death (Mt. 26:54; 1 Cor. 15:3).   So was His treatment by Judas and His other enemies (Mt. 26:56; Mk. 14:49; 15:28 in some manuscripts, Jn. 13:18; 19:24, 37). So was the fate of Judas (Jn. 17:12; Acts 1:16).   So were details of the Crucifixion (Jn. 19:28, 36).   So was His Resurrection (Jn. 20:9; 1 Cor. 15:4).   Everything in fact was the fulfilment of God's promise (Rom. 1:2).

Reference to Scripture has often been made too mechanical and literal.   God never intended us to take irrelevant texts in the Old Testament and force them into prophecies of the coming of Christ.   All the same, however, the whole history of Israel is the account of God's saving work.   He first redeemed Israel that she might be the channel of His saving power, and when she failed as His chosen people He sent one individual prophet after another, culminating in His own Son.   He would not be turned aside from His work of redemption.   It is no surprise that in the early stages of this history of salvation we get many indications of its final climax in Jesus.

2.   Yet, though the Scriptures were there to guide men, there were many then, as now, who misused them.   There were those who erred because they did not see what they meant, like the Sadducees who were so stupid (or worse) about the resurrection (Mt. 22:29; Mk. 12:24).   There were the other Jewish leaders who had never accepted the meaning of the Scripture about 'the stone which the builders rejected' (Mt. 21:42; Mk. 12:10). There were those who searched the Scriptures to find eternal life and would not come to Christ (Jn. 5:39).   There were those Jews who did not even believe the writings of Moses because of their prejudice against Jesus (Jn. 5:47), and who refused to accept Him because they said that the Scriptures said that the Christ would be a descendant of David and they did not believe that Jesus was (7:42).   2 Pet. 3:16 refers to some, presumably Christians, who misinterpret the Scriptures to their own ruin. Their race has not died out.   And even St. Paul sometimes used Scripture in ways that he could hardly have justified.   He is of course following the Old Testament when he says that Scripture

told Pharaoh that God had raised him up in order that He might punish Egypt for Pharaoh's obstinacy (Rom. 9:17, quoted from Ex. 9:16), but it might have been better for Paul to have left that verse alone. In Gal. 4:30 he quotes the jealous words of Sarah: 'Cast out the handmaid and her son' (Gen. 21:10) as though they were the message of God Himself. Even a great man like Paul can go too far in his enthusiasm.

3. But such cases are rare. The Scripture is the certainty that cannot be broken (Jn. 10:35), and that does not speak in vain (Jas. 4:5). Happy are those who know it from their childhood, like Timothy (2 Tim. 3:15), who examine it daily, like the people of Beroea (Acts 17:11), who are powerful in their use of it, like Apollos (18:24). The Church has been built up by those who have interpreted it. Our Lord began that work. To the two disciples on the Emmaus road He interpreted in all the Scriptures the things concerning Himself (Lk. 24:27), and they realised afterwards how their hearts had been burning within them while He had been opening the Scriptures to them (24:32). He continued the process with the Eleven, opening their mind that they might understand the Scripture (24:45), and the Apostolic Church went on with the work. Philip, 'beginning from this Scripture' (the passage in Isaiah), preached Jesus to the Ethiopean (Acts 8:35). Paul reasoned with the Jews in Thessalonica from the Scriptures (17:2), and Apollos in Corinth showed by the Scriptures that Jesus was the Messiah (18:28). And, as 2 Pet. 1:20 emphasises, true interpretation of Scripture is not just a task for human wisdom. Scripture was originally inspired by the Spirit of God, and it needs the help of His Spirit to interpret it.

4. And what else does Scripture do for us besides showing us Christ? It shows us the great men of old, that we may learn from them. 'What says the Scripture? Abraham believed God, and it was reckoned unto him for righteousness' (Rom. 4:3); 'The Scripture was fulfilled which says, Abraham believed God, and it was reckoned unto him for righteousness' (Jas. 2:23). Paul underlines Abraham's *faith*, James his *action* in offering up Isaac — two complementary qualities in a great man. Paul brings in Abraham again in Gal. 3:8, saying that Scripture was really preaching the universal Gospel of Christ when it said to Abraham, 'In thee shall all the nations be blessed'. Paul finds Scripture giving us a lesson from Elijah also (Rom. 11:2), and Philip has his opportunity with the eunuch from 'the place of the Scripture' about the Suffering Servant (Acts 8:32). There was something

peculiarly Christ-like about the Servant, but we cannot over-estimate how much we have gained from reading of so many of the heroes of old.

The Scriptures also offer us all the major requirements of life. 'As the Scripture has said, Out of his belly shall flow rivers of living water '(Jn. 7:38). We cannot be sure what the Old Testament reference is, nor whether the meaning is that refreshment will come from Christ to the believer, or from the believer to others, but the promise of refreshment is there in both cases. The Scriptures also offer comfort and hope (Rom. 15:4) — and how many have proved that offer true! They also reveal the mysteries of the universe (16:26), declare the seriousness of sin so that men may seek release in Christ (Gal. 3:22), guide men with regard to the principles of payment for work done (1 Tim. 5:18), and enjoin the royal law of love (Jas. 2:8). 'Every inspired Scripture is profitable', says 2 Tim. 3:16. This is often translated 'Every Scripture is inspired and profitable', and used as a text to prove the inspiration of all Scripture. That is not, however, the writer's primary purpose. He takes inspiration for granted. His chief aim is to show the value of Scripture for making the man who belongs to God efficient and equipped for good work of every kind (N.E.B.).

This is what Scripture can do for us when we 'believe it' (Jn. 2:22), and when we believe on Him who is contained in it (1 Pet. 2:6). As 'the Scripture says, Whosoever believes on Him shall not be put to shame' (Rom. 10:11). 'He will not be disappointed' says J. B. Phillips in his translation. Others may know failure and frustration, but he who is fed and guided by God's Word will experience the fulfilment that God gives to those who receive it. I pray that this book may help many to prove this true.

INDEX OF UNDERLYING GREEK WORDS

N.B.—Though the book can be fully used without Greek, this index is included for the sake of those who wish to refer to the Greek.

Etc. after many words indicates that other forms from the same root are examined along with the form given.

The Table of Contents at the beginning of the book serves as an English index.